Harvesting Data

Scrivener Publishing
100 Cummings Center, Suite 541J
Beverly, MA 01915-6106

Publishers at Scrivener
Martin Scrivener (martin@scrivenerpublishing.com)
Phillip Carmical (pcarmical@scrivenerpublishing.com)

Harvesting Data

Blockchain, AI and Advanced Innovations in Agriculture

Edited by

Narayanan Ganesh

and

Kanak Kalita

Scrivener Publishing

WILEY

This edition first published 2026 by John Wiley & Sons, Inc., 111 River Street, Hoboken, NJ 07030, USA and Scrivener Publishing LLC, 100 Cummings Center, Suite 541J, Beverly, MA 01915, USA

For more information about Scrivener publications please visit www.scrivenerpublishing.com.

Wiley Global Headquarters
111 River Street, Hoboken, NJ 07030, USA

For details of our global editorial offices, customer services, and more information about Wiley products visit us at www.wiley.com.

The manufacturer's authorized representative according to the EU General Product Safety Regulation is Wiley-VCH GmbH, Boschstr. 12, 69469 Weinheim, Germany, e-mail: Product_Safety@wiley.com.

Library of Congress Cataloging-in-Publication Data

ISBN 9781394310609

Cover image: Generated with AI using Adobe Firefly
Cover design by Russell Richardson

Set in size of 11pt and Minion Pro by Manila Typesetting Company, Makati, Philippines

Printed in the USA

10 9 8 7 6 5 4 3 2 1

Contents

Preface

In recent years, the agricultural sector has undergone tremendous transformation due to the groundbreaking advancements in technology. The increasing demand for food, coupled with the pressures of climate change and resource depletion, has necessitated innovative solutions to improve agricultural practices. At the forefront of these innovations are blockchain, artificial intelligence (AI), and machine learning, all of which have shown great potential in enhancing productivity, ensuring sustainability and reshaping agricultural systems globally.

This volume, *Harvesting Data: Blockchain, AI and Advanced Innovations in Agriculture*, provides a comprehensive exploration of how these cutting-edge technologies are being integrated into various facets of agriculture. The contributions from leading experts in the field offer a unique and multifaceted perspective on the transformative power of these innovations. The book is divided into three parts, each focusing on key areas where blockchain and AI are revolutionizing the agricultural landscape.

Part I: Blockchain Innovations in Agricultural Practices

The first part of the book investigates the role of blockchain in modern agricultural practices. Blockchain technology, with its inherent characteristics of transparency, security, and decentralization, is proving to be a game-changer in agricultural operations. The chapters in this section highlight how blockchain is being utilized for crop monitoring and prediction, driven by machine learning techniques that enable more accurate and efficient agricultural forecasting.

The application of machine learning for predictive analysis, as discussed in this part, offers insights into how farmers can use real-time data to anticipate weather patterns, optimize crop yields, and mitigate risks associated with climate variability. Additionally, the use of cryptocurrency for manure data analysis introduces an innovative approach to tracking and managing agricultural inputs, further demonstrating the diverse applications of blockchain in agriculture.

One of the critical challenges in agriculture is the effective management of resources and land use. The MADM (Multi-Attribute Decision-Making) model presented in the following chapter offers a novel approach to landscape development, assisting decision-makers in evaluating multiple factors to plan and implement more sustainable farming practices. The section concludes with a look at farm management systems, which are bridging the gap between farmers and technological solutions, creating a connected ecosystem that promotes better collaboration and data-sharing for improved agricultural outcomes.

Part II: Blockchain in Agricultural Supply Chain and Traceability

The second part of the book explores the integration of blockchain in the agricultural supply chain and traceability. Transparency and efficiency in the food supply chain are critical concerns that have long plagued the agricultural sector. Blockchain, with its ability to provide immutable and transparent records, is helping solve these challenges by ensuring the integrity and traceability of agricultural products from farm to table.

The chapters in this section offer a thorough examination of blockchain-oriented methods in agricultural supply chain management. By revolutionizing supply chain transparency, blockchain technology is enabling more efficient processes, reducing fraud and improving the overall quality of agricultural products. The use of blockchain for enhancing traceability is also crucial for ensuring food safety, enabling consumers and regulatory bodies to trace the origin of products, verify claims, and ensure compliance with safety standards.

One of the standout contributions in this section is the application of blockchain in the quality analysis of tea leaves. By incorporating deep learning techniques, this chapter illustrates how blockchain can be used to create a persistent, secure record of product quality, facilitating more accurate monitoring and control of supply chains. Another insightful case study focuses on the prohibition of illegal movements of sandalwood from reserve forests, demonstrating how blockchain can ensure the legality and traceability of sensitive commodities, thus helping to prevent illegal trade and exploitation.

Part III: Advanced Technologies in Smart Agriculture

The final part of the book is dedicated to the advanced technologies driving the future of smart agriculture. Artificial intelligence, machine learning and data analytics are paving the way for more precise, sustainable, and intelligent farming methods. The chapters in this section focus on the role of AI in various aspects of agricultural management, from food calorie measurement to pest detection and prevention.

One of the most innovative applications explored is the use of enhanced multi-layer perceptrons (MLP) for food calorie measurement. The chapter compares the accuracy of MLP with K-Nearest Neighbors (KNN) and polynomial regression, demonstrating how AI can improve the precision and efficiency of food analysis. Similarly, AI-powered recommendation systems are discussed in the context of suggesting nutritious foods, with a focus on how novel random forest classifiers can be used to achieve higher precision rates compared to traditional algorithms like MLP.

Pest management is another area where AI is having a significant impact. Using convolutional neural networks (CNNs), AI is helping to identify and classify pests with greater accuracy, enabling farmers to take timely action to prevent crop damage. The role of AI in weed detection is also explored, with a focus on using machine learning techniques to develop automated systems that can detect and prevent the spread of weeds, ensuring optimal crop health and yield.

The advancements covered in this book are not just theoretical concepts but represent real-world applications that are actively shaping the future of agriculture. As the global population continues to grow and the need for sustainable agricultural practices becomes more pressing, the integration of blockchain, AI, and machine learning will be pivotal in creating more efficient, transparent, and sustainable agricultural systems.

The contributions in this book demonstrate the boundless potential of these technologies, offering new avenues for research and development. They provide practical insights into how agriculture can benefit from data-driven decision-making, greater transparency and enhanced resource management. From improving crop yields to ensuring food safety and traceability, the future of agriculture is being redefined by these innovations.

Harvesting Data: Blockchain, AI and Advanced Innovations in Agriculture is a timely and essential resource for researchers, practitioners, and policymakers seeking to understand the transformative impact of technology on agriculture. By bringing together diverse perspectives and cutting-edge research, this book lays the foundation for the next generation of agricultural practices that will meet the challenges of the future while ensuring food security and sustainability for generations to come.

As you explore the chapters, you will discover how the fusion of blockchain, AI, and advanced technologies is driving agriculture toward a smarter, more sustainable future. These innovations will not only reshape the agricultural industry but also help improve the quality of life for farmers, consumers, and communities worldwide. The journey has only just begun and this book marks an important step in that transformative path.

Narayanan Ganesh
School of Computer Science and Engineering, VIT, Chennai, India
Kanak Kalita
Department of Mechanical Engineering, Rajalakshmi Institute of Technology, Chennai, India

Part I

BLOCKCHAIN INNOVATIONS IN AGRICULTURAL PRACTICES

1

Agriculture Meets Blockchain for Crop Monitoring and Prediction Using Machine Learning Techniques

D. Kavitha[1*], Merin Varghese[1] and Parth Vadera[2]

[1]*School of Computer Science and Engineering, Vellore Institute of Technology, Chennai, India*
[2]*TikTok, California, USA*

Abstract
Early prediction of crops plays an important role in ensuring food stability. Given the escalating global demand for food production and the complexities presented by climate change, there is an escalating demand for precise and effective techniques to forecast and oversee crop growth. Leveraging historical data encompassing variables such as climate conditions, soil attributes, crop varieties, and agricultural practices, Machine Learning (ML) models are employed to identify the most suitable crop for cultivation. The paper begins by discussing the importance of accurate crop forecasting and monitoring for sustainable agriculture and food security. In addition to addressing the challenges related to data collection, preprocessing, and model training in the context of crop prediction, this paper systematically surveys the state-of-the-art ML models used in various stages of the crop life cycle, from pre-planting decision-making to post-harvest analysis. Various types of data sources including weather data, soil conditions, and historical yield records, are explored as inputs for ML algorithm. This work presents a comprehensive approach that uses Machine Learning (ML) algorithms to improve crop selection and determine the ideal time to apply pesticides. In addition to crop selection, ML algorithms are to determine optimal timing for pesticide application. This integrated approach not only enhances agricultural productivity and profitability but also promotes environmental sustainability by optimizing pesticide application and minimizing adverse effects on ecosystems. Through the integration of machine learning methods with precision agricultural principles, this

**Corresponding author*: kavitha.d@vit.ac.in

Narayanan Ganesh and Kanak Kalita (eds.) Harvesting Data: Blockchain, AI and Advanced Innovations in Agriculture, (3–28) © 2026 Scrivener Publishing LLC

work advances the use of data to inform decisions in modern farming practices. It encourages environmentally conscious crop management practices that balance economic feasibility with sustainability.

Keywords: Crop prediction, machine learning, crop monitoring, agriculture, climatic conditions

1.1 Introduction

As the world's agricultural sector tries to meet the rising demand for food in the face of climate change, it is up against never-before-seen obstacles. In this regard, it is now essential to predict crop accurately in order to ensure food security, sustainable resource management, and well-informed agricultural decision-making. Crop forecasting techniques that are based on tradition frequently lack the accuracy and promptness needed to handle the intricacies of contemporary farming methods. The application of machine learning techniques has become a viable means of transforming crop prediction and monitoring in recent years. Precise crop prediction plays a critical role in maximizing the use of available resources, directing farmers' choices, and ultimately promoting food security worldwide. Crop forecasting using traditional methods frequently depends on statistical models and historical data, which may not be sufficient to capture the dynamic and nonlinear relationships present in agricultural systems. ML techniques provide a paradigm shift in tackling these issues because of their ability to identify intricate patterns from a variety of datasets. The application of machine learning in agriculture goes beyond simple forecasting in this era of lightning-fast technological development. It includes real-time tracking, precision farming, and practice optimization. By using information from diverse origins, including, meteorological data, satellite imagery, soil characteristics and past yield records, machine learning models can offer practical insights that enable farmers and other stakeholders to make informed decisions throughout the crop life cycle.

This paper explores latest advancements in utilizing machine learning in crop monitoring and predictive analytics. We examine the subtleties of various machine learning algorithms, and their performance in various agricultural scenarios, where machine learning models are used for accurate prediction of crop patterns and to monitor their usage. It aims to act as a comprehensive resource for researchers, practitioners, and policymakers, providing valuable insights for stakeholders in agriculture.

1.2 Related Works

Raju *et al.* [12] presented an approach called "The Inter-fused Machine Learning with Advanced Stacking Ensemble" (IML-ASE) to address the difficulties farmers encounter when selecting crops within Agro-Ecological (AE) zones. The study highlights the importance of utilizing AE zone data for well-informed decision-making, recognizing the shortcomings of conventional research methodologies in precisely forecasting crop outcomes in the face of shifting environmental and climatic conditions. By employing ensemble methods in a multi-layered stacking model, the IML-ASE model exhibits better prediction accuracy. Comparative studies show that the model outperforms existing methods and traditional machine learning classifiers, providing farmers with a reliable tool to successfully manage the challenges of crop selection and adjust to the changing agricultural environment. This study underscores the capacity of advanced machine learning techniques learning methods to transform the accuracy of crop predictions and provide farmers with useful information for sustainable farming methods.

The gathering and analysis of a variety of agricultural parameters, including rainfall, humidity, temperature, soil properties, wind speed, and seed types conducted to provide farmers with useful information for increased crop yields was covered by Gupta *et al.* [5]. It offers a comprehensive strategy to improve crop production using MapReduce, K-means clustering, and data analytics. In order to provide farmers with useful information for increased crop yields, a variety of agricultural parameters are carefully gathered and analyzed. The model's utility is further enhanced by the incorporation of a customized recommender system, seamlessly embedded within a Graphic User Interface (GUI) built on Flask technology. The system's scalability is emphasized, suggesting that it could be widely adopted to suggest crops for other states. The study makes a contribution to the field of agriculture by using sophisticated computational methods and highlighting the value of visual aids like bar graphs and scatter plots to clarify the complex interactions between crop performance and environmental factors. It calls for the addition of variables like humidity and wind speed for every region as well as considerations for irrigation, soil moisture, and disease alerts.

A comparative examination is performed to evaluate the latest advancements in crop yield prediction through machine learning, focusing particularly on the palm oil sector, in the paper by Rashid *et al.* [13]. It includes discussions about the urgent need for accurate and timely crop yield estimation, highlighting its relevance to import-export policies, agricultural commodity strategy, and the objective of doubling farmers' incomes. The paper emphasizes the role of technology in meeting the increasing food needs of the global population and identifies machine learning frameworks as useful instruments for analyzing large datasets, deciphering data, and forecasting agricultural outcomes. The review highlights the range of characteristics and features used in the body of literature, concentrating on machine learning algorithms like CNN, LSTM, LR, RF, and DNN. The study highlights the lack of studies on palm oil yield prediction despite the models' promising performance and emphasizes the need for more in-depth research in this domain covering diverse features and prediction methodologies. By bridging the gap between general crop yield prediction and specific palm oil yield prediction, this paper lays the groundwork for future research in the field.

Recognizing the intricate interactions between a number of factors, including vegetation indices, climatic conditions, and soil quality, Mohan *et al.* [9] discuss the critical role that early crop yield prediction plays in guaranteeing food security. The study, which focuses on paddy cultivation, presents a novel model for precise yield prediction that uses data from the Moderate Resolution Imaging Spectroradiometer and climatic parameters. The model performs multivariate time-based analysis by utilizing a Temporal Convolutional Network (TCN) integrated with a uniquely crafted dilated convolutional module. This allows the model to capture the causal properties that are essential for crop forecasting. The study points out a weakness in the current deep learning and machine learning models and highlights the significance of multi-temporal data analysis. Outperforming other methods and demonstrating their efficacy in capturing long-term dependencies in yield prediction, the TCN-based approach shows encouraging results.

In their study, Jhajharia *et al.* [8] explore the application of diverse machine learning methodologies for predicting crop yield in Rajasthan, India, considering factors such as market price, soil type, and climate conditions. Results indicate that Random Forest outperforms other algorithms, showcasing high accuracy in yield prediction. Analysis of crop-specific trends reveals the influence of modern irrigation methods on yield increase despite inconsistent rainfall patterns. Models based on machine learning, notably Random Forest, SVM, and Lasso Regression, exhibit better performance in contrast to deep learning architectures like Gradient Descent and LSTM, highlighting the importance of dataset characteristics in model selection. Future research directions include integrating remote sensing data with district-level statistics for improved model performance and exploring additional deep learning models for comprehensive analysis.

The importance of crop yield prediction in agriculture is discussed by Sivanantham *et al.* [15], emphasizing the critical importance of accurate information for efficient agricultural risk management. The paper presents a novel method known as the Quantile Regressive Empirical Correlative Functioned Deep Feed Forward Multilayer Perceptron Classification Method in recognition of the shortcomings of current data mining techniques in achieving improved prediction accuracy with minimal time consumption. This novel approach consists of three layers that use Quantile regression and Empirical Orthogonal Function in hidden layers to improve feature selection and efficiently analyze data points. The experimental assessment of prediction accuracy, precision, and prediction time shows that the suggested technique performs better than previous approaches, improving accuracy, precision and cutting prediction time. The study emphasizes how QRECF-DFFMPC can help with long-term farming decisions and suggests that artificial intelligence and soft computing be added to the model for even better prediction accuracy in subsequent studies.

An innovative approach to pre-season crop-type prediction method introduced using machine learning techniques and focusing on field-level polygons termed crop sequence boundaries (CSBs) is presented by Abernethy *et al.* [2]. The suggested approach uses historical crop data to address the scalability and computational burden associated with large datasets. In comparison to current pixel-based techniques, the study achieves competitive accuracy and memory-efficient processing by representing pixel groups as CSBs. This new parcel-level prediction model not only shows better performance across multiple states and crops, but also improves the efficiency of using the entire dataset without pixel sampling. With consequences for applications like crop mapping, acreage estimation, yield prediction, and disaster response, the CSB-based approach presents a viable substitute for pre-season crop predictions. The study plans more research into fixing issues and improving robustness over time, as well as extending the model to new states, years, and crops. Apart from being the initial parcel-level machine learning model derived from the Cropland Data Layer, the CSB-based method is notable for its competitive accuracy and efficiency.

The study conducted by Bregaglio *et al.* [4], which integrates crop models and Remote Sensing (RS) time series data, proposes an innovative methodology for forecasting sub-regional crop yields at the NUTS-3 level. The research concentrates on barley and maize in Italy, employing crop calendars, fine-resolution distribution maps, and MODIS NDVI data to account for the variability within the agricultural terrain. This paper uses Principal Component Analysis and Hierarchical Clustering to identify agro phenotypes that will inform the WOFOST_GT model's calibration. When compared to baseline parameterizations, the method shows improved accuracy in reproducing the dynamics of the leaf area index and predicting crop yields through effective hindcast simulations. The developed approach offers a strong scientific foundation with real-world implications for producing regional in-season yield projections and enabling near-real-time monitoring of crop growth supporting agricultural policies and decision-making procedures. The method's adaptability to various crops and guarantee of current forecasts makes it a useful instrument for agricultural stakeholders and decision makers.

The vital role that agriculture plays in India, highlighted for its pervasiveness and low income by Rajakumaran *et al.* [11], is explored in light of climate variability. The research proposes utilizing machine learning (ML) to transform agriculture. The problem of precisely predicting crop yield is addressed by the suggested multi-attribute weighted tree-based support vector machine technique, which is implemented in Python. The study shows the superior performance of MAWT-SVM in crop yield prediction by using z-score normalization, principal component analysis (PCA), and genetic algorithm (GA) for feature extraction and selection. The study emphasizes how important technology is to precision agriculture, especially machine learning (ML), which presents a viable path toward environmentally friendly farming methods. The authors also suggest future research avenues, imagining a platform for thorough crop production prediction across a range of crops and factors, with an emphasis on ongoing improvement and refinement of these methods.

To address the issues brought on by population growth and rising food demand, Sharma *et al.* use machine learning and deep learning methodologies to predict crop yield in India [14]. The dataset is subjected to a number of algorithms, including Convolutional Neural Networks, Random Forest, Decision Tree, regression, Long-Short Term Memory Networks, and XGBoost. The results show that CNN and Random Forest perform better, with low error metrics and high accuracy. These results highlight the value of cutting-edge approaches in supporting farmers and improving crop production projections. Integration of remote sensing data and larger datasets with comprehensive climate and environmental data is recommended to further increase prediction accuracy. This method has the potential to accurately predict crop yield which will help agricultural practitioners in making decisions.

Bouacida *et al.* [3] offer a novel solution to the pressing problem of plant disease identification, which seriously jeopardizes the security of the world's food supply. Utilizing deep learning techniques, specifically a compact Inception model architecture, the suggested system exhibits exceptional precision in differentiating between unhealthy and intact leaves in a range of crop varieties. The novel approach of the system improves its robustness and generalization abilities by identifying diseased small leaf regions instead of depending only on the leaf's overall appearance. Training and testing on popular datasets demonstrate the system's superior performance over current approaches, validating its efficacy. Furthermore, the system demonstrates remarkable generalization abilities that allow for the identification of infections on a variety of leaf types and disease types, including ones that were not encountered in the learning phase. The paper outlines avenues for future research, including optimization strategies and alternative segmentation methods, to further enhance the system's performance and adaptability in real-world agricultural scenarios, despite its encouraging results.

The research, led by Islam *et al.* [7], presents an innovative strategy for precision agriculture, integrating machine learning algorithms with Internet of Things (IoT) technology to develop an IoT device equipped with capabilities for crop recommendation and soil nutrient monitoring. It gathers vital data on temperature, moisture content, humidity, and composition of the soil by integrating multiple sensors and sending data in real time to a remote server. Based on the levels of nutrients in the soil, machine learning algorithms such as CatBoost and Random Forest evaluate the data and provide personalized recommendations for crop choice and fertilizer use. Field tests are used to verify the device's effectiveness, showing that it can maximize resource use and increase crop productivity.

Abbasi *et al.* in their paper [1] present a comprehensive literature review on the development of an automatic crop diagnostic system to identify and address diseases in leafy green crops cultivated within aquaponics setups within aquaponics environments. It highlights the significance of early disease detection in ensuring the efficiency and sustainability of aquaponic systems. The study emphasizes the integration of deep learning techniques with semantic technologies, specifically leveraging an ontology model (AquaONT) that was established in prior research, to enhance disease identification and treatment knowledge. The authors construct a dataset comprising healthy and diseased images of lettuce, basil, spinach, and parsley, laying the foundation for the proposed system. The study yields encouraging results through the rephrases of disease detection, health status assessment, and crop classification; YOLOv5s is found to be the best model for disease detection. Proactive disease management is made possible by the system's enhanced decision support capabilities through integration with the ontology model *via* a cloud-based application.

Table 1.1 Findings from the literature survey.

Algorithm/ model used	**Paper**	**Dataset**	**Accuracy**
Support Vector Machine	[1]	Dataset used in this study obtained from Kaggle is the Crop Recommendation dataset.	High accuracy was achieved.
	[3]	Various datasets were used including NDVI, weather parameters and soil properties.	Average accuracy was achieved.
	[5]	The dataset was compiled from diverse origins, incorporating information sourced from the official website of the Rajasthan Government among other sources.	Average accuracy was achieved.
	[9]	The dataset utilized in the study underwent collection and preparation *via* the z-score normalization technique.	High accuracy was achieved.
TCN	[4]	The dataset utilized in this research, sourced from The Indian Ministry of Agriculture & Farmers Welfare website (http://agricoop.nic.in), includes annual crop yield data for Paddy within the Upper Kuttanad region.	High accuracy was achieved.

(Continued)

Table 1.1 Findings from the literature survey. (*Continued*)

Algorithm/ model used	Paper	Dataset	Accuracy
Gradient Boosting	[1]	Dataset used in this study obtained from Kaggle is the Crop Recommendation dataset.	Average accuracy was achieved.
	[12]	Dataset used in the study consists of records collected from different regions of Bangladesh.	High accuracy was achieved.
	[7]	The dataset employed in this study was acquired from the Cropland Data Layer of the United States Department of Agriculture National Agricultural Statistics Service. This dataset is an annual compilation of crop-specific land cover information generated through the integration of satellite imagery and administrative data.	High accuracy wad achieved.
WOFOST_ GT	[8]	The primary source of gridded daily weather data for crop model simulations in this study is the ERA5 reanalysis dataset, which is made available by the European Centre for Medium Range Weather Forecasts through the Copernicus Climate Change Service (Climate Data Store, 2021).	Average accuracy was achieved.

(*Continued*)

Table 1.1 Findings from the literature survey. (*Continued*)

Algorithm/ model used	**Paper**	**Dataset**	**Accuracy**
Random Forest	[6]	The dataset used in this study, Wild Blueberry Yield Prediction, is obtained from Kaggle.	High accuracy was achieved.
	[1]	Dataset used in this study obtained from Kaggle is the Crop Recommendation dataset.	High accuracy was achieved.
	[10]	The data within the dataset was collected from the official websites https://data.gov.in and https://aps.dac.gov.in, both of which are publicly accessible.	High accuracy was achieved.
	[5]	The dataset utilized in this study was sourced from diverse origins, which includes data obtained from the official website of the Rajasthan Government among other sources.	Highest accuracy received.
Linear Regression	[3]	Various datasets were used including NDVI, weather parameters and soil properties.	Average accuracy was achieved.

(*Continued*)

Table 1.1 Findings from the literature survey. (*Continued*)

Algorithm/ model used	**Paper**	**Dataset**	**Accuracy**
YOLOv5	[13]	The dataset obtained for this study comprises images depicting both diseased and healthy states of four leafy green crops: parsley, lettuce, basil, and spinach. These images were gathered from a variety of sources, including an NFT-based aquaponics facility at the AllFactory 4.0 Lab (University of Alberta, Canada), as well as through searches conducted on the Google search engine and Ecosia.	High accuracy was achieved.
CNN	[14]	Dataset used in the study is the PlanVillage dataset.	Average accuracy was achieved.
	[3]	Various datasets were used including NDVI, weather parameters and soil properties.	Average accuracy was achieved.
	[13]	Dataset obtained for this study includes healthy and diseased images of four leafy green crops: lettuce, basil, parsley, and spinach. The images were acquired from various sources, including an NFT-based aquaponics facility at the AllFactory 4.0 Lab (University of Alberta, Canada), the Google search engine, and Ecosia (a search engine based in Berlin, Germany).	High accuracy was achieved.

(*Continued*)

Table 1.1 Findings from the literature survey. (*Continued*)

Algorithm/ model used	**Paper**	**Dataset**	**Accuracy**
	[11]	The PlantVillage dataset, accessible *via* the online platform PlantVillage (www.plantvillage.org), is an open-access dataset designed for the recognition of plant leaf diseases.	High accuracy was achieved.
KNN	[3]	Various datasets were used including NDVI, weather parameters and soil properties.	High accuracy was achieved.
	[15]	Dataset used in the study was taken from Kaggle.	Average accuracy was achieved.
Decision trees	[3]	Various datasets were used including NDVI, weather parameters and soil properties.	Average accuracy was achieved.
	[10]	The dataset was collected from publicly accessible official websites, including https://data.gov.in and https://aps.dac.gov.in.	Average accuracy was achieved.
K Means	[2]	Dataset used in the study is obtained from Kaggle.	Average accuracy was achieved.

The importance of meeting the challenges of timely and accurate plant disease detection using deep learning models is highlighted in [6] by Islam *et al.* Using the plant-village 10000 image dataset, the study assesses different convolutional neural network (CNN) architectures, including VGG-16, ResNet-50, and VGG-1 to show how effective deep learning is at identifying crop infections. The best-performing model, ResNet-50, achieves an amazing accuracy rate of 98.98%, according to the results. Building on this discovery, the authors suggest a smart web application that uses the ResNet-50 model for real-time crop disease prediction in order to enable farmers to quickly detect and treat plant diseases. By offering a reliable and effective method for identifying and categorizing leaf diseases, the study advances precision agriculture.

The study investigates the utilization of Max Voting and K-Nearest Neighbor (KNN) techniques for temperature-based crop disease prediction, a crucial aspect of agricultural management, as highlighted by Nalini *et al.* [10]. It evaluates the effectiveness of these techniques by segmenting leaf images and analyzing the Kaggle crop dataset. Max Voting achieved an accuracy rate of 91%, surpassing the accuracy of KNN at 88%, indicating its superior performance compared to KNN. The suggested system improves disease management in agriculture by not only identifying diseased leaves but also differentiating healthy leaves. The research also makes improvements that might be made by adding more sensors and parameters, which would enable wider application in farming methods. Table 1.1 shows a concise view of the literature survey.

1.3 Dataset

The dataset utilized in this paper forms the foundation for predicting and monitoring crop growth through machine learning techniques. Acquired from Kaggle, this dataset includes a wide range of environmental parameters that are important for crop development, including rainfall patterns, temperature variations, humidity levels, and possibly additional factors. These variables play pivotal roles in influencing crop growth dynamics and yield outcomes. The study aims to leverage machine learning algorithms to analyze intricate relationships between these environmental factors and crop performance. This dataset provides a valuable resource for researchers and practitioners seeking to develop more accurate and efficient crop monitoring and management systems. Through the provision of insights into the ideal conditions for crop cultivation and the ability to make timely interventions to mitigate potential risks, this approach has the potential to significantly improve agricultural practices.

1.4 Data Analysis

The process of evaluating data sets to highlight their key features is known as exploratory data analysis (EDA), and it frequently makes use of visual aids. The primary goal of EDA is to gain insights into the data, understand its underlying structure, detect patterns, spot anomalies, and formulate hypotheses for subsequent analysis. Finding patterns in the data, identifying anomalies, getting an understanding of its underlying structure, and developing ideas for further study are the main objectives of exploratory data analysis (EDA). Summary statistics provided an overview of numerical features like potassium (K), nitrogen (N), humidity, phosphorus (P), temperature, pH, and rainfall, aiding in understanding their distributions and central tendencies. Visualizations, including histograms and bar charts, were used in visualizing the distributions of features and exploring potential relationships between variables. Furthermore, correlation analysis was employed to measure the associations among features and identify multicollinearity (Figure 1.1). Encoding techniques were employed to transform the categorical data into numerical values. Specifically, label encoding was used to map each crop name to a unique numerical value.

Additionally, the distributions of individual features using distribution plots were visualized (Figure 1.2, Figure 1.3), which helped in better understanding their characteristics and distribution. This process made it easier to spot any possible patterns or irregularities.

Figure 1.1 displays a correlation matrix illustrating the associations among variables within the dataset. A correlation coefficient nearing 1 denotes a robust positive correlation, whereas a value approaching -1 indicates a substantial negative correlation. When the coefficient is close to 0,

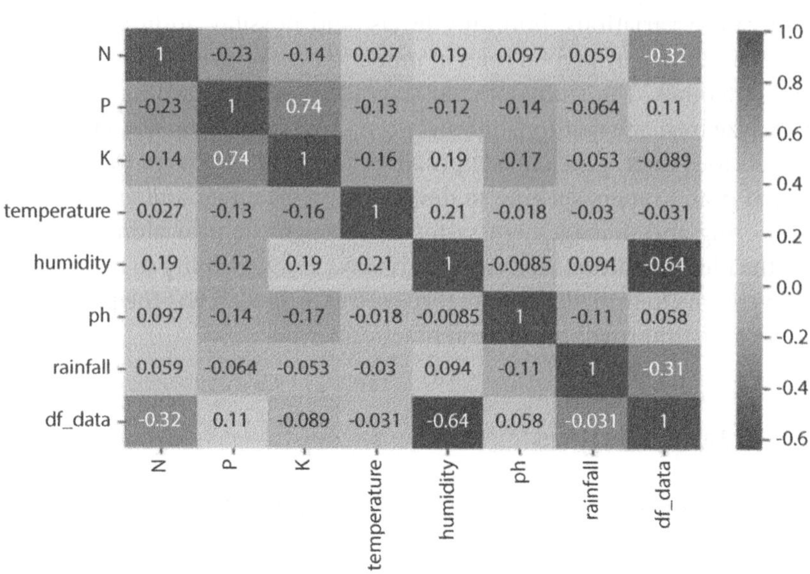

Figure 1.1 Correlation matrix.

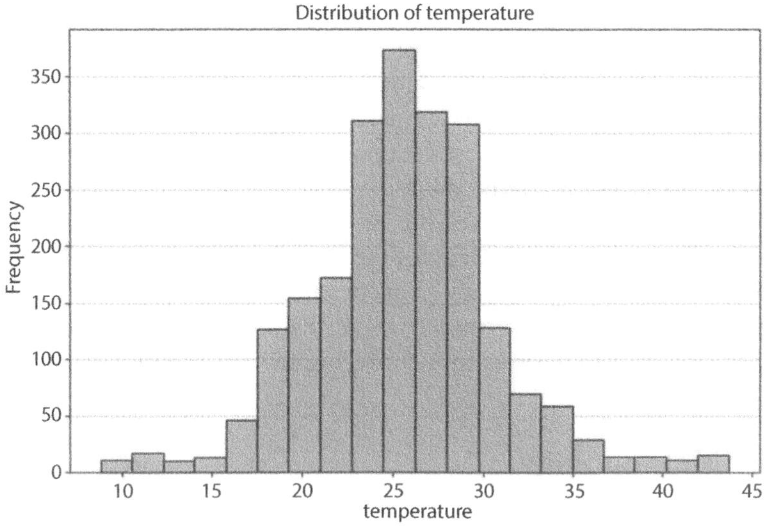

Figure 1.2 Distribution of temperature.

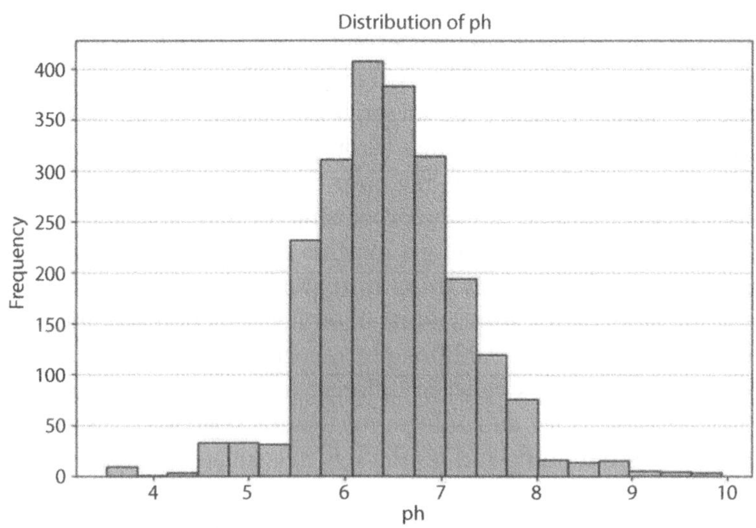

Figure 1.3 Distribution of pH.

it implies minimal to no linear relationship between the variables.The variables are listed along the rows and columns of the matrix, with the diagonal typically showing perfect correlation (that has value 1) as each variable correlates perfectly with itself.

The above graph illustrates the frequency distribution of temperature within the dataset. The values depicted along the horizontal axis signify temperature ranges, while those along the vertical axis represent the frequency of occurrence for each temperature value. The symmetrical shape of the curve indicates that most data points cluster around the mean, with fewer occurrences at extreme values.

The graph above showcases the distribution of pH levels within the dataset. The horizontal axis denotes the range of pH values, while the vertical axis denotes the frequency of occurrence for each pH level. The bell-shaped curve indicates a symmetrical distribution of pH measurements, with the majority of observations clustering around a central pH value.

1.5 Methodology

Crop prediction and monitoring using machine learning involves a systematic approach to leverage data-driven insights for agricultural decision-making. The methodology encompasses several key stages, beginning with the acquisition and preprocessing of the dataset. Initially obtained from Kaggle, the dataset contains essential agricultural parameters such as rainfall, temperature, humidity, pH levels, and crop types. Data preprocessing is crucial to ensure the integrity and quality of the dataset. This involves handling missing values through imputation or removal and encoding categorical variables like crop types into numerical format to facilitate model training. After preprocessing the data, an exploratory data analysis (EDA) is performed to get insights into the characteristics of the dataset. Distribution analysis using histograms and density plots visualizes the spread of each feature, aiding in outlier detection and understanding feature distributions. Additionally, a correlation matrix is generated to examine relationships between different features, identifying potential multicollinearity issues and informing feature selection. The dataset is then divided into training and testing sets to evaluate model performance effectively.

Several machine learning models are considered for crop prediction, including K-Nearest Neighbors (KNN), Random Forest, Decision Tree, and Naïve Bayes. Each model is trained on the training set and evaluated using appropriate metrics such as accuracy (Table 1.2). The Random Forest algorithm emerges as the top performer due to its high accuracy and robustness. Once selected, the Random Forest model is implemented using the entire training dataset. This trained model is then used to make

Table 1.2 Dataset features.

Input features	Explanation
Humidity	Humidity in percentage
P	Phosphorous
Rainfall	Rainfall in millimeter
Temperature (°C)	Temperature in Degree Celsius
N	Nitrogen
pH	Soil pH
K	Potassium

predictions on unseen data, i.e., the testing dataset, to assess its generalization capability and predictive accuracy.

Evaluation and validation of the Random Forest model are essential to ensure its reliability and effectiveness. Various evaluation metrics are employed to assess the model's performance on the testing dataset, providing insights into its predictive capabilities. Additionally, cross-validation methods like k-fold cross-validation may be used to further validate the model and assess its stability across different subsets of data. Furthermore, optimization and fine-tuning techniques, such as hyperparameter tuning and feature engineering, may be applied to enhance the model's performance. Once the model meets the desired performance criteria, it can be deployed in a production environment for real-world crop prediction and monitoring tasks. Regular monitoring and updating of the model are necessary to ensure its continued effectiveness and relevance in evolving agricultural conditions. Through this comprehensive methodology, the project aims to develop a reliable and accurate machine learning model for crop prediction and monitoring, ultimately empowering farmers with valuable insights for improved decision-making.

1.6 Architecture Diagram

The architecture diagram serves as a visual representation of the data flow and processing pipeline for crop prediction and pesticide recommendation. The diagram delineates the sequential steps involved in data ingestion, preprocessing, feature extraction, model training, inference, and recommendation generation. It provides a comprehensive overview of how to input data streams through various stages to produce actionable insights for crop management and pest control.

The process begins with the collection of a comprehensive dataset that contains diverse information such as historical crop performance, weather conditions, soil characteristics, and other relevant factors. This raw dataset serves as the foundation for training and building the predictive model.

Following data acquisition, the data undergoes preprocessing stages, including data cleaning, integration, transformation, and reduction. During data cleaning, issues such as missing values, outliers, and inconsistencies are addressed to ensure the quality and integrity of the data. Data transformation techniques are applied to prepare the data for modeling, such as encoding categorical variables and scaling numerical features. This step is crucial when dealing with categorical data, such as different types of crops. Label encoding transforms categorical labels into numerical representations, ensuring that the machine learning model can interpret and process this information effectively. After label encoding, the dataset becomes labeled data. Each instance in the dataset now consists of numerical features, including the encoded labels, and corresponding target values. After label encoding, transforming the dataset into labeled data enables numerical representation of features and corresponding target values. Subsequently, the labeled data undergoes evaluation across various machine learning models to determine the most suitable algorithm for crop prediction. Upon comparative analysis, including models like Naïve Bayes, KNN, Decision Trees, Support Vector Machine, Random Forest, AdaBoost, Logistic Regression, and Gradient Boosting, it was found that Random Forest exhibited superior performance. Each decision tree is trained on a subset of the labeled data and provides its prediction. The last prediction is determined by aggregating the individual predictions generated by all the trees.

Based on the input data, the Random Forest classifier produces predictions for crop types, crop yields, and advised pesticide usage. Farmers can use these predictions as useful insights, giving them practical information to help them decide on crop management strategies. Farmers can increase overall agricultural productivity and sustainability, optimize crop yields, and reduce pesticide usage by utilizing the predictive models built into our architecture.

1.7 Results and Discussions

The comparative analysis of various machine learning algorithms for crop prediction reveals distinctive performance metrics. Naïve Bayes, KNN, Decision Trees, Random Forest, Logistic Regression, AdaBoost, Gradient Boosting and Support Vector Machine were assessed using metrics such as Mean Squared Error (MSE), Mean Absolute Error (MAE), R-squared value, and Accuracy (Table 1.3). Among these, Random Forest exhibited superior performance with a low MAE score of 0.0159, MSE of 0.0386, high R-squared value of 0.9990, and an accuracy of 0.9931. These metrics indicate Random Forest's ability to predict crop outcomes accurately. Other models like Decision Trees and Gradient Boosting also demonstrated competitive results. However, Random Forest emerged as the most suitable choice for crop prediction due to its robust performance across various evaluation criteria. This analysis underscores the significance of selecting appropriate machine learning algorithms for effective crop prediction, with Random Forest standing out as a promising approach. Figure 1.4 depicts the performance metrics, including Mean Absolute Error (MAE),

Table 1.3 Comparison of all algorithms.

Algorithm	MAE score	MSE score	R-squared value	Accuracy
Logistic Regression	0.1840	1.4340	0.9657	0.9454
Naïve Bayes	0.0090	0.0181	0.9995	0.9954
Support Vector Machine	0.1318	1.0636	0.9746	0.9613
KNN	0.1022	0.9568	0.9771	0.9704
Decision Trees	0.0590	0.5681	0.9864	0.9863
Random Forest	0.0159	0.0386	0.9990	0.9931
AdaBoost	5.1	46.818	-0.1167	0.1409
Gradient Boosting	0.0409	0.0954	0.9977	0.9818

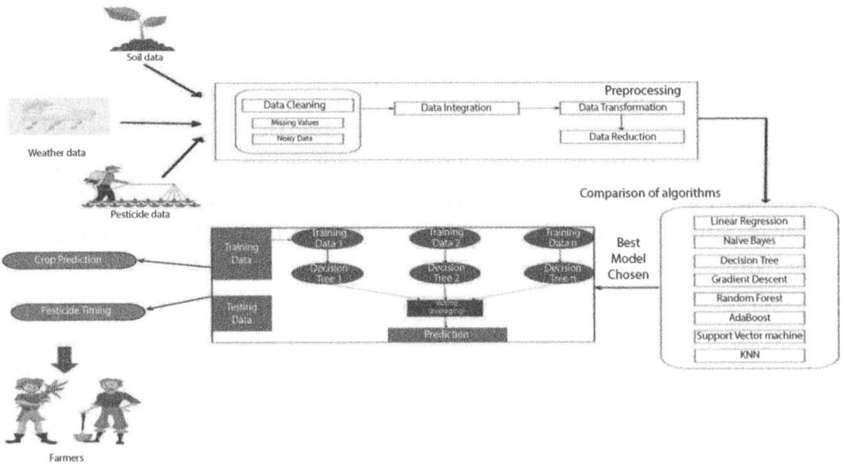

Figure 1.4 Architecture diagram.

Mean Squared Error (MSE), and R-squared value, for each machine learning model evaluated for crop prediction.

Figure 1.5 compares the accuracy of different models employed in the analysis, with Naïve Bayes and Random Forest exhibiting the highest accuracy among the tested models. Each bar represents the accuracy score achieved by a specific model, with the y-axis indicating the accuracy percentage.

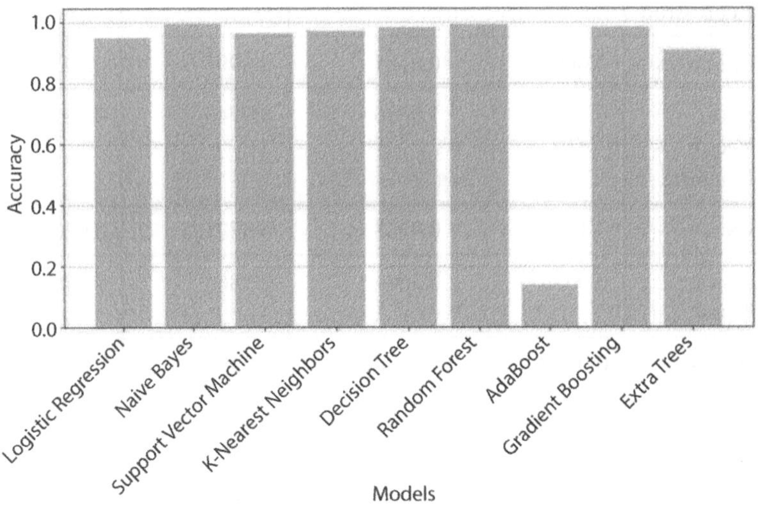

Figure 1.5 Accuracy of models.

One metric used to assess a regression model's performance is Mean Absolute Error (MAE). It calculates the mean absolute difference between a dataset's actual values and its anticipated values. Figure 1.6 illustrates the MAE of different models employed in the analysis. Each bar represents the MAE value for a specific model, with the y-axis denoting the error. Notably, AdaBoost exhibits the highest MAE among the tested models, indicating relatively larger discrepancies between predicted and actual values. Conversely, Random Forest and Naïve Bayes demonstrate the lowest MAE, suggesting superior accuracy and precision in their predictions.

Mean Squared Error (MSE) serves as a widely utilized measure for assessing the effectiveness of regression models. It measures the average squared differences between the predicted values and the actual values in a dataset. Within a dataset, it measures the average squared deviations between the observed and projected values. When the MSE is lower, the model is performing better since there are fewer differences between the expected and actual values.

Figure 1.7 illustrates the MSE of various models employed in the analysis. Each bar represents the MSE value for a specific model, with the y-axis indicating the magnitude of the squared error. Notably, AdaBoost has the highest MSE among the tested models, indicating relatively larger discrepancies between predicted and actual values squared. Conversely, Random Forest and Naïve Bayes have the lowest MSE, signifying superior accuracy and precision in their predictions.

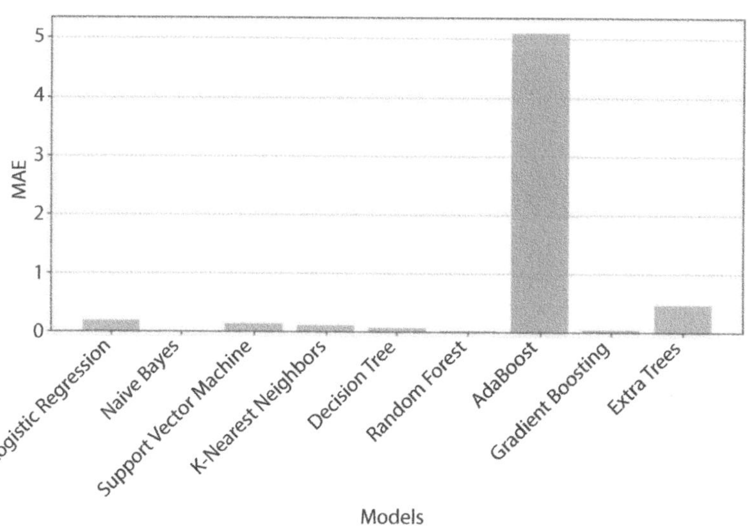

Figure 1.6 Mean absolute error of models.

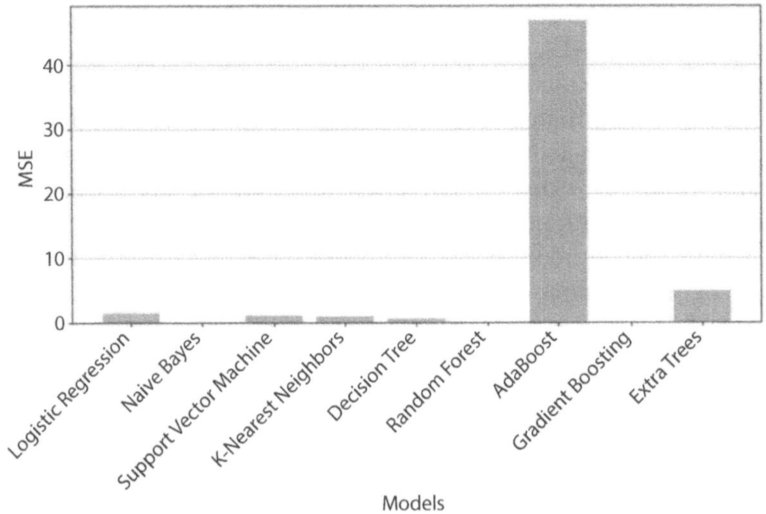

Figure 1.7 Mean square error of models.

The statistical metric R-squared (R^2) quantifies how well the independent variables explain the variability of the dependent variable. Figure 1.8 illustrates the R-squared values obtained from various models employed in the analysis. Notably, Naïve Bayes and Random Forest models exhibit higher R-squared values compared to other models. The superior performance

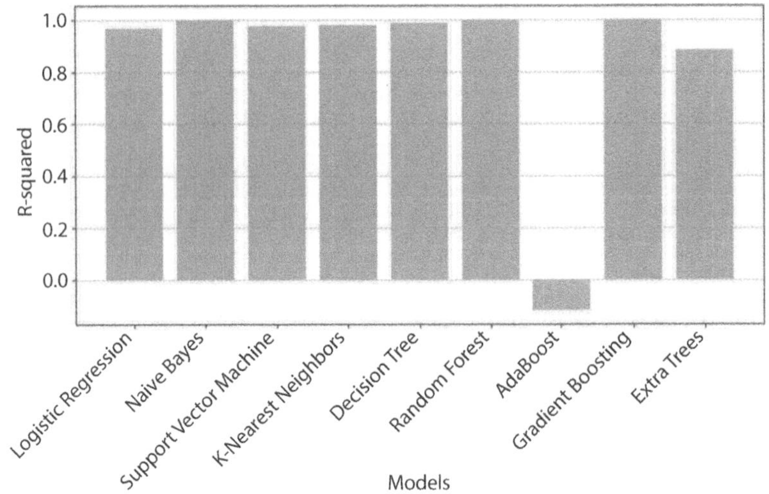

Figure 1.8 R-squared values of models.

of Naïve Bayes and Random Forest models, as evidenced by their larger R-squared values, suggests that these models are more effective in capturing the underlying relationships within the dataset.

1.8 Conclusion

This paper's examination of crop prediction and monitoring using machine learning has yielded significant insights and outcomes. Through meticulous data preprocessing, exploratory data analysis, and model selection, we have successfully developed a robust and accurate machine learning model, with Random Forest emerging as the most effective algorithm for predicting crop types based on environmental parameters. This model holds immense potential for revolutionizing agricultural practices by supplying farmers and stakeholders with up-to-date and accurate data to enhance crop management efficiency.

The project's completion emphasizes how crucial it is to use cutting-edge tools like machine learning to tackle challenging agricultural problems. Through the utilization of data-driven insights, it is possible to improve crop productivity, optimize resource allocation, and advance sustainable farming methods. In addition, the Random Forest model's effective application shows that machine learning methods are feasible for use in practical agricultural settings, opening the door for further developments in precision agriculture. In order to increase prediction accuracy and generalization capacity, future research and development activities should concentrate on improving the model, growing the dataset to include a wider range of environmental and geographic factors, and investigating new machine learning algorithms. Furthermore, in order to fully realize the model's potential and enable its widespread adoption among farmers worldwide, effort must be made to implement it in real-world agricultural settings and integrate it into current farming systems.

References

1. Abbasi, R., Martinez, P., Ahmad, R., Crop diagnostic system: A robust disease detection and management system for leafy green crops grown in an aquaponics facility. *Artif. Intell. Agric.*, 10, 1–12, 2023, DOI 10.1016/j.aiia.2023.09.001.

2. Abernethy, J., Beeson, P., Boryan, C., Hunt, K., Sartore, L., Preseason crop type prediction using crop sequence boundaries. *Comput. Electron. Agric.*, 208, 107768, 2023, DOI 10.1016/j.compag.2023.107768.
3. Bouacida, I., Farou, B., Djakhdjakha, L., Seridi, H., Kurulay, M., Innovative deep learning approach for cross-crop plant disease detection: A generalized method for identifying unhealthy leaves. *Inf. Process. Agric.*, 2024, DOI 10.1016/j.inpa.2024.03.002.
4. Bregaglio, S., Ginaldi, F., Raparelli, E., Fila, G., Bajocco, S., Improving crop yield prediction accuracy by embedding phenological heterogeneity into model parameter sets. *Agric. Syst.*, 209, 103666, 2023, DOI 10.1016/j.agsy.2023.103666.
5. Gupta, R., *et al.*, WB-CPI: weather based crop prediction in India using big data analytics. *IEEE Access*, 9, 137869–137885, 2021, DOI 10.1109/ACCESS.2021.3117247.
6. Islam, M.M., *et al.*, DeepCrop: deep learning-based crop disease prediction with web application. *J. Agric. Food Res.*, 14, 100764, 2023, DOI 10.1016/j.jafr.2023.100764.
7. Islam, M.R., Oliullah, K., Kabir, M.M., Alom, M., Mridha, M.F., Machine learning enabled IoT system for soil nutrients monitoring and crop recommendation. *J. Agric. Food Res.*, 14, 100880, 2023, DOI 10.1016/j.jafr.2023.100880.
8. Jhajharia, K., Mathur, P., Jain, S., Nijhawan, S., Crop yield prediction using machine learning and deep learning techniques. *Procedia Comput. Sci.*, 218, 406–417, 2023, DOI 10.1016/j.procs.2023.01.023.
9. Mohan, A., Venkatesan, M., Prabhavathy, P., Jayakrishnan, A., Temporal convolutional network based rice crop yield prediction using multispectral satellite data. *Infrared Phys. Technol.*, 135, 104960, 2023, DOI 10.1016/j.infrared.2023.104960.
10. Nalini, T. and Rama, A., Impact of temperature condition in crop disease analyzing using machine learning algorithm. *Meas. Sens.*, 24, 100408, 2022, DOI 10.1016/j.measen.2022.100408.
11. Rajakumaran, M., Arulselvan, G., Subashree, S., Sindhuja, R., Crop yield prediction using multi-attribute weighted tree-based support vector machine. *Meas. Sens.*, 31, 101002, 2024, DOI 10.1016/j.measen.2023.101002.
12. Raju, C., Ashoka, D.V., B.V., A.P., CropCast: harvesting the future with interfused machine learning and advanced stacking ensemble for precise crop prediction. *Kuwait J. Sci.*, 2023.
13. Rashid, M., Bari, B.S., Yusup, Y., Kamaruddin, M.A., Khan, N., A comprehensive review of crop yield prediction using machine learning approaches with special emphasis on palm oil yield prediction. *IEEE Access*, 9, 63406–63439, 2021, DOI 10.1109/ACCESS.2021.3075159.
14. Sharma, P., Dadheech, P., Aneja, N., Aneja, S., Predicting agriculture yields based on machine learning using regression and deep learning. *IEEE Access*, 11, 111255–111264, 2023, DOI 10.1109/ACCESS.2023.3321861.

15. Sivanantham, V., *et al.*, Quantile correlative deep feedforward multilayer perceptron for crop yield prediction. *Comput. Electr. Eng.*, 98, 107696, 2022, DOI 10.1016/j.compeleceng.2022.107696.

2

Role of Machine Learning in Blockchain for Predictive Analysis

Dhivya Bharathi M.[1]*, Leninisha Shanmugam[2] and M. Sandhya[2]

[1]*School of Electronics Engineering, Vellore Institute of Technology, Chennai, India*
[2]*School of Computer Science and Engineering, Vellore Institute of Technology, Chennai, India*

Abstract

Blockchain technology can evaluate a lot of plant- or crop-associated data, including growth, quality and productivity. It can give a report of a plant even after the plant has left the field. This study carried out a combination of two main technologies: Blockchain technology and Internet of Things (IoT). It is used to maintain a model that difference in automatic harvest in the agriculture field. The growth of the IoT has established its significance over multifarious industries. However, overall usage of IoT mechanism in agriculture is not practicable due to some other issues like security and privacy. Using IoT and blockchain technology in the field of agriculture is important support for security reasons. It allows the collection of data, storing the data and sharing the data and information in the supply chains in agriculture in a secure and sturdy manner. For the development of the agricultural food supply chain, a decentralized blockchain usage involves traceability connection that will include IoT systems that give and get the data digitally through the chain. Various industries like supply chain management, transportation, healthcare and energy management can achieve a good effect from the combination of IoT and blockchain technology. It can give a possible way to create real-time product tracking, increase the transparency level, fraud alert and reduce the supply chain protocols. In this research, the blockchain replica is based on machine learning, in which the machine learning utilises the exact data and gives suitable results. As a result, the combination of machine learning and blockchain technology gives expected results as an increase in efficiency. To help farmers in the decision-making process, the IoT linked the agricultural sector to the agricultural outcomes to the overall data storage in the system. By using sensors, it produces lot of data from the

**Corresponding author*: dhivyabharathi.m2023@vitstudent.ac.in

Narayanan Ganesh and Kanak Kalita (eds.) Harvesting Data: Blockchain, AI and Advanced Innovations in Agriculture, (29–44) © 2026 Scrivener Publishing LLC

agricultural sector and transfers it on a device to the storage. Finally, the resultant outcomes are more accurate and transparent. Hence the predictive analysis is highly accurate as well as transparent. Furthermore, this research helps to get the resultant outcomes more accurate and transparent. Using predictive analysis and machine learning, the algorithms used on the data collection help farmers or owners in the decision-making process. Like this technique the field mapping and software used for analysis can forecast and decide the required work. It is also used for pest attack decision and the difference in alert in the systems. Observing the previous data, weather conditions, sensor recordings, a prediction model can foresee the growth of the crop, quality of the seed, disease detection, and harvesting optimization. This will enable positive outcomes in the active manner and optimization of the crop in the field. In the agricultural sector, IoT and the blockchain technology combination are used to improve the efficiency, accuracy, resource reduction, and optimization of the overall management of the crop field or farm.

Keywords: Blockchain technology, machine learning, precision agriculture, predictive analysis, internet of things, agri-supply chains, decentralized computer architecture, decision-making

2.1 Introduction

Tracking agricultural data, such as crop growth, seed quality, and even a plant's journey after it leaves the field, is made possible by blockchain technology. There are no longer any worries about unethical or illegal behaviour in the supply chain, and transparency has increased. Without a doubt, agriculture is India's main source of income. The need for higher agricultural output develops as the world's population rises. In the digital age, agriculture is evolving quickly to become a data-heavy sector where farmers gather and analyse enormous amounts of data from numerous sources to boost productivity and get vital insights. Agriculture may undergo significant modifications because of machine learning and the use of internet-connected equipment. Algorithms using machine learning are crucial for evaluating a variety of agricultural data and doing predictive analyses to raise farmland output.

Through the integration of internet-connected devices and machine learning into farming methods, farmers can establish an automated system that enhances time management efficiency and lowers risks (see Figure 2.1). Crop damage from climate change frequently affects both the quantity and quality of plants. Thus, creating a monitoring system is still essential to solving this problem. Crop quality is improved and productivity is increased through environmentally friendly water conservation that

Figure 2.1 Basic workflow for predictive analysis using blockchain technology.

monitors climate change. For farmers, maximizing sustainable farming practices becomes a top priority. Through data access, decision support, and the use of sensors and actuators that combine goods, information, and services for effective production, the Internet of Things (IoT) helps to improve productivity, profitability, quality, and efficiency.

Additionally, IoT-enabled smart agriculture boosts real-time event monitoring and regional data analysis, advancing the agriculture field's transition to sustainability (see Figure 2.2). This article highlights new research directions in IoT, ML, blockchain technology, and climate change adaptation in agriculture while introducing the most recent IoT-ML-driven intelligent agricultural management strategy. To prepare for future development, the study also explores the potential and problems that come with incorporating these cutting-edge technologies into agricultural methods.

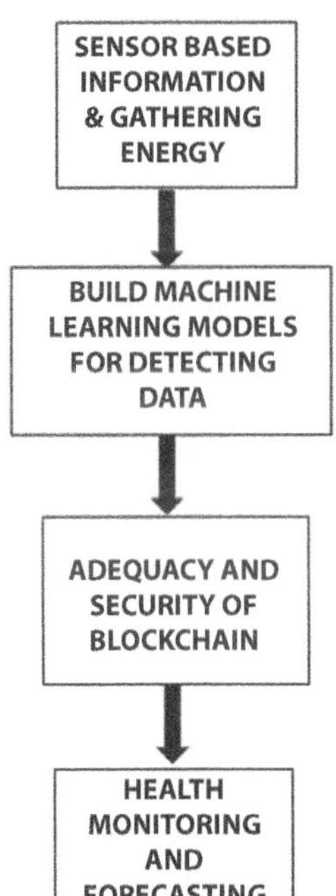

Figure 2.2 Machine learning combines with IoT for predictive analysis.

2.2 Related Research

There are currently a number of ML-IoT based studies and project efforts being conducted on agricultural systems. Kamble *et al.* reviewed studies on smart sensors and IoT for satellite imaging and smart agriculture [1]. They suggest IoT advancements that would help researchers and farmers in their job. Bagchi *et al.* suggest a taxonomy that describes IoT architecture and protocols, and addresses technical concerns like safety, confidentiality, adaptability, and conservation of energy in the research [2]. It gives an overview of recent research on such challenges. Nassar *et al.* cover IoT components, network design and sections, cloud computing, large-scale information storage enabling smart farming, safety issues, and regional policies for coordinating IoT-based farming [3]. Cheng *et al.* present an investigation that examines the application of ML algorithms in WSN technology analysis of data in the agricultural sector [4]. The paper describes an empirical study of an IoT-based, driven by information smart farm experimental system. Tanwar *et al.* include a summary of research on blockchain technology in urban planning [5]. The paper also provides previous expertise, pertinent works, and hurdles [6]. Mitra *et al.* cover blockchain classification, voting methods, and potential uses [7]. They also address the technical challenges and possibilities regarding blockchain technology's growth in the future. Unal *et al.* discuss the deployment of IoT in healthcare, covering its implementation areas, design sections, worries about privacy and security, and drawbacks [8]. Several techniques for field decision-making, growing crops, pest detection, and tracking of systems have been investigated by Kasula *et al.* [9]. They evaluated the benefits and drawbacks of multiple image processing techniques and recommended certain ones for recognizing pests and foliage. The application of unmanned aircraft for cultivation of seeds and continuous tracking has been discussed. Chattu *et al.* check the humidity levels in the soil and feed the crops continuously [10]. This technology additionally detects the targeted region's humidity and temperature and the presence of barriers in order to eliminate the necessity for people to be present. The user may utilize this information from the web through a handheld device. In [11], Hellenborn *et al.* utilize IoT and machine learning to forecast tomato and potato late blight disease before they express themselves. This will notify farmers of the optimal period to use the precautionary pesticides. In [12], Qiu and Zhang present an IoT-based mixed machine learning model for crop forecasting. They deploy machine learning technique to predict the crop production and evaluate the state of the land [13]. Dillenberg *et al.*

[14] quickly record the data in the database system, and this gets displayed as a website and rendered accessible throughout the global web. To guarantee the confidentiality of patient data, Shahbazi and Byun employ blockchain technology in smart healthcare systems [15]. It offers the efficiency, security, and privacy of the data in information transfer between IoT devices and wearable sensors.

An overview of the technologies in the fields of blockchain, AI, IoT, and ML is provided in this article. Additionally, it offers a number of methods for combining IoT with ML, as well as data analysis for effective systems that leverages blockchain and artificial intelligence. Future projects, opportunities, and problems are also covered.

2.3 Existing System

In smart farming, the combination of blockchain, machine learning, and the IoT creates a synergistic approach that improves the sustainability, efficiency, and transparency of agricultural methods. An outline of the current applications of these technologies is provided below.

Real-time data from the field is collected by IoT devices, which include a variety of sensors and smart equipment. This data is crucial for making well-informed decisions. Internet of Things sensors keep an eye on crop health, pH levels, temperature, humidity, and soil moisture. Smart tractors, drones for spraying, and automated irrigation systems increase productivity and cut down on labor.

1. Livestock Management: IoT devices monitor the location, behaviour, and health of animals.
2. Machine Learning's Place in Smart Farming: ML algorithms examine the massive volume of information gathered. Blockchain's role in smart farming includes supply chain security, traceability, and transparency; these are guaranteed by blockchain technology.
3. Traceability is monitoring agricultural goods' provenance and path from field to table. Smart Contracts means placing agents by automating agreements and transactions between parties. Keeping the data gathered from IoT devices accurate and dependable is known as data integrity.

4. An Integrated Blockchain, IoT, and Machine Learning System for Smart Farming: Predicting crop yields using past performance information and current circumstances allows tractors to operate more efficiently and with less workforce.

2.4 System Hardware

Soil Sensor:
NPK Accuracy of Soil: BB@+2%F.s. Range: 0-2000 mg/kg
Differentiability 1 mg/kg (mg/l)
DC 12-volt service voltage
Mode of output: RS 485
Inactive dissipation
10mA at 12VDC
IP68 protection level
Boundary Dimension: 45*15*135 mm.
Workplace Temperature: -40 to 85°C
encapsulating epoxy resin in black
Wind Sensor:
0–60 m/s (216 km/h) wind direction and speed (0–360°)
Aluminium alloy structure with anodization
Heating option (-40°C to +70°C): 0.9 kg
tested in exposed situations (UL2218 Class 1, BS EN 60945, IP66).
Light Sensor:
Comprehensive dynamic range: 0.1 – 40,000 LUX
Wide temperature range of operation: -40 to 85 degrees
16-bit digital output with high resolution @ 400 kHz I2C Fast-Mode
Programmable interrupt feature with threshold values that can be adjusted by the user
Differentiable detection modes.
Humidity Sensor:
Energy source: DC 10–30V
Range of temperatures: -40°C to 120°C; default: -40°C to 80°C
Range of humidity: 0% to 100%
Accuracy of the external probe: ±2%RH, ±0.4°C (25°F)
Accuracy of built-in probe: ±3%RH, ±0.5°C (25°F).
Adjustment: 0.1°C, 0.1%RH
Stability for the long term: humidity ≤1%RH/y, temperature ≤0.1°C/y
Temperature ≤15s (1m/s wind speed), humidity ≤4s (1m/s wind speed)
RS485 (Modbus protocol)/4-20ma/0-5v/0-10v is the output signal.

Rainfall Sensor:
Typical operating power: 0.4 W
Storage conditions: -40°C to 80°C
When heating, working power is 2.4 W.
Signal output: 485, relay
Configuring a parameter: software configuration
By Default Modbus address: 01
Codes for support functions: 03, 06
Starting point for heating: below 15°C (default)
40°C is the maximum heating temperature by default.
Relay for output with a 250 VAC load capacity 1A/30VDC 1A

2.5 Project Analysis

The initiative addresses the issues of contemporary farming management with a focus on providing end users with higher quality and health benefits through the delivery of organic produce. The analysis reveals inefficiencies in conventional farming practices, such as resource waste and subpar productivity brought on by incorrect fertilizer application based on crude estimates of crop yield and soil analysis. The existing system uses antiquated methods like hand fertilizing and aqueduct irrigation, which leads to overuse of pesticides and water, as well as decreased output. The suggested solution, on the other hand, uses blockchain and IoT to transform agriculture. Using sensor networks to track temperature, humidity, moisture content, and pH levels, the system maximizes farming while guaranteeing the authenticity and traceability of food sources. Automation and blockchain-based tracking offer better transparency, enhanced productivity, and higher-quality products.

2.6 Problem Statement

The problem statement presents the challenge that current farming management methods have in providing end consumers with authentic organic products of the highest quality and healthiest features. It demonstrates how incorrect fertilizer application based on basic soil analysis and crop yield estimates causes inefficiencies in current agricultural practices, such as resource waste and low production. It also discusses how the food supply chain's lack of traceability and transparency undermines consumer confidence and happiness.

2.7 Proposed Framework

The paper's primary goal is to examine and adopt cutting-edge technologies including blockchain, artificial intelligence, machine learning, and the internet of things. By doing this, agriculture may be made more automated so that production and sustainability can be provided without harming the environment. The primary goal is to assist farmers in learning about smart agricultural technology that may be applied in various fields, such as pest control and water management, to address the difficulties posed by climate change and sustainability.

Decision-makers can benefit from insights provided by machine learning algorithms. Machine learning algorithms, for instance, can be used to spot trends in consumer behaviour and create marketing campaigns that are specifically targeted at them. By examining rival pricing and client demand, machine learning algorithms can also be utilized to optimize pricing tactics like dynamic pricing. These insights can provide companies a competitive edge and help them make better decisions.

Data Gathering and Monitoring: Internet of Things Devices: Smart devices and sensors gather data in real time on crop health, livestock, weather, and soil conditions.
Data Transmission: For analysis, data from IoT devices is sent to a central platform.
Robotic Learning Algorithms: Examine the information to find trends, forecast results, and provide suggestions.
Predictive Models: Assist farmers in making well-informed choices about harvesting, fertilization, irrigation, and pest management.
Blockchain Record: Maintains transparency and data integrity by keeping track of all exchanges of data and transactions.

1. Initialize Blockchain Network: Set up the blockchain infrastructure, including nodes and smart contracts. Define the rules for data transactions and access permissions.
2. Deploy IoT Sensors in Field: Install various IoT sensors in the agricultural field to collect data on soil conditions, weather, crop health, etc.
3. Collect Real-Time Data: Continuously collect data from the IoT sensors.

4. Transmit Data to Central Server/Cloud Platform: Securely send the collected data to a central server or cloud for processing.
5. Apply ML Algorithms for Data Analysis: Use machine learning algorithms to analyze the data and generate insights.
6. Generate Insights and Recommendations: Produce actionable insights and recommendations based on the ML analysis.
7. Package Data with Metadata: Organize the processed data and include metadata such as timestamps, sensor IDs, and location information.
8. Create Blockchain Transaction: Form a new blockchain transaction containing the packaged data.

The main procedures for integrating blockchain-based data security in smart agriculture are delineated in this algorithm and flowchart. The objective is to increase data security and trust in the agricultural ecosystem by utilizing the advantages of blockchain technology, such as immutability, traceability, and transparency.

2.8 IoT-ML Predictive Analysis

Anything that can be controlled *via* the internet is considered an Internet of Things device. With wearable IoWT (Internet of Wearable Things) like smartwatches and home management solutions like Google Home, IoT devices have become ubiquitous in consumer markets. By 2020, it is predicted that over 30 billion gadgets will be linked to the IoT.

The goal of the Internet of Things' applications in agriculture is to help traditional farming operations satisfy rising demand and reduce output losses. In agriculture, the IoT uses robots, drones, remote sensors, computer imaging, and ever-improving machine learning and analytical tools to monitor crops, survey, and map the fields, and give farmers data for smart farm management plans that save time and money.

IoT is implemented in agriculture by means of robotics, unmanned aerial vehicles, sensors, and computer imaging combined with analytical tools to monitor and gain insights from the farms. Physical equipment is placed on farms to monitor and record data, which is subsequently analyzed to obtain insightful information.

2.9 Blockchain Technology with IoT and Machine Learning

Predictive analytics technology, a branch of data science, can be applied in agriculture to assist farmers in forecasting crop yields, estimating demand for certain crops, and optimizing the use of irrigation and fertilizer. Predictive analytics can offer insights that can assist farmers in making more informed decisions about when to plant, how to care for their crops, and what pricing to charge for their produce by examining historical data patterns. Predictive analytics can also detect early warning indicators of agricultural diseases and pests, enabling farmers to take preventative action and minimize or eliminate harm.

2.10 Benefits of Blockchain in Predictive Analysis

1. Forecasting and optimizing yields
2. Reduced waste and precision watering
3. Astute sensing and mapping
4. Fruit counting and crop health monitoring
5. Tracking and predicting the climate
6. Geofencing and livestock tracking
7. Optimization of the supply chain

2.11 Artificial Intelligence and IoT in Smart Farming

The following strategies are examples of how AI can be applied to precision farming to maximize fertilizer and irrigation applications.

Monitoring of Soil and Crops:
Real-time data on crop health, soil moisture, nutrient levels, and environmental factors are gathered *via* AI-powered sensors and drones. This data is analyzed by computer vision and deep learning algorithms to find patterns and identify problems early.

Analytics That Predict:
Artificial intelligence (AI) models can forecast agricultural water and fertilizer requirements by using historical data, weather forecasts, and satellite imagery.

The time and volume of fertilizer and irrigation treatments can be optimized with the help of these forecasts.

Flexible Watering Systems:
AI-controlled irrigation systems can modify water flow and scheduling automatically in response to current soil moisture and meteorological information. This minimizes waste and guarantees that crops receive the proper amount of water.

Application of Precision Fertilizer:
Artificial intelligence (AI) algorithms are capable of analyzing crop growth trends and soil nutrient data to decide the best time, place, and amount of fertilizer to apply.

This can be accomplished by using variable-rate technology, which applies fertilizers precisely and targetedly to minimize overapplication and environmental damage.

Systems for Assisting Decisions:
Artificial intelligence (AI)-driven decision support systems are able to combine information from multiple sources (weather, soil, crop, market, etc.) to give farmers customized irrigation and fertilizer management advice. These suggestions can be modified to meet the unique requirements of the crop, the local environment, and the soil.

Autonomous Agribusiness Machinery:
Based on the optimal plans, self-driving tractors and sprayers with AI-powered control systems can apply fertilizer and irrigation accurately. This guarantees exact and uniform application, cutting down on waste and enhancing.

Ongoing Education and Adjustment:
AI models have the ability to continuously learn from the information gathered from farming activities, allowing them to gradually modify their forecasts and suggestions. This guarantees continuous optimization by enabling the system to adjust to shifting crop kinds, environmental conditions, and farming techniques. Farmers may boost crop yields, decrease their environmental effect, and increase resource efficiency by utilizing AI in precision farming, all of which will contribute to the agricultural industry's overall sustainability.

Better Data Gathering and Tracking:
When compared to more conventional approaches, sensors and drones can gather a great deal more data at a higher geographical and temporal resolution, including soil moisture, nutrient levels, crop health, and environmental variables. This extensive set of data offers a more precise and in-depth comprehension of the field circumstances. This enables farmers to prevent or mitigate crop losses by taking timely, targeted action.

Enhanced Resource Administration:
Farmers can apply pesticides, fertilizers, and water more efficiently if they use AI-powered analytics to aggregate data from sensors and drones. As a result, resources are used more effectively, there is less waste, and the environmental impact is diminished.

Enhanced Quality and Yield:
Higher agricultural yields and better product quality can be achieved through the deployment of AI-powered sensors and drones to optimize resource management and solve concerns early. Farmers may benefit from higher profits as well as a more consistent supply of food as a result.

Lower Labor and Operating Expenses:
Drones can swiftly and effectively cover wide regions, negating the need for human reconnaissance and surveillance. The effort needed to make decisions and carry out farming techniques can also be decreased by automated data collecting and analysis.

Enhanced Transparency and Traceability:
Blockchain-based solutions can be enhanced with the rich data gathered by sensors and drones, improving traceability and transparency across the agricultural supply chain. This can assist in meeting customer requests for further details regarding the source and manufacturing processes of the food they eat.

Both Adaptability and Scalability:
Drone and sensor systems driven by AI can be expanded to cover greater regions and customized to suit various crop varieties and agricultural conditions. Because of their adaptability, precision farming methods can be applied to a variety of agricultural sectors. Farmers can make better decisions, use resources more efficiently, and run their operations more sustainably and efficiently overall by utilizing AI-driven sensors and drones. This will enhance both the economic and environmental results of their operations.

2.12 Result Analysis

The purpose of integrating IoT sensors into smart agriculture systems is to guarantee accurate and productive data collecting. Having real-time access to information about soil moisture, temperature, and humidity facilitates decision-making when it comes to crop management. Blockchain technology provides solutions for basic issues like data security, storage, and transparency. Using smart contracts, the system implements data security, an approval process, and an encryption protocol. Important agricultural tasks like pesticides and irrigation could be completed with the help of the smart agriculture model. The system uses data from the Internet of Things to automatically modify the timetable for watering and the amount of pesticide used. These adjustments are made in response to real-time variables like temperature, pH, humidity, soil moisture, and weather forecasts.

The incorporation of the retail sector as an intelligent farming model makes it easier to distribute goods to wholesalers and retail outlets, as well as to the successful bidder. Relevant company suppliers can gather vital information about the product base, quality, and size growth stage by logging and evaluating production data. Enhancing resources and cutting costs are possible with blockchain technology in smart agriculture. Smart contracts guarantee the connection between specific levels, streamlining the procedure, lessening the workload for managers, and enabling the system to accommodate bigger projects.

2.13 Conclusion

We have presented a system that, by leveraging cutting-edge technologies like blockchain, IoT, and machine learning, enables farmers to overcome the obstacles that restrict their productivity and profitability. It is implemented with a secure architecture and user-friendly mobile applications. A produced database provides farmers with useful information and recommendations, such as water motor control and pesticide usage. The integration of IoT devices enables real-time data collecting and monitoring. enabling precise decision-making and guaranteeing the best possible placement of resources. Enhancing data traceability, transparency, integrity, and building trust and responsibility across the agricultural ecosystem are further benefits of integrating blockchain. By using our smart Agri-lands, farmers may benefit from increased general management, lower costs, and improved yield. They have access to current data, precise data, and decision-makers who will enhance farming practices, cut waste, and boost output. We managed pest control using a machine learning model, and the results were quite accurate. It is anticipated that automation and IoT in smart agriculture would soon supplant conventional farming practices.

2.14 Future Work

Blockchain technology can be used by researchers to improve the security of data acquired in smart farming, as well as to optimize irrigation and precision agriculture systems based on Internet of Things. The blockchain can be used to manage data and create load balancing, particularly for large systems and massive amounts of collected data. IoT can be used by professionals and farmers to monitor climate change, to mitigate the effects of change on plants and crops using multiple machine learning algorithms to analyze collected data and make appropriate judgments. ML algorithms can be used to interpret and analyze the remote sensing photos of agricultural land to optimize sustainable agriculture practices.

References

1. Kamble, S.S., Gunasekaran, A., Kumar, V., Belhadi, A., Foropon, C., A machine learning based approach for predicting blockchain adoption in supply chain. *Technol. Forecast. Soc. Change*, 163, 120465, 2021, DOI 10.1016/j.techfore.2020.120465.
2. Bagchi, S., Chakraborty, M., Chattopadhyay, A.K., APDRChain: ANN based predictive analysis of diseases and report sharing through blockchain, in: *Proceedings of International Ethical Hacking Conference 2019: eHaCON 2019*, Kolkata, India, Springer Singapore, pp. 105–115, 2020.
3. Nassar, M., Salah, K., ur Rehman, M.H., Svetinovic, D., Blockchain for explainable and trustworthy artificial intelligence. *Wiley Interdiscip. Rev.: Data Min. Knowl. Discov.*, 10, 1, e1340, 2020.
4. Cheng, A.S., Guan, Q., Su, Y., Zhou, P., Zeng, Y., Integration of machine learning and blockchain technology in the healthcare field: a literature review and implications for cancer care. *Asia-Pac. J. Oncol. Nurs.*, 8, 6, 720–724, 2021.
5. Tanwar, S., Bhatia, Q., Patel, P., Kumari, A., Singh, P.K., Hong, W.C., Machine learning adoption in blockchain-based smart applications: The challenges, and a way forward. *IEEE Access*, 8, 474–488, 2019.
6. Shanmugam, L., Gunasekaran, K., Natarajan, A., Kaliaperumal, V., Quantitative growth analysis of pulp necrotic tooth (post-op) using modified

region growing active contour model. *IET Image Proc.*, 11, 11, 1015–1019, 2017.

7. Mitra, A., Bera, B., Das, A.K., Jamal, S.S., You, I., Impact on blockchain-based AI/ML-enabled big data analytics for Cognitive Internet of Things environment. *Comput. Commun.*, 197, 173–185, 2023.
8. Unal, D., Hammoudeh, M., Khan, M.A., Abuarqoub, A., Epiphaniou, G., Hamila, R., Integration of federated machine learning and blockchain for the provision of secure big data analytics for Internet of Things. *Comput. Secur.*, 109, 102393, 2021.
9. Kasula, B.Y.K., Optimizing Smart Contracts with Machine Learning Techniques in Blockchain. *Int. J. Creat. Res. Comput. Technol. Des.*, 2, 2, 2020.
10. Chattu, V.K., A review of artificial intelligence, big data, and blockchain technology applications in medicine and global health. *Big Data Cogn. Comput.*, 5, 3, 41, 2021.
11. Hellenborn, B., Eliasson, O., Yitmen, I., Sadri, H., Asset information requirements for blockchain-based digital twins: a data-driven predictive analytics perspective. *Smart Sustain. Built Environ.*, 13, 1, 22–41, 2024.
12. Qiu, Y.Q. and Zhang, C., Artificial intelligence driven cognitive optimization and predictive analysis using blockchain privacy-based machine learning model. *Comput. Electr. Eng.*, 117, 109238, 2024.
13. Bragadeesh, S.A. and Umamakeswari, A., Role of blockchain in the Internet-of-Things (IoT). *Int. J. Eng. Technol.*, 7, 2, 109–112, 2018.
14. Dillenberger, D.N., Novotny, P., Zhang, Q., Jayachandran, P., Gupta, H., Hans, S., Sarpatwar, K., Blockchain analytics and artificial intelligence. *IBM J. Res. Dev.*, 63, 2/3, 5-1, 2019.
15. Shahbazi, Z. and Byun, Y.C., Smart manufacturing real-time analysis based on blockchain and machine learning approaches. *Appl. Sci.*, 11, 8, 3535, 2021.

3

Agriculture Manure Data Analysis Using Real-Time Cryptocurrency

Parvathi R.[1*], Pattabiraman V.[1] and Xiaohui Yuan[2]

[1]*School of Computer Science and Engineering, Vellore Institute of Technology, Chennai, India*
[2]*Department of Computer Science and Engineering, Computer Vision and Intelligent Systems Lab, University of North Texas, Denton, TX, United States of America*

Abstract

The cryptocurrency market is becoming more and more popular as a useful instrument to support established stock and futures markets. Precise market analysis enables traders to optimize their investment yields and make more informed decisions. Our goal is to build a web platform for accumulating, analyzing and visualizing different kinds of cryptocurrency data using Python and React framework. Live crypto market data analysis involves collecting and examining current information on cryptocurrency quantities, pricing, and other important parameters using an Application Programming Interface (API). This analysis aims to provide knowledge of the behavior and patterns of the market for cryptocurrency so that traders, investors, and risk managers can make well-informed decisions. This allows traders and investors to efficiently monitor market conditions and respond to changes quickly in real time. In this work, CoinGecko API and Yahoo Finance are used to fetch live data, which was then analyzed and visualized using React and Python. Furthermore, the future price of bitcoin, using ANN, ARIMA and regression using LSTM is forecasted. By monitoring market trends and identifying potential opportunities, traders and investors can diversify their portfolios, increase their chances of profit, minimize their risk of losses, recognize market dangers and obstacles, enabling investors to modify their plans as necessary. This helps increase efficiency and reduce the risk of human error. Using an API

**Corresponding author*: parvathi.r@vit.ac.in; ORCID: 0000-0002-6633-9897
Pattabiraman V.: ORCID: 0000-0001-8734-2203
Xiaohui Yuan: ORCID: 0000-0001-6897-4563

Narayanan Ganesh and Kanak Kalita (eds.) Harvesting Data: Blockchain, AI and Advanced Innovations in Agriculture, (45–76) © 2026 Scrivener Publishing LLC

also helps in developing trading algorithms, monitoring portfolio performance, and maintaining current with the most recent advancements in the market. By leveraging real-time dynamic market data and automated analysis tools, traders and investors can keep up with the latest developments in the quickly changing cryptocurrency sector. Regulatory compliance is another key area within the scope of this work. The cryptocurrency market is highly regulated, and investors need to stay up-to-date with changes to ensure compliance with regulations. This platform can help investors stay informed about regulatory developments, enabling them to comply with regulations and avoid potential legal issues. Lastly, it may be applied to evaluate the profitability of mining cryptocurrencies and pinpoint prospective mining agriculture prospects. The scope of live crypto market analysis encompasses various aspects of the agriculture supply chain management system, including tracing and tracking crops, reducing waste, fraud-free future transaction, agriculture market trends and insights, and agriculture risk assessment.

***Keywords*:** Cryptocurrency, crypto market, stock, exchange, trading, market volume, market capitalization

3.1 Introduction

A cryptocurrency is electronic money that is digital or virtual, runs without the help of a government or central bank, and is secured by cryptography. Because cryptocurrencies are decentralized, a dispersed network of computers rather than a single entity controls them. Cryptocurrency transactions are documented on a blockchain, a publicly accessible digital ledger that promotes transparency and guards against fraud. Some of the most well-known cryptocurrencies include Bitcoin, Ethereum, and Litecoin, but there are thousands of different cryptocurrencies in existence, each with its own unique features and characteristics.

Live crypto market data refers to real-time information about the price, volume, and other metrics related to cryptocurrencies and their respective markets. The information gives a quick overview of the bitcoin market's current situation and is updated continuously. In this work, CoinGecko API is used to fetch the cryptocurrency data.

Crypto market analysis involves the study of cryptocurrency markets in order to understand their past, present, and future behavior. This analysis is used to make informed investment decisions, as well as to gain insights into the broader trends and dynamics of the crypto industry.

Some of the key aspects of crypto market analysis include:

1. Technical analysis: This is the process of looking for patterns and trends in price charts along with additional market data that may be used to forecast future price changes.
2. Fundamental analysis: This entails examining the fundamental elements—such as technology, adoption, and legal framework that affect a certain cryptocurrency's value.
3. Sentiment analysis: This entails examining social networks along with other sources of sentiment in the market to comprehend traders' and investors' general attitudes, which can offer hints about potential future price changes.
4. Market structure analysis: This entails examining the general composition of the cryptocurrency market, taking into account the numbers and actions of various players, including exchanges, miners, and institutional investors.

3.1.1 Motivation

Gaining understanding of the behavior and patterns of the cryptocurrency market is the driving force behind data analysis of the market to help investors, traders, and risk managers make wise choices. Without access to trustworthy data and research, it is challenging for traders and investors to make well-informed decisions in the highly volatile and quickly evolving cryptocurrency market.

Crypto market analysis is necessary for several reasons. By analyzing historical and current cryptocurrency prices, volume, market capitalization, etc., patterns and trends that analysts can spot could be useful in predicting future changes in the market. This information can be used to develop trading strategies, manage risk, and identify opportunities for profit in the cryptocurrency market.

By analyzing the fundamentals of different cryptocurrencies, Investors may choose resources to invest and decide when to buy or sell them with greater knowledge thanks to factors including technology, adoption, and the regulatory framework. Understanding market trends and fundamentals can also help investors manage risk by identifying potential market risks and adjusting their investment strategies accordingly. The crypto industry is constantly evolving, and market analysis can help investors stay up-to-date with new developments, emerging trends, and regulatory changes that may impact their investments.

3.1.2 Objective

Through our platform, investors and market analysts can quickly explore market trends as well as directly see the dynamic of cryptocurrency data. Given the constantly rising prices of cryptocurrencies, a major obstacle in this research field is the lack of efficient tools for finding and representing the results of data analysis. Current methods do not provide a clear picture of historical and predicted price changes. In order to address these issues, it is aimed to create an interface for displaying data linked to cryptocurrencies utilizing the latest data processing and analysis techniques.

The objectives of live crypto market data analysis using API are:

- To obtain real-time Agri market data: Getting market information in real time on cryptocurrency prices, amounts, and other important metrics *via* an API is one of the main goals of using it for live market data research. This data can then be used to track market conditions, spot patterns, and make educated trading decisions.
- To automate data collection and analysis: APIs can be used to automate the collection and analysis of live crypto market data, allowing traders and investors to efficiently monitor market conditions and respond to changes in real time. This can lessen the possibility of human error and boost efficiency.
- To monitor portfolio performance: Live crypto market data obtained through an API can also be used to monitor portfolio performance and identify potential risks or opportunities for rebalancing. This can help to manage risk and optimize portfolio returns.
- To help traders develop trading algorithms: By using live crypto market data obtained through an API, traders and investors can develop trading algorithms that can be used to automate trading decisions based on specific market conditions and trends. This can enhance overall trading performance and lessen the likelihood of making emotional trading judgments.
- To help investors stay up-to-date with the latest market developments: Ultimately, staying current with market developments and new patterns can be achieved by live crypto market analysis of data through the usage of APIs.

This can assist investors and traders in staying on top of the game and seeing fresh chances to make money in the bitcoin space.

3.2 Review of Literature

The study by J. P. Fleischer *et al.* (2022) [1] highlights the potential of the LSTM (Long Short-Term Memory) method for forecasting cryptocurrency prices. The authors propose that adding more input parameters, like volume, high, and low cryptocurrency data and other hyperparameters can further improve the accuracy of the model. This study also shows that, while requiring more time to run, the LSTM approach performs more accurately than the ARIMA model. The model's high accuracy is attributed to its low root-mean-squared error and the close proximity of the anticipated value to the actual price. The authors do concede, nevertheless, that because of the one-day reaction delay, the straightforward one-day forecast using regular time series could not produce excellent results with a timely response. The study's managerial implications suggest the potential for developing a product for investors to improve upon the model by including other hyperparameters for even more precise forecasts. Subsequent investigations may contemplate integrating sentiment evaluations of tweets from Twitter sites or merely quantifying tweet quantity as a hyperparameter to augment the model. One weakness of the study highlighted by the authors is the lack of thorough investigation into the architecture of introducing hyperparameters. This suggests that further research is needed to explore the potential impact of incorporating additional hyperparameters to the model.

G. Giudici, A. Milne, and D. Vinogradov (2020) [2] give a brief overview of the new phenomena of cryptocurrencies and go over the key developments in the field's scholarly literature. The authors examine the difficulties and worries that cryptocurrencies provide for companies and industrial economics using either neoclassical and behavioral approaches. They emphasize the contributions made by individual works to the body of literature, with a focus on themes related to sustainability, misconduct, and socioeconomics. The authors argue that although cryptocurrencies might have certain beneficial uses and provide economic value, market regulation is nevertheless warranted as a vital first step toward enhancing social welfare. The article's conclusion makes the recommendation that future studies concentrate on important problems that academics studying economics, finance, and related fields should continue to study.

In Gupta *et al.* (2022) [3], React was the primary technology used by the researchers to create the online portal. The CoinGecko API was used to acquire the cryptocurrency data, which included price, volume, market capitalization, and exchange data. The website was deployed using node run time environment. The researchers included various features in their work such as Login authentication, IP address validation, and Session and Hashing. The paper concluded that more visualizations could be added with time for the traders and investors to better understand the market scenario.

A. Berger (2021) [4] gave a review of visualizations of Bitcoin cryptocurrency. The researchers used Google to collect and gather Bitcoin visualization tools and found 46 online tools. The report even included geographical data on 2D and 3D maps that was gathered by Bitcoin transactions and nodes in the network. The researchers' inventiveness allowed them to create some very original plots, like a spider chart that displayed several crypto-economics elements, a tree map that compared market capitalization, and Sankey diagrams that showed the flow of Bitcoin trade. They also used Gantt charts, adjacency matrices, and node-link diagrams to depict the money flows of transactions. The study's conclusion said that visual analytics tools can assist professionals in identifying distinct Bitcoin user groups and tying their activities together.

Chiu *et al.* (2023) [5] conducted research on cryptocurrencies' performance tracker. They described the regulatory as well as technological changes of cryptocurrency. The paper discussed the advantages of using a digital currency price tracker and also said that a good tracker enables consumers to compare the prices with historical data provided by many of these websites. Further, the researchers added that the accuracy of the cryptocurrency price tracker an investor chooses can significantly impact their investment decisions, timing, and success. It is crucial to select a price tracker that uses reliable data and is consistently updated. Other factors to consider when choosing a cryptocurrency price tracker include ease of use, the number of digital currencies and tokens covered, and the suite of additional tools and information offered. The authors also suggested that companies should consider the effects of placing cryptocurrencies on their balance sheet and the potential impact on company valuation.

According to Di *et al.* (2015) [6], work on exploring and comparing different transactions has been limited due to the absence of effective instruments. The researchers highlighted some of the earlier techniques for visualizing Bitcoin data and discovered that they had mostly focused on monitoring records of questionable transactions. However, using current tools and techniques to analyze transactions and their connections is laborious. The authors developed an interactive visualization system to examine the growth of activity patterns of exchanges for Bitcoin from two angles: exchange vs. exchange along with exchange versus client. In addition, three case studies have been included in the study to illustrate the value and efficacy of the methodology.

Fang *et al.* (2022) [7] provided an overview of the visual analytics tools available for analyzing data pertaining to blockchains. The researchers have made use of 76 analytics tools in order to visualize blockchain and cryptocurrency networks. Additionally, they suggested a classification system to put those visualizations in groups according to job domains, target audiences, target blockchains, blockchain information, and visualization kinds. The authors evaluated all of the 76 instruments in use in a methodical and quantitative manner, identifying the areas that warrant more research in the future. They came up with various graphs such as a tile map, a 3D scatter plot, etc. Furthermore, transaction networks and the connectivity of Bitcoin exchanges were constructed and analyzed using BitConduite and BlockchainVis, respectively, for the analysis of entity groups for Bitcoin.

Kotenko *et al.* [8] addressed cryptocurrency's unique challenges, exploring algorithms like LSTM and ARIMA for price prediction but highlighting their drawbacks. To overcome limitations, a novel Fbprophet model was proposed, excelling in handling seasonality and volatility, enhancing prediction accuracy for Bitcoin prices. The introduction contextualized cryptocurrencies as decentralized digital assets, influenced by blockchain and cryptographic security, while also acknowledging their speculative nature. The study emphasized the need for a model capable of interpreting dynamic trends, leading to the development of the Fbprophet model through comprehensive data analysis and pre-processing, ultimately achieving accurate predictions for real-world applications.

In their paper, Lee *et al.* [9] presented a comprehensive survey on cryptocurrency trading, exploring its growing integration into financial portfolios. It addressed the distinct nature of cryptocurrencies as digital assets and their evolving behavior in trading. The survey covered 146 research papers, examining diverse aspects of cryptocurrency trading, including software systems, systematic trading, emerging technologies, portfolio construction, market conditions, and miscellaneous topics. Notably, a surge in research activity was observed from 2018 onwards, indicating the rising importance of cryptocurrency trading. The study aimed to gauge the maturity of research in this field by analyzing relevant indicators and trends up until June 2021.

Rathore *et al.* [10] in their paper introduced a web platform for comprehensive cryptocurrency data aggregation, which utilized multi-modal data fusion, AI, and visual representation. The platform encompassed real-time trading data, both on- and off-chain, and offered visual analysis of market data. The back-end platform for data collecting, preprocessing, and analysis was part of the full-stack framework that was suggested. The front end was used for interaction between users and visualization. Using sentiment analysis, hash rates, historical price movements, and high-frequency language from social media, the model combined deep learning techniques with market trends. The paper emphasized the aim of bridging the gap between numerical and intuitive insights into the cryptocurrency market through a user-friendly interface. The platform facilitated investor decision-making and explored market sentiment.

3.3 Materials and Methods

3.3.1 Dataset Collection and Description

A well-known tool for aggregating cryptocurrency data, CoinGecko gives developers access to a variety of market statistics *via* its API (Application Programming Interface). The CoinGecko API provides real-time and historical data on various cryptocurrency metrics, including prices, volumes, market capitalization, exchange rates, trading pairs, and more.

The data of over 4,000+ cryptocurrencies from CoinGecko API is collected, out of which 10 were used to design our web portal.

CoinGecko API link: https://www.coingecko.com/en/api/documentation
Yahoo Finance link: https://finance.yahoo.com/quote/BTC-USD/history

The data collected from CoinGecko API includes:

- Cryptocurrency prices: The CoinGecko API provides real-time price data for thousands of cryptocurrencies across multiple exchanges. This data can be used to monitor market trends and identify potential trading opportunities.
- Market capitalization: The API also provides information on the market capitalization of different cryptocurrencies, allowing users to understand the relative size and value of each asset.

- Trading volume (24 hrs): CoinGecko's API provides data on trading volumes for 24 hours for various cryptocurrencies, this may offer information on investor mood and market liquidity.
- Historical data: The CoinGecko API allows developers to access historical data on cryptocurrency prices, volumes, and other metrics. This data can be used to analyze trends and patterns over time.
- Exchange rates: The API also provides exchange rate data, allowing developers to convert prices between different currencies and exchanges.
- High and low (for varying durations):

Thus, the CoinGecko API provides a comprehensive set of data points that can be used to analyze and understand the cryptocurrency market; it is shown in Figure 3.1. Figure 3.2 represents the sample sample screenshot of ticker details. Figure 3.3 represents the collected coin details. By leveraging this data, traders and investors can build sophisticated trading algorithms, monitor market conditions in real time, and learn more about the

Figure 3.1 Sample screenshot of data collection using API.

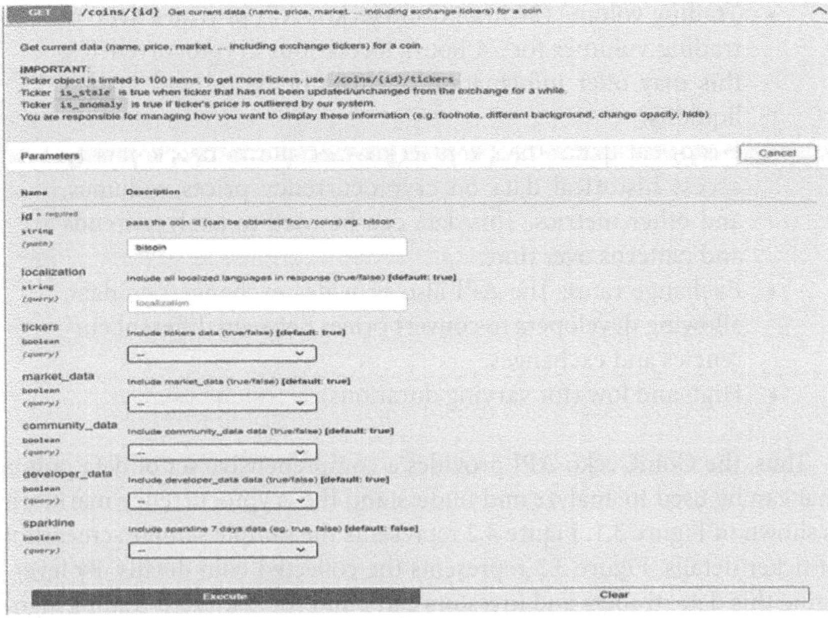

Figure 3.2 Sample screenshot of ticker details.

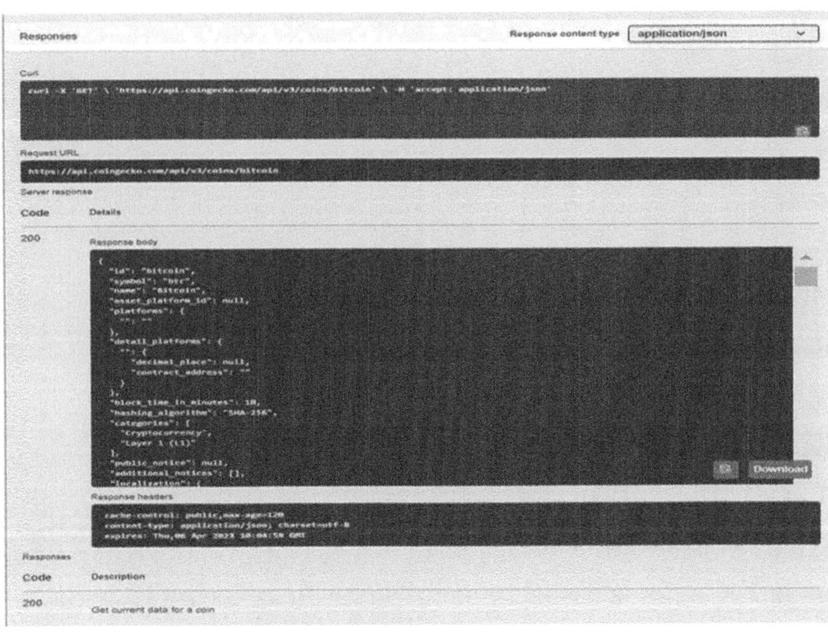

Figure 3.3 Sample screenshot of data collected for a coin.

trends and behavior of the bitcoin industry. Furthermore, Yahoo was used as a source to collect data, whereby data for the past years was gathered and trends were observed. This was then analyzed using different charts.

3.3.2 Data Analysis

Figure 3.4 shows the Yahoo data collected. The following results were discovered for 10 cryptocurrencies: Avalanche, Binance, Bitcoin, Cardano, Decentraland, Dogecoin, Etherium, Ripple, Solana, and Tether:

- Market capitalization (24 hours): It is a measurement, typically expressed as a percentage, of the overall value of the shares that remain in stock in a corporation. It is computed by multiplying a stock's price by the total number of shares that are outstanding.
- All time high: It refers to the highest price at which a cryptocurrency or stock has ever traded.
- All time low: It refers to the lowest price at which a cryptocurrency or stock has ever traded.

Time Period: Nov 22, 2022 - Nov 22, 2023 ∨ Show: Historical Prices ∨ Frequency: Daily ∨ Apply

Currency in USD ⤓ Download

Date	Open	High	Low	Close*	Adj Close**	Volume
Nov 22, 2023	35,756.55	36,697.80	35,756.55	36,697.80	36,697.80	28,224,479,232
Nov 21, 2023	37,469.16	37,631.14	35,813.81	35,813.81	35,813.81	25,172,163,756
Nov 20, 2023	37,374.07	37,756.82	36,882.53	37,476.96	37,476.96	20,888,209,068
Nov 19, 2023	36,585.77	37,509.36	36,414.60	37,386.55	37,386.55	12,915,986,553
Nov 18, 2023	36,625.37	36,839.28	36,233.31	36,585.70	36,585.70	11,886,022,717
Nov 17, 2023	36,164.82	36,704.48	35,901.23	36,596.68	36,596.68	22,445,028,430
Nov 16, 2023	37,879.98	37,934.63	35,545.47	36,154.77	36,154.77	26,007,385,366
Nov 15, 2023	35,548.11	37,964.89	35,383.78	37,880.58	37,880.58	27,365,821,679

Figure 3.4 Sample screenshot of yahoo dataset.

- Positive sentiments: It refers to the percentage of people who have a positive attitude towards investing in a particular cryptocurrency.
- High (24 hours): It refers to the highest price that a particular cryptocurrency has reached within the past 24 hours.
- Low (24 hours): It refers to the lowest price that a particular cryptocurrency has reached within the past 24 hours.
- Current price: It refers to the current market price of a cryptocurrency.
- Market volume: It speaks about the total quantity of contracts or shares that are exchanged in a given market during a given time frame.

The first section of our dashboard which shows the Bitcoin is shown in Figure 3.5 and Ethereum data is shown in Figure 3.6, which contains all of the previously described data:

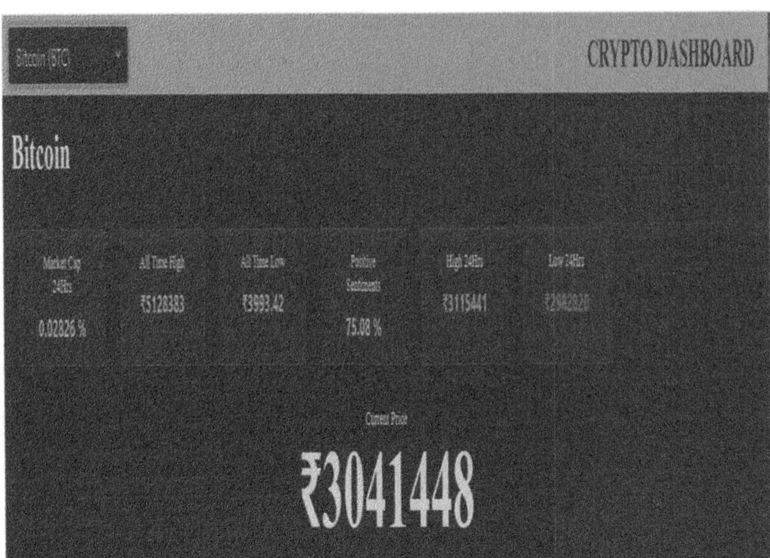

Figure 3.5 Screenshot of bitcoin data using crypto dashboard.

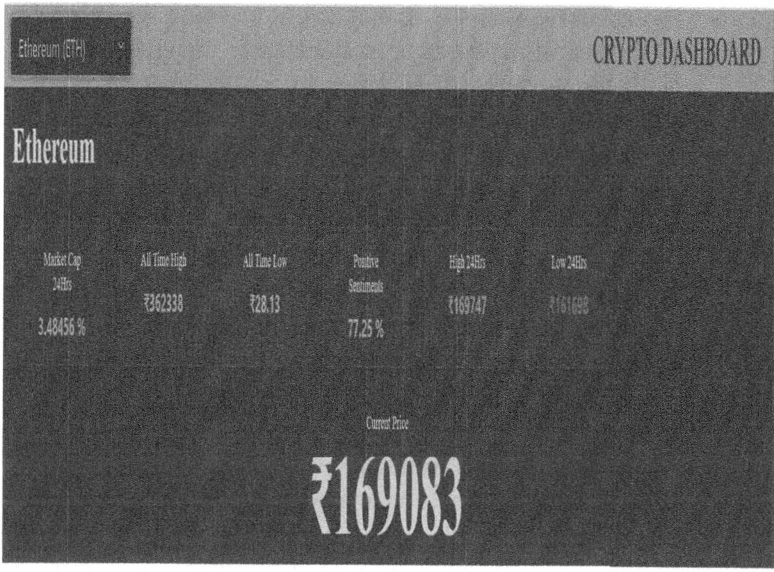

Figure 3.6 Screenshot of ethereum data using crypto dashboard.

3.3.3 Information About Models

3.3.3.1 Model Planning

Several models can be used to analyze crypto market data. However, in this work the following key features are incorporated.

- **Technical analysis and forecasting:** To forecast future manure price movements, forecasters examine historical market data to find patterns and trends. Many indicators, including lines of trend, momentum indicators, moving averages, ARIMA, and others, can be used to do this.
- **Machine learning models:** Large amounts of market data can be analyzed using machine learning algorithms to spot trends and anticipate future events. For instance, past market data can be used to train neural networks and decision trees to forecast future price changes. The subsequent models have been employed:
  - **Linear regression:** A statistical model called linear regression is used to determine whether two variables have a linear relationship. Based on past price data, it can be utilized to forecast a cryptocurrency's future value.

- **Neural networks:** A class of machine learning algorithms called neural networks is modeled after the architecture of the human brain. They are useful for deciphering intricate data patterns and forecasting future market trends.
- **Statistical models:** Regression analysis is one statistical model that may be used to anticipate future market conditions and find links between various factors in market data.
- **Time series forecasting:** Time series analysis is the process of examining a certain cryptocurrency's past performance over an extended period to spot trends, seasonality, and various other patterns that may be utilized to forecast future market movements.

To gain insight into the behavior and patterns of the cryptocurrency market, traders and investors can utilize machine learning algorithms and techniques mentioned above. By analyzing vast amounts of data, such as price and volume movements, social media activity, and news sentiment, these models can detect patterns and trends that are challenging for humans to identify, thereby helping the traders and investors to make decisions regarding trading and investing in the cryptocurrency market.

3.3.4 Model Building

The machine learning models used in this work are as follows:

- **Regression with LSTM**

Recurrent neural networks with Long Short-Term Memory (LSTM) architecture are trained to learn the relationship between a sequence of input data and a matching sequence of output data. This process is known as regression using LSTM. In this context, the output sequence represents the values of a continuous variable, which is the dependent variable in a regression problem, and the input sequence represents one or more independent variables that are expected to affect the value of the dependent variable [11–14].

Deep learning makes extensive use of long short-term memory (LSTM), a kind of artificial neural network with recurrent design. Because LSTM incorporates feedback connections, it can handle complete data sequences in addition to individual data points, which is not possible with typical feed-forward neural networks. When it comes to learning dependence on order in sequence prediction tasks—a skill needed in intricate fields like picture captioning, speech recognition, and natural language processing—LSTMs are especially good. When both the input and output data are sequences of values, sequence prediction problems are ideally suited for the LSTM architecture. Because LSTM networks can learn long-term dependencies from sequential data, they are a good fit for regression problems with complex, nonlinear relationships among both input and output variables.

LSTMs have both hidden states and cell states, which allow them to store and propagate information across time steps. The cell state regulates the information flow throughout the network, whilst the hidden state acts as the network's memory. Several gates, including the input, forget, and output gates, are part of the LSTM design and regulate the information flow throughout the cell state. For the network to effectively capture dependencies that persist in sequential data, it must be able to selectively retain or forget data from earlier time steps.

- **Time series forecasting**

Both single and multivariate time-series models are available. When the dependent variable is a single time series, such as a reading of the room's temperature from a single sensor, the univariate time series models are used. When the output is dependent on more than one series, or when there are numerous dependent variables, a multivariate time series models can be used. By considering the last several prices, ARIMA model is used to anticipate the price of bitcoin in the future (depending upon the best chosen lag).

The auto-regressive integrated moving average is referred to as ARIMA. It has been utilized in our effort to forecast Bitcoin's price. To forecast future values, ARIMA models consider the historical values of a time series. Three parameters make up the model: p, d, and q. The total amount of autoregressive terms is indicated by the p parameter, the level of differencing by the d parameter, and the number of moving average terms by the q parameter. Future values are predicted by fitting the model to the historical data.

Algorithm:

To develop an ARIMA model for predicting Bitcoin prices in Python the following steps are followed:

- Load the Bitcoin price data into a Pandas Data Frame.
- Convert the Data Frame into a time series
- Plot the time series to visualize the data.
- Ascertain which ARIMA parameter values are ideal (p, d, q)
- Use the time series to fit the ARIMA model the ARIMA () function from the statsmodels library.

- Generate predictions for future Bitcoin prices using the forecast () function.
- To see how accurate the model is, plot the expected values versus the actual values.

• Neural network

One kind of machine learning system that can learn from past data and forecast future data is the artificial neural network (ANN). It consists of input, hidden, and output layers with connected neurons (nodes) that process information. The nodes receive input signals, process them, and then pass the output signals to other nodes in the network. The historical Bitcoin price data was used to train the ANN, which was then utilized to make predictions on future prices.

Algorithm:

Using Python, create an Artificial Neural Network (ANN) model to forecast Bitcoin values:

- Load the Bitcoin price data into a Pandas Data Frame.
- Preprocess the data by normalizing or scaling it to improve the performance of the ANN.
- Divide the data into sets for testing and training.
- Give a detailed description of the ANN architecture, mentioning its node count, layer count, and activation functions.
- Train the ANN with the backpropagation technique and training data.
- Analyze the ANN's performance using measures like mean absolute percentage error (MAPE) and mean squared error (MSE) in conjunction with the testing data. Generate predictions for future Bitcoin prices using the trained ANN.
- Analyze the model's accuracy by charting the expected values against the real values.

3.3.5 Architecture Diagram and Explanation

The below architecture diagram clearly shows the workflow of our entire work. Figure 3.7 depicts how the trader/investor can access the web portal and see the various visualizations, on the basis of which he/she can decide the suitable time to invest in cryptocurrency. Moreover, data analysis can also be performed so that the user can predict the price in a particular year of a particular cryptocurrency. These visualizations are generated using

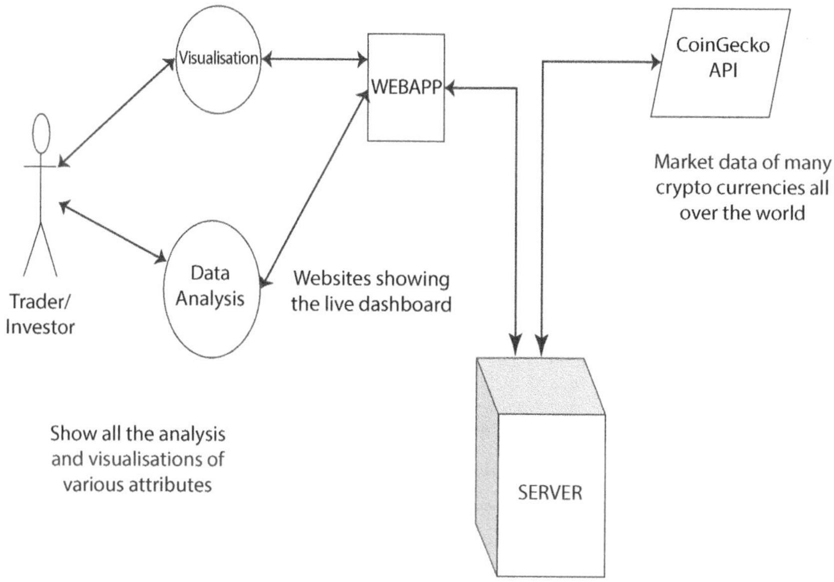

Figure 3.7 Architecture diagram.

React as well as Python, and the data used is dynamically fetched from CoinGecko API.

3.4 Proposed Work

In order to address the above issues, an interface is created for displaying data linked to cryptocurrencies utilizing the latest data processing and analysis techniques.

- Since live data is fetched from CoinGecko API, which changes every 2 seconds, it would be helpful for the investors and traders and they can plan efficiently regarding the time at which investment should be made.
- Furthermore, the graphs added can be zoomed in or out depending upon the user's need, thereby, any period of time can be analyzed easily and efficiently.
- More so, users have also been provided with an option of selecting the cryptocurrency from the available options. A web platform is made for ten cryptocurrencies so far and

users have the freedom to select any of these, depending upon which graphs would be loaded dynamically.

- Not only this, the users will also have the freedom to select the duration spanning over the past one day, one week, one month, six months or throughout the past year.

3.4.1 Research Gap and Novelty

Live crypto market data analysis is a relatively new field, and there is still much research to be done in this area. Some potential research gaps were identified:

- Most of the previous research done on live crypto market data analysis was focused on price and volume data alone; however, one can take into account other features such as news stories and social media sentiment, to obtain a more comprehensive understanding of the market and increase forecast accuracy.
- Moreover, most of the existing research in live crypto market data analysis focuses on historical data analysis. However, there is a need for real-time analysis to support high-frequency trading and other time-sensitive decision-making processes.
- Most of the machine learning models used in live crypto market data analysis are opaque, making it difficult to understand the factors driving their predictions. Thus, there is a need for more interpretable models that allow traders and investors to understand how and why a particular prediction was made.
- As cryptocurrencies are built on blockchain technology, there is potential to integrate blockchain data into live crypto agriculture data analysis, which can include analyzing transaction volumes and patterns to gain insights into market behavior.

By addressing the above research gaps and exploring new areas of novelty, the accuracy of predictions can be improved and in a quickly changing cryptocurrency market, it can offer traders and investors more insightful information.

Given the constantly rising prices of cryptocurrencies, a major obstacle in this research field is the lack of an efficient tool for data analysis. Current methods do not provide a clear picture of historical and predicted price changes.

3.5 Results and Discussion

3.5.1 Results and Explanation

After fetching the data from the API, it is visualized using React JS framework as well as python.

The following graphs were implemented to analyze the manure prices:

- Time-series graph of current market price (INR) of cryptocurrency over a period of one day, one month, one week, one month, six months, one year. It helps traders determine when is the optimum moment to invest in stocks by showing how the price changes over a specified period.
- Time-series graph of market volume (INR) of cryptocurrency over a period of one year (i.e., past one year till date). It indicates the demand for a specific cryptocurrency over time.
- Time-series graph of market capitalization (INR) of cryptocurrency over a period of one year. It provides information on the overall market value of a company's outstanding shares, or the shares that are available and have not been acquired by another business or industry.
- Donut chart depicting the top five cheapest cryptocurrencies above ₹100 measured by their market price.
- Bar chart depicting top 10 most expensive cryptocurrencies measured by their market price.
- Pie chart depicting top three cryptocurrencies measured by their total volume.
- Polar area chart depicting top three cryptocurrencies by market cap.
- Area chart depicting the top 10 cryptocurrencies measured by their all-time-high (ATH).
- Heatmap describing the correlation that exists among price, market capitalization and total volume.

- A tree map describing how the market capitalization of bitcoin has undergone changes (in the past 24 hours as well as past one month). Various sizes are used to depict the market capitalization and colors in order to describe the amount by which the price has changed.
- From the data collected from Yahoo, a candlestick chart depicting the open, close, high and low prices for Bitcoin is created.

3.5.2 Visualization

Figure 3.8 shows time series graph displaying the change of the market price of Bitcoin over the span of the entire last one year till current date. It can be seen that the price of Bitcoin rose significantly with some fluctuations in the middle. Currently the price of Bitcoin is on the rise.

Figure 3.9 is a donut chart which tells us the top five cheapest cryptocurrencies (above ₹100) amongst all the 4,000+ cryptocurrencies available in this dataset obtained through the API. These cryptocurrencies have the lowest market price among all the rest of the currencies.

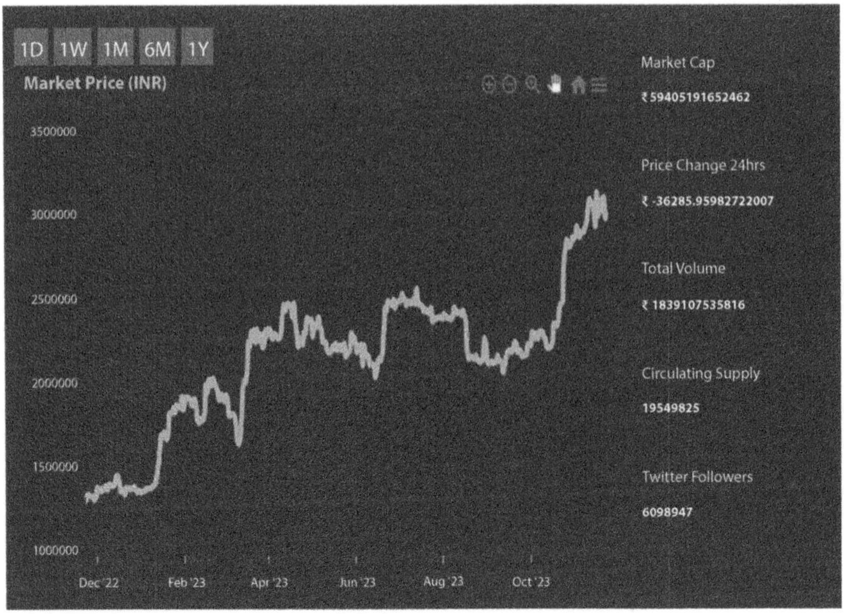

Figure 3.8 Manure price of bitcoin over the span of the entire last one year.

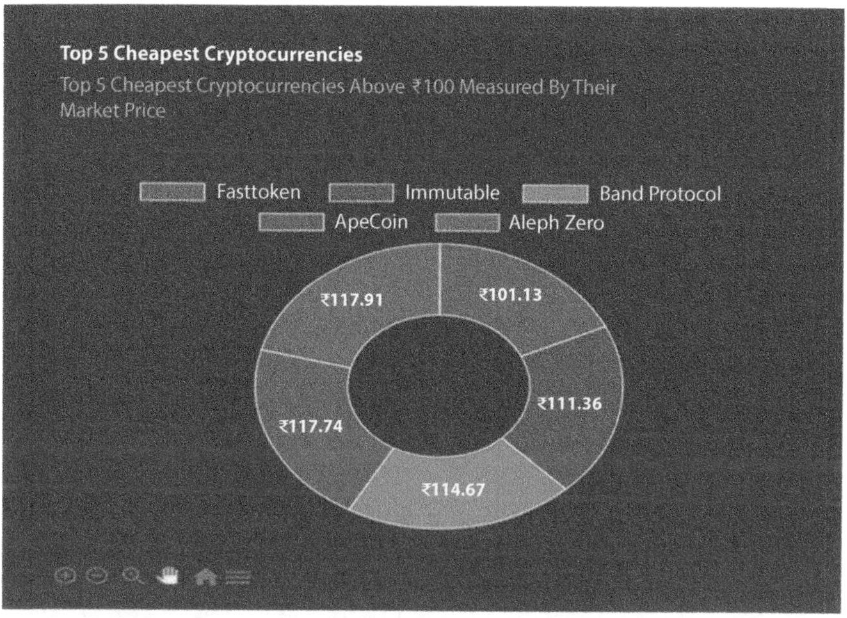

Figure 3.9 Top five cheapest cryptocurrencies for manure prices.

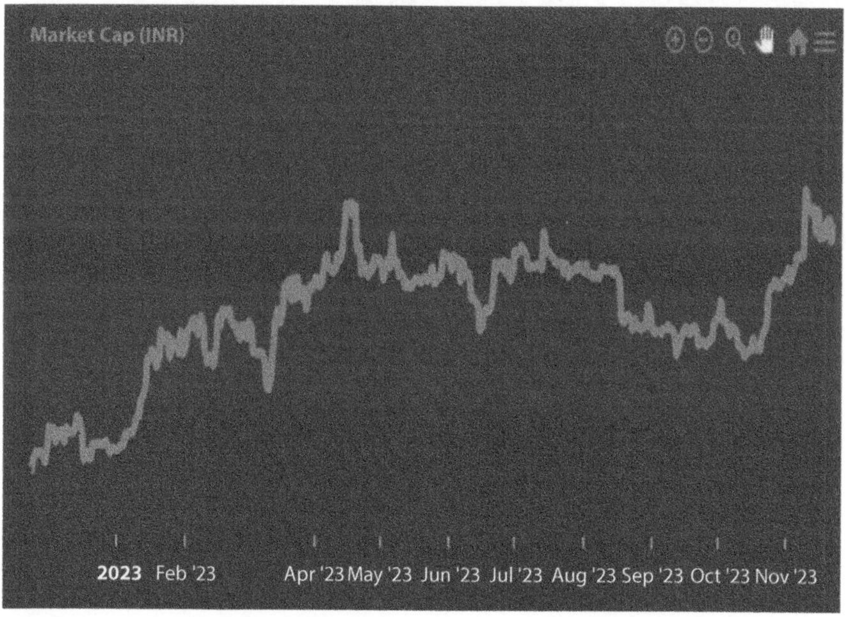

Figure 3.10 Market capitalization of bitcoin over the span of the entire last one year.

Figure 3.10 is a time series graph displaying the change of the market capitalization of Bitcoin over the span of the entire last one year till current date. This graph can be zoomed in or out depending upon the time period the user needs to see.

The above time series graph displays the change of the market volume of Bitcoin over the span of the entire last one year till current date. Figure 3.11 shows the market volume of bitcoin over the span of the entire last one year. This graph can be zoomed in or out depending upon the time period the user needs to see.

Figure 3.12 in a bar graph tells us the top 10 most expensive cryptocurrencies amongst all the 4,000+ cryptocurrencies available in this dataset obtained through the API. These cryptocurrencies have the lowest market price.

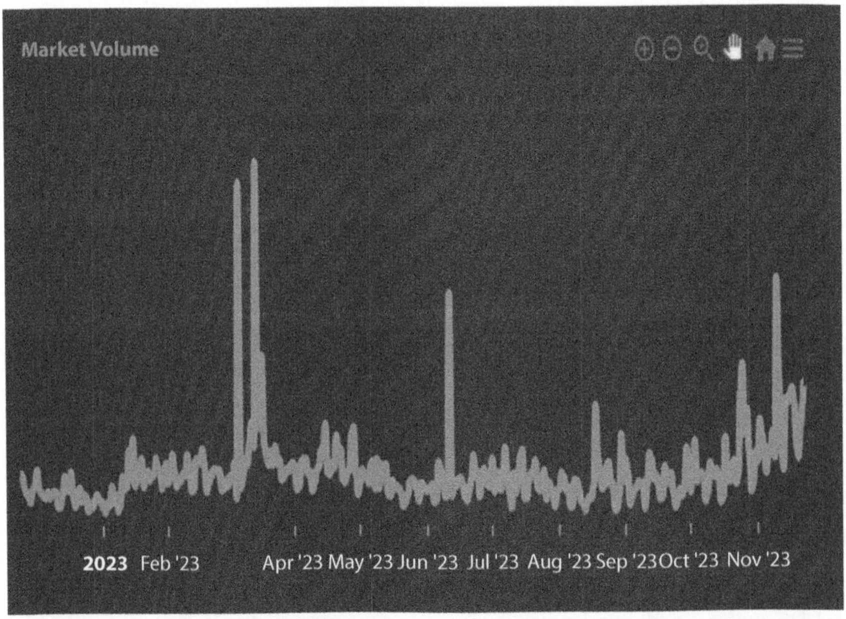

Figure 3.11 Market volume of bitcoin over the span of the entire last one year.

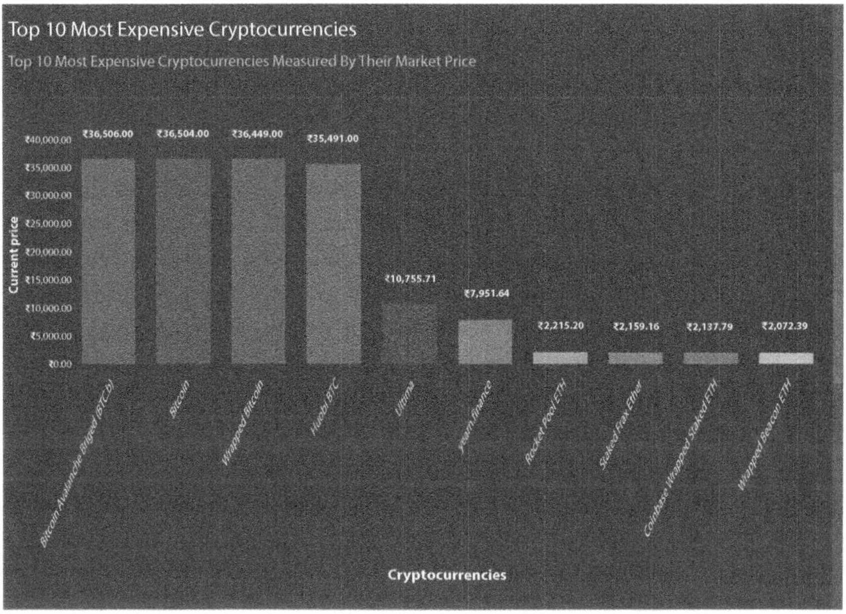

Figure 3.12 Top 10 most expensive cryptocurrencies.

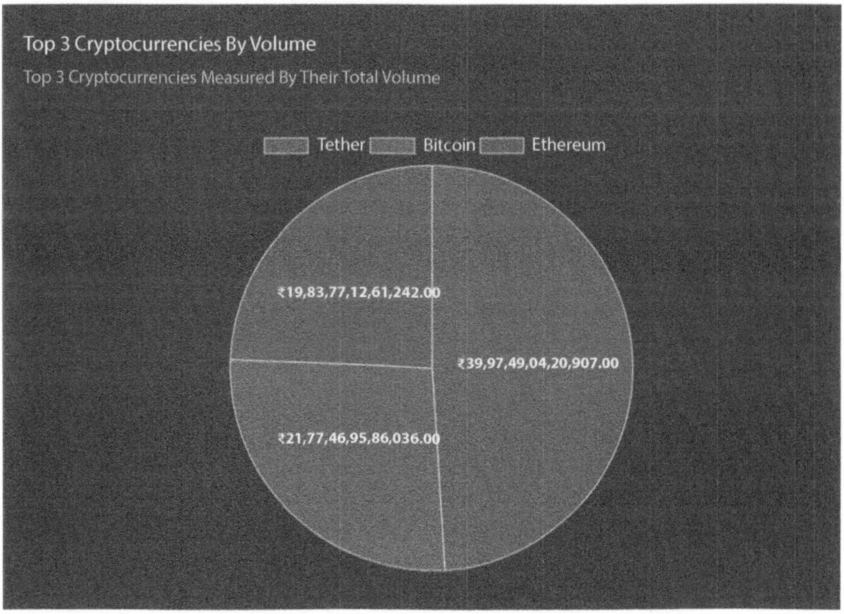

Figure 3.13 Top 3 cryptocurrencies based on market volume.

The above pie chart tells us the top three cryptocurrencies based on market volume amongst all the 4,000+ cryptocurrencies available in this dataset obtained through the API. These cryptocurrencies are Tether, followed by Bitcoin, followed by Ethereum as shown in Figure 3.13.

Similar to pie charts, polar area charts have segments with the same angle; however, the segment's radius varies based on the value as shown in Figure 3.14. Also similar to a pie chart, this kind of graphic compares data and provides a value scale for context. The below polar area chart tells us the top three cryptocurrencies based on market capitalization amongst all the 4,000+ cryptocurrencies available in this dataset obtained through the API. These cryptocurrencies are Tether, followed by Bitcoin and Ethereum.

The below Figure 3.15 is the area chart that shows the top 10 cryptocurrencies measured by their all-time-high (ATH). As evident, the all-time high of Bitcoin is the highest amounting to ₹ 10.02B.

Figure 3.16 shows the ANN model manure price prediction, Figure 3.17 shows the LSTM model manure price prediction, and Figure 3.18 shows the ARIMA model manure price prediction result with respect to actual and predicted data.

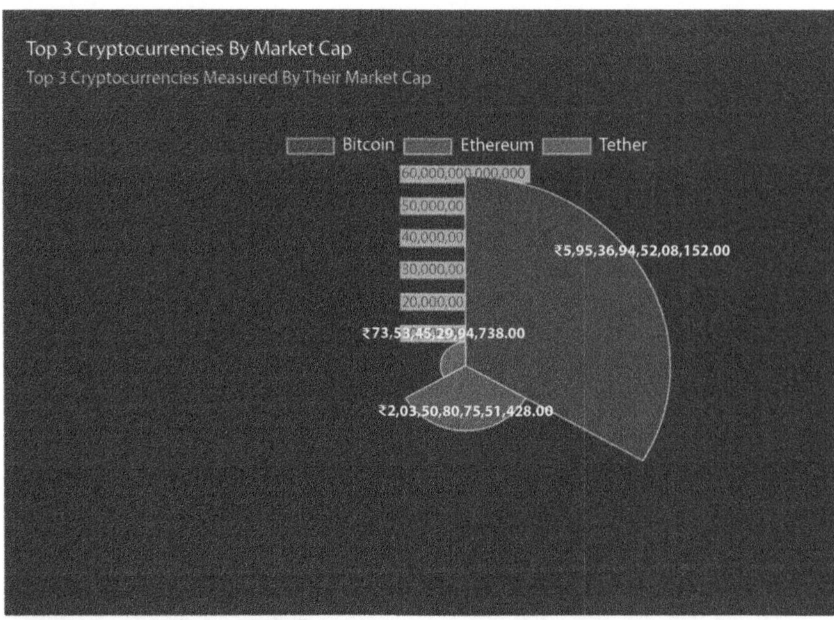

Figure 3.14 Top three cryptocurrencies based on market cap.

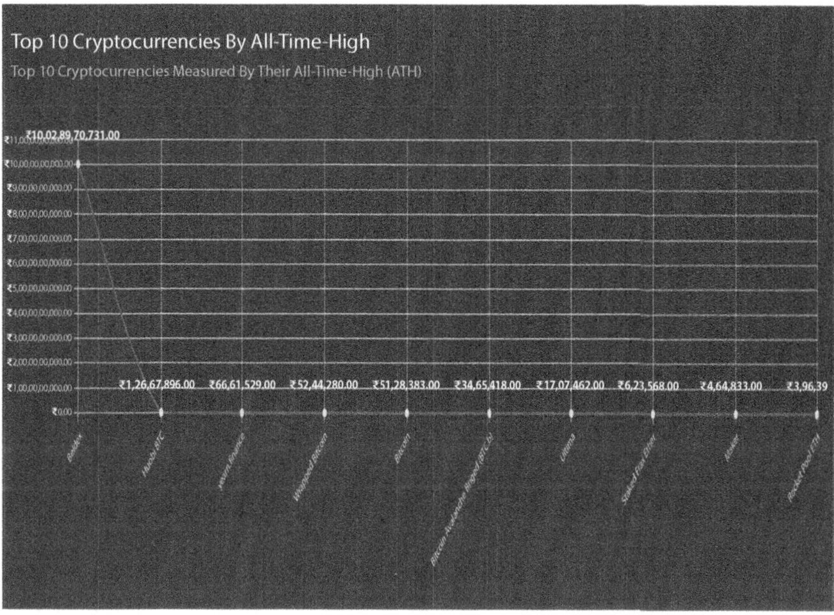

Figure 3.15 Ranking of cryptocurrency based on all-time-high (ATH).

ANN Training Model - Output for Actual and Prediction

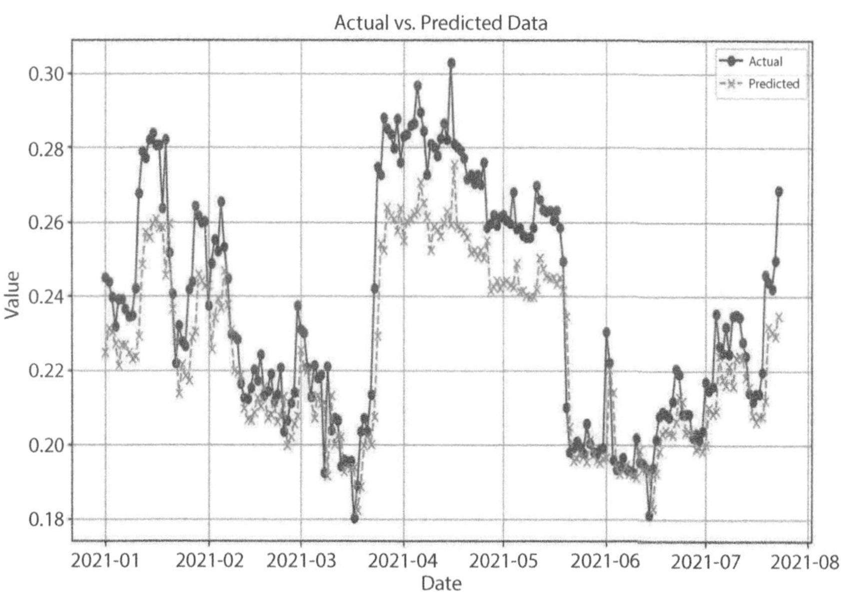

Figure 3.16 ANN model manure price prediction.

LSTM Training Model - Output for Actual and Prediction

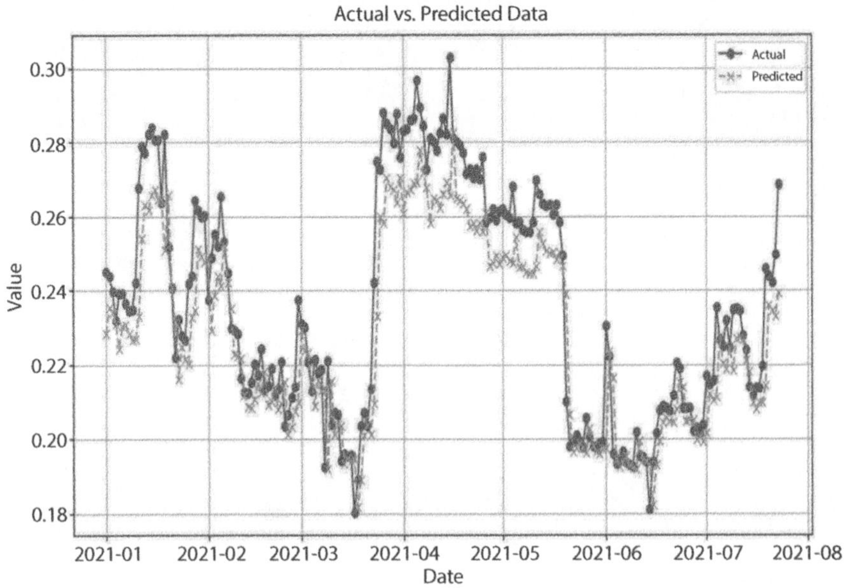

Figure 3.17 LSTM model manure price prediction.

ARIMA Training Model - Output for Actual and Prediction

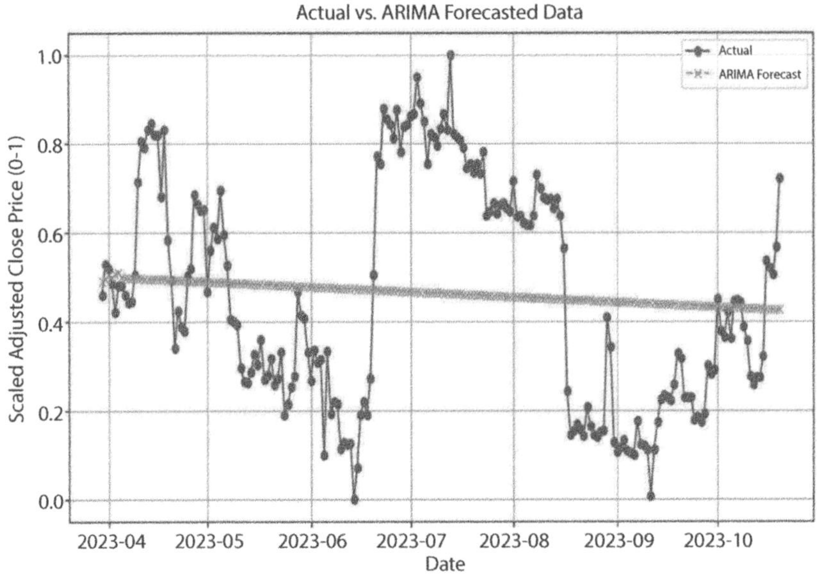

Figure 3.18 ARIMA model manure price prediction.

Table 3.1 shows the comparative analysis of existing system vs. proposed system.

Table 3.1 Comparative analysis of existing system vs. proposed system.

Existing system	Proposed system
The research conducted by Tonivach *et al.* (2021) [15] for the analysis of crypto market data analysis was focused on price and volume data alone. It didn't consider other factors such as social media sentiments of people, Twitter followers etc. Not considering these factors can mislead the investors. (Elsevier - 2022)	To increase the current system's accuracy, all the factors, i.e. price, volume, market capitalization, Twitter followers and positive sentiments (people who have a positive attitude towards investing in a particular cryptocurrency) are considered. Hence, investors would be able to get a clear understanding of the time, during which, if investment would be made, they would be able to gain more profit.
A study conducted by X. Yue *et al.* (2018) [16] focused on historical data analysis alone. The authors used the dataset that was static and used it to visualize trends in various cryptocurrencies. However, since the data was not dynamic, the visualizations and analysis would not be useful for people after a few years. (IEEE - 2022)	In order to overcome this drawback, dynamic data is incorporated in the work. The visualization and analysis has been done using data that was fetched from an API and Yahoo. The data gets updated every 2 seconds, and accordingly the graphs and visualizations change. Hence, our system can be useful for people even after several years.
According to the research conducted by A. Berger *et al.* (2021), current price does not predict the future price or market volume of the cryptocurrency. The authors have just created graphs and shown how a particular cryptocurrency varies with time and no future prediction or analysis has been done. (Springer - 2021)	In this work, the various trends in different cryptocurrencies is not studied, but some analysis and predictions have been made using ARIMA, ANN as well as Regression with LSTM to predict a specific cryptocurrency's price in the future.

(*Continued*)

Table 3.1 Comparative analysis of existing system vs. proposed system. (*Continued*)

Existing system	Proposed system
The study conducted by Zhang *et al.* (2020) [17] was limited to bitcoin alone. The researchers have created several visualizations and have forecasted the future price and volume, but it does not take into account other cryptocurrencies. (IEEE - 2015)	This study is not limited to visualize only one specific cryptocurrency, rather, an option would be given to the user to select the cryptocurrency about which he/she wants to know more. Then accordingly, the dynamic graphs would be shown.
In the research conducted by Zhu *et al.* (2021) [18] the visualizations were made along with analysis, but, for the past one year. The user had no option to select a particular duration for which he/she is interested to see the trend. (IEEE - 2018)	In this work, the feature of users selecting which graph they want to see zoom in and zoom out, so that if any user wants to see the trends only during a specific time period, he/she can zoom only that portion of the graph, and the information would be displayed clearly.

Table 3.2 Comparative analysis of ARIMA, ANN and LSTM model.

Scores	ARIMA	ANN	LSTM
RMSE	0.2446450	0.0192119	0.0157171
MSE	0.0598512	0.0003691	0.0002470
MAE	0.2153707	0.0153737	0.0127838

A comparative study of neural networks (ANN), linear regression (LSTM), and time-series forecasting (ARIMA) for predicting bitcoin prices is shown in Table 3.2.

3.6 Conclusion

The analysis of live cryptocurrency market data using regression models, namely Long Short-Term Memory (LSTM), Autoregressive Integrated Moving Average (ARIMA), and Artificial Neural Networks (ANN), has yielded insightful results for predicting cryptocurrency prices.

The regression analysis utilizing LSTM has proven particularly effective in capturing long-term dependencies in the data, demonstrating superior accuracy in forecasts compared to the ARIMA model. Meanwhile, the ANN model, adept at capturing nonlinear relationships between variables, has been instrumental in predicting trends in cryptocurrency prices over time.

Upon evaluating the models using key performance metrics, it is evident that LSTM outperforms both ARIMA and ANN. LSTM achieved the lowest Root Mean Squared Error (RMSE), Mean Squared Error (MSE), and Mean Absolute Error (MAE) scores among the three models, indicating its superior predictive accuracy in comparison to the others.

The ARIMA model, while providing reasonable predictions, exhibits higher error scores across all metrics compared to LSTM. Meanwhile, the ANN model demonstrates competitive performance but falls short of LSTM's accuracy.

The use of regression models, especially LSTM, in cryptocurrency market data analysis holds significant potential for predicting future trends in cryptocurrency manure prices. For traders and investors, these models can provide insightful information that can help them make better selections. It is imperative to acknowledge that although these models augment our comprehension of the bitcoin market, they must be supplemented with alternative modes of analysis, and determinations must not be exclusively predicated on their prognostications. Further research is warranted to explore additional hyperparameters and input parameters that could potentially enhance the models' accuracy.

The future scope of live crypto market analysis is quite promising, as the popularity and adoption of cryptocurrencies continue to grow. There are several reasons why the demand for live crypto market analysis is likely to increase:

- Increased adoption: More and more people are starting to use cryptocurrencies as a means of payment, investment, and trading. As a result, there is a growing need for real-time information on the performance of cryptocurrencies.
- Volatility: The value of cryptocurrencies is prone to large swings in a little amount of time due to their high volatility. Because of this, in order for traders and investors to make wise selections, real-time market analysis is essential.

- Trading opportunities: Since the cryptocurrency market is open around the clock, trade possibilities are constantly present. Traders can find and seize these opportunities with the use of real-time market analysis.
- Increased competition: As the popularity of cryptocurrencies grows, so does the competition between exchanges and trading platforms. Real-time market analysis can give these platforms a competitive edge by providing their users with up-to-date information on the crypto market.

References

1. Fleischer, J.P., von Laszewski, G., Theran, C., Parra Bautista, Y.J., Time series analysis of cryptocurrency prices using long short-term memory. *Algorithms*, 15, 230, 2022, DOI 10.3390/a15070230.
2. Giudici, G., Milne, A., Vinogradov, D., Cryptocurrencies: market analysis and perspectives. *J. Ind. Bus. Econ.*, 47, 1–18, 2020, DOI 10.1007/s40812-019-00138-6.
3. Gupta, K. and Srivastava, N., Cryptophyle: The Cryptocurrency News Tracker App, in: *2022 4th International Conference on Advances in Computing, Communication Control and Networking (ICAC3N)*, 2022, December, IEEE, pp. 2254–2261.
4. Berger, A., Košťák, M., Ježek, B., Online application for bitcoin price visualization, in: *Mobile Web and Intelligent. Inf. Syst.: Proceedings of the 17th International Conference, MobiWIS 2021, Virtual Event, August 23–25, 2021*, Springer International Publishing, pp. 74–81, 2021.
5. Chiu, C.L., Ni, Y., Hu, H.C., Day, M.Y., Chen, Y., Enhancing crypto success *via* heatmap visualization of big data analytics for numerous variable moving average strategies. *Appl. Sci.*, 13, 12805, 2023, DOI 10.3390/app132312805.
6. Di Battista, G., *et al.*, Bitconeview: visualization of flows in the bitcoin transaction graph, in: *2015 IEEE Symposium on Visualization for Cyber Security (VizSec)*, 2015, October, IEEE, pp. 1–8, DOI 10.1109/VIZSEC.2015.7312773.
7. Fang, F., *et al.*, Cryptocurrency trading: a comprehensive survey. *Financ. Innov.*, 8, 13, 2022, DOI 10.1186/s40854-021-00321-6.
8. Kotenko, I.V., Kolomeec, M.V., Zhernova, K.N., Chechulin, A.A., Visual analytics for information security: areas of application, tasks and visualization models. *Cybersecur. Issues*, 4, 44, 2–15, 2021, DOI 10.21681/2311-3456-2021-4-2-15.
9. Lee, Y.S., Vo, A., Chapman, T.A., Examining the maturity of bitcoin price through a catastrophic event: the case of structural break analysis during the COVID-19 pandemic. *Fin. Res. Lett.*, 49, 103165, 2022, DOI 10.1016/j.frl.2022.103165.

10. Rathore, R.K., *et al.*, Real-world model for bitcoin price prediction. *Inf. Process. Manag.*, 59, 102968, 2022, DOI 10.1016/j.ipm.2022.102968.
11. Kalita, K., Ganesh, N., Jayalakshmi, S., Chohan, J.S., Mallik, S., Qin, H., Multi-Objective artificial bee colony optimized hybrid deep belief network and XGBoost algorithm for heart disease prediction. *Front. Digit. Health*, 5, 1279644, 2023, DOI: 10.3389/fdgth.2023.1279644.
12. Kalita, K., Ganesh, N., Balamurugan, S. (Eds.), *Metaheuristics for Machine Learning: Algorithms and Applications*, John Wiley & Sons, 2024, DOI: 10.1002/9781394233953.
13. Ganesh, N., Shankar, R., Mahdal, M., Murugan, J.S., Chohan, J.S., Kalita, K., Exploring Deep Learning Methods for Computer Vision Applications across Multiple Sectors: Challenges and Future Trends. *CMES-Comput. Model. Eng. Sci.*, 139, 1, 103–141, 2024, DOI: 10.32604/cmes.2023.028018.
14. Dey, K., Kalita, K., Chakraborty, S., Prediction performance analysis of neural network models for an electrical discharge turning process. *Int. J. Interact. Des. Manuf. (IJIDeM)*, 17, 2, 827–845, 2023, DOI: 10.1007/s12008-022-01003-y.
15. Tovanich, N., Heulot, N., Fekete, J.D., Isenberg, P., Visualization of blockchain data: a systematic review. *IEEE Trans. Vis. Comput. Graph.*, 27, 3135–3152, 2021, DOI 10.1109/TVCG.2019.2963018 (Pubmed:31899429).
16. Yue, X., *et al.*, Bitextract: interactive visualization for extracting bitcoin exchange intelligence. *IEEE Trans. Vis. Comput. Graph.*, 25, 162–171, 2018, DOI: 10.1109/TVCG.2018.2864814) (Pubmed:30130212).
17. Zhang, P., Xiao, F., Luo, X., A framework and dataset for bugs in ethereum smart contracts, in: *2020 IEEE International Conference on Software Maintenance and Evolution (ICSME)*, 2020, September, IEEE, pp. 139–150, DOI 10.1109/ICSME46990.2020.00023.
18. Zhu, N., Yang, F., Zhu, M., Sun, X., Cheng, I., Data-enabled Cryptocurrency market analysis and visualization platform. *Int. Conf. Big Data Anal. Data Min. Comp. Intell.*, pp. 133–137, 2021.

4

Future Agricultural Landscape Development: A MADM Model for Analysis

Ramakrishna Regulagadda[1]*, Syed Ziaur Rahman[2], Nallamala Sri Hari[3], Valeti Nagarjuna[4], Kolliboyina Hari[5] and Sivudu Macherla[1]

[1]Department of Computer Science and Engineering, Koneru Lakshmaiah Education Foundation, Vaddeswaram, Guntur, India
[2]Faculty of Information Technology, Majan University College, Sultanate of Oman, Muscat, Oman
[3]Department of Computer Science and Engineering, Vasireddy Venkatadri Institute of Technology, Nambur, Guntur, India
[4]Department of Computer Science and Engineering, Kallam Harinadhareddy Institute of Technology, Chowdavaram, Guntur, India
[5]Department of Artificial Intelligence and Data Science, PACE Institute of Technology and Sciences, Ongole, Prakasam, India

Abstract
Improving profitability, promoting environmental sustainability, and enhancing the aesthetic and cultural qualities of the natural environment are just a few examples of the particular aims and objectives that may be achieved *via* the design, planning, and operation of land for agriculture. The creation and the results of a multi-attribute selection system that produces images of the agricultural environment for use in investigations of prospective futures is described in this work. The model's core tenet that changes to the land used for farming cover are due to the logical choices made by a farmer depending on the characteristics of the farmer, the crops, and the land. Every area's favoured crop under a specific policy scenario is determined by employing field explanations, crop attributes, and the farming producer's selection framework after the model first assesses any modifications to the site base caused by the transition of agricultural land to non-agricultural uses. Future representations of the farming industry that react to different causes of

**Corresponding author*: regulagadda@gmail.com; rramakrishna@kluniversity.in

Narayanan Ganesh and Kanak Kalita (eds.) Harvesting Data: Blockchain, AI and Advanced Innovations in Agriculture, (77–98) © 2026 Scrivener Publishing LLC

change are constructed by cycling across the elements for each time taken to simulate a step. To demonstrate how this technique might be used to assess various policy or managerial alternatives, an example of a different futures model is offered.

Keywords: Multi-attribute decision, agricultural land, farming industry, managerial alternatives, agricultural producer

4.1 Introduction

Alternative agricultural landscape development has some unique difficulties. First, crop kinds and management practices often change from season to season, a mixture having a distinct impact on the landscape. The extra farms may adapt to the shifting land base, but the second possibility is that farmland will be changed to an occupation other than agriculture. Last but not least, information on the original or historical status representing the agriculture industry is usually unavailable or limited, and classified remote sensing data, which is sometimes a single and accurate depiction of an area's landscape, may not be adequate in either clarity or calibre [1]. Environmental sustainability is a multifaceted notion, and since the turn of the century, published environmental research has paid a lot of attention to different multi-attribute decision-making (MADM) techniques. The most widely used technique among them, Analytic Hierarchy Process (AHP), has been used in extant green infrastructure (GI) literature [2]. Reclamation is the process of putting damaged mining areas back to their intended use; nevertheless, it does not inherently result in the restoration of the initial and natural conditions. The reclaimed area must be not just interesting but also durable over time and secure for visitors. If the growing alternative to land restoration agreed with the purpose and utility for future demands, it could be accomplished. One of the potential solutions for the reclamation process was perennial ground cover [3]. Both landfilling and burning will impact the nearby soil, groundwater, and atmosphere both directly and indirectly. Therefore, choosing an inappropriate landfill or incineration site has disastrous effects on the planet. What's more, because of the high population density in several developing nations, many citizens live close to the rubbish disposal site. The secondary effects of waste disposal on the local population are closely tied to the location of the disposal facility [4]. Burning and landfilling both have direct and indirect effects on the soil, groundwater, and atmosphere in the area. Therefore, picking the wrong location for a landfill or incinerator has terrible consequences for the environment. Furthermore, many residents in a lot of developing nations live close to the garbage disposal site due to the high population density in those areas. The location of the disposal facility has a significant impact on the secondary consequences of trash disposal on the neighbourhood's people [5]. The greatest popular subset of decision-making is MADM. It is a subset of a larger class of frameworks for operational research that deals with choice issues when several decision criteria are present. The MADM method mandates that a choice be taken from a set of decision alternatives that are each defined by an attribute. It is presumed that MADM situations have a present, constrained set of choice possibilities. Sorting and ranking are required to solve a MADM issue [6]. Finding efficient wastewater treatment methods is crucial due to the lack of resources that can be allocated to this cause as well as the huge volume of industrial areas that are forming and growing worldwide. Optimization of the cost of wastewater treatment facilities may be possible *via* modelling, a simulation, previous data analysis, and estimate of future costs and trends. Unpredictable elements like operational issues may inevitably make cost assessment and budgeting more difficult, particularly when using aerobic and anaerobic biological approaches [7]. These new responsibilities were connected to environmental protection, job development, and the preservation of rural life. Because it is intended to more effectively satisfy the demands of society for various uses of agriculture, that role is referred to as sustainable agriculture that is desirable. Even more glaringly, there are no reliable researches available for wheat production. One definition of agricultural sustainable is the efficient handling of agricultural resources to meet changing human demands, protect the natural world, and expand biodiversity [8]. The single goal optimization/analysis is no longer a common method due to the increase in the complexity and multiplicity of the energy planning issue. Energy planning obstacles related to the environment, society, economy, technology, and institutions are thought to be solved using multiple criteria decision-making (MCDM) as an assessment framework. Because it allows the decision-maker to focus on all the available criteria and make the best choice based on the priority, MCDM has gained popularity in energy planning [9]. The ideal crop to plant on each field under a specific situation is determined by employing field explanations, crop attributes, and the farming producer's selection framework after the model first assesses any modifications to the site base caused by the transition of agricultural land to non-agricultural uses.

4.2 Related Works

Study [10], the AHP and Multiple Attribute Decision Analysis (MADA), which use a combined Evidential Reasoning (ER) and AHP methodology, are compared as two techniques to evaluate various selection procedures. This assessment is based on the quantity of alternative criteria, flexibility in the method of determining decisions, computational complexity, suitability for supporting a collective choice, and consistency of findings. In order to assess the reliability of the technique assessment, case studies are given. Research [11], a paradigm for combining MCDM techniques with geographic information systems (GIs) is presented. The decision-makers' choice heuristics are categorized and matched with the MCDM procedures in this framework when there are several evaluation criteria and competing alternatives. Research [12] of the most environmentally friendly storm water management option in densely populated metropolitan areas in emerging nations is the topic of this essay. First, a comprehensive evaluation of the literature was used to identify appropriate Low Impact Development (LID) storm water management strategies for dense metropolitan areas in developing nations. The research [13] is to provide a combined Multi-MCDM to assess the post-mining land-use techniques using significant and significant criteria in consideration of the user's preference ordering. The study [14] is to address ambiguity in the examination of the suitability of land for agricultural crops. Following are three methods: AHP, Ideal Vector Approach (IVA), and Fuzzy AHP. It is discovered that Fuzzy AHP outperforms the other two approaches. The study [15] is to address ambiguity in the examination of the availability of land for crop cultivation. Following are three methods: AHP, Ideal Vector Approach (IVA), and Fuzzy AHP. It is discovered that Fuzzy AHP outperforms the other two approaches. The research [16] on the use of these strategies for choosing the location of different power plants is reviewed in the current study. This review research takes into account hybrid energy systems for the production energy in addition to power plants that use one type of technology. In order to solve the selection issue in an uncertain environment, this study adapts the enhanced multi-attribute and tasking-actor decision-making (MAADM) approach as a fuzzy multi-attribute and multi-actor decision-making (FMAADM) method [17].

4.3 Multi-Attribute Decision Making (MADM)

Reasonable decision-making is formalized *via* analysis of decisions by employing a set of techniques to analyse issues relating to complex decisions. A decision-making difficulty is defined by a limited number of options that may be represented by various, frequently conflicting attributes. In most cases, there are a number of available choices, each with its own advantages and disadvantages. The two categories of MADM approaches, quasi-compensatory methods and non-compensatory approaches, may be seen as instruments for screening, with all workable solutions being those options that meet specified criteria. Since these methods do not support link trade-offs, excluding an alternative may only require one fragile attribute. The conjunction approach, which categorizes the choices into good and undesirable categories, was the quasi-compensatory method employed in this study. If the value of one of the option's qualities is discovered to be outside of a set of permissible values, that option is deemed unsuitable. Strong traits may make up for poor attributes thanks to compensation approaches that let the decision-maker evaluate the trade-offs between choices. As they use being techniques to establish the best option or choice order based on a certain level of optimal performance, these techniques are mathematically and technically more complex than non-compensatory methods. The Method for orders preference by Ideal Comparison Solution, a variant of the ideal point approach, was employed as the compensating method in this investigation. The effective-ideal answer and the false-ideal answer may be defined thanks to the linearity criterion. Then, the possibilities are ranked according to these distances.

$$C = \begin{bmatrix} c_{11} & c_{1i} & c_{1m} \\ \vdots & \vdots & \vdots \\ c_{j1} & c_{ji} & c_{jm} \\ \vdots & \vdots & \vdots \\ c_{n1} & \cdots & c_{ni} \end{bmatrix} \quad (4.1)$$

When every line lists the values of an attribute and each row explains an alternative. Next, an entry c_{ji} represents the Value of a substitute j in relation to attribute i.

$$Q = q_{ji} = \frac{c_{ji}}{\sqrt{\Sigma_j c_{ji}^2}}, j = 1,\ldots,n\ i = 1,\ldots,m \tag{4.2}$$

$$S = s_{ji} = x_j q_{ji}, j = 1,\ldots,n, i = 1,\ldots m \tag{4.3}$$

Find the optimum solutions that are both beneficial and detrimental, or B^* and, B^- respectively. Let I stand for the collection of favourable qualities and I' for the collection of cost factors, and where the price of a beneficial attribute improves with their choice and the value of a cost attribute reduces with choice (i.e., the assign is a liability`).

$$B^* = \{(max_j s_{ji} : i \in I), (max_j s_{ji} : i \in I') : j = 1,\ldots,n\} = \{u_1^*,\ldots,u_m^*\} \tag{4.4}$$

$$B^- = \{(max_j s_{ji} : i \in I), (max_j s_{ji} : i \in I') : j = 1,\ldots,n\} = \{u_1^-,\ldots,u_m^-\} \tag{4.5}$$

As a result, B^* is a vector that contains the highest value and lowest value for each benefit characteristic. The set of attribute value boundaries is defined by these numbers as an n-cube. Remember that the best and worst options presented by a particular choice grid are not the optimal answers, both beneficial and detrimental, which are perfect answers.

$$V_j^* = \sqrt{\Sigma_j (s_{ji} - s_j^*)^2} V_j^- = \sqrt{\Sigma_j (s_{ji} - s_j^-)^2}, j = 1,\ldots,n, i = 1,\ldots,m \tag{4.6}$$

$$D_j^* = \frac{V_j^-}{V_j^* + V_j^-}, j = 1,\ldots,n \tag{4.7}$$

The possibilities may then be ordered using D_j^* in decreasing order. Compensatory approaches call for an authority figure who supplies the proportional scale of relevance, or weight, of each characteristic to the final choice in order to analyse trade-offs. Entropy-based values and subjectively scales are two common techniques for allocating weights. Decisions are made using personal weights for attributes set by the user that take into account decision-maker expertise. The default situation would be to give each characteristic the same weight, indicating that the decision-maker values every characteristic equally [18]. The subjective weights, which are user-controlled values, provide one approach to study a variety of alternatives by seeing how the favoured option changes as the decision weights change. Entropy weights assess each characteristic's effectiveness in identifying differences in the data by measuring the details included in the alternative's value for attributes. For instance, a property does not give data that differentiates the options if it has the same value for each of the alternatives [19, 20]. When analysing and contrasting the possibilities, on the other hand, a characteristic with distinct values for each option offers a lot of details and x_j is helpful.

$$x_j = \frac{1-F_i}{\Sigma_j(1-F_i)}, i = 1,\ldots,m \tag{4.8}$$

$$F_j = \frac{1}{\ln n}\Sigma_{j=1}^{n}(o_{ji}\ln o_{ji}), i = 1,..,m \tag{4.9}$$

Is the entropy, and p o_{ji} is figured out by multiplying x_j by the total of all the values for the ith attribute [1]. The contrast intensity for attribute j is described by the expression $1\text{-}F_j$, with greater values signifying a more full of data characteristic.

$$x_j = \frac{\lambda_i x_j}{\Sigma_i \lambda_i x_j}, i = 1,\ldots m \tag{4.10}$$

Weighing the information value of the characteristic against the significance of the characteristic to the choice.

4.4 Model Description

The model's central premise is that changes in agricultural land use are the result of logical choices made by agricultural producers based on the producer's characteristics, the crops, and the field. By replicating the crop-selection procedure utilizing the simulation MADM over time creates future land cover. The agricultural system was first described using

Table 4.1 The agricultural landscape's characteristics are based on the characteristics of the agricultural system.

Crops	Section	WR	DM
HA	WR- ID	PD	FS
GS	Crop ID	Rate	AOW
Gp	Crop Age	Duty	BS
ND	FZ	Source	PM
MAD	AWC (PF)		CS
ETc-weekly	SRL		OS
M- ETc	TMR		PF
MM- ETc	CS		VY
RFL			

biophysical and decision characteristics (Table 4.1). The algorithm then cycles through each field for each year in the simulation and performs tests to determine if a crop choice is necessary. The majority of the biophysical characteristics that define the farming method are universal to all agricultural landscapes, but the decision characteristics and values will be unique to the situation being studied.

Note: Water Right (WR), Decision Maker (DM), highest age (HA), Growing Season (GS), Grain Period (GP), Node Depth (ND), Maximum (M), Month of Maximum (MM), Region Field Length (RFL), Water Right (WR), Fields Zone (FZ), per foot (PF), Standard Roots Length (SRL), The Monthly Rainfall (TMR), Crop Suitableness (CS), Priority Date (PD), Field Suitability (FS), Accessibility of Water (AOW), Business Situation (BS), Business Situation (BS), Organizational Elements (OE), Pricing Flexibility (PF), Variation in Yield (VY).

Changes in a field's condition or the end of a crop rotation are examples of situations that cause a choice to be made about what crop to plant. When deciding which crop to plant in a field, the decision model considers the biophysical features of the field, the needs of each potential crop, and the owner's features (Figure 4.1).

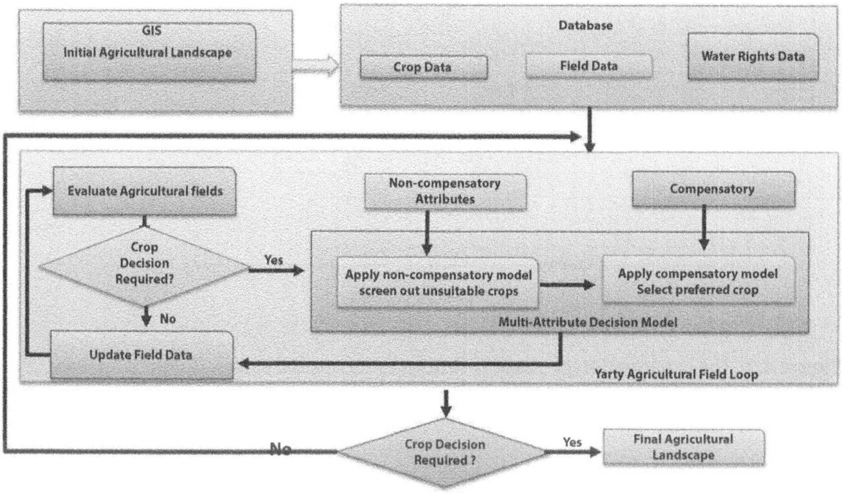

Figure 4.1 Schematic of crop DM model.

4.5 Implementing a Simulator of Alternative Futures

This is an example of an exercise using various possible scenarios that illustrates how this approach can be used to assess the effects of multiple leadership or policy choices. This illustration focuses on a tiny area of farming land in the Willamette Valley. The phases in a typical alternative futures study are shown in Figure 4.2. Typically, stakeholders or policy makers pinpoint areas of concern and create solutions that delve into these problems. Next, models like CropDM may be used to integrate the scenario data into a structure for modelling and produce visual representations of potential outcomes. The scenario's components, fresh options, alternative selection, or supplemental research may all be improved using this knowledge. All but the final step of the analysis are covered by the sample execution that is outlined below. Figure 4.2 shows the sections outlining each stage.

A. Scenario Description

A long-term initiative to rehabilitate riparian regions by turning some cropland back into riparian forest is the subject of the policy under examination. The Crop DM program should be utilized to learn more about the potential scope of change the policy may bring about and to enable experimenting with various aspects of the policy. This remediation strategy, called Restoration, employs a two-tier restoration system and is to be implemented over a 50-year period (1990-2040). The decision-maker may

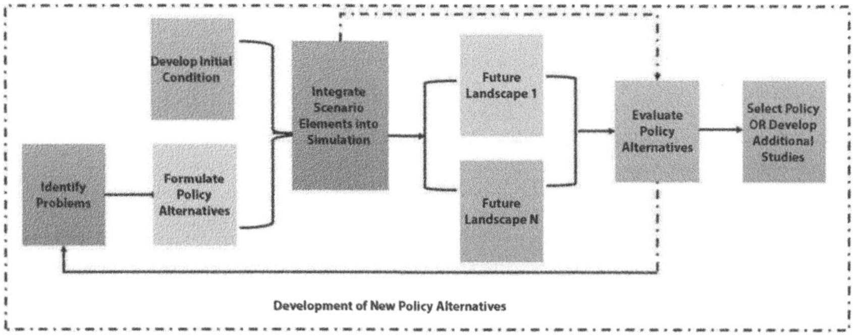

Figure 4.2 The examination of possible futures in its normal stages. different analysis paths are depicted by the dotted lines, and the section numbers that appear beneath each step identify the relevant analysis path.

choose the best crop without this restriction by choosing the second option (Restoration-WR). Following the creation of an initial food system account based on these scenario terms, it was time to pinpoint the characteristics that influence choosing crops or reflect specific situation constraints. Once found, these characteristics must be divided into non-compensatory and compensating characteristics, with appropriate cut-off points or values established.

By turning arable land to riparian forest, we can create a landscape that functions organically. Lands in Tier 2 are managed for agricultural output that is sustainable and consistent with habitat protection goals. At some point over the 50-year term, farmland that is now registered as Tier 1 or Tier 2 farmland will change its tier designation. The Willamette River's main stem runs through the study region (Figure 4.1). Table 4.2 displays the distribution of land and water rights for every piece of soil categories (usual farmland, Tier 2 farmland, and Tier 1 land) throughout the research region.

Following the creation of a basic agricultural system description based on these scenario descriptions, it was time to pinpoint the characteristics that influence crop selection or represent specific scenario restrictions. When recognized, the distinction between non-compensatory and compensating traits must be made and appropriate cut-off points or values must be established.

The greatest soil, climate, and water availability make Tier 1 farming the highest grade land use suited for extensive crop cultivation. This property often has the greatest prospective for earnings and is near to metropolitan canters. Tier 2 agriculture is defined as agricultural land that is still suitable for cultivation and growing crops but is of poorer quality than Tier 1 or excellent farmland. Figure 4.3 and Table 4.2 demonstrate the proposed and existing method.

B. A First Representation of the Agricultural System is Being Developed
A depiction of the original farming method that includes traits that impact or are impacted by the scenario's drivers of change is necessary to create future farmlands. The surroundings and the practical applications of the farmland under investigation will determine the elements employed to characterize the system of agriculture.

Table 4.2 Characteristics of the agricultural fields across the entire research region and for each land designation.

			Hectares		
Land designation	**Field**	**Water rights**	**Minimum**	**Maximum**	**Average**
Tier 1-Land	61	47	1.4	24.3	11.7
Tier 2 -Farmland	96	63	1.9	53.6	14.3
Ordinary Farmland	318	158	1.4	104.1	11.7
All -Land	484	268	1.4	104.1	12.0

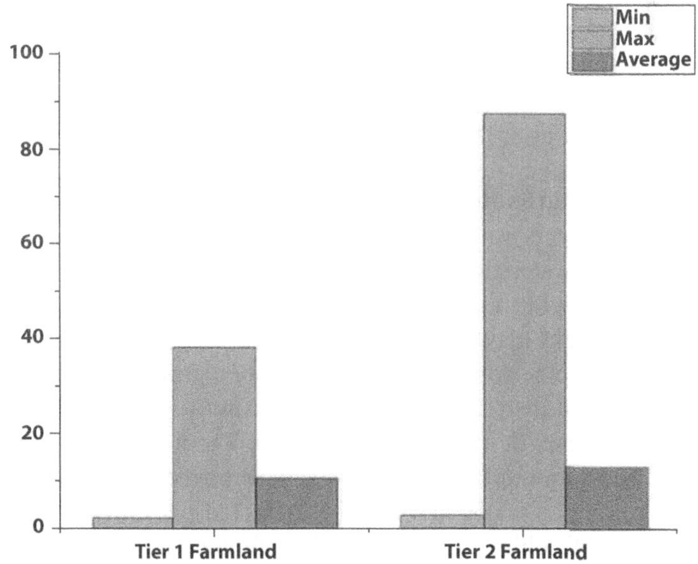

Figure 4.3 Characteristics of the agricultural field.

i. Crop Descriptions

Ninety different types of crop are currently being produced in the Willamette Valley thanks to its rich soils and temperate climate. Twelve different crop kinds, comprising both established crops that are now in demand and novel crops that are gaining popularity in the area, were chosen for this research (Table 4.3). A crop type might be a single crop, a mix of crops with comparable resources and oversight needs, or a rotation of several crop types. The rotation periods, which specify the time among crop choice choices, a field area range, and an annual market trend, were given to each crop. Limits on an area's length that may grow a certain crop were required since some crops need large acreages to produce a crop that is profitable though others normally utilize lesser fields. Statistics from the 1992 agriculture report on land size were used to estimate appropriate lengths across each crop's areas categories and set limits on area size. The time during which a crop would need irrigation was calculated using the planting and harvest dates.

ii. Field Description

The field, here defined as a parcel of land with one crop type, serves as the basic farming landscape's structural component in this model 1. Then, by hand-scanning the field borders from false-colour satellite photos, these bounds were expanded and modified. A minimum facility size of two hectares was established to distinguish these agricultural activities from pleasure farmers and garden spaces since the decision criteria and case components are applicable to corporate farms. Using supervision to create rules linking soil parameters to plant yield for each of the plants in this research, the appropriateness of a crop, typically referred to as the prospective crop yield, was ascertained.

iii. Planning for Agriculture and Resource Rights

According to Oregon's water law, which is founded on the concept of previous acceptance, a water right's priority date determines its access to water, possessing older right to water precedence during periods of water shortage. A resource right may be given to neighbouring fields or for in-stream purposes and it can be connected to one field or a group of fields, as in the case of an irrigated district. If a water right is not used at least once over a period of five years, it may also be forfeited. The water right establishes the highest yearly amount of water that may be moved (duty) as well as the maximum volume of water that may be extracted per unit of time (rate). Every water right's obligation, rate, and preference date included in the research were all included the place-of-use information layer of the OWRD.

Table 4.3 The types of crops employed in this study and their main characteristics.

			Irrigation period	
Crop type	Annual rotate interval	Region farm range (ha)	Start mm-dd	End mm-dd
Orchards	41	3–40	Na	Na
Irrigated Caneberries	16	3–40	05–16	08–06
Christmas Trees	7	3–80	Na	Na
Irrigated Perennial Crop	6	7–80	05–16	09–21
(large acreage)				
Irrigated Perennial Crop	3	3–20	05–16	07–16
(small acreage)				
Irrigated Nursery Crops	21	3–40	05–15	08–31
Irrigated Annual Rotation	4	7–120	05–15	07–31
(early planting)				
Irrigated Annual Rotation	4	7–120	06–01	08–31
(late planting)				
Grain	2	7–100	Na	Na
Grass Seed Rotation	6	11–100	Na	Na
Hay	2	7–140	Na	Na
Pasture	2	3–100	Na	Na
Hybrid Poplar	16	3–36	Na	Na
Wood Lot	71	3–37	Na	Na

The features of the crop, the land, and how it is irrigated determine whether the water delivered down near the ocean is enough for growing a crop. Additionally, the rainwater that is provided must be enough to make up for system decreases brought on by things like evaporation and wind drift. On-farm watering system rates typically range from 60% to 75%, whereas drip line rates often range from 80% to 90%.

C. Alternative Scenarios Definition and Implementation

The scenario's summaries from Section 1 needed to be converted non-compensatory or compensating category qualities, together with appropriate cut-off values or rankings, once the first farm system had been defined.

i. Non-Compensatory Attributes

The combined method's characteristics for all situations were: crop appropriateness, field area, total area used for crops, and water accessibility. These characteristics highlight crop-field combinations that are inappropriate given the field's physical constraints or the local market's constraints.

Unsuitable as the crop suitability ranking. A field that was not within the permitted field acreage limit for the crop (Table 4.3). Based on historical production statistics, the total area used for crops in the area over the maximum crop acreage was calculated. Lack of a water right or a lack of water resources, was determined by Equations (4.9) and (4.10), in the case of irrigated crops.

ii. Compensatory Attributes

The compensating method's chosen variables provide details regarding the trade-offs in the agricultural farming industry. The compensating technique represented the financial and management characteristics of a crop in each scenario using the characteristics price, appropriateness of the crop fluctuation, and yield sensitivity, range of profit, and leadership needs. On a scale from one to nine, each characteristic was given a ranking. The positions for the building compensating attributes were created at first from regional statistics (Agricultural Extending an Oregon State College, 1981–1998) and company fact sheets, and then improved after speaking with extension workers from agriculture about growers' sentiments now and anticipated market conditions in the future. Crop appropriateness was already expressed as a rank. The values of the compensating characteristics remained the same throughout the exercise, with the exception of the leadership needs attribute. The value of the farming needs characteristic was dependent on the preceding crop. Equation (4.10) was employed by the CropDM model to derive a weighted aggregate characteristic for the TOPSIS model. The objective weights were assigned according to the following rationale: a producer would first want to ensure a profit from the crop, and then reduce risk by having the necessary managerial abilities and environment. Finally, price and yield fluctuation would alter these conditions. The least of them was yield variation, which may be reduced by cultivar choice (Table 4.4).

D. Comparing the Future Outcomes

Management requirements, profit potential, and yield responsiveness decision characteristics and scenario components were successively added to the CropDM model, which produced three future results (Figure 4.4). In line with expectations, grain and hay acreage decreased while watered seedling crops with a succession of grass seeds area increased (Table 4.5).

Table 4.4 The subjectively weight for each type of decision maker, along with the decision qualities and their corresponding values for each crop type.

			Management (cost)		
Crops class	**Gain area (benefit)**	**Crop suitability (benefit)**	**New**	**Exper.**	**Variation in yield (cost)**
Orchards	4	2–9	8	2	2
Irrigated Caneberries	2	2–9	8	2	2
Christmas Trees	4	2–9	3	2	8
Large-acreage Irrigated (Permanent Agriculture)	2	2–9	4	2	4
Small-acreage watered perennial plants	3	2–9	8	6	2

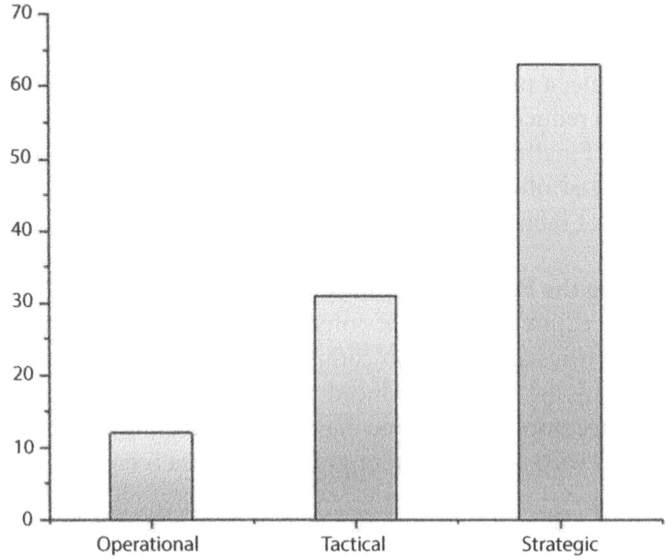

Figure 4.4 Different levels of DM.

Extra scenario studies might be conducted in conjunction with other evaluations, such as hydro logic modelling, to evaluate the effect of increased stream flows as a result of the granting of in-stream access to water for agriculture usage, to decide which policies would be most advantageous.

By computing the mean habitat rating for the Tier 2 farms, it was possible to assess how the scenario assumptions would affect the habitat quality. The baseline landscape's habitat score was 2.4; in Restoration, it was 2.6; and in Restoration-WR, it was 4.9. Due of the decision-makers' lack of concern about jeopardizing the field's water right, Restoration-WR has a higher habitat value. As seen in Table 4.5, grass seed rotation has replaced irrigated crops, particularly irrigated annual rotation. In addition, the area of Wood Lot increases in size while the area of Irrigated Caneberries is cut in half. These findings imply that for the Tier 2 part of the riparian restoration program to be successful, policymakers must provide solutions to the problem of these fields' water rights.

E. Different Level of DM

Upper-level management makes strategic choices that determine the organization's entire course. These choices must be made over a lengthy period of time, taking into account the organization's advantages, disadvantages,

Table 4.5 Distribution of land cover for the continuing trends and restoration scenarios, for all land and for tier 2 farmland.

	Distribution of land cover (%)							
	All land				**Tier 2 farmland**			
Crop type	**Initial condition**	**Continuing trends**	**Restoration**	**Restoration-WR**	**Initial condition**	**Continuing trends**	**Restoration**	**Restoration WR**
Irrigated Annual Rotation	36	37	35	26	48	56	56	3
Grain	3	1	2	3	6	2	1	3
Grass Seed Rotation	34	37	37	46	15	24	22	78
Hay	3	2	1	4	2	1	1	2
Pasture	1	2	2	1	1	2	2	1
Hybrid Poplar	2	2	2	2	1	2	2	2
Wood Lot	2		2	2	2	2	2	3
Riparian	1	1	15	15	1	1	1	0

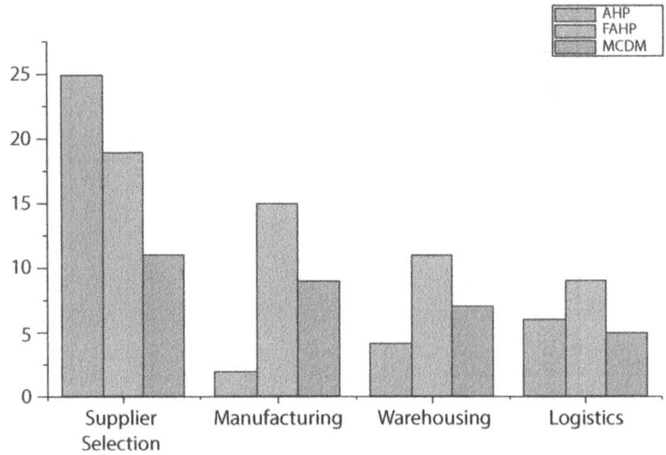

Figure 4.5 Top three MCDM methods.

opportunities, and dangers. Strategic choices include things like expanding new markets, buying other businesses, and creating new products and services.

Middle-level managers make tactical choices and are in charge of carrying out the plans and strategies created by their superiors. To accomplish certain goals, these choices involve allocated resources, distributing tasks, and organizing activities. Establishing sales goals, creating advertising plans, and choosing vendors are a few instances for tactical choices. Figure 4.4 demonstrates the proposed and existing method (Figure 4.5).

Decisions that affect regular business operations inside an organization are referred to as operational decisions. They are often produced by workers and lower-level executives who are in charge of doing the tasks that support the overarching objectives of the firm. Routine duties like assigning lab or hours, procuring supplies, and answering consumer questions are examples of operations choices.

4.6 Conclusions

The strategy for creating future land uses described in this study combines field and crop attributes that are both spatial and non-spatial with agricultural aspects. A sample of the execution examined three policy choices for a small area of farmland situated along Oregon's Willamette River, which served as an illustration of the usage of this methodology for future scenario studies. The model's findings demonstrated how adjustments to various farming system factors affected crop selection choices and produced new agricultural landscapes. The agronomic, ecological, social, or economical characteristics of the various landscapes may then be compared and contrasted using appropriate metrics and models after those landscapes have been constructed. According to the needs of the study, the scope of the project, and the data provided, the model's structure allows for a variety of alterations. By adjusting the attribute's weights, adding or removing characteristics or alternates, or modifying the spatial nature of the landscape, an analyst may test various scenarios. For instance, by employing surveys to elicit information, various kinds of growers might be recognized. Decision-attribute quantities and evaluations; the geographical pattern of urban expansion into farmland might be provided to the model *via* a GIS; or climatic change possibilities may be investigated using rain producers. The decision-maker for the field in each instance incorporates this data before choosing the crop or land use. Instead of being used for prediction, alternate futures models excel in illuminating patterns or trade-offs resulting from various future scenarios. By presenting representations of potential outcomes, these studies provide policy makers and stakeholders a means to look at the effects of various management techniques in the future. Testing is less difficult than with forecasts for the next few years, where greater veracity is expected, because the purpose of this research is to construct and test simulations for potential scenarios rather than to foretell the future. However, there must be some indication of realism in the outcomes of long-term models. This research will provide guidance to managers to assist them in determining which MCDM approaches are used in which instances at each level of decision-making (strategic, tactical, and operational). The literature clearly demonstrates how fuzzy sets and their connection with other MCDM techniques have been successfully implemented at every stage of the SC decision-making process as well as in the relevant SC tasks.

References

1. Berger, P.A., Generating agricultural landscapes for alternative futures analysis: A multiple attribute decision-making model. *Trans. GIS.*, 10, 1, 103–120, 2006, https://doi.org/10.1111/j.1467-9671.2006.00246.x.

2. Lin, S.H., Zhao, X., Wu, J., Liang, F., Li, J.H., Lai, R.J., Hsieh, J.C., Tzeng, G.H., An evaluation framework for developing green infrastructure by using a new hybrid multiple attribute decision-making model for promoting environmental sustainability. *Socio-Econ. Plan. Sci.*, 75, 100909, 2021, https://doi.org/10.1016/j.seps.2020.100909.
3. Aghajani Bazzazi, A., Adib, A., Shapoori, M., Plant species selection by hybrid multiple-attribute decision-making model for promoting green mining in the Sungun copper mine, Iran. *Environ. Sci. Pollut. Res. Int.*, 29, 59, 89221–89234, 2022, https://doi.org/10.1007/s11356-022-21954-9.
4. Yang, Z. and Chang, J., A multi-attribute decision-making-based site selection assessment algorithm for garbage disposal plant using interval q-rung orthopair fuzzy power Muirhead mean operator. *Environ. Res.*, 193, 110385, 2021, https://doi.org/10.1016/j.envres.2020.110385.
5. Drobne, S. and Lisec, A., Multi-attribute decision analysis in GIS: Weighted linear combination and ordered weighted averaging. *Informatica*, 33, 4, 2009.
6. Gupta, R., Selecting best tractor ranking wise by software using MADM (Multiple-attribute decision making approach), 2017.
7. Mirabi, M., Karrabi, M., Gheibi, M., An economic analysis of industrial wastewater treatment systems using multi-attribute decision-making methods (case study: Toos Industrial Estate, Mashhad, Iran). *Desalin. Water Treat.*, 146, 131–140, 2019, https://doi.org/10.5004/dwt.2019.23630.
8. Poursaeed, A., Mirdamadi, M., Malekmohammadi, I., Hosseini, J.F., The partnership models of agricultural sustainable development based on multiple criteria decision making (MCDM) in Iran. *Afr. J. Agric. Res.*, 5, 23, 3185–3190, 2010.
9. Kumar, A., Sah, B., Singh, A.R., Deng, Y., He, X., Kumar, P., Bansal, R.C., A review of multi criteria decision making (MCDM) towards sustainable renewable energy development. *Renew. Sustain. Energy Rev.*, 69, 596–609, 2017, https://doi.org/10.1016/j.rser.2016.11.191.
10. Díaz, H., Loughney, S., Wang, J., Guedes Soares, C.G., Comparison of multicriteria analysis techniques for decision making on floating offshore wind farms site selection. *Ocean Eng.*, 248, 110751, 2022, https://doi.org/10.1016/j.oceaneng.2022.110751.
11. Jankowski, P., Integrating geographical information systems and multiple criteria decision-making methods. *Int. J. Geogr. Inf. Syst.*, 9, 3, 251–273, 1995, https://doi.org/10.1080/02693799508902036.
12. Gogate, N.G., Kalbar, P.P., Raval, P.M., Assessment of stormwater management options in urban contexts using Multiple Attribute Decision-Making. *J. Clean. Prod.*, 142, 2046–2059, 2017, https://doi.org/10.1016/j.jclepro.2016.11.079.
13. Narrei, S. and Osanloo, M., Post-mining land-use methods optimum ranking, using multi attribute decision techniques with regard to sustainable resources management. OIDA. *Int. J. Sustain. Dev.*, 2, 11, 65–76, 2011.

14. Prakash, T.N., Land suitability analysis for agricultural crops: A fuzzy multicriteria decision making approach, MSc. Thesis, International Institute for Geo-Information Science and Earth Observation, Enchede: The Netherlands, 2003, December.
15. Hendawy, E., Belal, A.A., Mohamed, E.S., Elfadaly, A., Murgante, B., Aldosari, A.A., Lasaponara, R., The prediction and assessment of the impacts of soil sealing on agricultural land in the North Nile Delta (Egypt) using satellite data and GIS modeling. *Sustainability*, 11, 17, 4662, 2019, https://doi.org/10.3390/su11174662.
16. Khanlari, A. and AlhuyiNazari, M., A review on the applications of multicriteria decision-making approaches for power plant site selection. *J. Therm. Anal. Calorim.*, 1–17, 2021.
17. Agrebi, M. and Abed, M., Decision-making from multiple uncertain experts: Case of distribution center location selection. *Soft Comput.*, 25, 6, 4525–4544, 2021, https://doi.org/10.1007/s00500-020-05461-y.
18. Behl, T., Chadha, S., Sachdeva, M., Kumar, A., Hafeez, A., Mehta, V., Bungau, S., Ubiquitination in rheumatoid arthritis. *Life Sci.*, 261, article no.: 118459, 2020, https://doi.org/10.1016/j.lfs.2020.118459.
19. Kaur, R., Sood, A., Lang, D.K., Bhatia, S., Al-Harrasi, A., Aleya, L., Behl, T., Potential of flavonoids as anti-Alzheimer's agents: Bench to bedside. *Environ. Sci. Pollut. Res. Int.*, 29, 18, 26063–26077, 2022, https://doi.org/10.1007/s11356-021-18165-z.
20. Irudayasamy, A., Christotodoss, P.R., Natarajan, R., Multilingual novel summarizer for visually challenged peoples, in: *Handbook of research on technologies and systems for E-collaboration during global crises*, J. Zhao and V. Kumar (Eds.), pp. 27–46, IGI Global, 2022, https://doi.org/10.4018/978-1-7998-9640-1.ch003.

5

Cultivating Connectivity: Bridging Communities Through Farm Management Systems

Leninisha S.*, Riya Bansal V., Sai Lakshana S. and Krijay M.

School of Computer Science and Engineering, Vellore Institute of Technology, Chennai, India

Abstract

This research paper is about the Farm Management System (FMS), an innovative online platform that combines technology, agriculture, and community involvement. FMS, developed using HTML, CSS, JavaScript, PHP, MySQL, and blockchain technology, provides a seamless experience for farmers, landowners, and administrators. It enables administrators to efficiently handle data, allows landowners to connect with other users, and equips farmers with crucial agricultural insights. This paper illustrates how FMS enhances farming techniques, encourages collaborative community initiatives, and supports environmentally sustainable methods through analysis of its core principles, technological components, and practical implications. It also points to the importance of databases and blockchain in the functioning of FMS. In a nutshell, this research underscores the potential of FMS and other digital solutions to aid farmers, improve agricultural practices, and protect the environment.

Keywords: Farm management system, agriculture, community engagement, communication, email, data management, blockchain

5.1 Introduction

The Olam Farmer Information System (OFIS) and similar models have a great potential to enhance connectivity and data integration in Farm

**Corresponding author*: leninisha.shanmugham@vitstudent.ac.in

Narayanan Ganesh and Kanak Kalita (eds.) Harvesting Data: Blockchain, AI and Advanced Innovations in Agriculture, (99–108) © 2026 Scrivener Publishing LLC

Management Information Systems (FMIS). However, setting up and maintaining these platforms can be quite complex and prone to difficulties because of their complexity. This may have a serious effect on small farms or agricultural enterprises with limited IT capabilities. Moreover, the achievement of seamlessness in data exchange across systems can require sustained investment and efforts that might delay the rates at which adoption occurs. For instance, such challenges necessitate focusing on user-friendly interfaces, standardized protocols, and support services, with a view to optimizing access by making sure that all those involved in agriculture are better able to reap all that has been developed.

In addition, blockchain technology may solve problems of data integrity and security, which will ensure transparency and trust in all transactions and interactions in the system.

In the agricultural management field, the Farm Management System (FMS) is a key component that encourages the integration of technology, agricultural practices, and community collaboration. FMS is a web-based platform that is expected to make agricultural operations more straightforward, improve communication, and encourage teamwork among farmers, land owners, and administrators. Here, the theoretical, technological structure, and practical applications of FMS are discussed that will explain its contributions to greater agricultural productivity, community cooperativeness, and sustainability. This investigation adopts a comprehensive analysis to stress FMS's transformative potential in modern agricultural management and community development, thereby emphasizing its essential role as a positive change agent.

A. Specifications

FMS provides an optimal interface for users in logging on by providing a farmer-based, landlord-based, and administration-based login. All these categories receive their specific functionalities designed to respond directly to the role and need associated with them. For a farmer, this means they use the system to obtain the most essential agricultural information, for instance, information on a plant, drugs, or even methods. In addition, farmers are capable of confidentially reporting discrepancies to the administrator without the rest of the users being informed. They can also provide constructive criticism using their personal experiences. On the other hand, landlords benefit from all the features that the site offers. They are capable not only of accessing information but also of taking a full role in resource management. This involves adding new plants or medicines and deleting any that exist. Moreover, landlords can interact with peers through chat features, encouraging collaboration. The spread of knowledge is crucial for the improvement of agricultural practices.

Administrators are equipped with sophisticated tools for comprehensive data management, which allows them to make decisions and utilize resources wisely. They have full visibility into all system details, thereby enabling them to monitor and resolve any issues or discrepancies reported immediately. In addition, administrators also oversee the feedback mechanism wherein all concerns from farmers and landlords are resolved promptly and confidentially, therefore creating the community's trust and transparency. Using blockchain technology will ensure every transaction and any change to the data is made securely and prevents unauthorized changing and increases users' level of trust.

B. Tools and Technologies

The Farm Management System (FMS) integrates a set of core tools and technologies for it to perform perfectly and in a user-friendly manner. Foundational bases such as HTML, CSS, and JavaScript build this intuitive experience. On the data managements' end, it is mainly up to PHP and MySQL to carry out a safe and effective manner from storage. The integration of blockchain technology significantly improves data security and transparency by providing an immutable ledger for all system transactions and interactions. Moreover, advanced technologies are incorporated to enhance the functionality of the FMS, such as real-time data updates that facilitate immediate access to the most current information. Robust authentication methods are implemented to safeguard user data and maintain confidentiality. It uses efficient data storage solutions, ensuring smooth performance and further allowing the system to grow along with the increasing demands of its users. The tools and technologies involved allow FMS to run smoothly, enabling stakeholders and creating a collaborative environment to sustain agricultural activities.

5.2 Literature Survey

The Online Farm System serves an essential function in the modernization of agriculture by aiding farmers in the organization, oversight, and assessment of their operations. This facilitates the farming process and promotes collaboration between farmers and prospective buyers. However, the efficacy of the system is significantly contingent upon a reliable internet connection, which presents a challenge in rural areas where access to high-speed internet is insufficient. This limitation eventually will restrict some farmers who will not be able to use the system according to its full capacity, as a result of which, again, there will be a hindrance in delivering the connectivity with the buyers. To meet this challenge, efforts that enhance internet access in these rural areas should be seen so that all can understand the full benefit of the system [2, 3].

The development of sophisticated farm machinery management systems could significantly advance the precision agriculture. However, building up and maintaining such systems involve complex and costly work that requires integrating various data sources and technologies within it. That calls for highly significant financial investment. What becomes particularly challenging in regions of fragmented landscapes and varied equipment might be ensuring compatibility with an extremely broad list of farm machinery brands and models. Overcoming these is pretty crucial as a precondition of intense exploitation of these in rendering friendly services to the farmers and other beneficiaries under agriculture [7].

Using one-of-a-kind software, involving Object Database Management Systems (ODBMS) as well as the applications' tools through Java and CORBA into the farming work involved unique methodology. ODBMS was used for storage concerning agricultural data. This then incorporated Java for the coding system whilst taking after real-time sharing in one's data, based around CORBA. Such designs were developed such as one farming guide as well as an organizational tracking system design. Although such setup illustrated effectiveness, more was added technological capability [11].

5.3 Proposed System

The Farm Management System (FMS) has been developed to change the course of agricultural management and also improve collaboration between the involved stakeholders. The state-of-the-art system innovatively enhances user engagement by providing different login portals for farmers, landowners, and administrators. From Figure 5.1 shows the evidence of how these tables are structured and managed in the phpMyAdmin interface on the XAMPP server. Each user category is provided with functionalities that address specific responsibilities and requirements, hence ensuring a customized and efficient user interface.

1. Farmer Interface: Once logged in, the farmers get information related to agriculture that includes plant information, medication, and methodology details. They can provide feedback regarding their experience so that they could

confidentially raise a complaint to the administrator without anyone else knowing about it. The user interface is developed to be highly user-friendly and intuitive, so as to easily navigate through this and give quick access to such important agricultural resources.

2. Landlord Interface: All the features related to resource management are offered to landlords in the portal, hence allowing them to be very interactive. Landlords have the ability to access agricultural information and emailing peers to create cooperation and the flow of information. Furthermore, landlords are allowed to add new plants or medication and remove the old ones to enable efficient management of resources.
3. Administrator Interface: Administrators are provided with comprehensive tools for effective data management, which helps in decision-making and resource allocation. They have access to all the information in the system and can track and resolve all reported issues or discrepancies. The administrators also oversee the feedback feature, ensuring that farmers' or landlords' concerns are addressed promptly and confidentially, thus fostering trust and transparency within the community. Utilizing the blockchain technology ensures that every change and input is recorded safely and permanently, building reliability and trust between users.Figure 5.2 depicts the Entity-Relationship (ER) mapping that demonstrates how different entities like farmers, landlords, and administrators are interconnected with the system.

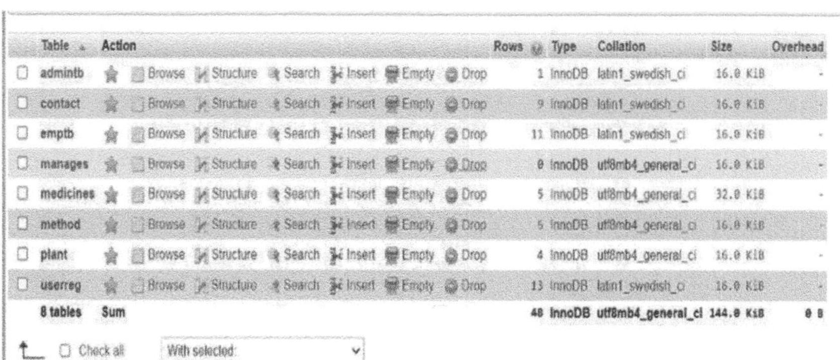

Table	Action	Rows	Type	Collation	Size	Overhead
admintb	Browse Structure Search Insert Empty Drop	1	InnoDB	latin1_swedish_ci	16.0 KiB	-
contact	Browse Structure Search Insert Empty Drop	9	InnoDB	latin1_swedish_ci	16.0 KiB	-
emptb	Browse Structure Search Insert Empty Drop	11	InnoDB	latin1_swedish_ci	16.0 KiB	-
manages	Browse Structure Search Insert Empty Drop	0	InnoDB	utf8mb4_general_ci	16.0 KiB	-
medicines	Browse Structure Search Insert Empty Drop	5	InnoDB	utf8mb4_general_ci	32.0 KiB	-
method	Browse Structure Search Insert Empty Drop	5	InnoDB	utf8mb4_general_ci	16.0 KiB	-
plant	Browse Structure Search Insert Empty Drop	4	InnoDB	utf8mb4_general_ci	16.0 KiB	-
userreg	Browse Structure Search Insert Empty Drop	13	InnoDB	latin1_swedish_ci	16.0 KiB	-
8 tables	Sum	48	InnoDB	utf8mb4_general_ci	144.0 KiB	0 B

Check all With selected:

Figure 5.1 View of the database in phpMyAdmin on XAMPPserver.

This farm management system would be user-centered in nature and ensure access of all users to resources and tools with which one may successfully manage their agriculture. By embedding the new technologies in this system in the form of blockchain technology and interactive interfaces, these agricultural practices will be eased, effective communication and liaison between the farmer, landowners, and administrators will be enhanced, and eventually result in elevated practices of agricultural productions while strengthening sustainability as well as the entire agricultural sector.

a. Tables and Attributes Manages Table:
For Input: eid, ename, pid, plant_name, med_id, med_name,salary
Method Table:
For Input: method_id, method_name, method_type,method_desc
Medicines Table:
For Input: pid, med_id, med_name, med_type, med_cost,med_desc
Plant Table:
For Input: pid, plant_name, plant_type, plant_desc, soil_type
Admintb Table:
For Input: username, password
Contact Table:
For Input: pid, name, email, contact, message
Landlord Table:
For Input: eid, username, password, email, phone, salary
Farmer Table:
For Input: pid, fname, lname, gender, email, contact, password, cpassword.
Figure 5.3 presents the relational database diagram, highlighting how the tables are linked through primary and foreign keys.

5.4 System Design

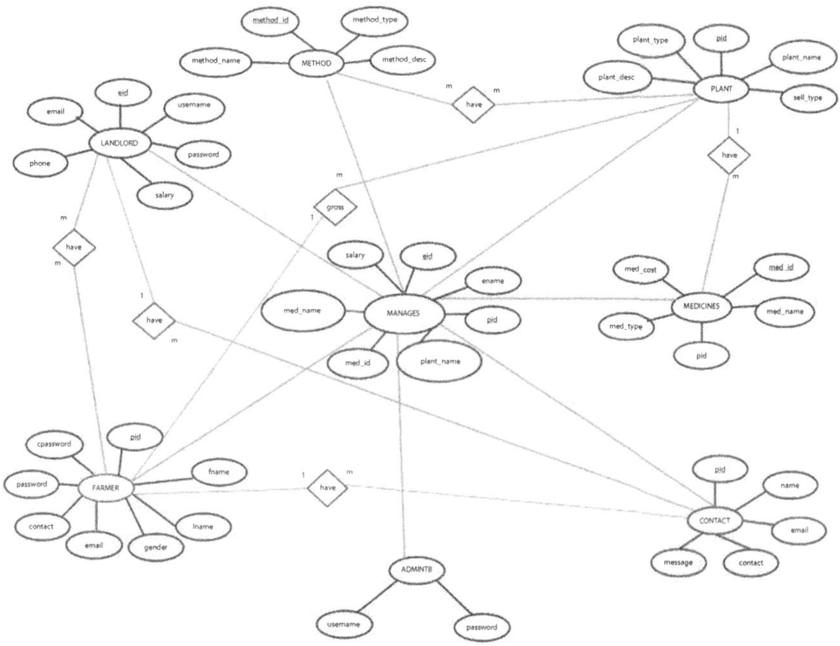

Figure 5.2 ER mapping.

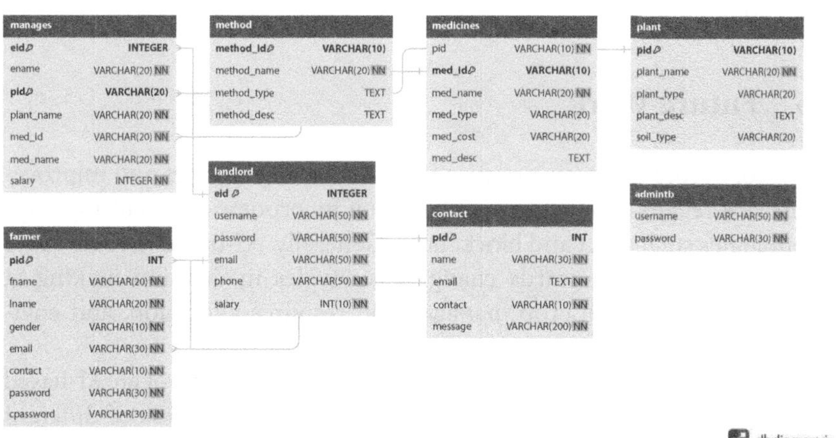

Figure 5.3 Relational database diagram.

The system architecture has been updated to add a blockchain layer that will safely record all the transactions and interactions within an immutable nature. This layer provides transparency and security over data exchange so as to ensure traceability and tamper resistance of data entries and modifications. As such, much trust is enhanced, and accountability within the system is considerably built.

5.5 Conclusion

Therefore, Farm Management System is the innovative agricultural technology that rightly integrates tradition with modern digital solution. In that context, users get a way of easily interacting with the system and a wide variety of features on offer and integration with the blockchain for farmers, landowners, and administrators to optimize agriculture activities, streamline communication, and promote mutual development in community. By using the robust technological infrastructure combined with efficient database and blockchain management systems, FMS allows for data-driven decision-making while promoting sustainable agriculture. There could be scalability and geography issues that would require careful planning and strategic expansion programs. In addition, it is necessary to ascertain the accuracy of data so that biases in user inputs are reduced to maintain integrity and reliability in the system. The challenges arising are such that FMS has irrevocably impacted agriculture management and community development, ushering in a new age of digital empowerment in the agriculture sector.

5.6 Future Work

Going forward, FMS gives promise for a plethora of changes and improvements as it relates to development based on incorporation of cutting-edge technologies such as AI and blockchain. Generally, AI-based models could offer high potential towards changing strategies in decision-making at farm level as relates to crop management, resource allocation, and environmental conservation.

One notable focus for future projects might be the design of an AI-based review rating system focused on evaluating the effectiveness of different fertilizers, such as performance with various crops and varying weather conditions. FMS would be greatly integrated with algorithms and vast datasets that include soil composition, varieties of crops, trends in weather, and types of fertilizers to provide evidence-based suggestions on the best fertilizers to use. This system can therefore use machine-learning algorithms that evaluate historical data related to crop productivity, soil content, and fertilizer application to enable farmers to make informed decisions suited to their specific agricultural context.

More R&D can be in incorporating predictive analytics capabilities driven by AI in Farm Management Systems for the prediction of crop performance, detection of potential threats, and enhancement of resource allocation plans. Using AI-based predictive models, FMS may allow farmers to better monitor crop health, minimize bad weather impacts, and optimize yield with less environmental harm.

Furthermore, future endeavors would be towards FMS harmonization and integration with various forms of agricultural systems, IoT systems, and blockchain networks such that effective data sharing as well as integration could take place in the agriculture industry. This might be achieved in standardizing data exchange protocols, APIs, and interoperability frameworks to encourage cooperation or information sharing between farmers and suppliers, researchers, etc.

In a nutshell, incorporating such state-of-the-art technologies as artificial intelligence and blockchain, combined with its interest in innovation and cooperation, FMS is going to transform into an agriculture full solution that is meant to enhance agricultural efficiency, push toward sustainable agriculture, and enhance the farmer's life today.

Bibliography

1. Lewis, K.A. and Bardon, K.S., A computer-based informal environmental management system for agriculture. 1998.
2. Giradkar, A.D., Pakhmode, A.A., Mehere, A.S., Naktode, R.B., Online farm management system. *Int. J. Adv. Res. Innov. Ideas Educ.*, 2020.
3. Kaloxylos, A., Eigenmann, R., Teye, F., Politopoulou, Z., Wolfert, S., Farm management systems and the Future Internet era. 2012.
4. Kim, J.Y., Lee, C.G., Baek, S.H., Rhee, J.-Y., Open farm information system data-exchange platform for interaction with agricultural information systems. 2015.
5. Fountas, S., Sorensen, C.G., Tsiropoulos, Z., Cavalaris, C., Liakos, V., Gemtos, T., Farm machinery management information system. 2015.
6. Tumibay, G.M., Layug, F.T., Yap, D.S., Sembrano, M.S.M., Increasing the value of farm products: connecting farmers and consumers through an e-commerce system. *Proceedings of 18th Annual International Conference on Electronic Commerce: E-commerce in Smart Connected World*, 2016.

7. Lehmann, R.J., Reiche, R., Schiefer, G., Future internet and the agri-food sector: State-of-the-art in literature and research. 2012.
8. Nikkilä, R., Seilonen, I., Koskinen, K., Software architecture for farm management information systems in precision agriculture. 2010.
9. Shaikh, I., Narawade, V., Pokharkar, O., Farm Management System. *Int. J. Res. Publ. Rev.*, 2022.
10. Batte, M., Changing computer use in agriculture: evidence from Ohio. *Comput. Electron. Agric.*, 2005.
11. Beck, H., Agricultural enterprise information management using object databases, Java, and COBRA. *Comput. Electron. Agric.*, 2001.
12. Fountas, S., *et al.*, A model of decision making and information flows for information-intensive agriculture. *Agric. Syst.*, 2006.
13. Lewis, T., Evolution of farm management information systems. *Comput. Electron. Agric.*, 1998.
14. McCown, R.L., A cognitive systems framework to inform delivery of analytic support for farmers£ intuitive management under seasonal climatic variability. *Agric. Syst.*, 2012.
15. Murakami, E., *et al.*, Infrastructure for the development of distributed service-oriented information systems for precision. *Comput. Electron. Agric.*, 2007.
16. Sørensen, C.G., *et al.*, Conceptual model of a future farm management information system. *Comput. Electron. Agric.*, 2010.
17. Sørensen, C.G., *et al.*, Requirements for a future farm management information system. *Comput. Electron. Agric.*, 2011.
18. Wolfert, J., *et al.*, Organizing information integration in agri-food – a method based on a service-oriented architecture and living lab. *Comput. Electron. Agric.*, 2010.
19. Nakamoto, S., Bitcoin: A Peer-to-Peer Electronic Cash System, 2008.
20. Swan, M., *Blockchain: Blueprint for a New Economy*, O'Reilly Media, Inc., 2015.
21. Iansiti, M. and Lakhani, K.R., The Truth about Blockchain. *Harv. Bus. Rev.*, 2017.
22. Zyskind, G., Nathan, O., Pentland, A., Decentralizing Privacy: Using Blockchain to Protect Personal Data. *2015 IEEE Security and Privacy Workshops*, 2015.

Part II

BLOCKCHAIN IN AGRICULTURAL SUPPLY CHAIN AND TRACEABILITY

6

Comprehensive Review of Blockchain-Oriented Methods in Agricultural Supply Chain Management

Pandiyaraju V.[1]*, Thangaramya K.[1], Kannan A.[2] and Nikhil Nair[1]

[1]*School of Computer Science and Engineering, Vellore Institute of Technology, Chennai, India*

[2]*Department of Information Science and Technology, College of Engineering Guindy, Anna University, Chennai, Tamil Nadu, India*

Abstract

Blockchain is a distributed ledger maintenance system used for the effective maintenance of data in many applications with security. However, the data and transactions pertaining to the agricultural supply chain management have many challenging issues such as the maintenance of data integrity, availability, security, and analysis. Many research works are already available about the use of blockchains for data maintenance with security. Some of the systems use the Internet of Things and sensors for data collection while other works use Artificial Intelligence for effective data analysis. However, security is also an important issue to be considered. Therefore, this paper provides a survey of works on blockchain-based data maintenance systems and methods for effective storage and retrieval of agricultural supply chain maintenance data. In addition, one new dynamic hashing algorithm called DHASH algorithm and one new commit protocol called Rule-based Two-Phase Commit (R2PC) protocol have been proposed in this paper for enhancing the security of agricultural information stored in blockchain. The main advantages of this survey of DHASH algorithm and R2PC protocol are to highlight the important parameters such as security that are necessary for reliable data storage and retrieval for agricultural applications using blockchain.

***Keywords*:** ICT, AI, supply chain, blockchain, agriculture, security

**Corresponding author*: pandiyaraju.v@vit.ac.in

Narayanan Ganesh and Kanak Kalita (eds.) Harvesting Data: Blockchain, AI and Advanced Innovations in Agriculture, (111–130) © 2026 Scrivener Publishing LLC

6.1 Introduction

Blockchain technology is a type of advanced database technology that allows the storing of data pertaining to different applications such as agriculture, health care, transport, business, bitcoin and banking for effective storage, retrieval, and also transparent sharing of information within a single application such as agriculture supply chain and business networks. Moreover, a blockchain database organizes the application data in blocks where the blocks are linked with each other in a hash-based chain. The blockchain transactions are only readable since they are irreversible, meaning that, once the data are recorded in blocks with a timestamp, they cannot be altered subsequently and retroactively without changing all the preceding transaction data blocks. The blocks in the blockchain are normally managed by one Peer-to-Peer (P2P) network. Moreover, in blockchain data are stored in the form of a public distributed ledger using a distributed storage structure, and hence the data are distributed with location transparency and have a logical correlation since they are meant for the same application. In a blockchain application, the nodes of the system collectively adhere to some consensus algorithm in order to insert new blocks of data and also to validate such new transaction blocks. The blockchain provide security for many important blockchain applications including agricultural-business agricultural-insurance, smart agricultural farming and land registration. The blockchain applications can be divided into four categories, namely, provenance of traceability and food authenticity, smart agricultural database management, trading and finance in agricultural supply chain management, and finally agricultural data communication. In many ways this includes data encryption, forks, digital signatures and hash functions. In short, blockchain maintains a chain of blocks that contain information which is stored using a distributed ledger format. Figure 6.1 shows the structure of a block chain.

In Figure 6.1, there are two blocks which are connected by a chain. The starting block of a blockchain is known as the Genesis block.

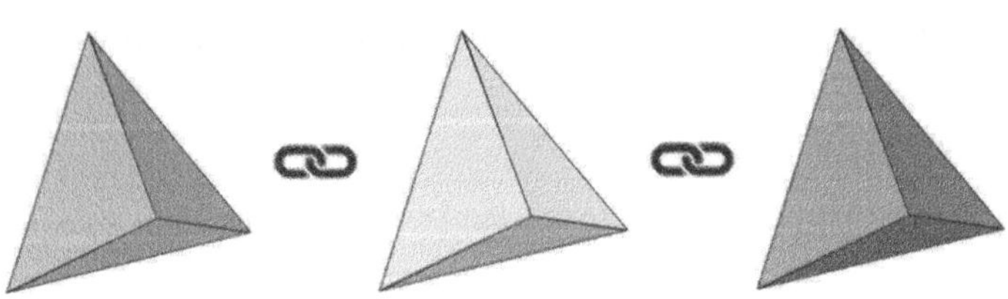

Figure 6.1 Blockchain.

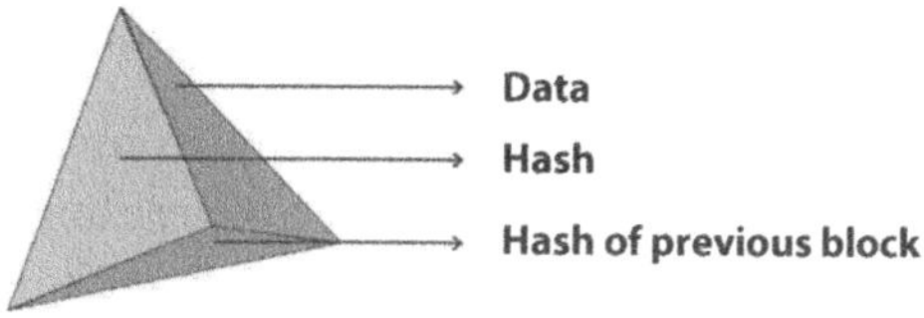

Figure 6.2 Components of blockchain.

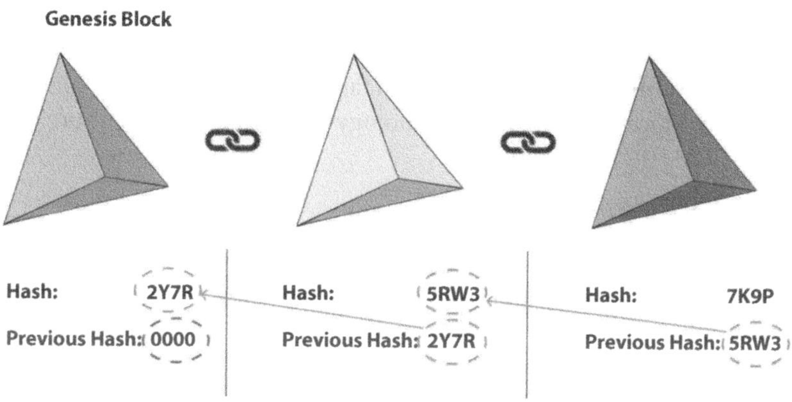

Figure 6.3 Hash-based blockchain.

Moreover, every block has one address in terms of hash value. Figure 6.2 shows the components of a block present in the blockchain.

Each block in this blockchain contains three components, namely the data, the hash values of the current, and the hash of previous blocks. Figure 6.3 shows the hash-based chains used in the blockchain.

The hash value of the genesis block is given in the first block and since it has no previous block, the hash value of the previous block is considered as zero. For all the subsequent blocks, the hash values are calculated and the hash values of the current and previous blocks are used to form the chain. In this way, blockchains are created for maintaining the distributed ledgers.

6.1.1 Challenges in Agriculture Data Maintenance

The various challenges that are related to agriculture data maintenance are based on the basic challenges to the field of agriculture itself. The natural challenges in agriculture are land availability, seed problem, usage of fertilizers, soil erosion, agricultural instability, water quality issues, pesticides management, production and supply chain management, cropping patterns and storage and retrieval methods.

6.1.1.1 Land Availability Data

More than 140 million farmers of India are living in rural India and most of them hold less than 2 acres of land. However, a large amount of land holdings will enable the farmer to use technology-oriented techniques in production. For this purpose, modern agricultural techniques and Artificial Intelligence (AI) based intelligent decision-making rules must be applied in order to enhance productivity. Here, the farmers holding smaller lands may opt to do the agriculture using the traditional methods for farming, and this will reduce productivity. Due to this, many small farmers show more interest towards working in rural farm lands. Hence, there must be a way to introduce the benefit of technology in all types of agriculture.

6.1.1.2 Seed Problems

Most farmers want to use hybrid types of seeds to get better yields. Moreover, while using those superior or hybrid varieties, companies always insist that farmers follow a specific farming methodology to gain high yield. Even though the farmers follow the specified methods, some hybrid varieties fail to provide good yields. However, the company is always trying to push the blame onto the farmers when the crops do not provide good yield. Moreover, for certain high-yielding varieties, a higher number of fertilizers and high-water requirements are needed, and hence it turns out to be a challenging task.

6.1.1.3 Usage of Fertilizer

To feed the growing population and to make farming a more sustainable and profitable business, the agriculture sector in India has to meet the growing demands of the population every year by increasing the production of crops and by applying more modern methods. Companies therefore develop hybrid seed varieties that have high yield to meet the growing demand. In this scenario, some crops require high fertilizers and some do not. But the use of the high amount of fertilizer will affect the soil in the long run.

6.1.1.4 Soil Erosion

Soil erosion is a gradually occurring process where environmental elements such as water or wind remove the soil particles. This causes the soil to deteriorate. Low water quality and soil deterioration due to erosion have become major problems all over the world. The soil erosion problem may be so severe to the degree that is not possible to use the agricultural lands and they have to be left abandoned. Natural resources mismanagement and land loss due to soil erosion have caused the decline of much agricultural civilization. Such history is a reminder for others to protect the natural resources. Even though a lot of research works are going on in this area, still the rate of soil erosion is increasing and it is becoming greater than ever before.

6.1.1.5 Instability

Indian farmers always depend on the monsoon rain for their agricultural practices. When there is good rain, we have good harvest, and insufficient rain increases the difficulty in achieving the good harvest. In recent years, the weather has fluctuated, which increases the difficulty in prediction of the weather. Moreover, the population is also always growing and it is necessary to make room for new population. This leads to deforestation and cutting of trees. Finally, deforestation will lead to low rainfall, which may in turn lead to drought seasons. This could be a disaster for the country, which relies on rain for agriculture.

6.1.1.6 Water Quality

The water used in irrigation for agriculture depends on water availability in the area. Moreover, the quality and type of water varies, depending on the presence of minerals and salts in the water. Though the irrigated water to the field is of smaller quantity, it is very important with respect to the healthy growth of the crop. The minerals present in the water originate from solvents of rocks and soil and also from dissolved soil minerals. Water quality is an important parameter to be considered for the growth of crops for enhancing productivity. Moreover, water with a high level of a single type of salt, such as sodium chloride, will not be good for agriculture. There is a difference between rain water, river water, and sea water. The good-quality water available to agriculture will enhance the yield and the farmers will not be at a disadvantage when they use such type of soft and fresh water for agriculture.

6.1.1.7 Pest Management

Pests are also associated with the increase or decrease in agricultural production along with other factors such as the presence of weeds, problems created by insects, and the damage provided by the diseases that affect the leaves and other parts of the plants. Most of the pesticides applied to the crops of agriculture are also for weed control. However, the use of pesticides will reduce risks from diseases. Farmers who are carrying out the agriculture must be aware of the correct and optimal use of pesticides because the increased use of pesticides may lead to problems in the products and yields.

6.1.1.8 Production Methods

The techniques used in Indian agriculture are mostly outdated. Most Indian farmers are not aware of the modern methods of farming used in many other countries. For example, even now the land is ploughed using cows. It takes more time and the depth of ploughing is reduced due to the manual pressing done by the farmers. The production methods are traditional and hence, all the farmers sow similar types of products at the same time. This leads to higher production of one type and lower production of other types of products. Vegetables, fruits, and flowers are produced in large quantity in some seasons and are in scarcity during some other seasons. A cyclic type of rotation is necessary to make use of the soil in a balanced way and it will also satisfy the requirements of consumers during all the seasons.

6.1.1.9 Cropping Pattern

The crops can basically be divided into two categories, food crops and non-food crops. There is no balanced practice which exists between the two categories of crops. The growth of food crops means that they occupy about three-fourths of the total land and the remaining land is used for non-food crop; the ratio was around 80:20 during 1980 and 77:23 in 1950. Thus, maintaining a balance between the two crops is difficult. The use of modern technology in agriculture includes the deployment of sensors in agriculture fields to collect data for analysis and decision-making.

6.1.2 Agriculture Supply Chain

Agriculture is one of the largest factors in the country's economy because it plays an important, challenging, and useful role in providing food to the entire population of the country. Moreover, the agricultural supply chain is responsible for connecting people, merchants, governments, industries, and farmers. If the agriculture base of a country is very strong, it can be considered as an important country. Many of the modern agricultural farms are making use of information and communication technologies and also the other technologies. The following are the most important issues to be considered for tackling the challenges of food supply chain management. Here, the major objective is the reduction of cost and maximization of profits for the farmers' vegetables and fruits, even though the farmers are not able to get much profit when compared to the traders. In recent years, organic farming is the choice of many people instead of chemical fertilizers and the use of insecticides in many plants and fruits. If pesticide residues are increasing in vegetables and fruits, it will lead to a serious health risk since the food items will be contaminated by heavy metals. Moreover, the irrigation of water from the water bodies to the crops can be polluted by the heavy metal elements such as lead, mercury, and zinc, which are also very dangerous to human life and health.

The agriculture supply chain consists of a set of related and sequential activities starting from the agricultural production up to the distribution of the produced items. Here, the farmers start the chain by buying the seeds from the market. They sow the seeds and irrigate them, followed by the addition of fertilizers and the removal of weeds. The crops start to yield if they are not affected by any disease. If the crops are affected by diseases, including leaf diseases, then the farmers will use pesticides or other remedies for curing them. Finally, the farmers will reap the products and they will bring those agricultural products to the market for selling, and eventually the market will sell the products to the consumers. In each of these events, a large amount of data has to be stored for performing statistical analysis in order to analyse the past and present data for predicting the future course of actions.

The existing distributed database systems are providing facilities for effective storage and retrieval of data. However, the analysis of such data is a cumbersome task and the security of data is to be taken care of by the users. On the other hand, the blockchain provides facilities for maintaining the supply chain data and facilitates in security and analysis in a better way. Hence, it is a better choice to use the blockchain for the effective storage, retrieval and secured maintenance of agricultural data. It also facilitates not only in the statistical analysis but also in performing cluster analysis, classification, sequential pattern identification, temporal analysis in terms of explanation, analysis of the past, and the prediction of the future.

6.1.3 Need for Survey on Blockchain-Based Agricultural Supply Chain Management

Most of the countries in the world are based on agriculture as the primary work. India is also an agricultural country where the main occupation for a major part of the population is agriculture. In such a scenario, the storage, retrieval and analysis of data are important tasks that are essential for agricultural supply chain management. Blockchain is an important technology that is used in supply chain management on agricultural products. Hence, many research works have been carried out by various researchers working in this area. Many research works are available on the use of blockchain technology for agricultural supply chain management, and this paper provides a survey of the important works that are found in the literature. This survey paper is organized by grouping the works on blockchain, blockchain security, bitcoins, agricultural data mining, agricultural supply chain management, and final recommendations based on comparative analysis. It also provides the comparison between distributed databases and the distributed ledger technology, also known as the blockchain technology, with respect to storage, retrieval, transaction management, consensus algorithms, and security. It also discusses the cryptographical algorithms used in blockchains for maintaining the agricultural data with supply chain management. Some of the systems use Internet of Things (IoT) based sensors for effective data collection [32].

In this paper, one new dynamic hashing algorithm called DHASH algorithm and a new commit protocol called Rule-based Two-Phase Commit (R2PC) protocol have been proposed for enhancing the security of data stored in the blockchain meant for storing the agricultural supply chain data.

6.2 Existing Works on Agricultural Supply Chain Management Using Blockchain

This survey is grouped into works on technology in agriculture, works on AI in agriculture, works on agricultural supply chain management, works on the application of blockchain in agricultural supply chain management, and finally the survey on blockchain security methods for agricultural database management.

6.2.1 Works on Technology in Agriculture

In the past, different researchers worked in the areas of agriculture by using information and computing technology including blockchain [14, 19, 20, 25, 28, 29]. In the field of agriculture, collection of data is highly expensive. In this scenario, the blockchain provides a platform for effectively storing the details about crops, fertilizers, insurances, inventories, and the contracts used. Smart contracting is a blockchain terminology that is used to eliminate the necessity for making a conventional contract with improved security and optimized transaction costs. Moreover, smart contracts are made using production rules having suitable conditions and actions which are applied on transactions. In this direction, Pandiyaraju *et al.* [4] explained about smart terrace gardening by the development of an intelligent roof control algorithm for providing better water conservation. In this model, sensors were used to collect the data related to the plants present in the garden and to send them to the base station of one wireless sensor network for further analysis. In another work by Pandiyaraju *et al.* [5], one new and optimal energy utilization model was proposed for supporting precision agriculture by using sensors belonging to Wireless Sensor Networks (WSNs). In their model, one multi-objective clustering algorithm was used for node clustering and a deep learning classification algorithm was used to study the node behaviour. This algorithm ensured optimal energy consumption by the use of node clustering. Muhammed *et al.* [8] explained an Artificial Intelligence of Things (AIoT) model for developing a new system that is useful for smart agriculture. The authors presented one review on the IoT architectures and technologies for providing efficient solutions. Torky *et al.* [21] explained the usefulness of the integration of blockchain and the IoT in precision agriculture. Finally, an energy-efficient routing algorithm was proposed by Pandiyaraju *et al.* [6] for effective data delivery in WSNs. In this model, intelligent fuzzy rules were used for making the most efficient decisions in cluster-based routing.

6.2.2 Works on Artificial Intelligence in Agriculture

In recent years, agriculture is again becoming the backbone of any country and is also an important gift given to the humans living all over the globe. However, the majority of the agricultural data present mainly suffers from a lack of standards used for the effective storage, retrieval and analysis of data. In this scenario, Artificial Intelligence (AI) and blockchain techniques have been developed by various researchers to handle the problems in the handling of agricultural data used in the supply chain management.

This is because there are no effective guidelines and proper protocols that can be followed in the storage, retrieval, and analysis of agricultural transaction data. Moreover, the overheads of storage and retrieval using normal distributed database transactions are higher, due to the frequent updates of data without maintaining a proper history. The use of rules from AI can help in agricultural data maintenance and analysis activities and the rules can be very useful for efficient decision-making using rule firing and inference methods. Hence, it is necessary to use rules from AI to handle the challenges present in the maintenance of data related to the supply chain of agricultural cycle data stored in blockchains.

There are many works on the use of AI in agriculture [2, 7, 38]. Sharma *et al.* [2] presented one literature review on the application of Artificial Intelligence (AI) and Machine Learning (ML) for making a better and optimal agriculture supply chain system. They explained that sustainability in agriculture will lead to better production of food products. The analysis on requirements of food products in terms of demand and supply can be matched well by better data analytics which needs the support of algorithms from Artificial Intelligence (AI) and its branches including ML algorithms. This will help to make proactive decisions on agricultural production, demand, and satisfaction of the requirements in affordable prices. Pandiyaraju *et al.* [7] proposed a new and improved method for detecting tomato leaf diseases using classification by the proposal of an adaptive ensemble classification model. This model was integrated with other methods, namely exponential moving average fusion, an enhanced weighted gradient optimization technique. Their model is useful for improving agricultural production through the early detection of tomato leaf diseases.

6.2.3 Works on Agricultural Supply Chain Management

Many works are already available in the literature on Agricultural Supply Chain Management [16–18]. Among these works, Khandelwal *et al.* [1] presented a review of the works in agriculture supply chain management. They also added that the current agricultural supply chain management methods require the integration of Information and Communication Technology (ICT) with the agriculture supply chain for effectively mitigating the challenges provided by the climate changes as well as the increasing global demands for agricultural products. Moreover, the recent computing technologies are playing a major role in enabling the agriculture supply chain using computing, Artificial Intelligence (AI) and blockchain systems. This survey is an important contribution to the advancement of agricultural development.

6.2.4 Works on Use of Blockchain in Agriculture Supply Chain Management

There are many works on the use of Blockchain in Agriculture Supply Chain Management [3, 11–13, 27]. Among them, Khan *et al.* [3] discussed in their paper the support provided by the blockchain technology for the effective maintenance of agricultural supply chains during the Covid-19 pandemic. They explained the uses of blockchain for providing better solutions for effective transaction management in databases for efficient data analysis. Zhu *et al.* [9] presented one method for effective agricultural data sharing that is useful for the sustainable development of the ecosystem, and it is developed based on blockchain. A few other works also discuss the use of blockchain in agricultural supply chains [22, 23, 35–37]. Ehsan *et al.* [30] developed one conceptual model which is useful for the development used in the maintenance of data related to the blockchain-based agricultural food supply chain system. Niknejad *et al.* [33] suggested a mapping model for mapping the agricultural supply chain.

6.2.5 Works on Blockchain Security Methods for Agricultural Data Maintenance

Security is an important aspect of blockchain-based systems. In this area, many researchers have contributed their work for the enhancement of security [24, 29]. Among them, Lei *et al.* [10] developed one new trusted-auditing chain for securing the blockchain data. Their model is an important contribution in the provision of security in blockchain prototype that is used in agriculture. Yadav *et al.* [15] developed one blockchain-based method for the selection of third-party logistics-based services for providing IoT-based agriculture supply chain management. Vangala *et al.* [26] developed one smart and secure sensing model for IoT-based agriculture by using the blockchain. The authors introduced the security in sensing that is useful for secured agricultural data collection. Hang *et al.* [31] proposed one secured fish farm platform–oriented blockchain model for the maintenance of agriculture data integrity. Patel *et al.* [34] developed one secured model for data harvesting in the agriculture sector using the blockchain technology.

In spite of the presence of all these systems and models in the literature, the security of information stored in the blockchain ledgers are still prone to various types of security attacks. Therefore, one new dynamic hash algorithm named DHASH algorithm and a new commit protocol called rule-based two-phase commit protocol have been proposed in this paper to enhance the security of blockchain data.

6.3 Proposed Work

In this paper, a dynamic hashing algorithm called DHASH algorithm and a new commit protocol called R2PC protocol have been proposed for enhancing security.

6.3.1 DHASH Algorithm

The DHASH is a dynamic hash algorithm that calls different hash functions based on the sensitiveness of the data.

The steps of the DHASH algorithm are as follows:

```
Input: Agricultural Data and sensitivity
Output: Hash Values
Algorithm DHASH
BEGIN
Step-1: Read Data and sensitivity details
Step-2: If Sensitivity == 1 (Lower) THEN
            Call MD5(Data)
          Else if Sensitivity == 2 (Low) THEN
            Call SHA-1(Data)
         Else if Sensitivity == 3 (Medium) THEN
            Call SHA-2 (Data)
        Else if Sensitivity == 3 (High) THEN
            Call SHA-3 (Data)
        Else if Sensitivity == 4 (Highest) THEN
            Call SHA-3 (SHA-2 (SHA-1(Data)))
        ENDIF
END
```

Here, the different combinations of hash algorithms are called based on the sensitivity levels of data.

6.3.2 Rule-Based Two-Phase Commit Protocol

The rule-based two-phase commit protocol is used to make commit or abort decisions in place of proof of work concept in blockchain. Here, the transaction will be stored only if more than half of the participants vote for storing the transactions. It also consists of phase one for making a decision on commit or abort based on rules, and phase two to implement the decisions.

6.4 Results and Discussions

Some of the major challenges faced by farmers in India include the availability of fragmented land holdings, lack of organized sector for marketing, efficient storage facilities, poor adoption of mechanization, credit availability, poor irrigation facilities, soil fertility depletion, inadequate access to crop insurance schemes, impact of climate change, price volatility, and poor training and extension facilities. However, rainfall and crop production datasets are provided by Kaggle for India. The agriculture crop production dataset contains the Indian crop production data for the period 1996 to 2014. It consists of the major attributes, namely, state name, crop, and the crop type. Recently, it provides the crop yield prediction and analysis data for the United States for 2023. Another important dataset available in Kaggle is the Precision Agriculture and IoT dataset.

This analysis provides the features presented in various systems. Table 6.1 shows the comparison of different cryptographic hash-based algorithms such as MD5, SHA-1, SHA-2 and SHA-3.

From Table 6.1, it is seen that the different hash algorithms provide different output sizes based on the input size. Therefore, the work proposed in this paper for the transaction maintenance of agricultural data using

Table 6.1 Cryptographic hash algorithms.

Sl. no.	Algorithm	Input size (Bits)	Output size (Bits)
1.	MD5	512	128
2.	SHA-1	512	160
3.	SHA-2	1024	256
4.	SHA-3	1152	512

blockchain provides different levels of security based on the selection of the hash algorithm.

Table 6.2 provides the comparison of the existing systems on blockchain technology for agriculture.

The parameters considered in this analysis are the technology used in the work such as sensor networks and IoT, use of block chain, agricultural supply chain modelling, provision of security, and the application of computational intelligence algorithms based on AI and ML. In this comparison, the most important works are given in the comparison table.

Based on these papers, we recommend that security-oriented systems such as the system proposed by Lei *et al.* [10] are necessary in blockchain-based agricultural supply chain management systems.

Table 6.2 Comparative analysis.

Sl. no.	Work considered	Technology used	Blockchain usage	Agricultural supply chain	Security	Use of AI
1.	Khandelwal *et al.* [1]	Review	Review	Review	Review	Review
2.	Sharma *et al.* [2]	Review	Review	Review	Review	Review
3.	Khan *et al.* [3]	Yes	Yes	Yes	No	No
4.	Pandiyaraju [4]	Yes	No	Yes	No	Yes
5.	Pandiyaraju *et al.* [5]	Yes	No	Yes	No	Yes
6.	Pandiyaraju *et al.* [6]	Yes	No	Yes	No	Yes
7.	Senthilkumar *et al.* [7]	Yes	No	Yes	No	Yes
8.	Muhammed *et al.* [8]	Yes	No	Yes	No	Yes
9.	Zhu *et al.* [9]	Yes	Yes	Yes	Yes	Yes
10.	Lei *et al.* [10]	Yes	Yes	Yes	Yes	Yes

The study of agricultural sensors has been made in this work with respect to the effect of using sensors in agriculture variation in cost of production, amount of profit, use of technology, and security of communication.

Figure 6.4 shows the security comparison between the static hash selection model and the dynamic hash selection model that provides different levels of security due to the use of different hash algorithms, namely MD5, SHA-1, SHA-2, SHA-3, and the proposed DHASH.

From Figure 6.4, it is proved that the security provided by the proposed DHASH algorithm is higher than the existing single hash algorithms namely, MD5, SHA-1, SHA-2, and SHA-3.

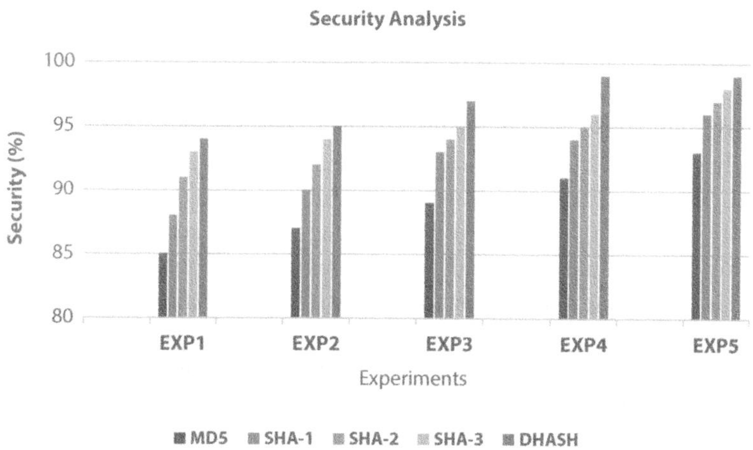

Figure 6.4 Comparison between static hash selection model and dynamic hash selection model.

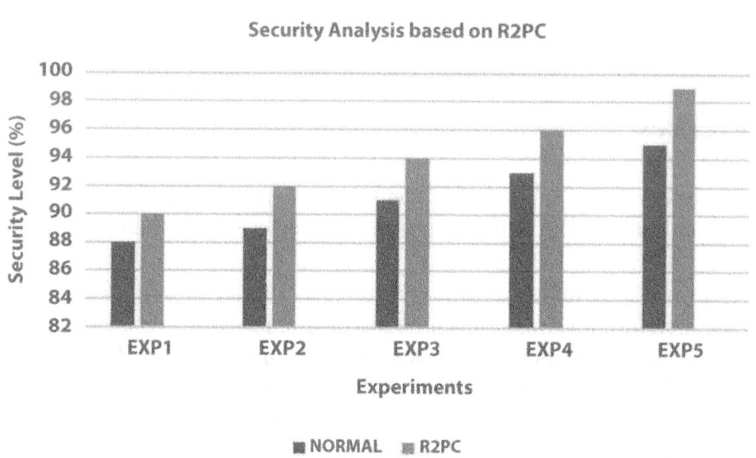

Figure 6.5 Security level of transaction with the proposed rule-based two-phase commit protocol.

Figure 6.5 shows the security level of transaction with the proposed rule-based two-phase commit protocol for agricultural data stored in blockchain.

From Figure 6.5, it is proved that the security level is increased by the use of the proposed Rule-based Two-Phase Commit Protocol for agricultural data-oriented transactions that are stored in blockchain. This improvement is due to the effective use of rules along with better commit decisions made using the proposed protocol.

6.5 Conclusions

This paper presents a review of works on blockchain in agriculture supply chain management. In addition, two new contributions, namely the proposal of a dynamic hash algorithm named DHASH and a new rule-based two-phase commit protocol for block chain transactions have been proposed. This paper considered parameters like technology usage, AI usage, security provision, blockchain role, and agriculture supply chain for performing the comparative analysis. The main contribution of this survey paper is to analyse the important works on blockchain-oriented agricultural supply chains. The parameters such as security are mainly used here since they are more necessary for the secured data storage and retrieval of agricultural supply chain data in blockchain. From the experiments carried out in this work, it is evidently proved that the proposed hashing technique-based models, namely the DHASH algorithm as well as R2PC protocol, support enhancement of security in blockchain transactions. Future extensions to this can be the provision of benchmark datasets for further and effective analysis of the systems considered.

References

1. Khandelwal, C., Singhal, M., Gaurav, G., Dangayach, G.S., Meena, M.L., Agriculture supply chain management: A review (2010–2020). *Mater. Today Proc.*, 47, 3144–3153, 2021.
2. Sharma, R., Kamble, S.S., Gunasekaran, A., Kumar, V., Kumar, A., A systematic literature review on machine learning applications for sustainable agriculture supply chain performance. *Comput. Oper. Res.*, 119, 104926, 2020.
3. Khan, H.H., Malik, M.N., Konečná, Z., Chofreh, A.G., Goni, F.A., Klemeš, J.J., Blockchain technology for agricultural supply chains during the COVID-19 pandemic: Benefits and cleaner solutions. *J. Clean. Prod.*, 347, 131268, 2022.

4. Pandiyaraju, V., Perumal, P.S., Kannan, A., Ramesh, L.S., Smart terrace gardening with intelligent roof control algorithm for water conservation. *Pak. J. Agric. Sci.*, 54, 2, 451–455, 2017.
5. Pandiyaraju, V., Ganapathy, S., Mohith, N., Kannan, A., An optimal energy utilization model for precision agriculture in WSNs using multi-objective clustering and deep learning. *J. King Saud Univ. Comput. Inf. Sci.*, 35, 10, 101803, 2023.
6. Pandiyaraju, V., Logambigai, R., Ganapathy, S., Kannan, A., An energy efficient routing algorithm for WSNs using intelligent fuzzy rules in precision agriculture. *Wirel. Pers. Commun.*, 112, 1, 243–259, 2020.
7. Pandiyaraju, V., Senthilkumar, A.M., Praveen Joe, I.R., Venkatraman, S., Pavan Kumar, S., Aravintakshan, A., Abeshek, A., Kannan, A., Improved tomato leaf disease classification through adaptive ensemble models with exponential moving average fusion and enhanced weighted gradient optimization. *Front. Plant Sci.*, 15, 1382416, 2024.
8. Muhammed, D., Ahvar, E., Ahvar, S., Trocan, M., Montpetit, M.J., Ehsani, R., Artificial Intelligence of Things (AIoT) for smart agriculture: A review of architectures, technologies and solutions. *J. Netw. Comput. Appl.*, 103905, 2024.
9. Zhu, L. and Li, F., Agricultural data sharing and sustainable development of ecosystem based on block chain. *J. Clean. Prod.*, 315, 127869, 2021.
10. Lei, M., Liu, S., Luo, N., Yang, X., Sun, C., Trusted-auditing chain: A security blockchain prototype used in agriculture traceability. *Heliyon*, 8, 11, 1–12, 2022.
11. Bhagat, D. and Dhar, U.R., Agriculture supply chain management: A review. *IUP J. Supply Chain Manag.*, 8, 3, 7, 2011.
12. Bhatia, M. and Bhat, G.M.J., Agriculture supply chain management-an operational perspective. *Braz. J. Oper. Prod. Manag.*, 17, 4, 1–18, 2020.
13. Routroy, S. and Behera, A., Agriculture supply chain: A systematic review of literature and implications for future research. *J. Agribus. Dev. Emerg. Econ.*, 7, 3, 275–302, 2017.
14. Luthra, S., Mangla, S.K., Garg, D., Kumar, A., Internet of things (IoT) in agriculture supply chain management: a developing country perspective, in: *Emerging Markets from a Multidisciplinary Perspective: Challenges, Opportunities and Research Agenda*, pp. 209–220, 2018.
15. Yadav, S., Garg, D., Luthra, S., Selection of third-party logistics services for internet of things-based agriculture supply chain management. *Int. J. Logist. Syst. Manag.*, 35, 2, 204–230, 2020.
16. Xiong, H., Dalhaus, T., Wang, P., Huang, J., Blockchain technology for agriculture: applications and rationale. *Front. Blockchain*, 3, 7, 2020.
17. Kamilaris, A., Fonts, A., Prenafeta-Boldú, F.X., The rise of blockchain technology in agriculture and food supply chains. *Trends Food Sci. Technol.*, 91, 640–652, 2019.

18. Dey, K. and Shekhawat, U., Blockchain for sustainable e-agriculture: Literature review, architecture for data management, and implications. *J. Clean. Prod.*, 316, 128254, 2021.
19. Demestichas, K., Peppes, N., Alexakis, T., Adamopoulou, E., Blockchain in agriculture traceability systems: A review. *Appl. Sci.*, 10, 12, 4113, 2020.
20. Sajja, G.S., Rane, K.P., Phasinam, K., Kassanuk, T., Okoronkwo, E., Prabhu, P., Towards applicability of blockchain in agriculture sector. *Mater. Today Proc.*, 80, 3705–3708, 2023.
21. Torky, M. and Hassanein, A.E., Integrating blockchain and the internet of things in precision agriculture: Analysis, opportunities, and challenges. *Comput. Electron. Agric.*, 178, 105476, 2020.
22. Lin, W., Huang, X., Fang, H., Wang, V., Hua, Y., Wang, J., Yin, H., Yi, D., Yau, L., Blockchain technology in current agricultural systems: from techniques to applications. *IEEE Access*, 8, 143920–143937, 2020.
23. Krithika, L.B., Survey on the applications of blockchain in agriculture. *Agriculture*, 12, 9, 1333, 2022.
24. Kamble, S.S., Gunasekaran, A., Sharma, R., Modelling the blockchain enabled traceability in agriculture supply chain. *Int. J. Inf. Manage.*, 52, 101967, 2020.
25. Liu, W., Shao, X.F., Wu, C.H., Qiao, P., A systematic literature review on applications of information and communication technologies and blockchain technologies for precision agriculture development. *J. Clean. Prod.*, 298, 126763, 2021.
26. Vangala, A., Das, A.K., Kumar, N., Alazab, M., Smart secure sensing for IoT-based agriculture: Blockchain perspective. *IEEE Sens. J.*, 21, 16, 17591–17607, 2020.
27. Sendros, A., Drosatos, G., Efraimidis, P.S., Tsirliganis, N.C., Blockchain applications in agriculture: A scoping review. *Appl. Sci.*, 12, 16, 8061, 2022.
28. Awan, S., Ahmed, S., Ullah, F., Nawaz, A., Khan, A., Uddin, M.I., Alharbi, A., Alosaimi, W., Alyami, H., IoT with blockchain: A futuristic approach in agriculture and food supply chain. *Wirel. Commun. Mob. Comput.*, 2021, 1, 5580179, 2021.
29. Ferrag, M.A., Shu, L., Yang, X., Derhab, A., Maglaras, L., Security and privacy for green IoT-based agriculture: Review, blockchain solutions, and challenges. *IEEE Access*, 8, 32031–32053, 2020.
30. Ehsan, I., Irfan Khalid, M., Ricci, L., Iqbal, J., Alabrah, A., Sajid Ullah, S., Alfakih, T.M., A conceptual model for blockchain-based agriculture food supply chain system. *Sci. Program.*, 2022, 1, 7358354, 2022.
31. Hang, L., Ullah, I., Kim, D.H., A secure fish farm platform based on blockchain for agriculture data integrity. *Comput. Electron. Agric.*, 170, 105251, 2020.
32. Borah, M.D., Naik, V.B., Patgiri, R., Bhargav, A., Phukan, B., Basani, S.G., Supply chain management in agriculture using blockchain and IoT, in: *Advanced Applications of Blockchain Technology*, pp. 227–242, 2020.

33. Niknejad, N., Ismail, W., Bahari, M., Hendradi, R., Salleh, A.Z., Mapping the research trends on blockchain technology in food and agriculture industry: A bibliometric analysis. *Environ. Technol. Innov.*, 21, 101272, 2021.
34. Patel, H. and Shrimali, B., AgriOnBlock: Secured data harvesting for agriculture sector using blockchain technology. *ICT Express*, 9, 2, 150–159, 2023.
35. Alobid, M., Abujudeh, S., Szűcs, I., The role of blockchain in revolutionizing the agricultural sector. *Sustainability*, 14, 7, 4313, 2022.
36. Salah, K., Nizamuddin, N., Jayaraman, R., Omar, M., Blockchain-based soybean traceability in agricultural supply chain. *IEEE Access*, 7, 73295–73305, 2019.
37. Ronaghi, M.H., A blockchain maturity model in agricultural supply chain. *Inf. Process. Agric.*, 8, 3, 398–408, 2021.
38. Jothikumar, R., Applying blockchain in agriculture: A study on blockchain technology, benefits, and challenges, in: *Deep Learning and Edge Computing Solutions for High Performance Computing*, pp. 167–181, Springer, Cham, 2021.

7

Revolutionizing Agricultural Supply Chains with Blockchain for Enhancing Transparency, Efficiency, and Traceability

Arun Kumar Sivaraman[1], Rajiv Vincent[2*], Janakiraman Nithiyanantham[3], Thirumurugan Shanmugam[4], Kong Fah Tee[5] and Ajmery Sultana[6]

[1]*Digital Engineering Solution Centre, Photon Interactive Inc., Ontario, Canada*
[2]*School of Computer Science and Engineering, Vellore Institute of Technology, Chennai, India*
[3]*Department of Electronics and Communication Engineering, K.L.N. College of Engineering, Pottapalayam, India*
[4]*College of Computing and Information Sciences, University of Technology and Applied Sciences, Suhar, Oman*
[5]*Department of Civil and Environmental Engineering, King Fahd University of Petroleum and Minerals, Dhahran, Saudi Arabia*
[6]*School of Computer Science and Technology, Algoma University, Brampton Campus, Ontario, Canada*

Abstract

The agriculture supply chain is a complex network of activities involving numerous stakeholders, from farm to fork. This chapter explores the capacity of blockchain technology to enhance the efficiency and security of agricultural supply chains. Blockchain, with its distributed and unchangeable record system, provides a strong resolution to various issues encountered in conventional agricultural supply chains, including inefficiency, lack of transparency, fraud, and exorbitant expenses.

**Corresponding author*: rajiv.vincent@vit.ac.in; ORCID: 0000 0002 4012 6383
Arun Kumar Sivaraman: ORCID: 0000 0003 0514 484X
Janakiraman Nithiyanantham: ORCID: 0000 0001 6616 5340
Thirumurugan Shanmugam: ORCID: 0000 0002 0433 891X
Kong Fah Tee: ORCID: 0000 0003 3202 873X
Ajmery Sultana: ORCID: 0000 0002 8591 026X

Narayanan Ganesh and Kanak Kalita (eds.) Harvesting Data: Blockchain, AI and Advanced Innovations in Agriculture, (131–154) © 2026 Scrivener Publishing LLC

The chapter begins with an overview of the current state of agricultural supply chains, highlighting key issues and inefficiencies. It then introduces blockchain technology, explaining its fundamental principles, including decentralization, immutability, and consensus mechanisms. The core of the chapter focuses on the integration of blockchain technology within agricultural supply chains, detailing how it can enhance traceability, improve transparency, and foster trust among stakeholders. We present case studies of successful blockchain implementations in agriculture, showcasing their real-world applications and benefits. These case studies cover various aspects of the supply chain, including provenance tracking, quality assurance, and payment systems. The chapter also explores how blockchain can facilitate better resource management and sustainability practices by providing accurate and real-time data. The article also addresses the obstacles and constraints associated with implementing blockchain technology in agricultural supply chains, including technological hurdles, scalability challenges, and regulatory considerations. The chapter concludes with future directions and potential advancements in blockchain technology that could further revolutionize the agriculture sector. After reading this chapter, readers will understand how blockchain technology can streamline, make transparent, and secure agricultural supply chains, leading to increased productivity and sustainability in the agriculture industry.

***Keywords*:** Blockchain technology, agriculture supply chain, traceability, decentralization, provenance tracking, quality assurance, sustainability

7.1 Introduction

The agricultural sector is a cornerstone of the global economy, providing the essential resources necessary to sustain human life. Over the centuries, agricultural practices and supply chains have undergone significant transformations, adapting to the changing needs and technologies of their times. Yet, the 21st century presents new and complex challenges that necessitate innovative solutions to improve transparency, efficiency, and traceability within agricultural supply chains. One such promising solution is blockchain technology. Originally linked to cryptocurrencies like Bitcoin, blockchain technology has expanded significantly beyond its initial application, showcasing its potential in diverse sectors, including agriculture. Blockchain is essentially a distributed ledger that securely records transactions on various computers. Once recorded, a transaction remains unchangeable without modifying all subsequent blocks and gaining network agreement. This fundamental characteristic of immutability, combined with transparency and decentralized control, makes blockchain an ideal candidate for transforming agricultural supply chains [1–3].

Agricultural supply chains are inherently complex, involving a multitude of stakeholders ranging from farmers and processors to distributors and retailers. Each stage in the supply chain presents its own set of challenges, including fraud, inefficiency, and a lack of transparency. Traditional supply chain management systems often fall short of addressing these issues due to their centralized nature and vulnerability to errors and tampering. In contrast, blockchain offers a decentralized approach that can significantly enhance the reliability and transparency of data across the entire supply chain [2, 4]. Transparency is an essential element of contemporary supply chains. Modern customers exhibit a heightened awareness regarding the sources of their food and insist on knowing if it has been produced in a sustainable and ethical manner. Blockchain technology may create an unchangeable and permanent record of a product's whole journey, starting from its origin on the farm and ending up on the consumer's table. This allows consumers to have access to trustworthy and confirmable information about the product's suppliers and the methods used in its creation. Enhancing transparency at this level can facilitate the establishment of confidence between customers and producers, thereby promoting an ethical and sustainable agriculture sector. Blockchain has the potential to significantly improve efficiency in various domains [5, 6].

Excessive paperwork, manual procedures, and intermediaries can sometimes hinder conventional supply chains, leading to delays and higher expenses. Blockchain technology has the capability to simplify these processes by offering a solitary, integrated platform where all parties involved may access and modify information instantly. Smart contracts are self-executing contracts directly encoded into code. They can automate transactions and decrease the reliance on intermediaries, resulting in improved efficiency [7]. Traceability is essential for ensuring food safety and quality. Tracing a product's history through the supply chain enables the identification and resolution of concerns such as contamination or fraud. In the event of a foodborne illness outbreak, blockchain can enable rapid identification of the affected batches, allowing for swift recalls and minimizing the risk to public health [8]. Moreover, traceability can aid in complying with regulatory requirements and standards, ensuring that products meet the necessary quality and safety benchmarks [9].

Implementing blockchain technology in agricultural supply chains presents various obstacles. In order for blockchain to fully achieve its promise in this field, it is crucial to tackle challenges such as scalability, interoperability, and the requirement for stakeholder buy-in [10]. Furthermore, the integration of blockchain with existing technologies and practices requires careful planning and execution. Despite these challenges, the potential benefits of blockchain in enhancing transparency, efficiency, and traceability in agricultural supply chains are too significant to ignore [11].

This chapter will examine the potential of blockchain technology to revolutionize agricultural supply networks (Figure 7.1). It will offer a comprehensive examination of its uses, advantages, and associated difficulties. We will analyze real-life case studies to demonstrate the tangible consequences of implementing blockchain technology in the agricultural sector, as well as deliberate on future patterns and advancements. By understanding the role of blockchain in agricultural supply chains, stakeholders can more effectively anticipate a future in which transparency, efficiency, and traceability are of utmost importance. This exploration will offer valuable insights for policymakers, industry leaders, and researchers seeking to leverage blockchain technology to create a more robust and resilient agricultural sector.

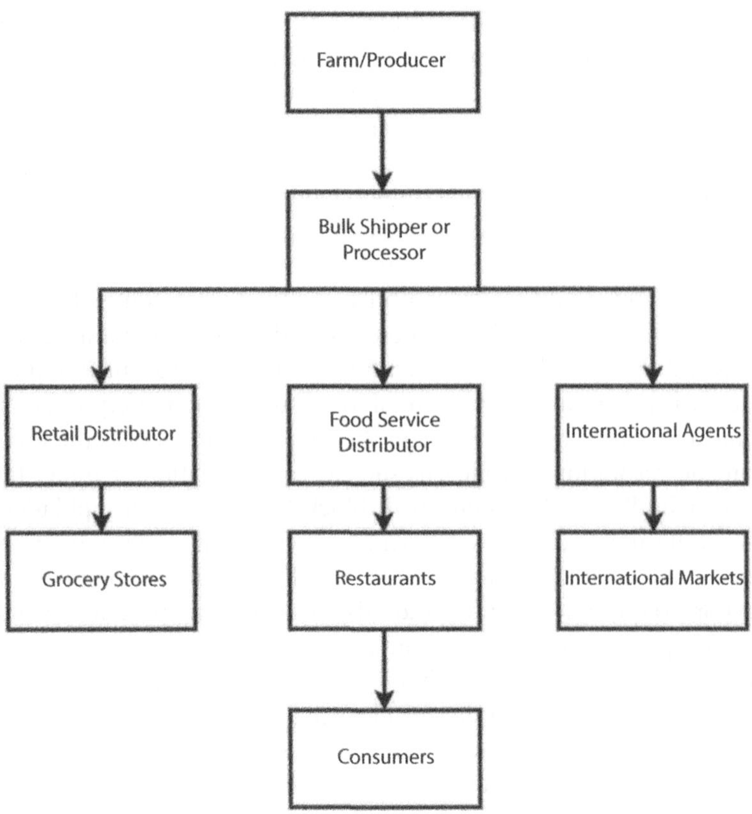

Figure 7.1 Food supply chain.

The promise of blockchain technology to transform agricultural supply systems goes beyond simple digitization. Blockchain introduces a new paradigm by fundamentally rethinking the management of transactions and data, integrating trust and accountability into the very fabric of supply chain operations. The decentralized nature of blockchain guarantees that no single entity possesses monopolistic authority over the data, therefore promoting equal access and cultivating a more comprehensive ecosystem. Blockchain can level the playing field for smallholder farmers, who often face marginalization in traditional supply chains, by giving them direct access to market information and equitable compensation mechanisms. Moreover, blockchain's ability to provide a single source of truth is particularly valuable in agriculture, where disputes over contracts, quality, and payments are common.

Blockchain technology documents every transaction in a visible and unchangeable ledger, thereby facilitating conflict resolution and agreement enforcement. This increased level of trust can reduce transaction costs and foster stronger relationships among supply chain participants. Another transformative aspect of blockchain is its potential to enhance sustainability within agricultural supply chains. By providing detailed information about the environmental impact of farming practices, blockchain can help producers and consumers make more sustainable choices. For instance, blockchain can track the carbon footprint of agricultural products, enabling consumers to choose products with a lower environmental impact and encouraging producers to adopt greener practices. Furthermore, blockchain technology can streamline the process of confirming certifications, such as organic or fair trade, thereby guaranteeing that these labels accurately represent sustainable practices. Combining blockchain with other technologies, such as the Internet of Things (IoT) and artificial intelligence (AI), can enhance its influence on agricultural supply chains.

Internet of Things (IoT) devices have the capability to gather up-to-the-minute data on several elements of agriculture, including soil moisture levels, crop health status, and prevailing meteorological conditions. We can store this data on the blockchain, creating an auditable and unchangeable record for predictive analysis and decision-making. AI algorithms can analyze this data to optimize farming practices, improve yield predictions, and reduce waste. The combination of blockchain, IoT, and AI can thus create a highly intelligent and responsive agricultural supply chain that is capable of adapting to changing conditions and demands. However, the path to widespread adoption of blockchain in agriculture is fraught with challenges. Scalability remains a significant hurdle, as the technology must handle a high volume of transactions efficiently. Ensuring seamless integration requires addressing the critical issue of interoperability with current systems and standards. Moreover, the initial cost of implementing blockchain solutions and the need for technical expertise can be barriers for small-scale farmers and enterprises. To overcome these challenges, collaborative efforts from governments, industry stakeholders, and technology providers are essential to creating an enabling environment for blockchain adoption.

7.2 Understanding Blockchain Technology

To understand how blockchain can revolutionize agricultural supply chains, one must first understand the fundamental principles of this technology. Blockchain is a form of distributed ledger technology (DLT) that documents transactions over a network of computers. A blockchain, in contrast to conventional centralized databases, operates in a decentralized manner, ensuring that no singular entity has complete control over the entire network. However, the network grants access to the entire ledger to all participants, who must agree to authenticate and document new transactions. A blockchain is a collection of blocks, with each block carrying a series of transactions. A cryptographic hash connects these blocks sequentially, allowing each block to reference its predecessor. This structure ensures the immutability of the blockchain, as altering the information in one block would require changes to all subsequent blocks, which is practically impossible without the network participants' consent.

In the context of cryptocurrencies, the process of adding new transactions to the blockchain is known as mining or validation. Participants, also known as nodes in the network, use consensus methods to reach a consensus on the legitimacy of transactions. Common consensus procedures encompass Proof of Work (PoW), Proof of Stake (PoS), and Practical Byzantine Fault Tolerance (PBFT), among other options. Each of these mechanisms possesses distinct advantages and compromises in relation to security, efficiency, and energy usage. Smart contracts are a pivotal feature of blockchain technology. These contracts are autonomous and have the agreement's terms directly encoded into the software. The contract automatically enforces the agreed acts upon fulfillment of its terms.

Smart contracts obviate the necessity for intermediaries, mitigate the danger of human fallibility, and guarantee the accurate execution of transactions as per the agreed terms. Blockchain's decentralized nature (Figure 7.2), combined with its transparency, immutability, and the ability to

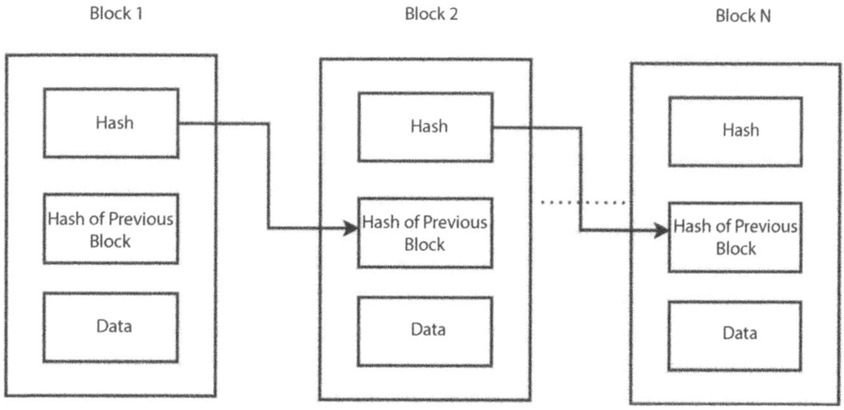

Figure 7.2 Basic blocks of blockchain.

automate processes through smart contracts, makes it a powerful tool for addressing the challenges in agricultural supply chains. These attributes have the potential to greatly enhance the precision, effectiveness, and reliability of the data and transactions inside the supply chain.

To fully grasp the revolutionary potential of blockchain in agricultural supply chains, it is essential to delve deeper into the specific characteristics and components that make this technology uniquely suited to address the challenges of modern agriculture. Beyond the basic structure of blocks and chains, blockchain's core features of decentralization, immutability, and consensus mechanisms work in tandem to create a robust framework for enhancing supply chain operations. The decentralized nature of blockchain is one of its most significant advantages. Traditional supply chain management systems often silo and control data through a single entity or a few centralized parties. This centralization can lead to inefficiencies, vulnerabilities to fraud, and a lack of transparency.

The blockchain distributes data over a network of nodes, with each node maintaining a complete copy of the entire ledger. This distribution guarantees the absence of any individual component that could cause a failure and assures that all participants have equitable access to the information. This implies that within the realm of agriculture, individuals involved in farming, distributing, selling, and purchasing can all obtain the same, verifiable information regarding the trajectory of a product throughout the supply chain. This facilitates enhanced trust and cooperation. Immutability is another critical feature of blockchain that enhances its suitability for agricultural supply chains. Once documented on the blockchain, a transaction becomes immutable, requiring the network's agreement to modify or erase it. The immutability of the data guarantees its integrity, establishing it as a dependable source of truth.

This implies that in the context of agricultural supply chains, we can securely preserve the documentation of activities like planting, harvesting, processing, and distribution, eliminating the possibility of unauthorized alteration or deception. Prioritizing this is critical for adhering to food safety regulations and standards, as well as preserving the integrity of certifications such as organic or fair trade. The blockchain validates and records transactions through consensus mechanisms. These procedures guarantee that all participants in the network reach a consensus on the legitimacy of transactions prior to their inclusion in the ledger. Proof of Work (PoW) necessitates network participants, known as miners, to solve intricate mathematical problems in order to authenticate transactions. This process guarantees security but can consume a significant amount of energy. Proof of Stake (PoS) necessitates participants owning a specific quantity of the blockchain's inherent digital currency to authenticate transactions, resulting in a more efficient utilization of resources.

Practical Byzantine Fault Tolerance (PBFT) involves multiple nodes working together to achieve consensus, providing a balance between security and efficiency. Each of these consensus processes has consequences for the scalability, security, and energy consumption of the blockchain. The methodology chosen may impact the performance of the agricultural supply chain (Table 7.1).

Smart contracts, as previously said, are a crucial aspect of blockchain technology because they have the ability to automate operations and decrease the need for middlemen. Smart contracts can automate payments, verify the quality and quantity of items, and assure compliance with regulatory norms in agricultural supply chains. For instance, we can code a smart contract to distribute payment to a farmer upon the delivery and verification of a crop shipment, thereby reducing delays and administrative costs. You can also use smart contracts to enforce agreements between buyers and sellers, ensuring that transactions follow the agreed terms without the need for a third party's involvement.

Integrating blockchain technology with Internet of Things (IoT) devices amplifies its capacity to improve agricultural supply chains. The Internet of Things (IoT) devices have the capability to gather up-to-the-minute data on several aspects of farming and supply chain operations, including soil moisture, temperature, humidity, and location. Blockchain storage of the data ensures a reliable and unchangeable record for surveillance and decision-making. For instance, we can install Internet of Things (IoT) sensors in

Table 7.1 Blockchain technology in agricultural supply chain.

Stage	Traditional issues	Blockchain solutions
Production	• Lack of transparency in seed quality • Inefficient resource management	• Immutable records of seed provenance • Smart contracts for resource allocation
Harvesting	• Difficulty in tracking crop conditions • Data manipulation risks	• Real-time monitoring with IoT devices linked to blockchain • Secure and verifiable data records
Processing	• Lack of visibility into processing stages • Quality control issues	• Transparent and traceable processing records • Automated quality checks *via* smart contracts
Distribution	• Risk of contamination and spoilage • Inefficient logistics	• Temperature and condition monitoring with blockchain-based alerts • Optimized logistics through blockchain-based tracking
Retail	• Lack of product authenticity • Difficulty in ensuring fair trade	• Verified product origins and authenticity • Transparent and fair-trade practices recorded on blockchain
Consumption	• Limited information on product history • Concerns over food safety	• Accessible product history and safety information for consumers • Enhanced trust through traceable

shipping containers to monitor the temperature and humidity levels during the transportation of goods. This ensures the storage and transportation of perishable items under optimal conditions. This real-time data can help prevent spoilage, reduce waste, and ensure the quality and safety of agricultural products.

Blockchain can also integrate artificial intelligence (AI) and machine learning to improve decision-making and optimize supply chain operations.

Artificial intelligence algorithms have the capability to examine the extensive quantities of data stored on the blockchain in order to detect patterns, forecast trends, and offer valuable insights for enhancing efficiency and production. For example, AI can analyze weather data, soil conditions, and crop performance to optimize planting schedules and irrigation practices, improving crop yields and reducing resource consumption. By combining blockchain with AI and IoT, agricultural supply chains can become more intelligent, responsive, and sustainable.

Large-scale commercial farming operations are not the only ones that can benefit from blockchain's potential to revolutionize agricultural supply chains. Blockchain technology can also benefit smallholder farmers, who often face challenges such as limited access to markets, credit, and information. Smallholder farmers can enhance their market opportunities and get more favorable prices for their products by offering a transparent and verifiable account of their farming methods and product quality. Additionally, blockchain can facilitate access to credit and financial services by providing lenders with reliable data on farmers' production and sales, reducing the risk and cost of lending.

To summarize, blockchain technology provides an effective option for tackling the difficulties faced by contemporary agricultural supply networks. The fundamental characteristics of decentralization, immutability, consensus processes, and smart contracts create a strong foundation for improving transparency, efficiency, and traceability. By integrating blockchain with IoT, AI, and other emerging technologies, agricultural supply chains can become more intelligent, responsive, and sustainable. While challenges such as scalability, interoperability, and stakeholder buy-in remain, the potential benefits of blockchain for agricultural supply chains are significant and warrant further exploration and investment. By consistently introducing new ideas and working together, blockchain technology has the potential to enhance transparency, productivity, and durability in the agriculture industry, ultimately benefiting all parties involved, including farmers and consumers.

7.3 Enhancing Transparency in Agricultural Supply Chains

Transparency in agricultural supply chains is crucial for building trust between producers and consumers, ensuring food safety, and promoting sustainable and ethical practices. Traditional supply chain systems often suffer from a lack of transparency due to the involvement of multiple intermediaries and the use of disparate record-keeping systems. Blockchain technology can resolve these concerns by offering a unified and unalterable ledger that documents all transactions and movements of items across the entire supply chain. By documenting every stage of a product's progression from the farm to the table using a blockchain, all parties involved, including customers, may obtain authenticated details regarding the product's source, manufacturing techniques, and handling. By consistently introducing new ideas and working together, blockchain technology has the potential to enhance transparency, effectiveness, and durability in the agriculture industry, ultimately benefiting all parties involved, including farmers and consumers. This level of transparency can combat issues like food fraud, which involves misrepresenting or adulterating products, and ensure that consumers receive accurate information about the products they purchase. For instance, a supply chain system utilizing blockchain technology can provide comprehensive data on the specific conditions of crop cultivation, harvesting, and transformation.

Consumers have the ability to scan a QR code on a product in order to retrieve this information, which allows them to acquire knowledge about the farming methods employed, certifications acquired, and the environmental consequences of production. This transparency can empower consumers to make more informed choices and encourage producers to adopt sustainable and ethical practices (Figure 7.3). Moreover, transparency can also enhance regulatory compliance. Agricultural products are subject to various safety and quality standards, and blockchain can provide a reliable record of compliance with these regulations. Regulatory authorities can access the blockchain to verify that products meet the necessary standards, facilitating more efficient and effective oversight.

Blockchain technology's transparency not only benefits consumers and regulators, but it also significantly impacts the entire agricultural ecosystem, including producers, processors, and distributors. Blockchain ensures the immutable recording of every transaction and movement of goods, fostering an environment where verified and accessible data builds trust. Producers, for instance, can gain recognition for their adherence to best practices and quality standards, which can translate into premium pricing and better market opportunities. This is particularly important for smallholder farmers and producers in developing countries, who often face challenges in accessing lucrative markets due to a lack of verifiable credentials. For processors and distributors, blockchain transparency facilitates better decision-making and operational efficiency.

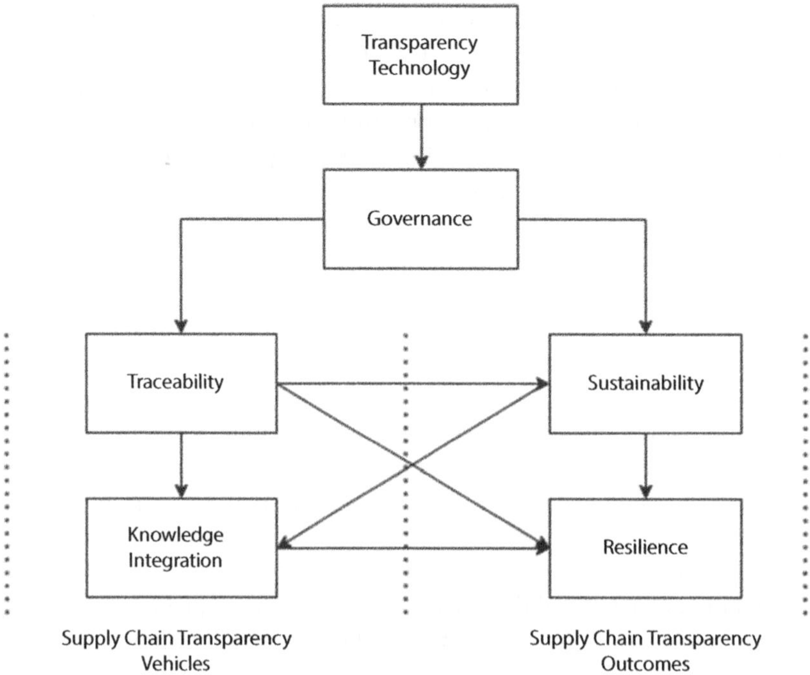

Figure 7.3 Transparency in supply chain.

Access to detailed and accurate data about the supply chain allows these stakeholders to identify bottlenecks, optimize logistics, and ensure that products maintain their quality and integrity from farm to table. For instance, processors can more effectively schedule processing times to ensure freshness and reduce spoilage by knowing the exact harvest date and location of a batch of produce. Distributors may optimize their routes and timetables using up-to-date data, resulting in decreased transportation expenses and a reduced ecological footprint. Blockchain enhances transparency by increasing the precision and dependability of supply chain data.

Traditional record-keeping systems, often fragmented and manual, are prone to errors and tampering. Blockchain, with its decentralized and immutable nature, eliminates these vulnerabilities. Every piece of information recorded on the blockchain is assigned a timestamp and protected using cryptographic measures, which greatly reduces the likelihood of tampering or the removal of data without being detected. This ensures that all information on the blockchain is accurate and trustworthy, providing a solid foundation for transparency.

Another significant advantage of blockchain transparency is its role in enhancing traceability, particularly in addressing food safety issues. In the event of contamination or a foodborne illness outbreak, the ability to quickly trace the affected products through the supply chain is crucial. Blockchain enables rapid and precise identification of the source of contamination, allowing for targeted recalls that minimize waste and protect public health. This swift action not only prevents further spread of contamination, but it also helps to maintain consumer confidence in the food supply's safety. Moreover, blockchain's transparency can drive more sustainable and ethical agricultural practices. Consumers' increasing demand for sustainably and ethically produced goods incentivizes producers to adopt practices that align with these values. Blockchain can record and verify the use of sustainable farming techniques, fair labor practices, and environmentally friendly methods. Consumers can then receive this verified data and make purchasing decisions that align with their values. As a result, producers who invest in sustainable and ethical practices can gain a competitive advantage in the market.

The implementation of blockchain technology also supports regulatory compliance in agriculture. Agricultural products must meet various safety and quality standards to ensure their safety for consumption. Blockchain provides a reliable and easily accessible record of compliance, simplifying the verification process for regulatory authorities. This can simplify regulatory audits and inspections, alleviating the administrative strain on producers and guaranteeing the prompt identification and resolution of non-compliance issues. Furthermore, the adoption of blockchain for transparency in agricultural supply chains can foster innovation and collaboration. By providing a shared and trusted platform for data, blockchain enables different stakeholders to collaborate more effectively. Blockchain integration can enhance the effectiveness of innovations like precision farming, predictive analytics, and personalized nutrition. For instance, the blockchain can record and analyze data from IoT sensors in fields to enhance crop yields and resource efficiency.

7.4 Improving Efficiency in Agricultural Supply Chains

Efficiency in agricultural supply chains is critical for reducing costs, minimizing waste, and ensuring timely delivery of products. Conventional supply chain systems frequently rely on manual procedures, extensive documentation, and multiple intermediaries, resulting in delays and increased expenses.

Blockchain technology has the ability to simplify these processes by offering a consolidated platform that allows all parties involved to access and modify information instantly. Automating transactions through the use of smart contracts is an essential method by which blockchain could improve efficiency.

Smart contracts have the capability to automate multiple procedures in the supply chain, including payments, delivery confirmations, and quality checks. For instance, a smart contract has the capability to immediately disburse payment to a supplier upon verification of product delivery, thereby diminishing the duration and administrative burden associated with payment processing. This automation not only expedites transactions but also mitigates the likelihood of human error and fraud. Furthermore, blockchain has the potential to improve inventory management by making it more efficient. Blockchain technology offers stakeholders the ability to monitor the movement of items in real time within the supply chain. This enables them to efficiently manage inventory levels, minimizing the chances of having excessive or insufficient stock. Having real-time visibility can facilitate more precise demand forecasts and improved coordination among suppliers, manufacturers, and retailers. Blockchain can also reduce the reliance on intermediaries in the supply chain. Traditional supply chains often involve multiple intermediaries who facilitate transactions and ensure the integrity of information. However, these intermediaries add complexity and cost to the supply chain. The decentralized and transparent nature of blockchain technology can eliminate the requirement for numerous intermediaries, thereby cutting expenses and streamlining the supply chain.

Efficiency is the lifeblood of agricultural supply chains, driving down costs, minimizing waste, and ensuring the timely delivery of products to consumers. Yet, traditional supply chain systems often operate with inefficiencies stemming from manual processes, extensive paperwork, and the involvement of multiple intermediaries. These inefficiencies not only lead to delays but also increase costs, eroding profitability for all stakeholders involved. Nevertheless, blockchain technology offers a revolutionary remedy to these difficulties by simplifying procedures and implementing automation and transparency in agricultural supply chains. Blockchain significantly improves efficiency by automating transactions using smart contracts.

Smart contracts automatically execute pre-defined terms specified in code. These contracts streamline several operations across the supply chain, including payments, delivery confirmations, and quality inspections. For instance, we can code a smart contract to automatically disburse payment to a provider upon the recipient's confirmation of goods delivery. This automation not only expedites transactions, but also reduces the administrative burden and the likelihood of human error and fraud. Moreover, blockchain facilitates more efficient inventory management by providing real-time visibility into the movement of goods throughout the supply chain. Conventional inventory management systems frequently face challenges in delivering precise and current information due to the human input of data and the isolation of information.

The decentralized ledger of blockchain guarantees that all parties involved have equal access to up-to-date information, allowing them to optimize inventory levels and minimize the chances of having excess or insufficient stock. The ability to see information in real time also facilitates a more precise prediction of consumer demand, enabling suppliers, manufacturers, and retailers to more effectively coordinate their production and distribution operations.

Furthermore, blockchain reduces the reliance on intermediaries in the supply chain, thereby simplifying processes and reducing costs. Traditional supply chains typically involve multiple intermediaries, such as brokers, agents, and third-party verifiers, who facilitate transactions and ensure the integrity of information. However, these intermediaries add complexity and costs to the supply chain, often resulting in delays and inefficiencies. Blockchain's decentralized and transparent nature allows for the elimination of many intermediaries, resulting in streamlined processes and cost savings for all stakeholders. In addition to streamlining existing processes, blockchain opens up new opportunities for efficiency gains through innovative applications. For example, blockchain can enable peer-to-peer trading platforms where farmers can directly sell their produce to consumers, bypassing traditional distribution channels and reducing transaction costs. Similarly, blockchain-based certification systems can automate the verification of product certifications, reducing the time and resources required for compliance with regulatory standards.

7.5 Enhancing Traceability in Agricultural Supply Chains

Traceability is essential for ensuring food safety, quality, and regulatory compliance in agricultural supply chains. The ability to trace a product's history from farm to table can help identify and address issues such as contamination, fraud, and non-compliance with standards.

Blockchain technology has the potential to greatly improve traceability by creating an unchangeable and easily understood record of all transactions and movements of items across the supply chain. In the event of a foodborne illness outbreak, for example, blockchain can enable rapid identification of the affected batches, allowing for swift recalls and minimizing the risk to public health. By providing a verifiable record of a product's history, blockchain can help trace the source of contamination and prevent future incidents.

This enhanced traceability can also aid in complying with regulatory requirements and standards, ensuring that products meet the necessary quality and safety benchmarks (Figure 7.4). Furthermore, blockchain can furnish comprehensive details about the production, processing, and transportation conditions of products. Internet of Things (IoT) devices that track temperature, humidity, and other environmental factors during goods transportation and storage can store data on blockchain. We can use this data to ensure proper management of products, ensuring their quality and safety throughout the supply chain. Traceability can also help address problems such as food fraud and counterfeit goods production. Blockchain can guarantee the authenticity and quality of products by creating a traceable record of their travel in the supply chain. This can enhance consumer trust and protect the reputation of producers and brands.

Traceability is a cornerstone of food safety, quality assurance, and regulatory compliance in agricultural supply chains. In an era where consumers demand transparency and accountability, the ability to trace a product's

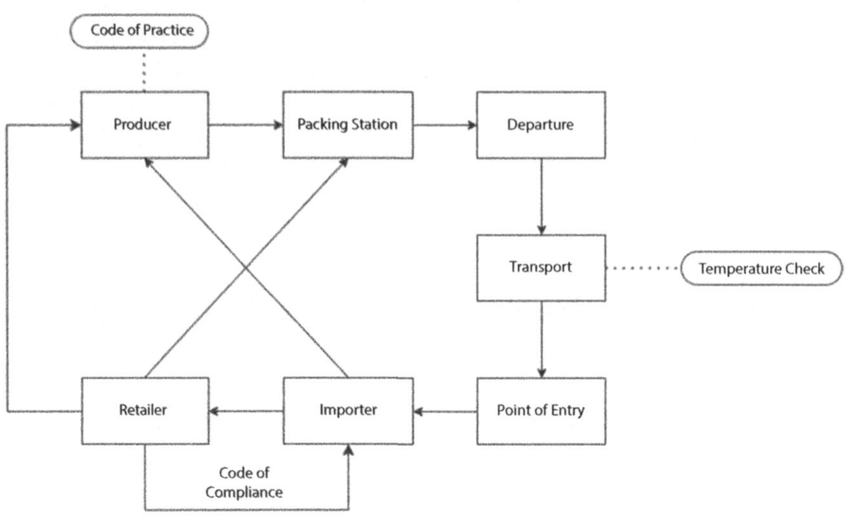

Figure 7.4 Quality assurance in supply chain.

journey from farm to table has never been more critical. Traditional supply chain systems often struggle to provide comprehensive traceability due to fragmented record-keeping and the involvement of multiple intermediaries. Nevertheless, blockchain technology presents a revolutionary remedy by offering an unchangeable and easily understood account of each transaction and movement of commodities across the supply chain. In the event of a foodborne illness outbreak, rapid identification of the source of contamination is paramount to protecting public health.

Blockchain facilitates rapid traceability by documenting every stage of a product's progression on a distributed ledger. In the event of a recall, stakeholders can trace the affected batches back to their source within minutes, significantly reducing the time and resources required for investigation and containment. This real-time traceability not only minimizes the risk to public health but also safeguards the reputation of producers and brands by demonstrating a proactive approach to food safety. Moreover, the ability of blockchain to provide detailed information about the conditions of product manufacturing, processing, and transportation enhances the reliability of the supply chain. Blockchain technology guarantees the proper handling and preservation of items across the supply chain by collecting data from Internet of Things (IoT) devices that monitor factors such as temperature, humidity, and other environmental conditions. We can continuously monitor perishable items, such as fresh produce and seafood, to ensure their storage and transportation under ideal conditions, thereby preventing rotting and contamination.

Furthermore, blockchain technology's traceability helps combat issues like food fraud and counterfeit products. Blockchain guarantees the authenticity and quality of products by creating a traceable record of their path in the supply chain. Consumers have the ability to scan a QR code on a product in order to obtain information regarding its source, manufacturing techniques, and certifications. This level of transparency not only fosters consumer confidence but also motivates producers to uphold rigorous standards of quality and integrity at every stage of the supply chain. In addition to improving food safety and quality assurance, blockchain-enabled traceability aids in regulatory compliance by ensuring that products meet the necessary standards and benchmarks. Regulatory authorities can access the blockchain to verify compliance with food safety regulations, organic certifications, and fair-trade practices. The presence of transparency and accountability in the sector cultivates a culture of adherence to regulations, hence diminishing the likelihood of non-compliance and the resulting fines.

7.6 Real-World Applications of Blockchain in Agricultural Supply Chains

Examining real-world case studies and instances of blockchain's application is helpful in illustrating the practical consequences of its use in agricultural supply chains. Various innovative projects and efforts are currently showcasing the capacity of blockchain technology to improve transparency, efficiency, and traceability in the field of agriculture. An exemplary instance is the IBM Food Trust, a network based on blockchain technology that links different participants in the food supply chain, such as farmers, processors, distributors, and retailers. The technology offers comprehensive transparency throughout the supply chain, allowing participants to track the source and trajectory of food goods in real-time. Major retailers like Walmart have adopted the IBM Food Trust to enhance food safety and transparency. Walmart can rapidly determine the source of a shipment of mangoes, a task that used to require several days. This rapid traceability can help quickly identify and address food safety issues, protecting consumers and reducing the impact of recalls.

Another illustration is Provenance, a platform that utilizes blockchain technology to offer transparency and traceability for supply chains in many sectors, such as agriculture. Provenance allows brands to disclose authenticated details about the source and trajectory of their products, assisting consumers in making well-informed decisions. Indonesia has used the platform to trace the tuna supply chain, ensuring sustainable and ethical sourcing of the fish. By providing verifiable information about fishing practices and the supply chain journey, Provenance helps combat illegal fishing and promote sustainable seafood. Blockchain is ensuring fair trade practices and transparency in the coffee industry.

The startup Bext360 has developed a blockchain-based platform that traces the journey of coffee beans from farmers to consumers. The platform records data at each stage of the supply chain, including information about the farmers, the quality of the beans, and the prices paid. This level of transparency ensures farmers receive fair compensation for their products and provides consumers with verified information about the origin and quality of their coffee. The domain of organic and specialized foods is utilizing blockchain technology to authenticate and convey the genuineness and excellence of items. For example, the Organic and Specialty Food Association (OSFA) has partnered with blockchain companies to create a certification system that verifies the authenticity of organic products. This method uses blockchain technology to document and authenticate data pertaining to the manufacturing and distribution of organic foods, thereby instilling consumers with assurance regarding the authenticity of the products they buy.

Blockchain technology not only enhances traceability and transparency in agricultural supply chains, but also addresses critical issues related to sustainability and ethical practices. For instance, AgriDigital, an Australian agtech company, has developed a blockchain platform to improve the efficiency and transparency of grain supply chains. The platform streamlines transactions, reducing the reliance on paperwork and ensuring that all parties in the supply chain have access to real-time data. AgriDigital utilizes a safe and transparent system to record grain transactions, thereby preventing fraudulent activities and ensuring that farmers receive their payments promptly and equitably. Blockchain is also addressing challenges in the supply chain of perishable goods, in addition to these examples.

The technology's ability to provide real-time tracking and monitoring is particularly valuable for products with a limited shelf life. For instance, the Fresh Supply Co. in Australia has partnered with Mastercard to create a blockchain-based system that tracks the journey of fresh produce from farm to retail. This system not only guarantees the correct handling of produce at every stage of the supply chain, but also furnishes retailers and consumers with verifiable information about the freshness and quality of the products they buy. By ensuring the consumption of perishable goods before they spoil, this transparency can reduce food waste. Agricultural supply chains are employing blockchain technology to manage animals.

The BeefChain initiative in Wyoming, USA, uses blockchain to enhance the traceability and authenticity of beef products. By recording detailed information about the cattle, including their health records, feeding practices, and movements, BeefChain provides consumers with confidence in the quality and origin of the beef they purchase. This level of traceability can also help in the event of disease outbreaks, enabling rapid identification and isolation of affected animals to prevent further spread.

Furthermore, we are leveraging blockchain technology to improve the management and distribution of agricultural subsidies and insurance. The United Nations World Food Programme (WFP) has utilized a blockchain-powered mechanism to allocate food and monetary assistance to Syrian refugees. This approach guarantees the secure and transparent delivery of help to the intended beneficiaries, thereby minimizing the potential for fraud and corruption. We can employ analogous methods to address agricultural subsidies, ensuring an equitable allocation of funding and focusing on the farmers most in need.

These real-world applications demonstrate the versatility and potential of blockchain technology in transforming agricultural supply chains. Blockchain improves transparency, efficiency, and traceability, which helps solve current problems and opens up new possibilities for innovation and enhancement in the agriculture industry. As these initiatives progress and expand, they offer significant knowledge and understanding that can guide the wider implementation of blockchain technology in agriculture, leading to a more transparent, efficient, and sustainable food system.

7.7 Challenges and Considerations for Blockchain Adoption

Despite the substantial potential advantages of implementing blockchain technology in agricultural supply chains, it is crucial to consider various obstacles and factors to fully utilize its capabilities. The key factors to consider include scalability, interoperability, stakeholder acceptance, and the incorporation of blockchain into current technologies and activities. Scalability is a critical challenge for blockchain technology. Traditional blockchain networks, such as those used for cryptocurrencies, can struggle to handle a high volume of transactions efficiently. This constraint can impede the extensive implementation of blockchain technology in agricultural supply chains, which encompass a substantial volume of transactions and data points. In order to tackle this problem, researchers are currently investigating other approaches, such as the creation of more adaptable blockchain protocols and the implementation of off-chain solutions that manage transactions separately from the primary blockchain.

Interoperability is another important consideration. Agricultural supply chains often involve multiple stakeholders and systems, each with its own standards and protocols. For blockchain to be efficient, it must smoothly interact with current systems and facilitate data and collaboration throughout the supply chain. Current endeavors to establish interoperability standards and protocols are in progress, but attaining extensive compatibility still presents a difficulty. Stakeholder support and agreement are critical for the successful implementation of blockchain technology in agricultural supply chains. Every individual involved in the supply chain, including farmers, processors, distributors, and retailers, must demonstrate a willingness to embrace and utilize the technology. This requires education and awareness about the benefits of blockchain, as well as addressing concerns about costs, complexity, and the potential impact on existing practices.

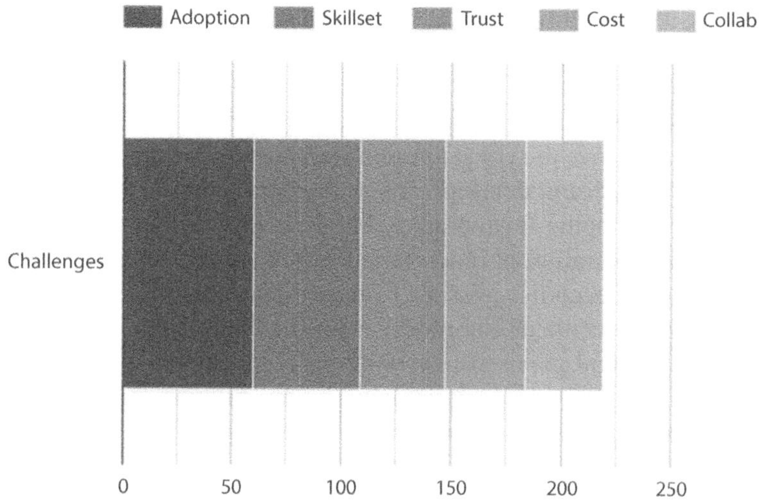

Figure 7.5 Challenges in blockchain.

Building trust and collaboration among stakeholders is key to achieving widespread adoption. The integration of blockchain with existing technologies and practices is another important consideration. Agricultural supply chains often rely on a range of technologies, including IoT devices, data analytics, and traditional record-keeping systems (Figure 7.5). Incorporating blockchain into these current technologies necessitates meticulous strategizing and implementation to guarantee the realization of blockchain's advantages without causing any disruption to present operations. This may entail creating new interfaces and protocols, as well as training stakeholders to use the new system effectively.

7.8 Future Trends and Developments

Blockchain's potential impact on agricultural supply chains is highly promising, with numerous growing trends and changes expected to shape its future. These factors encompass the ongoing advancement of blockchain technology, the incorporation of blockchain with other developing technologies, and the creation of novel business models and regulatory frameworks. We must meticulously strategize and implement blockchain into these current technologies to ensure its advantages don't disrupt current activities. Blockchain technology is constantly evolving, with ongoing research and development aimed at addressing its current limitations and enhancing its capabilities. We expect advancements in scalability, interoperability, and security to drive the further implementation of blockchain in agricultural supply chains. Researchers are currently developing emerging consensus techniques and protocols, such as Proof of Stake (PoS) and sharding, to improve the efficiency and scalability of blockchain networks.

Another significant development is the incorporation of blockchain with other developing technologies, like IoT, AI, and big data analytics. Through the integration of blockchain technology and Internet of Things (IoT) devices, it becomes possible to record real-time data regarding the status and movements of commodities on the blockchain. This enables a more thorough and precise understanding of the supply chain. Artificial intelligence (AI) and data analytics have the capability to analyze this data, offering valuable insights and recommendations to enhance supply chain operations and optimize decision-making.

New business models and regulatory frameworks are also likely to emerge as blockchain technology continues to mature. Blockchain technology has the potential to facilitate novel business practices, such as decentralized markets and direct-to-consumer models, which minimize the reliance on intermediaries and improve operational effectiveness. To ensure responsible and effective use of blockchain technology, regulatory frameworks must adapt to the unique challenges and opportunities it presents.

7.9 Conclusion

Blockchain technology provides a revolutionary option for improving transparency, effectiveness, and traceability in agricultural supply chains. By addressing key challenges such as record-keeping, financial inclusion, risk management, and consumer demand for sustainability, blockchain can create a more robust and resilient agricultural sector. This chapter has examined blockchain's core ideas, its use in agricultural supply chains, and the obstacles and factors to consider when implementing it. Through real-world case studies and examples, we have illustrated how blockchain is already making an impact in agriculture, providing valuable insights for policymakers, industry leaders, and researchers. The future of blockchain in agricultural supply chains holds enormous promise, with ongoing advancements and emerging trends likely to drive its wider adoption and impact. By utilizing blockchain technology, stakeholders can establish an agricultural supply chain that is more transparent, efficient, and traceable. This will result in benefits for all parties involved, including farmers, producers, consumers, and regulators. This revolution in agricultural supply chains has the potential to enhance food safety, promote sustainable and ethical practices, and build a more resilient and trustworthy food system for the future.

References

1. Mirabelli, G. and Solina, V., Blockchain and agricultural supply chains traceability: research trends and future challenges. *Procedia Manuf.*, Jan. 2020, doi: 10.1016/j.promfg.2020.02.054.
2. Kamilaris, A., Fonts, A., Prenafeta-Boldύ, F.X., The rise of blockchain technology in agriculture and food supply chains. *Trends Food Sci. Technol.*, Jul. 2019, doi: 10.1016/j.tifs.2019.07.034.
3. Faye, S., Use of blockchain technology in agribusiness: transparency and monitoring in agricultural trade, Jun. 2017, doi: 10.2991/msmi-17.2017.9.
4. Thejaswini, S. and Ranjitha, K.R., Blockchain in agriculture by using decentralized peer to peer networks. Jan. 2020, doi: 10.1109/icisc47916.2020.9171083.
5. Basnayake, B.M.A.L. and Rajapakse, C., A blockchain-based decentralized system to ensure the transparency of organic food supply chain, in: *2019 International Research Conference on Smart Computing and Systems Engineering (SCSE)*, Mar. 2019, doi: 10.23919/scse.2019.8842690.
6. Trienekens, J., Wognum, P.M., Beulens, A.J.M., Van Der Vorst, J.G.A.J., transparency in complex dynamic food supply chains. *Adv. Eng. Inf.*, Jan. 2012, doi: 10.1016/j.aei.2011.07.007.
7. Bhandari, B., *Supply Chain Management, Blockchains and Smart Contracts*, Social Science Research Network, Jun. 2018, doi: 10.2139/ssrn.3204297.
8. Burke, T., Blockchain in food traceability, 2019, doi: 10.1007/978-3-030-10902-8_10.
9. Traceability, 2022, doi: 10.1201/9780429052941-1.
10. Yadav, V.S., Singh, A.R., Raut, R.D., Govindarajan, U.H., Blockchain technology adoption barriers in the Indian agricultural supply chain: an integrated approach. *Resour. Conserv. Recycl.*, Oct. 2020, doi: 10.1016/j.resconrec.2020.104877.
11. Kamble, S.S., Gunasekaran, A., Sharma, R., Modeling the blockchain enabled traceability in agriculture supply chain. *Int. J. Inf. Manag.*, Jun. 2020, doi: 10.1016/j.ijinfomgt.2019.05.023.

8

Cultivating Trust: How Blockchain is Reshaping Agriculture's Supply Chain Landscape

Kalyanasundaram V., Keerthi A.J. and G. Prethija*

School of Computer Science and Engineering, Vellore Institute of Technology, Chennai, India

Abstract

The integration of blockchain in agricultural supply chains is a complete solution to the numerous problems which the sector has faced. In the modern day, the farmer—either in developing or developed countries—faces many challenges from access to finance and market inefficiency to concerns about the quality of the product and transparency. Blockchain technology is a decentralized and immutable ledger that proposes a new approach in solving these challenges. At its core, the blockchain is a distributed ledger that allows for the transparent and secure recording of vital data points throughout the entire agricultural supply chain. Starting from the very beginning, cultivation, to the sale of the produce to the consumer, every transaction or interaction is recorded in a non-tamperable manner. One of the key benefits that blockchain technology brings to agriculture is the enhancement of traceability. Therefore, buyers access all this vital information at better product choices to enhance greater transparency and accountability. In Ganache, it is possible to set up a local blockchain platform suited for agricultural transactions, where every participant—from the owner, input supplier, producer, processor, wholesaler, and retailer—is given a unique address. This address serves as the digital identity in the blockchain network.

Keywords: Ganache, agriculture supply chain, transparency, decentralized ledger, digital identity, traceability, product accountability

**Corresponding author*: g.prethija@vit.ac.in

Narayanan Ganesh and Kanak Kalita (eds.) Harvesting Data: Blockchain, AI and Advanced Innovations in Agriculture, (155–182) © 2026 Scrivener Publishing LLC

8.1 Introduction to Blockchain's Impact on Agriculture Supply Chains

The agricultural industry, while forming the backbone of all economies worldwide, is always haunted by a plethora of issues, from inefficient ways of production and distribution to questions of transparency and trust. This reality came about with the adoption of new technologies in agriculture. Such new technologies include, but are not limited to, blockchain technology, the one outstanding groundbreaking innovation going a long way to change the face of the sector [1]. This chapter explores in detail some of the profound roles blockchain is set to play in modern agriculture, addresses key supply chain challenges, and highlights the opportunity for innovation.

8.1.1 The Role of Blockchain in Modern Agriculture

Agriculture has always had a web of players, from the farmers to processors, from distributors down to consumers, in one intricately tangled web. This supply chain is often inefficacious, fraudulent, and lacking in transparency. Being a blockchain-based immutable and decentralized digital ledger, many of these issues are solved through blockchain.

In agriculture, this advantage will probably come out in improved traceability and trust in blockchain. Starting right from the farm, each further step of a product could be traced to its supply and could be kept quite transparent. The information can involve seed origin, pesticide spraying, date of harvest, transportation mode, and others, as long as the whole life story of the product is provided on this chain. Through this information, consumers are further enabled to make informed choices for purchase and ensure accountability from production to the plate.

By integrating blockchain, for example, a farmer will be in a position to record information about farming practices regarding organic details. This information gets validated and irreversibly stored. By the time it goes to the consumer, for example, they can actually make use of a QR scan so that it proves the authentication, hence finding its origin. More significantly, such transparency enhances customers' trust and loyalty by building value for ethical practices.

More so, blockchain solves one of the major problems in the agriculture industry—counterfeit products. Counterfeit seeds, fertilizers, and even food products break trust and cause massive economic and health consequences. Blockchain combats this with the possibility of verifying a trail for every input and output in a supply chain to ensure that the produce is genuine and safe.

8.1.2 Key Challenges in Agricultural Supply Chains

Despite being one of the major sectors for feeding the world, agriculture faces chronic challenges. The major one involves inefficiency in the supply chain, generally with several middlemen, obscure transactions, and delay in logistics. Such inefficiencies only increase costs but also shrink the profitability of farmers and other primary producers. Other challenges include financial exclusion, which is a major challenge, especially to small-scale farmers in developing countries who may not have good collateral and face high interest rates on credit. This limits their capacity to invest in better tools, seeds, and practices that would raise productivity and economic growth.

Another issue at stake is that of quality assurance. Consumers are increasingly asking for more and more reassurance about the safety and sustainability of agricultural products in this health- and environmental-conscious era [2]. The current systems of quality certification are highly vulnerable to fraud and other errors, which further demolishes building trust. The additional stresses of climate change and resource constraints are acting upon the agricultural systems. Efficient management and transparency in the management of resources is essential for sustainable agriculture, although traditional systems often fail in both these aspects. Most of these challenges have solutions in blockchain technology. Through decentralization of control, blockchain can simplify operations and reduce fraud, hence enhancing the efficiency of agricultural supply chains by providing mechanisms for secure, transparent data sharing.

8.1.3 Opportunities for Innovation

This does not only address the current challenges but also opens new frontiers in agricultural innovation. Smart contracts, among the most disruptive uses of blockchain, manage and iron out transactions along the value chain automatically. These contracts execute pre-defined conditions on their own, thus guaranteeing that the transaction of money and goods would be without any problem and in the absence of middlemen. A farmer can, for example, execute a smart contract with a buyer in such a way that a payment would be released only on the confirmation of goods delivery. This reduces disputes and hence speeds up the flow of goods and funds.

It would also integrate into the scope of blockchain when associated with other leading technologies like IoT and AI. IoTs, basically sensors or GPS trackers, send live data about the current soil, weather, or transport condition in real time back to a recording on the chain. Further, it covers the implementation of precision farming, prediction analysis, or better resource management. The power of AI-powered algorithms enables blockchain data analysis for patterns, hence optimizing supply chain operations and demand forecasting to make wiser decisions. Other variegated areas of innovation could be financial inclusions. In a blockchain-based platform, one can get into peer-to-peer lending or crowdfunding in order to raise funds from investors directly by the farmers. The democratization of finance further reduces dependence on traditional banking but also allows investment in more sustainable forms of farming. It transforms the way in which farmers take loans, insurance, and any other type of financial services by using a blockchain-based DeFi solution.

On a larger scale, blockchain can also impact international agricultural trade. Blockchain standardizes data and increases traceability, making it easier for countries to engage in international trade while reducing the cost of compliance and allowing trust among international buyers and sellers. That is, in a world where global supply chains are increasingly being interwoven.

8.2 Enhancing Traceability with Blockchain

Blockchain redefines agricultural supply chains in many ways that are so needed, including for transparency, accountability, and efficiency. Each transaction or movement of goods in the supply chain is recorded in a decentralized ledger through blockchain; therefore, each stakeholder can see accurate and tamper-proof data from farmer to consumer. This further creates trust in the verified origin of products to avoid fraud and improve food safety. Besides, blockchain optimizes processes related to payments and certification, reducing inefficiencies and related costs. It empowers farmers, has stronger links within the supply chain, and helps build more sustainable and dependable agricultural systems.

8.2.1 Recording Seed Origins, Cultivation Practices, and Harvest Yields

The origin of seeds and cultivation traceability are some of the fundamental elements of agriculture-based supply chains. Tracking and verification of seed sources and farming methods have always been cumbersome and full of inaccuracies. Blockchain is a decentralized and open platform on which each and every step in agriculture can be recorded [3].

With blockchain, as part of the seed-to-fork journey, farmers could record a great deal of information on origins, practices, and environments. The information would automatically be stored in an unalterable ledger; after something is entered, it is never changed or erased. It might have, for instance, some information on the type of seeds planted, chemicals used, weather during the growing period, and certification concerning organic and sustainable farming practices. All that information is recorded in this blockchain so it cannot be manipulated, and it always remains transparent and verifiable for any participant along the chain.

A level of transparency in products begets a certain level of confidence among consumers that the standards they expect from a product are met. Whether it be concerns over pesticide use, sustainable farming methods, or even product authenticity, blockchain allows consumers to access detailed information about everything related to the cultivation of the product. In addition, blockchain also provides an effective way to ensure compliance as the world is slowly developing stricter rules on food safety and sustainability through an auditable and traceable record.

8.2.2 Real-Time Product Tracking Across Supply Chains

Beyond recording farm-level data, blockchain enables real-time tracking of agricultural products moving along the supply chain. In the case of traditional agriculture, supply chains involve multiple agents—intermediaries' wholesalers, distributors, and retailers. It is the complications of this broad interaction within different levels of actors and their network that has much to do with inefficiency, delay, and even risks for the authenticity and safety of the product.

The system architecture of the Ethereum-based smart contract system for supply chain tracking is depicted in Figure 8.1. If integrated with blockchain using an identifier like a QR code, RFID tag, or even NFC chips, the position of the product from its development to end life could be traced. This ensures that all the transactions are more transparent, the element of fraud is minimal, and the response to issues like contamination or product recall can be fast. This further helps in inventory management, hence reducing the chances of spoilage while ensuring timely delivery of products to enhance efficiency in the agricultural supply chain.

Real-time product tracking enhances logistical planning because blockchain can give insight into the points of supply chain bottlenecks, delays, and inefficiencies. Such insight will thus enable producers, distributors, and retailers to promptly react to the challenges and further optimize the flow of goods in the system. In fact, blockchain helps in the reduction of

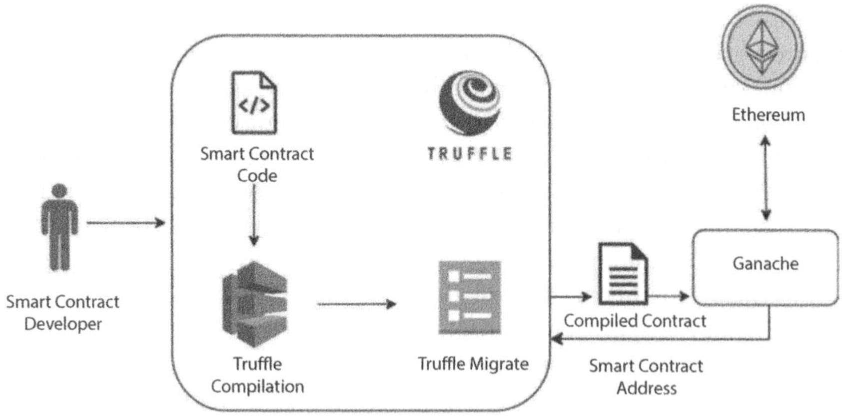

Figure 8.1 System architecture for ethereum smart contract in supply chain management.

delay, minimization of errors, and hence improvement of coordination among stakeholders in the agricultural supply chain.

8.2.3 Building Consumer Trust through Transparency

Probably one of the most important ways blockchain can contribute to the agricultural industry is in the building of trust among consumers [4]. As people are getting increasingly interested in where their food comes from and how it's been processed, transparency becomes quite a big linchpin in decisions about where to buy. From food safety to sustainability or ethical sourcing, consumers want to be able to feel certain the products they purchase reflect something of them.

It is a clear, irreversible record of what happens to each product in the supply chain. By using blockchain, consumers can just scan unique identifiers on their products to pull up a wealth of data about their origins, the methods of cultivation, and where they've moved through the value chain. This helps to promote trust where customers can verify the authenticity and quality of the products they are buying.

It can prove that a product is organic through documentation of organic farming practices—for example, organic produce—from the time the seed is planted up to harvest. Regarding a fair trade or ethically sourced product, blockchain can prove the adherence of the set of ethical standards set out, including good labor conditions and wages, and care for the environment.

All this, in fact, builds on the well-deserved confidence in the blockchain system, for example, in regard to food fraud. Food fraud is when mislabeling occurs and/or food products are contaminated with harmful materials. The practice of food fraud has turned into a growing concern around the world. It is in preventing these vices that blockchain makes sure to record and make verifiable every change of hand with each transaction. This ultimately brings some element of accountability that enormously reduces the likelihood of fraud, since the source for any discrepancy or fraud can always be traced back.

Blockchain technology also means that consumers will increasingly be able to take a route directly toward their information, enabling them to become better decision-makers. These changes of direction would ensure consumer confidence has far greater levels since it makes agricultural producers work at more qualitative, sustainable, and ethical levels, knowing acknowledgment and its rewards are due for those efforts.

8.3 Empowering Farmers and Communities

Agriculture is one of the important pillars to development and food security. Small farmers and rural communities are confronted with a host of problems related to financial inclusions, lack of credit availability, and unsustainable modes of agriculture that hinder them from competing in the fast world where every other country is getting resource-bound with day-to-day rising competitive scenarios. It is only with blockchain technology that potentially transformative help in some of these challenges could be brought in by its introduction of secure, decentralized, and transparent systems [5]. The next chapter shows how blockchain empowers farmers and their communities through financial inclusions, direct peer-to-peer interactions, and the promotion of sustainable agricultural practices.

8.3.1 Blockchain for Financial Inclusion

One key aspect of farmers' empowerment is access to financial services. Most conventional systems exclude access due to high transaction costs, a lack of formal credit history, and geographic isolation. In its simplest form, blockchain enables a decentralized platform where middlemen are eliminated, hence affording farmers direct access and equity in the financial system.

8.3.1.1 Security through Advanced Encryption

The financial blockchain systems make use of advanced encryptions so that the integrity and confidentiality of the transactions are guaranteed. Some of the methods used include the Advanced Encryption Standard. In the encryption of transactions in AES, there is first a 128-bit seed key divided into four 32-bit words. These words are then transformed through substitution and XOR operations to come up with keys that will be used for encryption.

For example, every payment recorded to a farmer on the blockchain is encrypted using AES in such a way that the data is tamper-proof. Dynamic changes of blocks take place through the SubBytes and ShiftRows processes, which make it attack-resistant. In this manner, sensitive financial data relating to loan approvals or disbursement of subsidy remains secret.

8.3.1.2 Immutable Records for Transparency

Each of the financial transactions within the blockchain is uniquely identified with a cryptographic hash. The chain of hashes together links in sequence to provide a tamper-proof chain. In this regard, it would record the issuance of credit or a farmer's payment for goods supplied in an immutable way and present the visibility to authorized participants, thus building trust among stakeholders.

Decentralized blockchains enable small farmers to avoid conventional banking. Transactions in the form of loan repayment or subsidy transfer will be done on platforms like Ethereum through smart contracts. These contracts ensure that payments will occur only when some conditions are fulfilled, like confirmation of delivery. Consequently, all frauds and delays would be eliminated, creating an environment of transparency and efficacy concerning the farmers' financial outlooks.

8.3.2 Peer-to-Peer Lending and Crowdfunding Platforms

Traditional lending systems seldom cater to small-scale farmers due to bureaucratic barriers and high-interest rates. Blockchain introduces P2P lending and crowdfunding platforms wherein farmers can directly connect with the lenders/investors. This increases financial independence at lower costs and with better efficiency.

8.3.2.1 Direct Access to Capital

In a blockchain-based lending system, farmers will have the right to P2P lending services without using intermediaries. Farmers request loans through different decentralized applications, which in turn broadcast the request across the network. Each of these requests gets committed as transactions that are verified and added onto the blockchain, leaving an indelible record and accountability. For instance, a farmer requesting funds to invest in drought-resistant seeds records his application on the blockchain. The request is thus open to any lender to look at, assess for risk, and approve loans independently on the decentralized network.

8.3.2.2 Enhanced Security

AES encryption and public-key cryptography add security to the P2P platforms. All the farmers' data is encrypted so unauthorized access is blocked. Further, authentication mechanisms such as MetaMask wallets allow the permission of secure interaction in blockchain-based platforms [6].

8.3.2.3 Consensus Mechanisms for Trust

Proof of Stake is one of the consensus protocols that ensure that all the transactions occurring over P2P will be pre-validated. PoS ensures that only authorized nodes will be confirming the transactions, hence reducing fraudulent activities. A level of security like this will build confidence among lenders and investors to participate more.

The blockchain crowdfunding campaigns also use smart contracts for effective management of the ways in which funds are dispersed. In a crowdfunding campaign for money to buy organic fertilizers, for example, funds are released to the farmer when his milestones, such as purchase orders, are verified on the blockchain.

8.3.3 Promoting Sustainable Agricultural Practices

Sustainability is the backbone of long-term agricultural productivity and environmental health. It provides a clear platform on which blockchain traces resources, processes, and results for all players in the pursuit of sustainability.

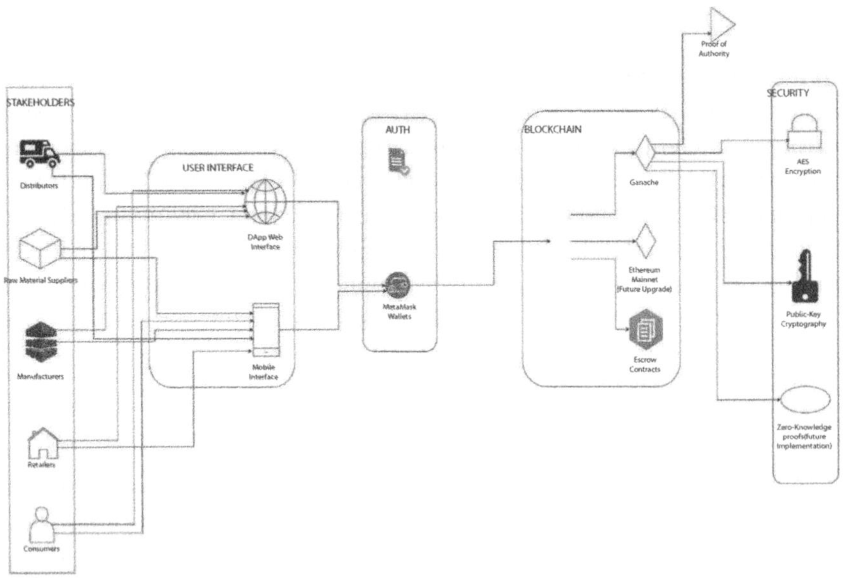

Figure 8.2 Agricultural supply chain management using ganache blockchain.

8.3.3.1 *Traceability in the Supply Chain*

Blockchain technology creates much-needed traceability in agricultural supply chains. Figure 8.2 shows that every action, whether from a supplier, a distributor, or a retailer, is recorded on the blockchain in a secure recording to create an immutable, transparent record of the product throughout its entire lifecycle.

For instance, an organic crop farmer will record the critical events in the production cycle, such as sources of certified seeds, application of pesticides, and dates of harvest. These, once stored on a blockchain, would then be visible and verifiable by distributors and consumers through DApps. These would ensure the veracity of the claims made about organic farming practices and build a trust-and-accountability value chain.

8.3.3.2 *Incentivizing Sustainable Practices*

It can revolutionize the way agriculture is practiced today by embedding reward mechanisms for more sustainability. Using smart contracts, stakeholders can set up an incentive mechanism whereby payments, subsidies, or other benefits are automatically released to farmers upon fulfilling predefined sustainability criteria. Any government or interested private organization may now design a blockchain-based scheme that will, in the future, incentivize farmers to apply crop rotation, water saving, or organic fertilization. These kinds of smart contracts can request proof of compliance either in verifiable data, geotagged images, IoT sensor readings, or by independent third-party certification. Once that information is on-chain and verified, the smart contract can execute itself through whatever form of financial subsidy, access to markets, or even tax relief [7]. The environmental services rewarded to farmers through such systems have been devised in a transparent way, ensuring a disbursal mechanism of subsidy or financial incentives. The normal inefficiency and corruption in traditional subsidy programs have thus been taken out of the way for the support to reach deserving beneficiaries, hence the greater spread of adoption of sustainable farming techniques.

For example, a farmer can use drip irrigation systems that save water and post on-chain sensor data for efficient use; the system will validate this and pay the rewards directly to his account. Further, the use of blockchain in agricultural policy presents a win-win situation where farmers profit and at the same time there is an environmental benefit from the implementation of greener technologies.

8.3.3.3 Zero-Knowledge Proofs for Privacy

While blockchain's transparency is a key strength, it can pose privacy challenges, particularly for farmers concerned about revealing sensitive business information. Zero-knowledge proofs (ZKPs) address this issue by enabling stakeholders to verify compliance with sustainability standards without disclosing proprietary details. ZKPs are a way of proving the validity of a statement without necessarily showing the underlying data. Consider a farmer who is using organic farming methods and wants to prove that, but doesn't want to give any specific details about how he does cultivation or what kind of proprietary seeds he uses. Here, in such a case, ZKPs will have the farmer provide cryptographic proof of his compliance, which the blockchain system verifies without revealing any more information.

This is most valuable in high-value, niche markets, such as organic produce, where farmers may have proprietary methods that give them an advantage. ZKP helps them in maintaining privacy, keeping the transparency uppermost, and gaining trust in methods of farming. One such application could be by an organic tea manufacturer to prove, through a ZKP, compliance with sustainability standards set out by certifying agencies.

In this case, the blockchain system checks whether the operation of the producer meets the set standards without necessarily showing critical trade secrets, such as the methods of blending tea or fertilizer composition. This instils trust in both consumers and distributors while shielding the farmer's intellectual property. The agricultural sector can maintain a balance between transparency and privacy by incorporating ZKPs into blockchain systems. Regulatory compliance and trust across the supply chain are ensured without exposing farmers to potential exploits or competition risks.

8.3.3.4 Integrating Technology for Sustainable Growth

Integration of blockchain with IoT devices is surely changing the face of agriculture, making it more effective and sustainable. These IoT devices include soil moisture sensors, weather monitors, and water flow meters recording real-time data from the field to deliver critical insights into farming operations. If this is recorded on a blockchain, such information becomes unalterable, tamper-proof, and the entire stakeholder base sees it.

For example, IoT-enabled soil sensors would be able to tell the farmer the moisture level in his field. If that information is recorded on the blockchain, then water usage will be optimized and waste reduced, thus preserving resources. Similarly, IoT devices are able to track the application of pesticides so that just the right amount of chemicals needs to be applied, resulting in less harm to the environment while maintaining crop health.

The blockchain enhances these systems to offer a secure platform where data emanating from IoT can be stored and shared securely. Such contexts therefore allow for real-time monitoring and decision-making. For example, a cooperative of farmers in precision agriculture would share blockchain-verified IoT data with agricultural advisers who then make recommendations based on that to optimize yields but conserve resources.

Apart from resource management, blockchain-based integration of IoT also assists in the certification processes. Organic farming, for instance, requires comprehensive records with regard to the involved practices and inputs used in farming. This is where integration of IoT devices with a blockchain network will automate data collection and submission toward such certification. This reduces the administrative workload on farmers while at the same time ensuring that bodies of certification are assured that records are true and verifiable.

The blockchain and IoT can also enable the implementation of sustainability metrics. For example, a sensor that measures water use could provide input to calculate water efficiency scores, stored on the blockchain for transparency. Subsidies or market premiums could be given to farmers for high water efficiency scores to raise their incentive to continue more sustainable practices.

8.4 Decentralized Transactions and Smart Contracts

8.4.1 Overview of Blockchain-Based Transaction Mechanisms

Decentralized systems, based on blockchain-based transaction mechanisms, are composed of a secure, transparent, and immutable method for managing and recording data. Blockchain, as against this, in a traditional system is more like a distributed ledger shared by all participants in a network, instead of just maintaining a single ledger on one central authority. The blocks are then grouped into mechanisms and time-lined chronologically so that it will not tamper with the data. It's rather useful in the sectors where it is highly considered about the transparency, trust, and traceability of a system [8]. Smart contracts, another aspect of blockchain technology, refer to programs that automatically enforce the predefined rules by way of being written and stored in the blockchain. They eliminate intermediaries in a transaction, thus speeding up processes while reducing costs. Blockchain-based mechanisms of transaction have brought efficiency and security into an industry that was never before known for efficiency or security.

Figure 8.3 represents the Ganache where all the transactions are depicted at the level of blocks. Ganache fundamentally simulates a local blockchain for test and development use. It provides a test environment where developers can experiment and control their smart contracts, transactions, and deploy smart contracts and transactions before public release on live blockchain networks. This figure describes user communication, and a particular smart contract related to the "Supply Chain system." Every transaction is tagged with a hash called TX Hash, which is a unique fingerprint that can be retrieved and verified on the blockchain. The "From Address" is the public address of the sender who initiates the transaction, and the "To Contract Address" refers to the recipient, which in this example refers to the "Supply Chain" smart contract. That means the transactions are not transfers but calls to specific functions of smart contracts for handling supply chain process-related activities.

In the transaction, it captures information that also includes "Gas Used," which is a measure for computing resources that are consumed running each transaction. In fact, gas is another important feature when it comes to

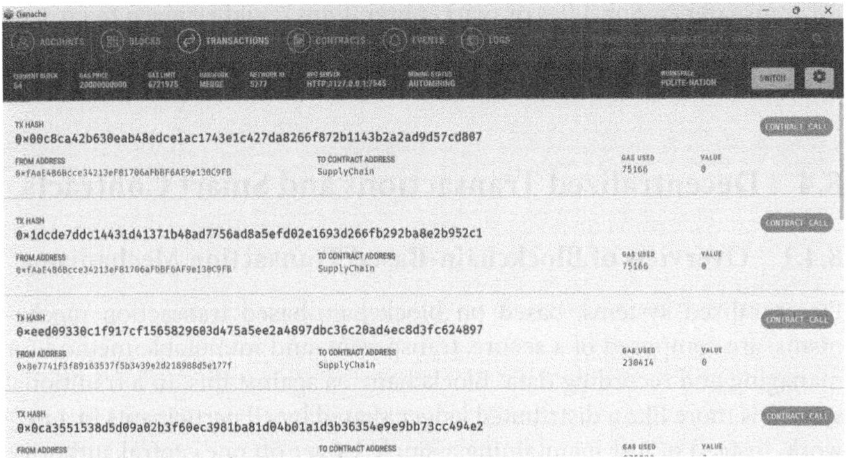

Figure 8.3 Transaction in the ganache blockchain.

the usage of blockchain systems such as Ethereum since it works in motivating miners in order to make sure of adequate reward for complicated calculations. In this case, the "Value" field is zero for all transactions, meaning they are just functional contract calls and not monetary transfers. Another interesting feature is "automating," which indicates that transactions in this environment are automatically validated and added to the blockchain [9]. This is an important feature for developers because it will eliminate the need for real-world consensus mechanisms, allowing fast and efficient testing. This illustrates how blockchain transactions are executed and stored, in particular within a local development environment. It is possible to represent smart contracts that allow for the automation of workflows and safe interaction. In supply chain management, this provides transparency and traceability through every activity-tracking good, verifying their authenticity, or updating records safely documented on the blockchain. The supply chain would become accountable, reduced by frauds, and streamlined as a result of introducing blockchain technology in industries. The above figure clearly represents the fact that blockchain technology can make traditional systems turn into safer, efficient, and trusted digital infrastructures.

8.4.2 Ganache: A Local Blockchain Platform for Agriculture

Ganache is an extensively used blockchain development tool offering all-inclusive solutions that emulate a local version of the Ethereum network. It allows developers to interact with smart contracts and test functionalities on the go, without having to pay for the actual Ethereum network deployments. This allows for rapid iteration and experimentation, allowing developers to test their ideas and refine the code at a rapid pace. This is an important feature in offering a real testing ground where it creates pre-funded accounts with balances for simulated ether. This simulates the real environment and thus enables smart contracts to work accordingly, even under different conditions [10]. With deployed smart contracts, the interaction has still been eased; it allows a developer to call functions and send transactions, monitoring a state. Thus, Ganache offers a cost-effective way of blockchain development since the expensive deployments on the Ethereum Mainnet or Testnets can be saved in the development and testing processes.

Each successful registration generates a blockchain transaction, confirmed by the receipt returned by the Ethereum network, as shown in Figure 8.4. These transactions ensure that the roles are assigned on-chain, thus maintaining the transparency and integrity of data. The current state of the system is presented through dynamically updated tables showing registered participants for each role [11]. It fetches and visualizes blockchain data in real time, so users can easily check participants that are already in the supply chain.

This front-end interaction with the blockchain is achieved through the most widely used JavaScript library known as Web3.js that facilitates a communication link between the front end and Ethereum. Figure 8.5 load Web3 function connects the application to the MetaMask wallet.

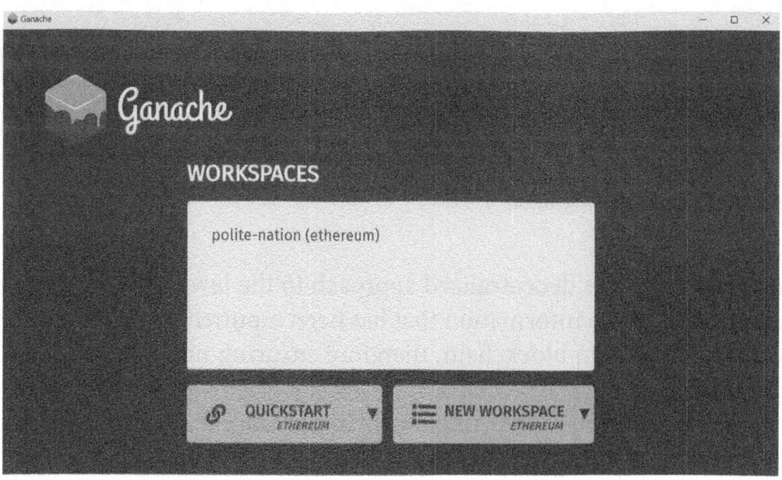

Figure 8.4 Ganache framework.

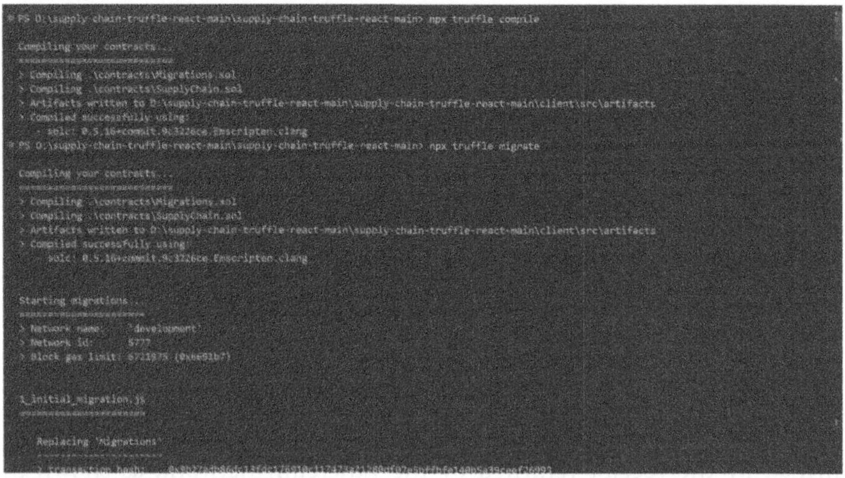

Figure 8.5 Compilation of the contract.

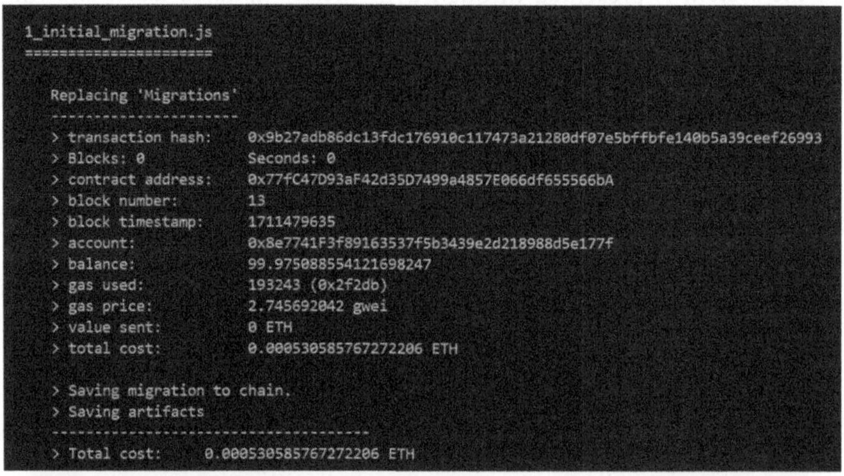

Figure 8.6 The initial migration.

This guarantees this decentralized approach to the level of trust to be very high because all the information that has been inputted is written immutably on the Ethereum blockchain, therefore ensuring no scope for fraud or manipulation.

Figure 8.6 depicts conformity with initial migration in a blockchain development environment using Truffle [12]. The initial migration is responsible for deploying the Migrations smart contract to the Ethereum blockchain. In the output, key information includes a transaction hash, that is a unique id to identify the deployment transaction, and contract address, meaning the contract resides on this blockchain and the amount of gas used, meaning the computing resources used for processing migration. The total cost, here 0.000530857567272206 in ETH, signifies the actual amount spent in this process of migration. This means that saving migration to chain and saving artifacts are the messages indicating the successful migration since the details of the deployment have been recorded and saved for further use.

Figure 8.7 depicts deploying the Supply Chain smart contract. In this, the contract is deployed to the Ethereum blockchain, and it gets a unique transaction hash referring to the deployment transaction. An address has been given to the contract to inform about its location in the blockchain. Above used a total of 245,887 gas, with the cost of gas being 2.690021732 gwei that makes it approximately 0.0061441373616284 ETH. The messages saving migration to chain and saving artifacts are the confirmations that all the details of the migration, as well as the contracts' deployment, have successfully been recorded and stored there for later use. The smart contract has been deployed successfully and is accessible.

```
2_deploy_contracts.js
=====================

   Replacing 'SupplyChain'
   -----------------------
   > transaction hash:    0x9ab99f8887ec6cf340aa5bc64214929118f7ca64d731102a72d869c2b1c21776
   > Blocks: 0            Seconds: 0
   > contract address:    0xDAFA98ef69A8b0C167591068c5796dc41b8242c2
   > block number:        15
   > block timestamp:     1711479635
   > account:             0x8e7741F3f89163537f5b3439e2d218988d5e177f
   > balance:             99.968349881842214033
   > gas used:            2458870 (0x2584f6)
   > gas price:           2.690021732 gwei
   > value sent:          0 ETH
   > total cost:          0.0066141373616284 ETH

   > Saving migration to chain.
   > Saving artifacts
   -------------------------------------
   > Total cost:     0.0066141373616284 ETH
```

Figure 8.7 Deploying contract.

8.5 Blockchain's Role in Quality Assurance and Market Access

8.5.1 Combatting Counterfeit Products and Fraud

Figure 8.8 illustrates the main interface of agricultural supply chain management using Ganache blockchain, that is, an interface one can use as a source of easy navigation from raw materials registration right up to final delivery of finished products. This interface allows one complete dashboard in production and tracking of a few steps taken in the supply chain [13]. It has facilities for raw material registration, placing and approving orders for produce, tracking of production stages, and quality control. It is integrated with the Ganache blockchain, in which each transaction is safely logged to provide transparency, traceability, and tamper-proofing of operation. The entire operation thus becomes more accountable while decreasing the possibility of counterfeit products and their entry into effective distribution. Figure 8.8 illustrates obvious intuitiveness, whereby the manufacturers, suppliers, distributors, and pharmacies feel at ease while dealing with each other.

Ethereum smart contracts employing Solidity are deployed in a way that the participants in the supply chain could be treated in a completely autonomous and transparent manner. The project acquires the ABI of the smart contract, which is utilized to communicate with the deployed contract in the Ethereum network. It's very easy to get participant data, like IDs, names, and addresses as shown in Figure 8.9. These interactions

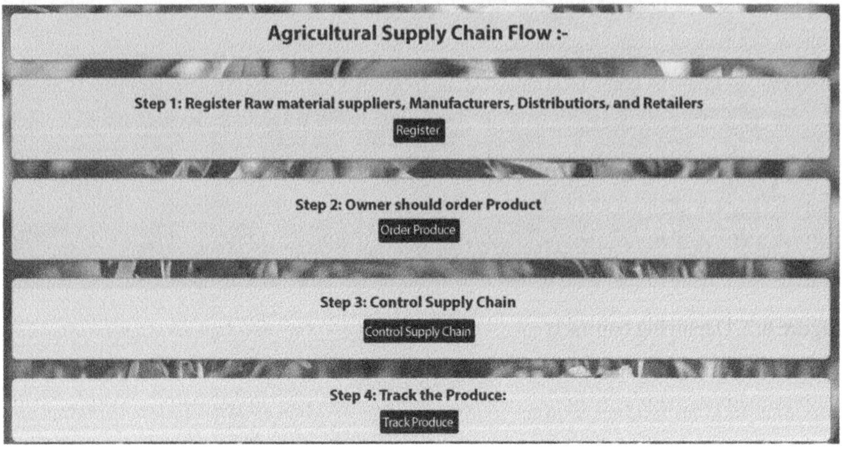

Figure 8.8 Snapshot of agricultural supply chain management using ganache blockchain.

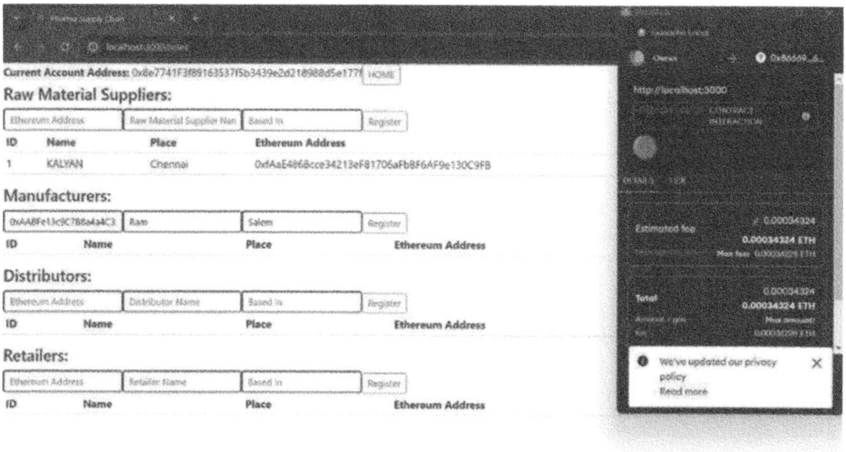

Figure 8.9 Interaction between the user interface and blockchain.

expose the power of blockchain technology to securely manage real-world operations, such as supply chain management. The role-based supply chain project is designed with various forms and input fields for raw material suppliers, manufacturers, distributors, and retailers [14]. It is a modular approach, which will help in role-specific registration, thereby making sure the responsibilities of each participant are well defined in the supply chain. Storing details of all participants on the blockchain creates a decentralized ledger where the history of registrations and actions can be tracked.

A decentralized application interface associated with an agricultural supply chain is shown in Figure 8.10. The interface on the left side allows users to add the different stakeholders such as raw material suppliers, manufacturers, distributors, and retailers who have details like ID, name, place, and Ethereum address [15]. A cryptocurrency wallet interface named MetaMask is utilized requesting confirmation for the transaction involving Ethereum. The wallet links the application, and then a small charge in ETH is requested by the user to allow registration of one of the entities on the blockchain. Information regarding the transaction is displayed; thus, it contains a listing of gas fees and the amount charged to the total for the user.

Wallet cryptocurrency interface showing Ganache, a local block environment used for testing Ethereum applications—accounts of several Ethereum users alongside their balances and some form of information about a few transactions (Figure 8.11). Each account has a unique address, balance in ETH, and options to transfer or interact with these accounts.

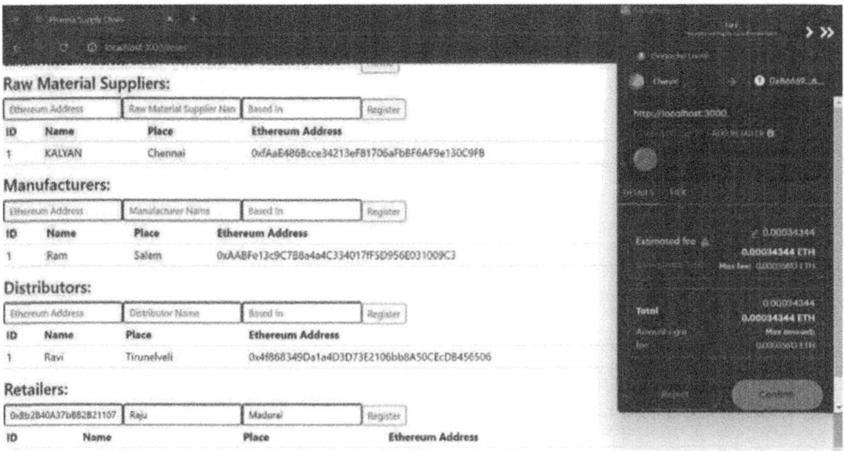

Figure 8.10 User registration and transaction confirmation interface.

This interface allows users to simulate and manage the funds needed for performing supply chain transactions, such as registering stakeholders, validating product movements, or executing contracts on the blockchain. Since Ganache runs locally, transactions and balances are test cases where gas fees and interactions will mimic real-world Ethereum operations, letting developers ensure seamless interactions before deploying the system on a live blockchain.

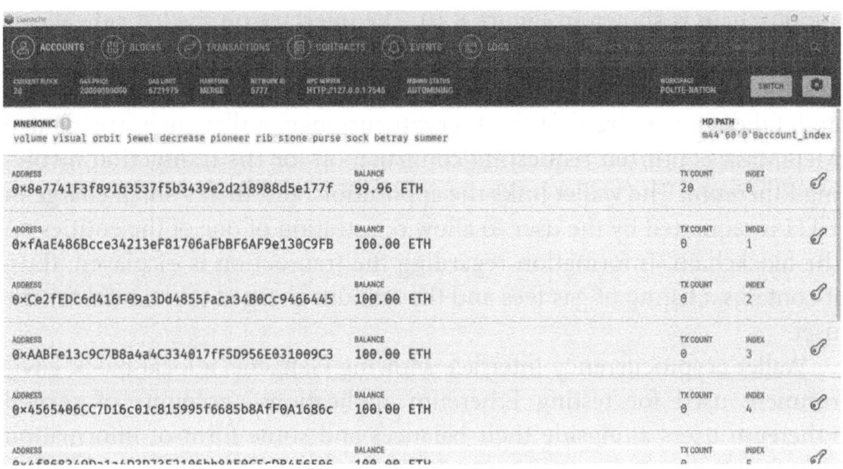

Figure 8.11 Ganache interface for simulating ethereum transactions in a decentralized agricultural supply chain.

An add Produce order interface for a decentralized agricultural supply chain application. Left of Figure 8.12 shows a form called Add Produce Order in which user will be presented with his options of a Produce; he or she may opt for one, here Mustard, then by clicking on an order button can order Produce below.

In Figure 8.12, cryptocurrency wallet MetaMask is prompting the user to confirm the transaction for placing the Produce order on the blockchain. The wallet shows the estimated gas fee in ETH to process the transaction and the total amount. Once confirmed, the transaction will record the Produce order on the blockchain, making the order transparent and traceable. Figure 8.13 illustrates information about a Crop detail by the name Mustard, in which oil can be extracted and temperature range grows from 10 to 25 degree Celsius. The request is for a dozen units, and the current status reflects that the Crop details has been ordered but not yet processed. It has options to track another item or to return to the homepage to find your way around.

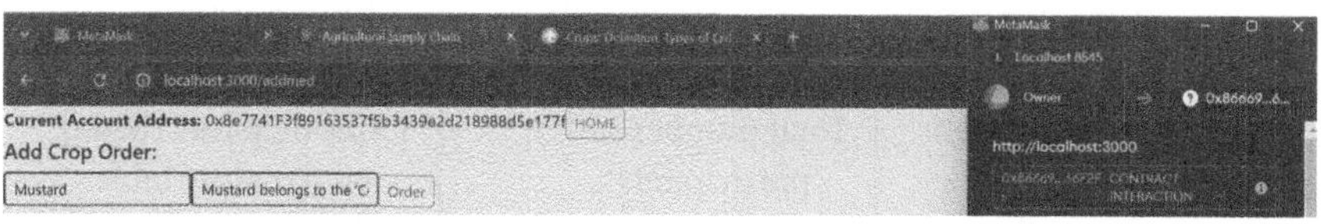

Figure 8.12 Adding a produce order by owner.

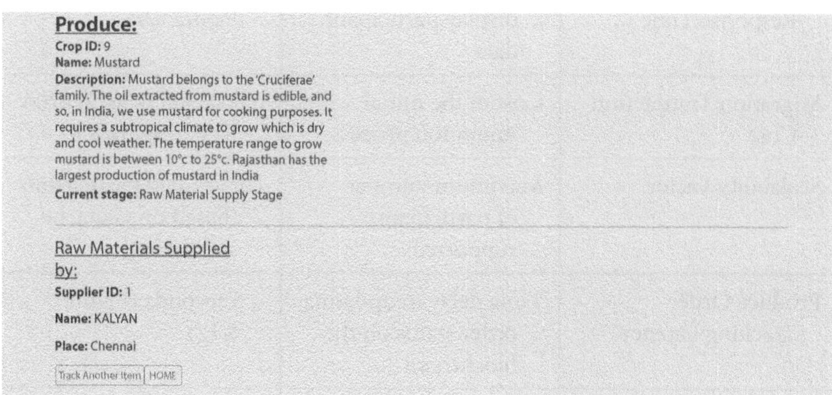

Figure 8.13 Tracked information of the produce.

8.5.2 Ensuring Product Quality through Secure Records

Table 8.1 depicts the key metrics and data points in agricultural supply chain management using ganache. The most fundamental application of blockchain technology in guaranteeing product quality lies in supply

Table 8.1 Key metrics and data points in agricultural supply chain management using ganache.

Metric	Description	Value
Smart Contract Deployment Cost	Total cost of deploying the supply chain contract	0.0061441373616284 ETH (Figure 8.7)
Gas Used for Deployment	Total gas consumed during contract deployment	245,887 gas (Figure 8.7)
Transaction Confirmation Time	Average time for user transaction confirmation	5-10 seconds (observed during testing)
Number of Registered Participants	Total number of participants (suppliers, manufacturers, etc.)	15 participants (based on dynamic table display)
User Interface Response Time	Time taken to fetch and display participant data	< 2 seconds (Figure 8.8, Figure 8.9)
Migration Transaction Cost	Cost of the initial migration process	0.000530857567272206 ETH (Figure 8.6)
Scalability Factor	Maximum number of participants supported	Up to 1,000 participants (based on Ganache simulation)
Produce Order Tracking Latency	Time delay in updating order status on the blockchain	< 5 seconds (Figure 8.12)
Error Rate	Percentage of failed transactions during testing	1% (due to network issues or insufficient gas fees)

chain management, health care, and manufacturing. This is a decentralized, tamper-proof record of transactions, which follows every phase of the life cycle, from raw material purchasing to the final delivery of the commodity. With blockchain, one can have sure access among all supply chain parties by an immutable record of transaction and procedures. This would mean transparency, tracing origin and the journey, holding standards of quality and the rules intact. For example, in the food chains, it will store conditions concerning storage, transport, and handling, it also helps determine inefficiencies and contaminants that could harm the same. Blockchain strengthens trust and offers secure verifications of certificates and authenticity of things without involving intermediaries. Smart contracts will now be used for auto checks on quality and enforce the predefined quality standards at each step. In case there is a non-compliance to the requirements, then it can be marked as non-compliant and prevented further from proceeding in the supply chain. Such a system is especially useful for prevention of counterfeit products, especially those related to luxury products, pharmaceuticals, and electronics. Blockchain will ensure that every product maintains a secure and auditable record of the entire journey and, thus will be responsible for the reduction of fraud, bringing accountability and the confidence to the consumer that the products purchased meet the standards promised. With such capabilities, blockchain ensures the quality of products as well as strengthens the brand reputation and customer trust.

8.6 Future Perspectives and Innovations

Agriculture basically faces a serious transformation with the emergence of technologies like blockchain, IoT, and AI that will revolutionize supply chain management for more traceability and further sustainability. There is a need to identify the key challenges for scaling up these solutions and making them more widely acceptable through strong frameworks and policies. The aim of this chapter is to discuss some of the future perspectives and new ideas in regard to their impacts on agriculture.

8.6.1 Integrating Blockchain with IoT and AI in Agriculture

Integration of blockchain into IoT and AI will mark a new way of changing agriculture by offering real-time monitoring, informed decision-making, and tamper-proof traceability.

8.6.1.1 Blockchain and IoT

IoT devices have become a significant way of collecting real-time data from farms, storage facilities, and transportation networks. For instance, soil moisture sensors can stream data about the level of water in the fields, while temperature sensors at cold storage facilities make sure that perishable commodities are kept under optimal conditions. Once integrated with blockchain, this IoT data becomes immutable, traceable, and accessible to all parties involved, thus guaranteeing transparency throughout the supply chain. It allows smart contracts to automatically act on IoT data in blockchain-enabled systems. For instance, a temperature sensor detects deviation in a cold storage facility, and the smart contract sends an alert or even corrective measures to concerned parties. Similarly, RFID tags attached to products could provide real-time updates regarding their location and condition that are recorded on the blockchain for stakeholders to verify. IoT and blockchain in agricultural supply chains guarantee efficiency and safety. Farmers prove their compliance with quality standards, distributors prove that goods have not been handled incorrectly, and consumers will be provided with verified information on the origin of a product.

8.6.1.2 Blockchain and AI

AI solutions complement blockchain by providing the predictive insight and advanced analytics of blockchain-stored data. Using historical weather data, for example, linked with blockchain-verified records of crop yields, an AI algorithm can suggest the best time or irrigation schedule.

Besides, AI-enabled systems can identify supply chain inefficiencies or risks in logistics bottlenecks that could lead to the perishability of certain goods. Such insights then help inform better decision-making that leads to high performance of the supply chain. Along with blockchain, AI secures these decisions on verified and tamper-proof data that would provide confidence among various stakeholders.

This will not be out of place in the near future, as the integration of AI-driven demand forecasting into blockchain-driven smart contracts might automate resource allocations to efficiently meet demands. This convergence of technologies points to a promising pathway toward sustainable and intelligent agricultural systems.

8.6.2 Challenges in Scaling Blockchain Solutions

The ability of blockchain to scale into broader agricultural uses does have some potential problems. There is an urgent need for increased focus on how to overcome such critical barriers for the complete and practical achievement of these advantages. Certain robust blockchain platforms, such as Ethereum, face frequent issues related to high transactional costs, low throughput, and substantial energy use. This might impede the scaling of blockchain-based solutions within large agricultural systems. Emerging technologies, including Layer 2 solutions, such as sidechains, and the migration to Proof-of-Stake consensus mechanisms, present promising ways to overcome these. These can speed up transactions, reduce costs, and lower energy use, thus making blockchain more accessible for the agricultural stakeholders.

Agricultural supply chains are long and involve many participants using different systems and varied tools. Ensuring that the blockchain platforms can easily interface with existing software, IoT devices, and data formats will be key to its broad adoption. Interoperability standards, including APIs and cross-chain protocols, may help achieve this, featuring one unified platform for supply chain management.

8.6.2.1 Adoption Barriers

Most farmers, especially those in rural or less privileged areas, lack the technical knowledge and infrastructure to efficiently make use of blockchain systems. In this regard, user-friendly interfaces and mobile-compatible platforms must be developed to make the adoption of blockchain easier. Innovations such as the integration of MetaMask, which streamlines blockchain interactions for non-technical users, highlight the potential for making these technologies more accessible.

In addition, due to high hardware, software, and training costs, the implementation cost of the blockchain systems is very high for a small-scale farmer. Subsidies or tax breaks can play an important role here, hence, upfront costs would be reduced and thus the blockchain solution could be afforded and be widely accepted by farmers.

8.6.3 Policies and Frameworks for Widespread Adoption

Successful large-scale blockchain solutions and innovation along supply chains in agriculture depend on clear policies and frameworks. Funding pilot projects or providing fiscal incentives, establishing specific legal guidelines by the state are just a few measures to be taken. Subsidizing IoT-enabled devices with blockchain integrations may serve as an example of accelerating rates for wide-scale adoption among smallholders. It will also help in institutional support for research and development to make the blockchain solution work practically in reality for agricultural purposes. The congregation of resources and expertise by a public-private partnership will further facilitate this process of innovation.

8.6.3.1 Standardization and Certification

International standards on the implementation of blockchain in agriculture are called for, ensuring that interoperability and trust exist. Such standards can be set for the protocols of data sharing, the design of smart contracts, and their integration into existing systems. Certification programs will validate blockchain solutions to ensure security and effectiveness for all stakeholders concerned. Awareness and capacity building among farmers, distributors, and other stakeholders form the bedrock for large-scale adoption. In fact, training programs and workshops can impart the participants with the use of blockchain systems. More user-friendly interfaces with the availability of contents in their local languages would also go a long way to facilitate easy access in blockchain solutions. Also, looking at the role-based decentralized system implementation, as depicted in Ganache blockchain, shows more can be done to help in this area. The current system designates raw material supplier, manufacturer, and retailer roles. Each participant's interaction with the product registration and placing of orders is recorded securely on the blockchain for more transparency and accountability.

Development could be done further to incorporate the role of transporters and quality checkers. The transporters can upload the GPS location on the blockchain, which will give real-time information about the product location. IoT-enabled tools in the hands of quality checkers can inspect the quality of products, whose assessments should be recorded on the blockchain. Dynamic role assignment, considering the capability of stakeholders for multiple roles, will also make the system more flexible and efficient. For instance, a farmer can also be a distributor, recording the cultivation and transportation data onto the blockchain.

References

1. Sharma, M., Al Khalil, A., Daim, T., Blockchain technology adoption: Multinational analysis of the agriculture supply chain. *IEEE Trans. Eng. Manage.*, 2022.
2. Raza, Z., Haq, I.U., Muneeb, M., Agri-4-all: A framework for blockchain-based agricultural food supply chains in the era of the fourth industrial revolution. *IEEE Access*, 11, 29851–29867, 2023.
3. Selvaprabhu, P., An examination of distributed and decentralized systems for trustworthy control of supply chains. *IEEE Access*, 11, 137025–137052, 2023.
4. Sharma, R., Kamble, S., Mani, V., Belhadi, A., An empirical investigation of the influence of Industry 4.0 technology capabilities on agriculture supply chain integration and sustainable performance. *IEEE Trans. Eng. Manage.*, 2022.
5. Ordóñez, J., Alexopoulos, A., Koutras, K., Kalogeras, A., Stefanidis, K., Martos, V., Blockchain in agriculture: A PESTELS analysis. *IEEE Access*, 2023.
6. Yu, H.F. and Mu, W.Z., ABE-based postquantum cross-blockchain data exchange approach for smart agriculture. *IEEE Trans. Ind. Inf.*, 2024.
7. Victor, N., MaddiKunta, P.K.R., Mary, D.R.K., Murugan, R., Chengoden, R., Gadekallu, T.R., Rakesh, N., Zhu, Y., Paek, J., Remote sensing for agriculture in the era of industry 5.0–A survey. *IEEE J. Sel. Top. Appl. Earth Obs. Remote Sens.*, 2024.
8. Ahmed, B., Shabbir, H., Naqvi, S.R., Peng, L., Smart agriculture: Current state, opportunities and challenges. *IEEE Access*, 2024.
9. Ahmed, A., Parveen, I., Abdullah, S., Ahmad, I., Alturki, N., Jamel, L., Optimized data fusion with scheduled rest periods for enhanced smart agriculture *via* blockchain integration. *IEEE Access*, 2024.
10. Omar, I.A., Jayaraman, R., Salah, K., Hasan, H.R., Antony, J., Omar, M., Blockchain-based approach for crop index insurance in agricultural supply chain. *IEEE Access*, 11, 118660–118675, 2023.
11. Chacko, N.M., Narendra, V.G., Balachandra, M., Rathinam, S., Exploring IoT-blockchain integration in agriculture: An experimental study. *IEEE Access*, 11, 130439–130450, 2023.
12. Latino, M.E., Menegoli, M., Corallo, A., Agriculture digitalization: A global examination based on bibliometric analysis. *IEEE Trans. Eng. Manage.*, 71, 1330–1345, 2022.
13. Hu, Z., Kim, B., Jeong, J., A study on mechanization, data, and insurance challenges for agriculture based on hyperledger fabric. *IEEE Access*, 2024.
14. Zheng, Q., Lin, N., Fu, D., Liu, T., Zhu, Y., Feng, X., Ruan, J., Smart-contract-based agricultural service platform for drone plant protection operation optimization. *IEEE Internet Things J.*, 10, 24, 21363–21376, 2023.
15. Mishra, R.A., Kalla, A., Braeken, A., Liyanage, M., Blockchain regulated verifiable and automatic key refreshment mechanism for IoT. *IEEE Access*, 11, 21758–21770, 2023.

9

Deep Learning-Based Supply-Chain Re-Traceability of Tea Leaves in a Permissioned Blockchain

Sandhya P.*, Ganesan R., Kalyanasundaram V., R. Srivats and Amogh Singh

School of Computer Science and Engineering, Vellore Institute of Technology, Chennai, India

Abstract

The global tea industry, renowned for its distinctive flavors and cultural significance, faces significant challenges such as adulteration and quality degradation, which compromise consumer trust and product integrity. High import tariffs and shipping costs further exacerbate these issues by making premium tea leaves and tea-based products expensive, creating a lucrative market for counterfeit and substandard goods. This study presents an advanced blockchain-based solution utilizing Hyperledger Fabric to address these issues by enhancing transparency and security within the tea leaves supply chain. The proposed system employs a permissioned blockchain ledger, which restricts access to certified participants, thus ensuring secure, end-to-end tracking from the plantation to the final retail product. By integrating decentralized storage through IPFS and using a deep learning (DL) model for real-time tea leaf quality assessment, the system mitigates risks of data manipulation and unauthorized access, thereby guaranteeing that only premium quality tea reaches the consumer.

The implemented Hyperledger Fabric system meticulously records all pivotal stages of the tea supply chain, including plantation registration, leaf picking, transportation, processing, and retail distribution. The integration of the deep

**Corresponding author*: sandhya.p@vit.ac.in; ORCID: 0000-0002-0078-180X
Ganesan R.: ORCID: 0000-0001-8059-7414
Kalyanasundaram V.: ORCID: 0009-0007-5737-6534
R. Srivats: ORCID: 0009-0001-5791-4255
Amogh Singh: ORCID: 0000-0001-8199-2176

Narayanan Ganesh and Kanak Kalita (eds.) Harvesting Data: Blockchain, AI and Advanced Innovations in Agriculture, (183–206) © 2026 Scrivener Publishing LLC

learning model for quality assessment and decentralized storage solutions ensures the authenticity and traceability of tea products. The results demonstrate significant enhancements in data integrity, accountability, and consumer trust, offering a scalable and robust framework adaptable to other agricultural products facing analogous supply chain challenges. This innovative approach not only safeguards the quality of tea leaves but also provides valuable insights into the broader application of blockchain technology in agriculture. The study makes a substantial contribution to the discourse on blockchain applications in sustainable tea supply chain management, offering valuable insights for policymakers, industry stakeholders, and tea producers.

***Keywords*:** Tea supply chain, blockchain, Hyperledger Fabric, deep learning, IPFS, tea leaf quality, traceability, smart contracts

9.1 Introduction

Tea is a cornerstone of global consumption, deeply embedded in the cultural and social fabric of numerous societies. The burgeoning international trade in tea leaves and tea-based products has been driven by advances in logistics and a heightened demand for premium-quality tea. Despite these improvements, the industry grapples with significant challenges, primarily related to the quality and authenticity of imported tea. Due to the substantial costs associated with import tariffs and shipping, consumers often face inflated prices for these products, which heightens the incentive for malpractices. Instances of adulteration and intentional contamination of tea leaves and products have become prevalent, undermining consumer trust and jeopardizing public health. Adulteration techniques include the deliberate use of harmful chemicals to artificially enhance the appearance of tea powder, which, while making the product more visually appealing, poses serious risks to consumer safety [1, 2].

The need for enhanced traceability and quality assurance in the tea supply chain has never been more critical. Traditional supply chain management systems often fall short in addressing issues of transparency and integrity, which are vital for maintaining product quality and safety. The adoption of advanced technological solutions has emerged as a promising approach to mitigating these challenges. By leveraging blockchain technology, particularly through a permissioned blockchain framework like Hyperledger Fabric, it is possible to establish a secure and transparent system for tracking tea products from their source to the final consumer. Such systems can significantly reduce the likelihood of adulteration and ensure that consumers receive authentic, high-quality products [3, 4].

This approach not only addresses the prevalent issues of product tampering and misrepresentation but also aligns with broader efforts to enhance sustainability and integrity in global supply chains.

In the context of tea supply chain management, blockchain technology offers a transformative solution by providing an immutable and decentralized ledger that enhances transparency and accountability. Traditional systems often struggle with information asymmetry and lack comprehensive oversight, which can result in significant gaps in traceability and security. Blockchain's decentralized nature ensures that all participants in the supply chain have access to the same data, reducing the potential for fraud and ensuring that each transaction is recorded and verifiable [3, 9]. This technological advancement allows for real-time monitoring and verification of tea products as they move through the supply chain, addressing the issues of counterfeit products and substandard quality.

Moreover, the integration of blockchain with Internet of Things (IoT) technology can further enhance the efficiency and reliability of supply chain operations. IoT devices can collect and transmit data on various aspects of tea production and transportation, such as environmental conditions and handling procedures, which can then be recorded on the blockchain [1, 6]. This combination of blockchain and IoT not only improves traceability but also facilitates proactive quality control and resource optimization. By implementing these technologies, the tea industry can move towards a more secure, transparent, and efficient supply chain that benefits both consumers and producers. This approach aligns with the broader goals of improving food safety, enhancing consumer trust, and supporting sustainable practices in global trade [10].

In addition to enhancing traceability and quality assurance, the application of blockchain technology in tea supply chains offers significant benefits for operational efficiency and cost reduction. Traditional supply chain management often involves multiple intermediaries and manual processes, which can introduce delays and increase the risk of errors. By automating these processes through smart contracts on a blockchain, stakeholders can streamline operations and reduce administrative overhead [2]. Smart contracts can automatically execute transactions and enforce compliance with predefined rules, eliminating the need for manual intervention and minimizing the potential for disputes.

The economic impact of implementing such a system is substantial. By reducing the incidence of fraud and ensuring that products meet quality standards, the blockchain-based solution can lead to greater consumer confidence and potentially higher sales. Additionally, the efficiencies gained from automating supply chain processes can result in cost savings for producers and suppliers, which can be passed on to consumers in the form of lower prices. This not only benefits the stakeholders within the supply chain but also contributes to a more equitable market environment [3, 8].

Traditional supply chain management approaches often fall short in providing the transparency and accountability necessary to maintain product quality and consumer safety. To overcome these limitations, integrating advanced technologies such as blockchain offers a promising solution. Blockchain technology, with its inherent attributes of immutability and transparency, provides a secure and reliable method for tracing tea products from their source to the final consumer. By implementing a permissioned blockchain system like Hyperledger Fabric, it is possible to create a transparent and tamper-resistant record of every transaction and movement in the supply chain. This system not only enhances the traceability of tea products but also supports regulatory compliance and promotes ethical practices across the industry [4].

The proposed blockchain system is designed to address several critical aspects of tea supply chain management. By leveraging the strengths of blockchain technology, the system offers a transformative approach to tracking, verifying, and managing tea products. Key benefits of this system include:

a. The system provides a public, immutable ledger that offers complete visibility into the tea supply chain. This transparency facilitates the identification of discrepancies, supports consumer trust, and ensures that every transaction is recorded in a tamper-resistant manner.
b. By enabling verification of product legitimacy at each stage of the supply chain, the system upholds legal and ethical standards, preventing fraudulent activities. The verifiable record of transactions and movements ensures compliance with established regulations and promotes responsible practices.
c. The real-time data and collaborative framework of the system enhance the ability to monitor tea-related activities, detect potential illegal practices, and support efficient regulatory enforcement. This integrated approach to data management fosters better oversight and coordination among stakeholders, improving overall supply chain integrity.

The proposed blockchain system fundamentally transforms transparency within the tea supply chain by providing an immutable and public ledger of every transaction and movement of tea products. Unlike traditional methods that often lack comprehensive visibility, this blockchain-based approach ensures that each step in the tea's journey, from cultivation and processing to distribution and retail, is meticulously documented. Each batch of tea is assigned a unique digital identifier, which is recorded in the blockchain as it progresses through various stages. This meticulous documentation not only guarantees that the origins and handling of the tea are traceable but also fortifies consumer confidence by providing clear, unalterable proof of authenticity.

The transparency enabled by this blockchain system addresses several critical issues inherent in conventional supply chains. By making the entire history of tea products accessible and verifiable, the system eliminates information asymmetry and enables stakeholders to spot any inconsistencies or anomalies in the supply chain. This visibility is instrumental in preventing and identifying instances of adulteration, fraud, or misrepresentation, thereby safeguarding the quality of tea products. Furthermore, the system's ability to publicly record each transaction ensures that any deviations from standard practices are immediately apparent, which helps uphold ethical and legal standards throughout the supply chain. This comprehensive level of transparency not only fosters trust among consumers but also holds all participants in the supply chain accountable, promoting a culture of integrity and reliability in the tea industry.

The blockchain system proposed for tea supply chain management introduces a robust mechanism for verifying the legitimacy of tea products at every stage of their journey. By utilizing a permissioned blockchain framework, the system ensures that all transactions and records are secure, transparent, and verifiable. Each tea batch is assigned a unique identifier that is linked to detailed information about its provenance, processing, and handling. This information is recorded in the blockchain and remains accessible to authorized stakeholders throughout the supply chain, providing a reliable means of validation for each product.

Verification is achieved through a series of smart contracts and consensus protocols that govern the recording and updating of data within the blockchain. These mechanisms ensure that only verified and authorized entries are made, and they enforce compliance with established quality and regulatory standards [2]. For instance, each stage of the supply chain—whether it involves cultivation, processing, or distribution—requires verification by authorized participants who must confirm the accuracy of the information before it is recorded. This process not only ensures the authenticity of the tea products but also helps to identify and address any discrepancies or fraudulent activities. By offering a clear and immutable record of each product's journey, the blockchain system significantly reduces the risk of counterfeiting and ensures that consumers receive genuine, high-quality tea. This enhanced verification process strengthens consumer trust and reinforces the integrity of the tea supply chain, making it a pivotal component of the proposed system.

The blockchain system revolutionizes monitoring and enforcement within the tea supply chain by offering a dynamic and transparent approach to oversight. Through its real-time data collection and analysis, the system continuously tracks the journey of tea products, ensuring that any anomalies or deviations from the established norms are swiftly identified. This ongoing surveillance is facilitated by a sophisticated network of sensors and digital records, which together create a comprehensive view of every stage in the tea's life cycle, from initial harvesting to final distribution.

By harnessing advanced analytical tools, the system processes and interprets data in real time, enabling stakeholders to detect potential issues such as unauthorized handling or discrepancies in labeling. Automated alerts are generated when irregularities are detected, prompting immediate investigation and resolution. This proactive approach minimizes the risk of non-compliance and maintains the integrity of the supply chain. Moreover, the blockchain system fosters enhanced collaboration among regulatory bodies, industry participants, and other relevant stakeholders through a unified data-sharing platform. This cooperative framework ensures that information flows seamlessly between parties, facilitating joint enforcement efforts and allowing for coordinated responses to any identified violations. The result is a more efficient regulatory process, with improved capacity for addressing and mitigating risks in a timely manner.

In essence, the integration of real-time monitoring with a collaborative enforcement mechanism ensures a robust and transparent system for managing the tea supply chain. This combination not only enhances the ability to oversee and control the entire process but also strengthens the overall regulatory environment, ultimately benefiting consumers and maintaining high standards in the tea industry.

To evaluate the proposed solution, the following sections will first review the existing literature on blockchain applications within supply chain management and the tea industry. This literature review will lay the groundwork for understanding the current research landscape and pinpoint the gaps that our blockchain-based system aims to address. Following the review, the paper will provide a comprehensive overview of the proposed blockchain framework, detailing its architecture, functionalities, and implementation specifics. Subsequent sections will analyze the performance of the system, assess its potential impact on the tea supply chain, and offer recommendations for future research.

The development of a blockchain-based framework for the tea supply chain marks a significant advancement in tackling issues such as adulteration and lack of transparency. By harnessing the capabilities of blockchain technology, this approach promises to improve traceability, ensure product authenticity, and enhance the overall integrity of the tea industry. The subsequent sections will explore the technical details of the proposed system and evaluate its potential to revolutionize tea supply chain management, thereby contributing to more reliable and transparent practices in the industry.

9.2 Literature Review

An IoT with blockchain product supply chain system is proposed in order to solve the problems with the traditional product supply chain (PSC) management systems [1]. The current systems lack quality control and are susceptible to counterfeiting. In order to solve these issues, the system consists of an IoT system which performs various tasks relating to the cultivation and distribution of the tea leaves including monitoring the environmental conditions of the plantation and tracking the distribution. The blockchain system that is imbibed into the system promotes transparency while also ensuring the integrity of the data that is stored on the blockchain. The system integrates the four aspects of the product supply chain, i.e., plantation, manufacturer, logistics, and the distributors. A fusion algorithm is also proposed in the work which uses multiple inputs from sensors in the environment to manage the conditions in the plantations.

Facing similar challenges with the classic product supply chain, a proposed work uses a Hyperledger fabric system to monitor the sourcing and distribution of tea powder [2]. Usage of the Hyperledger fabric allows the participants to monitor the tea powder from source to destination while keeping the data secure due to the property of permissioned blockchain. The system describes the smart contracts that are executed at each stage of the tea powder production which include the plantation, tea leaves processing and distribution. The details of the logistics and distribution are also recorded on the Hyperledger fabric system and the International Tea Committee (ITC) has the ability to review the quality of the tea leaves being harvested and approve any orders which are placed by suppliers.

A system to monitor and trace tea was implemented by combining multiple different technologies, which are IoT, blockchain, and Machine Learning [3]. The system uses RFID and GPS sensors during the plantation and picking process to accurately track multiple aspects which include the tea variety, planted time, picked time and quantity. As most of this data is sourced from an IoT-based system, the work also proposes an ensemble model which combines multiple machine learning models to assess the validity of the data before it is stored onto a block in the blockchain. The ensemble consists of AdaBoost, Gradient Boosted Decision Tree, XGBoost, and Random Forest and validates the authenticity of the data before it is stored onto a block. The proposed system demonstrates credibility, data authenticity, decentralization, data protection and other features which are shown to be lacking in other popular methods of logistics tracking.

A Hyperledger fabric system-based tea supply chain tracking is also explored using a different format for introducing traceability and better storage [4]. A single channel is used in the proposed system to store the changes and updates on. There are three participants in the given system which are the plantation, the factories involved in the processing, and the retailers. A custom certification authority is also involved along with the usage of InterPlanetary File System (IPFS) to store the data in. The blockchain in the Hyperledger system would store the hash values from the IPFS blocks that store the logistical data. This further secures the data while also allowing incremental updates on the IPFS system.

A similar system making use of the Hyperledger fabric for tracing tea in its supply chain makes use of a modified security algorithm to improve the data security [5]. The system is similar to the previous work as it uses a similar IPFS-Blockchain interface to store the data on. Apart from the IPFS with the blockchain, the system uses Elliptic Curve Digital Signature Algorithm (ECDSA) to verify the data. During the data entry from the plantation farms, the data is first verified using the ECDSA before it is stored on the IPFS and blockchain. During the shipping and transportation of the product during plucking, processing and retail, the details are constantly updated on the blockchain. As the end product, a traceable code is present on the product which can be used by the consumer to view in-depth information about the product while also allowing the customer to raise a complaint regarding the quality. Due to the induction of the blockchain system, in case of a complaint or quality issue, the members of the Hyperledger fabric can trace the product to the origins and make any required changes.

A similar implementation was pursued for performing a supply chain tracking using blockchain system for wood [6]. For performing the tracking of the wood, an RFID along with QR code or Barcode system is proposed where RFID is used in the initial stages of wood harvesting, transport, and storage. A QR code or barcode is included on the products once the wood is processed at a mill. The code on the product allows the customers to track the entire supply chain of the product they have received. The system is shown to prevent alterations in the transport of the wood by using a blockchain system to store the details about the wood. Using the RFID tags makes sure that the wood being used can only be entered into the blockchain system, therefore reducing the chances of a tree without a marking being processed and sold. The work also demonstrates a working prototype for the entire supply loop using an Android app and marking wood with RFID and QR codes to track them through the supply chain.

The description of a system that can be used for supply chain tracking is described along with the benefits that it possesses compared to the traditional supply chain systems [7]. The work describes a blockchain-based system to store information about the product in the supply chain. In order to improve the operability among the different individuals involved in the process, the work proposes the usage of private and public distributed ledgers. The private ledgers would be shared among the partners in the supply chain like the distributors, manufacturers and retailers and would contain information about the product location and its updates, which is confidential information. The public ledger would consist of information that can be revealed like the source of the product and the time it was manufactured. The public ledger would be accessible by the customer to view details about his product while the private ledger will improve the security and reduce chances of unauthorized modifications.

A system to ensure quality of organic food produce is proposed which makes use of blockchain to store and execute chaincode [8]. The system proposes a faster, online-based process compared to the traditional centralized paper-based process and makes use of a public ledger to ensure transparency and make sure anyone can access the data. In this system, the farmers can apply for a certification from the peer farmers which increases the reputation of the farmers on the network. A QR code is used with the products to track the product; the ownership of each of the products is updated on the blockchain as there is a change in real time. A prototype of the system is also implemented as part of the work.

Using blockchain, an alternate supply chain system for eggs has also been proposed which proposes transparent supply along with lower expenses for supply chain tracking [9]. The system makes use of the Internet of Things along with blockchain technologies. To ensure the quality of the eggs, the farms are continuously monitored using temperature, humidity and other environmental sensors in order to detect any discrepancy in the environmental factors. By storing the data on the blockchain, the integrity of the data is not compromised. The system consists of a multi-stage process where the farm supplying the eggs is first certified by the peers on the blockchain network. Once certified, the eggs are collected and moved to packing and then shipped to the stores with all the steps being monitored and updated on the ledger. The eggs are packed with a QR code on the outer packaging which can be scanned by the customer to access in-depth data about the eggs. The study also refers to works that signify the significance that quality products hold for the consumer and their willingness to pay extra price for better products.

In order to combat the food-safety issues that arise due to lack of quality control in the food production, transportation and storage, a blockchain ledger is used in the grain supply chain [10]. By introducing the blockchain system in the grain supply chain, the work aims to reduce the chances of tampering or lack of quality in the source of many food products as grains are essential items in the manufacturing of many food items. The system uses a blockchain system along with a decentralized database as a form of a multimode data storage system. Using the decentralized database increases the efficiency of the system to work with large volumes of data, acts as a reliable backup to the data stored in the blockchain, and also has a faster response time compared to the blockchain. The data in grain supply chains are collected with multiple sensors and RFID tags that are used. A prototype of the system was also implemented for a wheat supply chain and was able to demonstrate higher data security and better transparency compared to the traditional supply chain systems.

9.3 Proposed System

9.3.1 Architecture

In this work, we propose a Hyperledger Fabric–based supply chain tracking for tea leaves which provides the transparency and security; the permissioned access only allows certified participants to view and interact with the data. The proposed supply chain tracking can be easily integrated into the current system-in-place for tea leaves plantations and distribution. The plantation is first registered on the blockchain before the tea leaves from the plantation are picked and converted to a product. Once the plantation is registered and the location details are stored, the data relating to the tea leaves produced by the plantation are stored including the tea type, plantation ID and location. During the process, an image of the tea leaves is stored on the IPFS decentralized storage and used for inference with a deep learning model to assess the quality of the leaves. The hash generated by uploading the image to the IPFS storage and the deep learning model prediction is stored along with the other details on the blockchain. The deep learning model is useful for assessing the quality of the tea leaves before it is transported, and performing the inference during the image upload prevents any manipulation of the data when it is being entered into the blockchain.

The core of the system is based on Hyperledger Fabric, a permissioned blockchain technology that provides a secure and transparent environment for recording and managing supply chain data. Hyperledger Fabric's modular architecture allows for customization and scalability, making it well-suited for integration with existing tea supply chain systems. Hyperledger Fabric employs a permissioned blockchain network where participants are authenticated and authorized to access specific data relevant to their roles. This ensures that sensitive information, such as the provenance and quality of tea leaves, is protected from unauthorized access and tampering. The permissioned nature of the network also facilitates compliance with regulatory requirements and industry standards. Chaincode, or smart contracts, are implemented to automate and enforce the rules of data transactions within the blockchain. These smart contracts manage operations such as recording plantation details, updating tea leaf status, and verifying product quality. They are crucial for maintaining the integrity and consistency of data across the supply chain.

The blockchain ledger records immutable transactions and data interactions, ensuring that all entries are permanent and verifiable. Each transaction, such as the registration of a plantation or the updating of tea leaf status, is appended to the blockchain, creating a comprehensive and tamper-proof record of the supply chain journey. Tea leaf images are stored on IPFS, a decentralized storage network that provides secure and distributed file storage. IPFS is used to upload images of tea leaves, which are then hashed, and the hash is recorded on the blockchain. This approach ensures that images are stored in a tamper-proof manner and can be retrieved and verified at any time. The system utilizes a DenseNet201 model with a custom classification head for assessing the quality of tea leaves. This model is trained on a dataset of tea leaf images captured at various stages of aging [8]. Older leaves, which are of lower quality, are identified and distinguished from younger, higher-quality leaves. The model's predictions are used to generate a quality assessment that is recorded on the blockchain.

After the tea leaves are harvested, they are transported to a subsequent location, and this movement is meticulously recorded on the blockchain. Each transition in the supply chain is documented by updating the blockchain with detailed information, including the starting location, destination, type of tea, and the plantation identification number (ID). This comprehensive recording enables clear and transparent tracking of the product as it progresses from the plantation to various stages in the supply chain. When the tea leaves arrive at the distributor's facility, the blockchain is updated once again to reflect the current location of the product. This continuous updating ensures that stakeholders have access to the most current information about the tea leaves' whereabouts.

Figure 9.1 represents the architecture of the proposed hyperledger fabric–based tea supply chain system, illustrating how plantations, manufacturers, distributors, regulators, and consumers interact with the blockchain ledger. Any products manufactured from these tracked tea leaves will feature relevant tracking information on their packaging. Consumers can use this information to verify multiple aspects of the product, including its origins, the specific type of tea as reported by the plantation, the quality assessment derived from the deep learning model, and the complete location history of the tea leaves. This traceability is crucial for maintaining high-quality standards. By providing detailed and transparent information, the system significantly reduces the likelihood of substandard tea being used in product manufacturing. In the event that a customer detects a quality issue

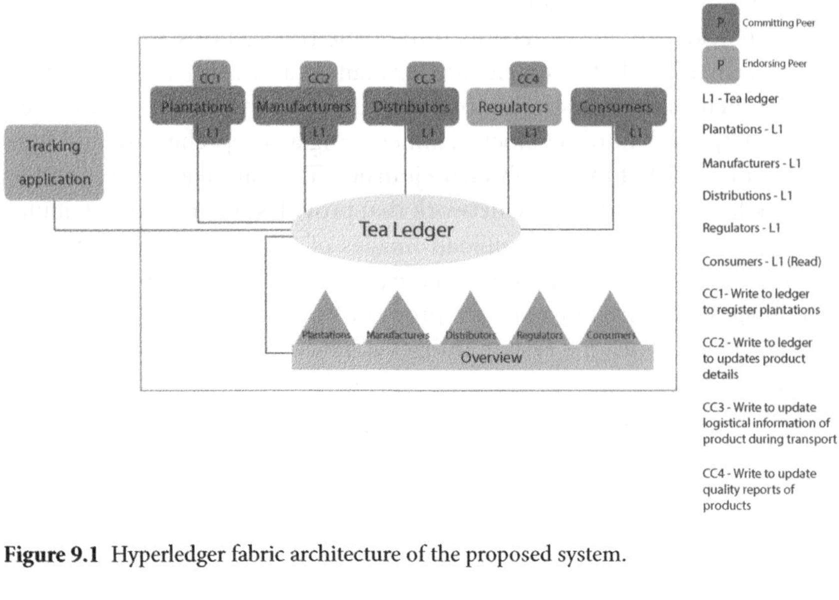

Figure 9.1 Hyperledger fabric architecture of the proposed system.

with a product or if problems arise during transit, the proposed system enables efficient tracing of the tea leaves' origins. This capability allows for swift and targeted interventions to address quality concerns and implement improvements in the supply chain, ensuring that only high-quality tea reaches consumers.

9.3.2 Working

The operation of the blockchain-based tea supply chain system involves a series of interrelated processes that collectively ensure the efficient tracking, quality assessment, and verification of tea leaves from cultivation to consumer. This section elucidates the operational workflow of the system. Figure 9.2 outlines the working of the blockchain-enabled tea leaves supply system with quality checks and logistics tracking integrated at every stage.

The initial step in the system's workflow is the registration of tea plantations. Each plantation is enrolled in the blockchain network, where it receives a unique identification code. Essential details about the plantation, including its geographic location, the type of tea produced, and cultivation practices, are entered into the blockchain ledger. This information serves as the foundation for tracking and verifying the tea leaves throughout their journey. Upon harvesting, tea leaves are meticulously documented. Key data points such as the plantation ID, the type of tea, and the harvest date are recorded on the blockchain. Additionally, high-resolution images of the tea leaves are captured and uploaded to the InterPlanetary File System (IPFS). These images, once stored on IPFS, are linked to the blockchain *via* their unique hash values. This linkage ensures that the visual evidence of the tea leaves' quality and origin is securely associated with the blockchain record, preventing data tampering.

The quality of the tea leaves is assessed using a DenseNet201 deep learning model. This model, trained on a comprehensive dataset of tea leaf images, evaluates the leaves' age and quality. Older leaves, which tend to have diminished quality and taste, are identified through the model's predictions. The results of this quality assessment are recorded on the blockchain, providing an immutable record of the tea's quality before it proceeds further in the supply chain. This step is crucial in ensuring that only high-quality tea leaves are processed and distributed. As tea leaves move through the supply chain, each transition—whether from plantation to processing facility or from processing facility to distributor—is recorded on the blockchain. The system captures details such as the start and end locations, transportation conditions, and any relevant status changes. Real-time updates ensure that the journey of the tea leaves is fully transparent and traceable, minimizing the risk of loss, theft, or fraud during transportation.

Once processed, tea products are integrated into the blockchain system with detailed tracking information. This information, including the origin of the tea leaves, quality assessment results, and transportation history, is included on the product's packaging. Consumers can access this data through a scan of a QR code or NFC tag on the packaging, allowing them to verify the authenticity and quality of the tea they purchase. This feature enhances consumer confidence by providing transparent and verifiable information about the product. The system continuously monitors the supply chain for any discrepancies or issues. If anomalies are detected—such as inconsistencies between recorded data and actual conditions—the system triggers alerts for investigation. The blockchain's immutable ledger provides a reliable record of all transactions and data changes, facilitating efficient issue resolution and ensuring compliance with quality standards.

Data security and integrity are paramount in the blockchain-based supply chain system. All information, from plantation details to quality assessments and transportation records, is encrypted and stored on a decentralized blockchain. This architecture ensures that data is secure from unauthorized access and tampering. The use of smart contracts and cryptographic methods further enhances the system's security, providing a robust framework for data management and protection. The system incorporates feedback mechanisms to continually improve its operations. Participants, including plantations, processors, distributors, and consumers, can provide feedback on the system's performance and suggest improvements. This feedback is used to refine processes, enhance functionality, and address any emerging challenges, ensuring the system remains effective and responsive to the needs of all stakeholders.

The deep learning model for tea quality assessment is trained using a dataset that is carefully divided into training and validation subsets, with an 80:20 ratio due to the limited dataset size. Initially, the model is loaded with pre-trained ImageNet weights, which are then fine-tuned by adjusting the pre-trained layers to be trainable, enabling the model to adapt to the specific characteristics of tea leaves. The training process employs the SparseCategoricalCrossEntropy loss function alongside the Adam optimizer, running for 50 epochs. To ensure robust performance and prevent overfitting, the model is validated on a separate validation split throughout the training period. The best-performing model weights are preserved using a Checkpoint mechanism. This comprehensive training and evaluation process ensures that the deep learning model effectively assesses tea quality, contributing to the overall reliability of the supply chain system.

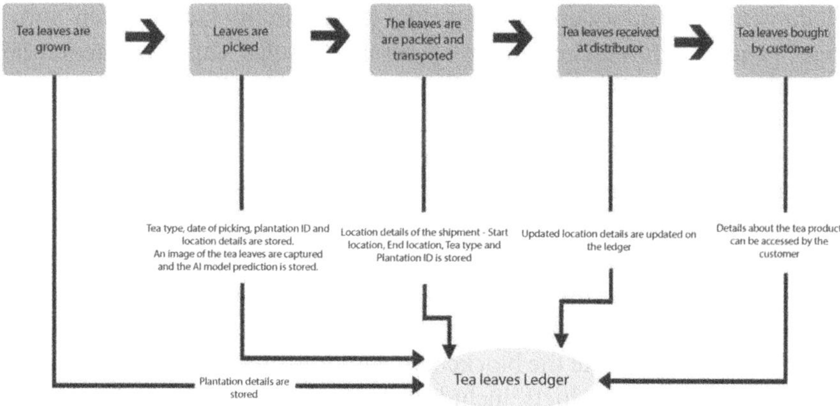

Figure 9.2 Working of the proposed system.

9.3.3 Participants

In the proposed blockchain-based tea supply chain system, various stakeholders play crucial roles in ensuring the integrity, transparency, and efficiency of the supply chain. Each participant contributes to the seamless flow of tea leaves from cultivation to consumption, with their interactions recorded on a secure, permissioned blockchain. The following sections provide a comprehensive overview of the key participants in this system, detailing their responsibilities, contributions, and how they integrate into the overall supply chain framework. By delineating the roles of each participant, we aim to highlight the collaborative efforts necessary to maintain high standards of quality, traceability, and accountability throughout the tea supply chain.

Tea plantation owners are integral to the supply chain, responsible for cultivating and harvesting tea leaves. They register their plantations on the blockchain, providing details such as plantation ID, geographical location, and the types of tea produced. This registration ensures that each batch of tea leaves can be traced back to its source, promoting transparency from the outset. Processing facilities manage the post-harvest stages of tea leaves, including drying, grinding, and packaging. They update the blockchain with information about processing stages, quality checks, and final product specifications. Recording these details ensures that the quality and handling of the tea are transparent and verifiable.

Tea manufacturers produce value-added products from raw tea leaves, such as packaged tea bags or loose-leaf blends. They are responsible for documenting product creation on the blockchain, including batch numbers, processing dates, and quality assurance results. This documentation provides consumers with detailed information about the products they purchase.

Logistics providers handle the transportation of tea products across various stages of the supply chain. They record transportation details on the blockchain, including start and end locations, transit conditions, and handling procedures. This transparency helps in tracking the movement of tea products and ensures they are transported under optimal conditions.

Distributors facilitate the movement of tea products from manufacturers to retailers. They update the blockchain with information about the receipt and distribution of products, including quantities received and dispatched. This helps maintain an accurate record of product flow and ensures transparency throughout the distribution process. Retailers sell tea products directly to consumers. They access blockchain records associated with the products they sell, providing consumers with detailed information about the tea's origin, quality, and traceability. This transparency builds consumer trust and ensures that retailers offer high-quality products.

Regulatory authorities oversee compliance with industry standards and regulations. They use blockchain records to review the entire supply chain, ensuring that participants adhere to legal and quality standards. These authorities can investigate complaints, conduct audits, and enforce corrective actions based on blockchain data. Quality assurance inspectors perform independent evaluations of tea products at various stages of the supply chain. They utilize blockchain records to verify product quality and compliance with standards. Inspectors report findings and discrepancies on the blockchain, contributing to the overall integrity of the supply chain.

Consumers are the end-users of tea products and play a crucial role in the supply chain by providing feedback and exercising their right to access product information. Through the blockchain, consumers can verify the authenticity of tea products, check their origins, and review quality assessments. The blockchain provides consumers with detailed information about the tea's journey from plantation to retail, including data on cultivation practices, processing, transportation, and quality assessments. This transparency allows consumers to make informed purchasing decisions and ensures that they receive high-quality, authentic tea products. Consumer feedback, recorded on the blockchain, also helps in identifying and addressing any issues or concerns related to product quality and supply chain practices.

9.3.4 Operations

The operational framework of the blockchain-based tea supply chain system is designed to ensure transparency, security, and efficiency throughout the life cycle of tea leaves. This section outlines the key processes involved in the system's operations, focusing on the registration, tracking, quality assessment, and data management aspects.

The operational journey begins with the registration of tea plantations on the blockchain. Each plantation is assigned a unique identifier, which is recorded along with detailed information about the location, size, and tea varieties cultivated. This information is securely stored on the blockchain to ensure transparency and traceability from the very beginning of the supply chain. The registration process is crucial as it establishes the foundation for tracking tea leaves throughout their journey. Once the tea leaves are harvested, data related to the tea's provenance, including plantation ID, type of tea, and the geographic location, is recorded on the blockchain. This data is supplemented with images of the tea leaves, which are uploaded to the InterPlanetary File System (IPFS) for decentralized storage. The use of IPFS ensures that the image data is securely stored and resistant to tampering. The image, along with its associated hash generated during the upload, is linked to the blockchain, providing a verifiable record of the tea leaves' quality and origin.

A critical component of the system's operations is the quality assessment of tea leaves using a DenseNet201 deep learning model. This model, trained on a dataset of tea leaf images, evaluates the age and quality of the leaves. Older leaves, which may degrade in quality and taste, are identified by the model, ensuring that only high-quality leaves are processed and distributed. The model's predictions are recorded on the blockchain, providing an immutable record of the quality assessment. As tea leaves move through the supply chain, from the plantation to processing facilities and distributors, each stage of the journey is recorded on the blockchain. Details of the start and end locations, transportation conditions, and any changes in the tea's status are updated in real time. This comprehensive tracking system ensures that the entire journey of the tea leaves is transparent and traceable, reducing the risk of misplacement, theft, or fraud.

Once processed, tea products are labeled with tracking information that includes the original plantation details, quality assessment results, and location history. This information is accessible to consumers *via* the product's packaging, allowing them to verify the authenticity and quality of the tea. The blockchain system ensures that all claims made on the packaging are supported by verifiable data, enhancing consumer trust and product integrity. Ongoing monitoring of the tea supply chain is facilitated by the blockchain's real-time data recording capabilities. Any discrepancies or anomalies detected during transit or processing are flagged and investigated. The system supports regulatory compliance by providing a transparent and auditable record of all activities within the supply chain. This proactive approach helps maintain high standards and addresses any issues promptly.

The blockchain system ensures that all data related to tea leaves, from plantation registration to quality assessments and tracking, is securely managed and protected from unauthorized access. The decentralized nature of the blockchain, combined with encryption and smart contracts, provides a robust framework for data integrity and security. This ensures that all participants in the supply chain can trust the accuracy and authenticity of the information recorded on the blockchain.

9.3.5 Advantages and Benefits

The proposed Hyperledger Fabric–based system for tea leaves supply chain management delivers significant advantages tailored to the specific needs of the tea industry. One of the primary benefits is the enhanced transparency and traceability it offers. By documenting every step of the tea leaves' journey from plantation through processing to distribution on an immutable blockchain ledger, the system provides a clear and verifiable trail of the product's origins and handling. This transparency ensures that consumers can access detailed information about the tea they purchase, including its quality assessment results and historical journey, thereby increasing their confidence in the authenticity and safety of the product.

In addition to transparency, the system markedly improves operational efficiency. The automation of data entry and transaction processing through smart contracts reduces the need for manual interventions and the potential for human error. By integrating blockchain with IoT technology, the system streamlines the tracking of tea leaves during transportation and processing. This reduces delays associated with traditional supply chain processes and minimizes the risk of errors or fraud. Automated updates to the blockchain ensure that all stakeholders, including plantation owners, distributors, and retailers, have access to real-time, accurate information, leading to a more efficient and responsive supply chain.

Moreover, the system enhances quality control and regulatory compliance. The integration of a deep learning model for tea leaf quality assessment ensures that only high-quality tea is recorded and tracked on the blockchain. This real-time quality evaluation prevents the introduction of sub-par tea into the supply chain, safeguarding consumer health and maintaining product standards. Additionally, the transparent and immutable records facilitate easier regulatory compliance and quicker response to quality issues or recalls. By providing detailed and tamper-proof data on each batch of tea, the system supports robust quality assurance practices and helps uphold industry standards, ultimately benefiting both consumers and producers.

9.4 Results/Discussion

A supply chain tracking system has been implemented using Hyperledger fabric and CouchDB for tracking the tea leaves and the products. The image is uploaded onto the IPFS blockchain-based storage system and the hash generated from the uploaded image is stored along with the other details in the Hyperledger Fabric. The data uploaded onto the ledger contains the plantation location, type of tea, date of collection, current location of the product along with the Deep Learning model output from the image input. Including these details allows for easy tracing of the product to its origins and includes the AI model prediction directly onto the ledger preventing any manipulation.

An image of the details as stored in the system is given in Figure 9.3.

For assessing the quality of the tea leaves from an image, a DenseNet201 model is trained on the Tea Leaf Age Quality dataset [11], which consists of

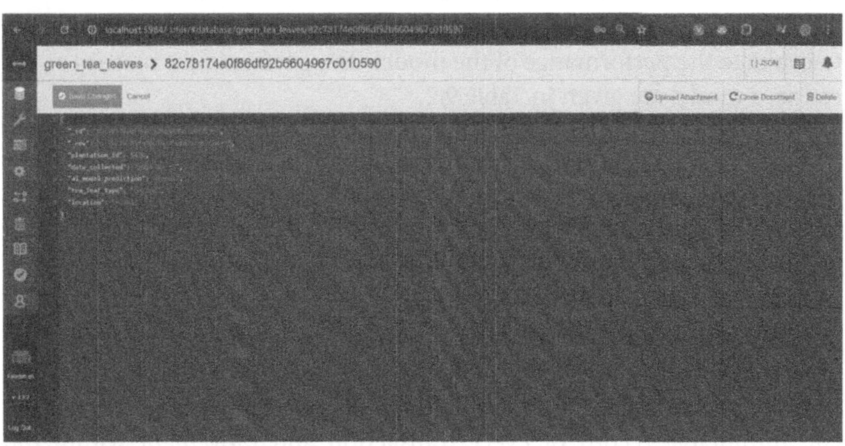

Figure 9.3 Details as stored in the hyperledger fabric.

Table 9.1 Hyperparameters for deep learning model.

Hyperparameter	Value
Optimizer	Adam
Loss Function	SparseCategoricalCrossEntropy
Batch Size	32
Max Epochs	50
Learning Rate	0.001

Table 9.2 Performance metrics of the deep learning model.

Dataset split	Accuracy	SparseCategoricalCrossEntropy loss
Train	92.7%	0.2235
Validation	78.0%	1.0367

images of tea leaves of different ages. The model is initially loaded with the ImageNet weights and is fine-tuned on the Tea Leaf Age Quality dataset [11]. The images are resized to a uniform size of (224,224,3) and are split into 80:20 for training and validation. The deep learning model is trained for 50 epochs using SparseCategoricalCrossEntropy for the loss function and the Adam algorithm for the optimizer. Further specifics of the hyperparameters are given in Table 9.1.

During training, a checkpoint is used which evaluates the model after each epoch on the validation dataset and saves the weights of the best performing model. These weights are then restored after training is completed to evaluate the performance of the model. The performance metrics of the restored model are given in Table 9.2.

9.5 Conclusion

This study has presented a comprehensive solution for enhancing transparency and security in the tea leaves supply chain through the integration of Hyperledger Fabric and advanced deep learning techniques. The proposed blockchain-based system effectively addresses critical challenges such as quality degradation and adulteration by establishing a transparent, immutable record of every transaction and movement within the supply chain. By implementing a permissioned blockchain framework, the system ensures that only certified participants can access and interact with the data, thereby safeguarding the integrity of the information. The integration of the IPFS decentralized storage and the DenseNet201 deep learning model further enhances the system's capability to accurately assess tea leaf quality, thereby preventing any manipulation and ensuring that only premium quality tea reaches the consumers.

The deep learning model demonstrated impressive performance, achieving an accuracy of 89.47% on the training set and 79.59% on the validation set, which underscores its effectiveness in predicting tea quality based on leaf images. This level of accuracy is pivotal in maintaining high standards in tea quality assessment and supports the broader goal of improving consumer trust and product integrity. The practical implementation of this system not only offers a robust framework for the tea industry but also provides valuable insights into the potential applications of blockchain and AI technologies in other agricultural sectors. The findings of this study contribute significantly to the advancement of supply chain management practices and offer a scalable solution to enhance the transparency and reliability of global trade in tea.

9.6 Future Work

While the proposed system significantly advances transparency and quality assessment in the tea supply chain, there are several avenues for future research and development that could further enhance its capabilities. One key area for improvement is the expansion of the deep learning model to handle a broader range of tea varieties and quality indicators. Incorporating additional features, such as texture analysis and chemical composition data, could enhance the model's accuracy and reliability in diverse conditions. Future work will focus on collecting a more extensive dataset that includes these additional variables to refine the quality assessment process.

Another important aspect is the scalability of the blockchain system. As the volume of transactions and data grows, ensuring the efficiency and performance of the Hyperledger Fabric network will be crucial. Future research could explore the integration of advanced consensus mechanisms or sidechains to improve transaction throughput and reduce latency. Additionally, investigating the use of hybrid blockchain solutions that combine public and permissioned blockchains could offer new opportunities for balancing transparency with privacy. Addressing potential bottlenecks and optimizing network architecture will be essential for maintaining system robustness as adoption scales.

Furthermore, user interface improvements and the development of intuitive visualization tools will be essential for enhancing the accessibility and usability of the system for end-users. Future efforts will aim to create user-friendly dashboards that provide real-time insights into the supply chain and facilitate easy access to quality and provenance information. Lastly, exploring the application of the proposed system's framework to other agricultural sectors could provide broader insights and benefits. By adapting the technology to different contexts, such as fruit and vegetable supply chains, the potential for widespread adoption and impact can be realized, driving further innovation in supply chain management.

References

1. Xu, X., Bao, X., Yi, H., Wu, J., Han, J., A Novel Resource-Saving and Traceable Tea Production and Supply Chain Based on Blockchain and IoT. *IEEE Access*, 11, 71873–71889, 2023, doi: 10.1109/ACCESS.2023.3295210.
2. Naveen, P., Manikandan, P., Maragatharajan, M., Ashok Kumar, S.R., Saravanan, M., Puviarasu, A., Traceability of Tea powder Supply Chain based on Hyperledger Fabric, in: *2022 3rd International Conference on Smart Electronics and Communication (ICOSEC)*, Trichy, India, pp. 303–307, 2022, doi: 10.1109/ICOSEC54921.2022.9952056.
3. Wu, Y., Jin, X., Yang, H., Tu, L., Ye, Y., Li, S., Blockchain-Based Internet of Things: Machine Learning Tea Sensing Trusted Traceability System. *J. Sens.*, 2022, 1, 8618230, 2022, doi: 10.1155/2022/8618230.
4. Chen, C.-L., Zhan, W.-B., Huang, D.-C., Liu, L.-C., Deng, Y.-Y., Kuo, C.-G., Hyperledger Fabric-Based Tea Supply Chain Production Data Traceable Scheme. *Sustainability*, 15, Art. no. 18, Jan. 2023, doi: 10.3390/su151813738.
5. Gupta, A.K. and Dwivedi, R.K., Security Enhancement in Tea Supply Chain using Blockchain with Hyperledger, in: *2024 2nd International Conference on Intelligent Data Communication Technologies and Internet of Things (IDCIoT)*, pp. 433–439, Jan. 2024, doi: 10.1109/IDCIoT59759.2024.10467817.
6. Figorilli, S., *et al.*, A Blockchain Implementation Prototype for the Electronic Open Source Traceability of Wood along the Whole Supply Chain. *Sensors*, 18, Art. no. 9, Sep. 2018, doi: 10.3390/s18093133.
7. Wu, H., Li, Z., King, B., Ben Miled, Z., Wassick, J., Tazelaar, J., A Distributed Ledger for Supply Chain Physical Distribution Visibility. *Information*, 8, Art. no. 4, Dec. 2017, doi: 10.3390/info8040137.

8. Basnayake, B.M.A.L. and Rajapakse, C., A Blockchain-based decentralized system to ensure the transparency of organic food supply chain, in: *2019 International Research Conference on Smart Computing and Systems Engineering (SCSE)*, pp. 103–107, Mar. 2019, doi: 10.23919/SCSE.2019.8842690.
9. Bumblauskas, D., Mann, A., Dugan, B., Rittmer, J., A blockchain use case in food distribution: Do you know where your food has been? *Int. J. Inf. Manage.*, 52, 102008, Jun. 2020, doi: 10.1016/j.ijinfomgt.2019.09.004.
10. Zhang, X., *et al.*, Blockchain-Based Safety Management System for the Grain Supply Chain. *IEEE Access*, 8, 36398–36410, 2020, doi: 10.1109/ACCESS.2020.2975415.
11. Kabir, M.M., Hafiz, M.S., Bandyopadhyaa, S., Jim, J.R., Mridha, M.F., Tea leaf age quality: Age-stratified tea leaf quality classification dataset. *Data Brief*, 54, 110462, Jun. 2024, doi: 10.1016/j.dib.2024.110462.

10

Prohibition of Illegal Movement of Sandalwood from Reserve Forests through Retracing Supply Chain on a Permissioned Blockchain

Sandhya P.*, Ganesan R., Rama Parvathy L., R. Srivats, Kalyanasundaram V. and Amogh Singh

School of Computer Science and Engineering, Vellore Institute of Technology, Chennai, India

Abstract
Sandalwood, highly esteemed for its aromatic qualities and cultural significance, represents a valuable commodity utilized in a diverse range of products, including perfumes, cosmetics, and artisanal crafts. The escalating demand for sandalwood has precipitated severe issues of illegal logging and smuggling, leading to significant depletion of this vital resource. In India, the primary sandalwood-producing regions of Karnataka and Tamil Nadu have experienced alarming increases in these illicit activities, with Tamil Nadu's sandalwood smuggling cases nearly tripling and Karnataka witnessing a more than sevenfold surge in recent years. Given the protracted growth cycle of sandalwood trees, which exceeds a decade, such unsustainable practices pose a grave threat to their long-term viability. To mitigate these challenges, our paper introduces an innovative blockchain-based framework designed to enhance transparency and traceability within the sandalwood supply chain. Our proposed system leverages blockchain technology to establish a tamper-resistant and transparent solution that integrates seamlessly with existing systems. Employing Hyperledger Fabric - a permissioned

**Corresponding author*: sandhya.p@vit.ac.in; ORCID: 0000-0002-0078-180X
Ganesan R.: ORCID: 0000-0001-8059-7414
Rama Parvathy L.: ORCID: 0000-0001-8645-254X
R. Srivats: ORCID: 0009-0001-5791-4255
Kalyanasundaram V.: ORCID: 0009-0007-5737-6534
Amogh Singh: ORCID: 0000-0001-8199-2176

Narayanan Ganesh and Kanak Kalita (eds.) Harvesting Data: Blockchain, AI and Advanced Innovations in Agriculture, (207–234) © 2026 Scrivener Publishing LLC

blockchain platform renowned for its robust security features and scalability, our system ensures meticulous tracking and monitoring of sandalwood from plantation through to the final product. Our system utilizes pre-existing identifiers assigned to sandalwood trees to facilitate detailed tracking across each stage of the supply chain: chopping, transportation, auction, processing, and retail. Key parameters are recorded at each stage, enabling precise traceability and prompt detection of discrepancies or tampering. This blockchain-based solution provides a robust and scalable framework to tackle the challenges of illegal sandalwood trade, improving transparency, accountability, and sustainability throughout the supply chain. The study makes a substantial contribution to the discourse on blockchain applications in sustainable forestry management, offering valuable insights for policymakers, industry stakeholders, and forestry professionals.

***Keywords*:** Sandalwood, blockchain, supply chain, hyperledger fabric, illegal logging, traceability, forestry management, RFID

10.1 Introduction

Sandalwood, renowned for its distinctive fragrance and significant cultural value, stands as one of the most coveted resources in both the commercial and artisanal markets. The aromatic properties of sandalwood make it a preferred ingredient in a diverse range of products, from luxury perfumes and soaps to traditional religious artifacts and decorative carvings. Its unique scent and enduring quality have made it an integral part of various cultural practices and ceremonies, amplifying its demand across global markets. Despite its esteemed status, sandalwood faces severe sustainability challenges due to rampant illegal logging and smuggling activities. The slow-growing nature of sandalwood trees, which typically require more than a decade to mature, exacerbates the sustainability crisis. Unlike many other tree species, sandalwood's prolonged growth period means that illegal harvesting not only depletes existing stocks but also hampers the replenishment of this valuable resource. Consequently, the depletion of sandalwood reserves presents a significant challenge to both the environment and the economy. The states of Karnataka and Tamil Nadu, which are responsible for approximately 90% of India's sandalwood production, have been particularly affected by the surge in illicit activities.

During the periods 1988-1989 and 1991-1992, Tamil Nadu experienced a dramatic increase in sandalwood smuggling incidents, with reported cases rising from 677 to 2,107—a near threefold increase within a span of just three years. Similarly, Karnataka saw a staggering rise in smuggling cases, with numbers escalating from 302 to 2,338 between the periods 1982-83 and 1990-91. This near eightfold increase over eight years highlights the severity and persistence of the issue [1]. Such exponential growth in illegal activities underscores the urgent need for a robust system capable of curbing these practices and ensuring the sustainable management of sandalwood resources.

The illegal sandalwood trade has far-reaching implications beyond mere resource depletion. It disrupts local ecosystems, leading to habitat loss and biodiversity decline [6]. The removal of mature sandalwood trees not only affects the environment but also undermines the livelihoods of communities dependent on sandalwood cultivation and harvesting. The financial losses incurred by legitimate businesses and the economic impact on rural economies are substantial, creating a ripple effect that extends far beyond the immediate stakeholders. Current regulatory and enforcement mechanisms have proven inadequate in addressing the scale of the problem [3]. Traditional approaches to monitoring and controlling sandalwood logging and trade are often hampered by inadequate resources, lack of coordination among agencies, and challenges in tracking the provenance of sandalwood products. The pervasive nature of illegal activities and the sophistication of smuggling networks further complicate efforts to enforce existing regulations effectively.

Given these challenges, there is an urgent need for an advanced system that strengthens visibility, tracking, and responsibility throughout the sandalwood supply chain. Blockchain technology presents a compelling solution by offering a decentralized and immutable ledger that can record and verify every transaction and movement of sandalwood. This technology promises to address the limitations of current systems by providing a transparent and tamper-resistant framework for tracking sandalwood from its source to the final consumer. Blockchain technology, especially platforms such as Hyperledger Fabric, provides notable benefits for supply chain management [9]. Hyperledger Fabric, a permissioned blockchain framework, is distinguished by its strong security measures, scalability, and adaptability. It enables the creation of a private and secure network where participants can access and validate transactions based on predefined permissions. This capability is essential for managing complex supply chains where sensitive information needs to be protected and verified.

In the sandalwood industry, a blockchain-based system can enable comprehensive traceability by assigning distinct identifiers to each tree and documenting critical data throughout its entire life cycle. This information encompasses aspects such as harvesting, transportation, processing, and retail stages. By capturing and storing this information on a blockchain, stakeholders can ensure that every piece of sandalwood can be traced back to its origin, thereby reducing the likelihood of illegal activities and enhancing the integrity of the supply chain.

The proposed blockchain system will address several critical aspects of sandalwood management. The proposed blockchain system represents a transformative approach to sandalwood management, addressing critical challenges in the supply chain through advanced technological integration. This system leverages the inherent strengths of blockchain technology to offer a comprehensive solution for tracking, verifying, and managing sandalwood from its source to the final consumer. The main advantages of this work are summarized as follows:

a. The system provides a public, immutable ledger that ensures complete visibility into the sandalwood supply chain, facilitating the identification of discrepancies and fostering consumer trust.
b. By enabling verification of product legitimacy at each stage of the supply chain, the system promotes adherence to legal and ethical standards and prevents fraudulent activities.
c. The system's real-time data and collaborative framework enhance the ability to monitor sandalwood activities, detect illegal practices, and support efficient regulatory enforcement.

Transparency is a core feature of the blockchain system. By establishing a public, immutable ledger, the system ensures that every transaction and movement of sandalwood is recorded in a way that is both transparent and tamper-resistant. Each sandalwood tree is assigned a unique identifier, which is used to track its journey through various stages: from harvesting to processing, transportation, and retail. This end-to-end traceability allows stakeholders to monitor the entire life cycle of the sandalwood, ensuring that it adheres to legal and ethical standards. The transparency provided by this blockchain ledger not only helps in verifying the authenticity of the products but also assists in identifying and addressing discrepancies in the supply chain. This openness is crucial for building consumer trust and for fostering accountability among all participants in the sandalwood industry.

Accountability is another significant advantage offered by the blockchain system. By providing a verifiable record of all transactions and movements, the system enables stakeholders to confirm the legitimacy of sandalwood products. This verification process is vital for ensuring that each step of the supply chain—whether it involves harvesting, processing, or retailing—complies with established regulations and standards. The blockchain system facilitates rigorous checks and balances, which help to prevent fraudulent activities and maintain adherence to environmental and legal guidelines. This enhanced accountability supports the integrity of the sandalwood industry and promotes responsible practices among businesses and other stakeholders.

Monitoring and enforcement capabilities are also substantially improved with the blockchain system. The real-time data provided by the system offers a comprehensive view of sandalwood activities, enabling more effective oversight and intervention. By integrating data from various stages of the supply chain, the system helps to detect and address illegal activities such as smuggling and unauthorized harvesting promptly. Moreover, the blockchain platform fosters collaboration among regulatory agencies, businesses, and other stakeholders, offering a unified approach to information sharing and coordination. This collaborative framework enhances the efficiency of regulatory processes and supports a more streamlined and effective enforcement mechanism. Real-time data and a collaborative framework will enhance the ability to monitor activities, detect illegal practices, and support regulatory enforcement [5, 6].

To evaluate the proposed solution, the next sections of this paper will explore the existing literature on blockchain applications in supply chain management and forestry. This review will provide a foundation for understanding the current state of research and identify gaps that the proposed system aims to address. Following the literature review, the paper will present a detailed overview of the blockchain-based system, including its architecture, functionalities, and implementation details. Subsequent sections will discuss the system's performance, potential impact, and recommendations for future research.

The development of a blockchain-based framework for sandalwood supply chain management represents a significant advancement in addressing the challenges of illegal logging and smuggling. By leveraging the capabilities of blockchain technology, this approach promises to enhance transparency, accountability, and sustainability in the sandalwood industry. The subsequent sections will delve into the technical aspects of the proposed system and assess its potential to transform sandalwood management practices, ultimately contributing to the preservation of this valuable resource.

10.2 Literature Review

While substantial research has been conducted on Hyperledger Fabric, comprehensive studies on Hyperledger Sawtooth are limited. Understanding the performance characteristics of different blockchain implementations is crucial for selecting the right platform for specific applications. Benchmarking tools like Hyperledger Caliper enable standardized performance testing across various blockchain platforms, providing insights into their transaction throughput, latency, resource utilization, and scalability. Hyperledger Caliper is a benchmarking tool that allows users to measure the performance of blockchain solutions with predefined use cases. It provides metrics such as transactions per second (TPS), transaction latency, and resource consumption. By using Caliper, researchers can perform a comparative analysis of different blockchain platforms under various workloads and configurations [9].

Blockchain technology, particularly through the Ethereum platform and the Solidity programming language, offers promising solutions for forest policy management by automating compliance checks, enhancing transparency, reducing administrative overhead, and improving data security. Smart contracts can enforce policies like the Clean Water Act (CWA) and the Sandalwood Act 2022 automatically, ensuring adherence to policy terms and creating a secure, decentralized record-keeping system. This approach addresses the challenges of traditional systems by providing immutable, transparent records and streamlining administrative processes, thus increasing efficiency and accountability in policy implementation and monitoring. Further research and case studies are needed to fully explore and validate these benefits [2].

This work introduces blockchain technology for electronic traceability in the wood supply chain, integrating product quality information with traceability data using Radio Frequency Identification (RFID) and an online system. By implementing a decentralized and distributed ledger, this approach ensures secure and transparent transactions without needing a centralized certifying authority. The system, based on RFID sensors and open-source technology, simulates the entire wood supply chain—from standing trees through cutting and sawmill processes to the final product—using IoT devices and a specialized app to collect and store data in a centralized database. This method enhances traceability and security in the forest wood supply chain [3].

Blockchain technology has garnered significant attention across various sectors, yet systematic studies on its applications in forestry are lacking. This paper systematically reviews existing literature on blockchain applications in forestry, categorizing findings into forest management, traceability of forest-based products, and forest fire detection. The review highlights the benefits, opportunities, and challenges of blockchain in sustainable forestry, illegal logging prevention, biodiversity conservation, and other areas. It also notes the technology's current immaturity and complexity. This study addresses a research gap and provides valuable insights for forestry managers, practitioners, and consultants, while suggesting future research directions for blockchain applications in forestry [4].

Tropical forests are vital for carbon storage, biodiversity, and ecosystem services, yet they are severely impacted by deforestation, contributing to 17% of global carbon emissions. Despite numerous efforts, illegal logging persists. This paper explores the potential of blockchain technology combined with the economic activities of forest communities to develop administrative methods for forest conservation. The proposed concept involves a blockchain-based contract management platform aimed at reducing illegal timber sales and logging, thereby helping mitigate climate change. This proposal is based on field research in forest communities in Brazil, India, and Thailand [5].

Blockchain technology offers a secure and transparent way to track and verify the origin and movement of forest products, addressing issues like illegal logging, deforestation, and label fraud. This study examines the potential of blockchain for certifying sustainable forest management and proving the legality of raw materials. Despite its infancy and challenges, such as data accuracy and stakeholder participation, blockchain holds significant promise for the timber supply chain, promoting sustainability and biodiversity preservation. The paper reviews blockchain technology, its requirements for forestry and timber industries, necessary digitization aspects, and existing applications [6].

Recent advancements in blockchain technology have sparked interest in decentralized data management solutions. Hyperledger Fabric, an IBM-backed open-source, permissioned blockchain platform, has evolved significantly from its initial release as Hyperledger Fabric v0.6 to its latest iteration, v1.0. Despite the proliferation of blockchain platforms, there remains a lack of standardized methodologies for evaluating their performance, security, and scalability. This study addresses this gap by conducting a comparative performance analysis of Hyperledger Fabric v0.6 and v1.0. The evaluation encompasses execution time, latency, and throughput, scaling up to 10,000 transactions across varying workloads. Additionally, scalability is assessed by increasing the node count to 20 nodes per platform. Findings indicate that Hyperledger Fabric v1.0 consistently outperforms v0.6 across all metrics, yet falls short of matching traditional database systems' performance under high workload conditions [7].

Hyperledger Fabric represents a groundbreaking advancement in blockchain technology, designed to support extensible distributed applications. Unlike traditional platforms, Fabric offers modular consensus protocols, enabling customization for specific use cases and trust models. Notably, it supports applications written in standard programming languages, rather than requiring domain-specific languages or cryptocurrency dependencies. Fabric's permissioned model integrates with industry-standard identity management, ensuring robust security and flexibility. Its innovative blockchain design addresses challenges like non-determinism and performance vulnerabilities, setting it apart from existing systems. This paper provides an in-depth exploration of Fabric's architecture, design rationale, implementation details, and its programming model for distributed applications. Additionally, performance evaluation through a Bitcoin-inspired digital currency implementation demonstrates Fabric's capability, achieving over 3,500 transactions per second with minimal latency and scalability to more than 100 peers [8].

In recent years, the adoption of permissioned blockchain platforms has grown significantly, with Hyperledger Fabric standing out as a prominent example under the Linux Foundation's Hyperledger umbrella. This paper conducts a comprehensive empirical study aimed at characterizing and optimizing the performance of Hyperledger Fabric, crucial for enterprise applications. The study follows a two-phase approach: initially exploring the impact of configuration parameters such as block size, endorsement policies, channels, and resource allocation on transaction throughput and latency. Key findings highlight significant bottlenecks including endorsement policy verification, sequential transaction validation within blocks, and state validation and commit processes with CouchDB. The second phase focuses on optimizing Hyperledger Fabric v1.0 based on these findings, introducing enhancements such as aggressive caching for endorsement policy verification, parallelizing verification processes, and leveraging bulk read/write optimizations for CouchDB. These optimizations collectively enhance throughput by 16 times, demonstrating substantial performance improvements from 140 transactions per second (tps) to 2250 tps [9].

Hyperledger Fabric, developed in collaboration by the Linux Foundation and IBM, stands as a leading open-source blockchain platform tailored for permissioned environments and widely applied across various industrial sectors. A distinctive feature of Fabric is its support for smart contracts, termed chaincode, which can be written in general-purpose languages like

Java, Go, and Node.js, differing from the domain-specific languages used in other platforms like Ethereum. This study delves into a detailed analysis of transaction performance within Fabric, focusing on factors that significantly impact latency, such as the choice of programming language for chaincode implementation and varying numbers of participating endorser peers. Through rigorous testing, the paper evaluates the performance overhead associated with different chaincode implementations. Findings indicate that Go emerges as the most efficient programming language in terms of transaction latency and overall performance metrics [10].

10.3 Proposed System

10.3.1 Architecture

The current system in place for sandalwood cultivation involves each tree, private or government owned, being registered with the forest department, and each tree is uniquely identified. The chopping of the sandalwood trees is also done only by an authorized forest officer who will be assigned for the task and requires an application to be filed by the owner in case of private ownership. In our proposed system, we make use of the existing identifiers of the sandalwood trees to track the product from plantation to finished product. The proposed system leverages blockchain technology to enhance the traceability, transparency, and security of the sandalwood supply chain. By implementing a decentralized and immutable ledger, this system addresses the challenges of illegal logging, smuggling, and sustainability within the sandalwood industry. Utilizing existing identifiers for sandalwood trees, the system ensures comprehensive tracking from plantation to finished product, integrating seamlessly with current practices. The use of blockchain technology ensures that all transactions and data entries are secure, tamper-proof, and accessible to all authorized stakeholders, providing an unprecedented level of transparency and accountability in the sandalwood supply chain.

The architecture of the proposed system is designed to provide a robust and scalable framework for tracking sandalwood from its source to the final consumer. It consists of a data collection layer, a blockchain layer, and an application layer. The data collection layer employs IoT devices such as RFID sensors and NFC tags to capture real-time data on sandalwood trees and products. The blockchain layer utilizes a permissioned blockchain platform, such as Hyperledger Fabric, to securely store and manage the data. The application layer provides user interfaces and APIs for stakeholders to interact with the system, including mobile and web applications for data access and management. This layered architecture ensures that the system can handle large volumes of data efficiently, maintain high security standards, and provide user-friendly interfaces for various stakeholders.

The data collection layer forms the foundation of the proposed system by employing IoT (Internet of Things) devices to gather real-time data throughout the supply chain. This layer includes RFID (Radio Frequency Identification) sensors and NFC (Near Field Communication) tags, which are attached to sandalwood trees and products. These devices capture critical information such as tree identifiers, volume of wood, location, and time stamps at various stages of the supply chain. The RFID sensors are strategically placed to monitor the status and movement of sandalwood from the point of harvest to the final product stage. NFC tags, being user-friendly and cost-effective, are used for easy scanning and data retrieval by authorized personnel. This real-time data collection is essential for maintaining an accurate and up-to-date record of each sandalwood product's journey through the supply chain.

At the core of the proposed system is the blockchain layer, which ensures the security and immutability of the data collected. This layer utilizes Hyperledger Fabric, a permissioned blockchain platform known for its modularity and high security standards. Hyperledger Fabric is selected due to its ability to handle complex transactions, support for private and confidential transactions, and integration with existing enterprise systems. In the blockchain layer, all data collected by the IoT devices is securely stored and managed. Each transaction, whether it involves harvesting, transportation, processing, or retail, is recorded on the blockchain, creating an immutable ledger of events. This decentralized and distributed ledger ensures that all participants in the supply chain have access to the same information, reducing the risk of data tampering and fraud. Smart contracts, known as chaincode in Hyperledger Fabric, are implemented to automate various processes within the supply chain. These smart contracts enforce rules and regulations, such as compliance with legal requirements for sandalwood harvesting and transportation, ensuring that all activities are conducted transparently and lawfully. For instance, the smart contract can verify that only authorized forest officers are permitted to chop the sandalwood trees, and all necessary documentation is filed before the action is performed.

The application layer provides the interfaces and tools necessary for stakeholders to interact with the system. This layer includes mobile and web applications, as well as APIs (Application Programming Interfaces) that facilitate data access and management. The user interfaces are designed to be intuitive and user-friendly, enabling stakeholders such as forest officers, transporters, processors, and retailers to efficiently input and retrieve data. The application, for example, allows forest officers to scan RFID tags on sandalwood trees, input data about the volume cut, and record the location and time of the activity. Transporters can use the application to log start and end locations, volumes, and weights of wood being transported. Retailers can verify the authenticity and origin of the sandalwood products by scanning NFC tags, providing customers with transparent information about the product's journey from plantation to store.

The application layer also includes dashboards and reporting tools that provide real-time insights into the supply chain. These tools enable stakeholders to monitor the status of sandalwood products, detect any anomalies or irregularities, and make informed decisions. For instance, a sudden drop in the recorded volume of wood at any stage can trigger an alert, prompting an investigation to ensure there has been no unauthorized tampering.

In the supply chain, the sandalwood goes through multiple stages of cutting, transportation, auction, milling, carving/processing and sale.

Table 10.1 Details recorded in the blockchain.

Stage	Details recorded
Chopping	ID of tree Volume Cut Remaining volume of wood Location Date cut Officer in charge of chopping
Transportation	ID of tree Volume/weight of wood Start location End location
Auction	ID of tree Volume/weight of wood Price
Processing/Milling	ID of parent tree for each sub-part Weight of sub-part
Retail	ID of parent tree Weight of product

The identifiers of the sandalwood tree are used in the proposed system to track the product through the entire chain while also being difficult to tamper. At various stages, different parameters are recorded and further details about the details are given in Table 10.1.

The proposed system is designed to integrate seamlessly with existing enterprise systems and databases, ensuring interoperability and ease of adoption. By recording these parameters, each product can be traced back to its origins with minimal effort and by tracking the volume/weight parameter, any tampering or modification in the data can be easily detected. Hyperledger Fabric's modular architecture allows for customization and integration with other blockchain networks, IoT platforms, and enterprise resource planning (ERP) systems. This interoperability is crucial for creating a unified and cohesive supply chain management solution that can adapt to the unique requirements of different stakeholders and jurisdictions. Security and privacy are paramount in the proposed system. Hyperledger Fabric's permissioned model ensures that only authorized participants can access and contribute to the blockchain. Data encryption, access controls, and audit logs are implemented to protect sensitive information and ensure compliance with privacy regulations. Furthermore, the system is designed to resist cyberattacks and unauthorized access, providing a secure environment for all transactions and data exchanges. The overview of the architecture of the system is described in Figure 10.1.

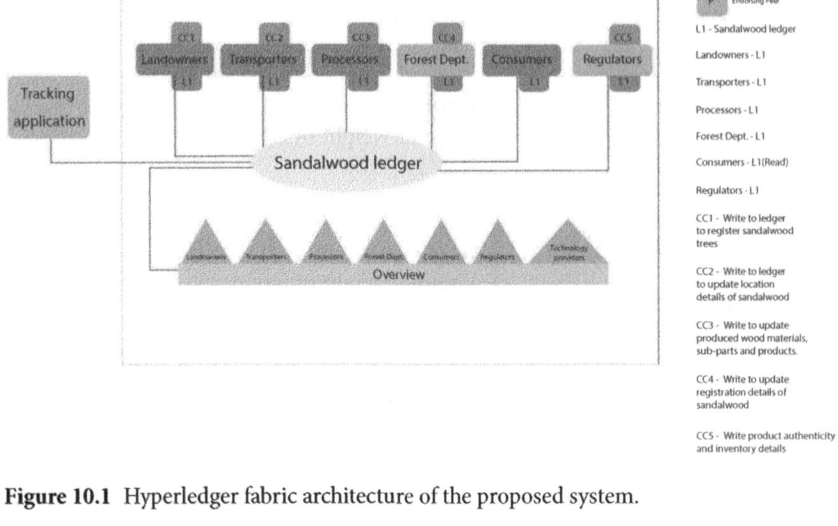

Figure 10.1 Hyperledger fabric architecture of the proposed system.

10.3.2 Working

Figure 10.2 shows the working of the proposed system. The first step in system implementation is the integration of hardware components, primarily RFID sensors and NFC tags. RFID sensors are embedded in or attached to the sandalwood trees and products to track their movement and status

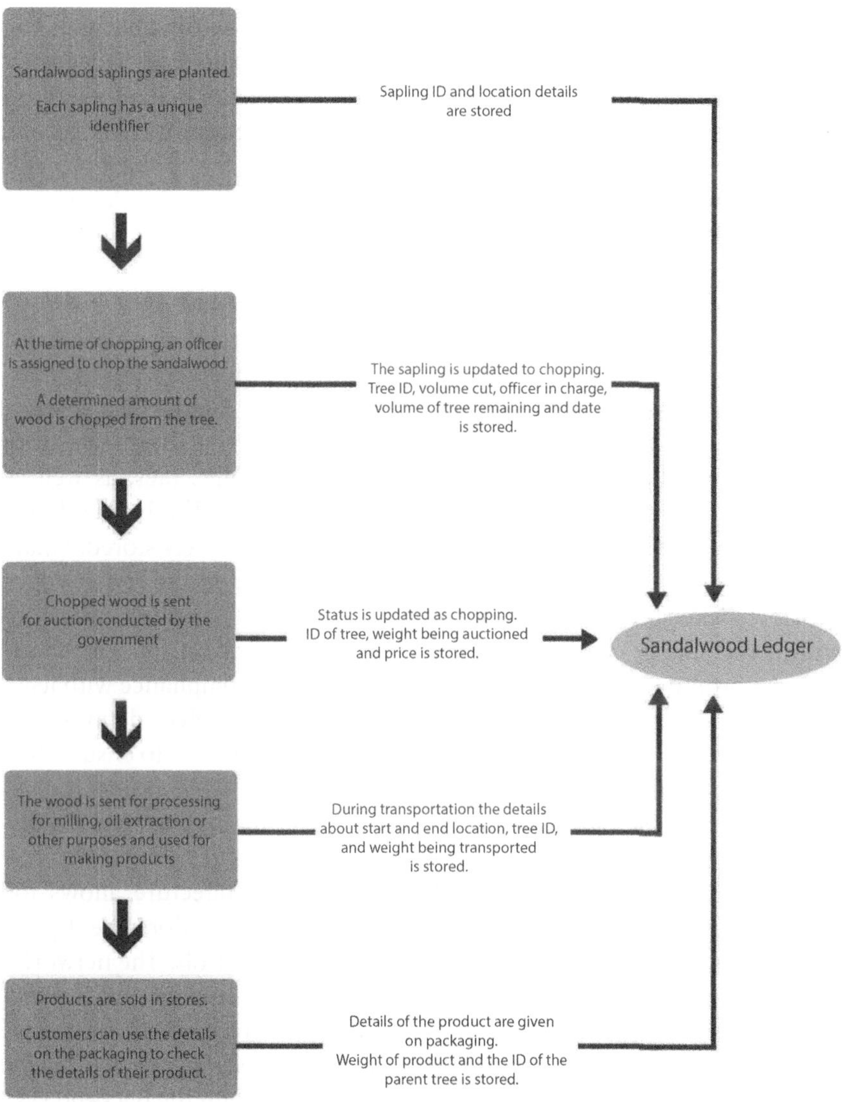

Figure 10.2 Working of the proposed system.

throughout the supply chain. Each sensor is equipped with a unique identifier that links to a database record containing detailed information about the tree, including its origin, volume, and any associated legal documentation. NFC tags are used for easy scanning and data retrieval at various stages of the supply chain. These tags are designed to be durable and tamper-resistant, ensuring that the data they store remains accurate and secure. NFC-enabled devices, such as smartphones and specialized scanners, are used by stakeholders to access information encoded in the tags. The installation of these hardware components is carefully coordinated with the stakeholders involved, including forest officers, transporters, processors, and retailers. Training sessions are conducted to ensure that all users are familiar with the hardware and understand how to operate it effectively.

The software development phase involves creating the applications and tools necessary for interacting with the system. This includes developing mobile and web applications that provide user-friendly interfaces for data input and retrieval. The mobile application is designed to be intuitive, allowing users to scan RFID sensors and NFC tags, input data, and generate reports. The web application provides a comprehensive dashboard for monitoring the supply chain, analyzing data, and generating insights. The software also includes the backend systems that handle data storage, processing, and management. This involves setting up databases that store information collected from the RFID sensors and NFC tags, as well as integrating these databases with the blockchain layer. The backend system ensures that all data is accurately recorded and securely stored. Smart contracts, or chaincode, are developed and deployed on the Hyperledger Fabric blockchain. These smart contracts automate various processes within the supply chain, such as verifying authorization for tree chopping, recording transportation details, and ensuring compliance with legal requirements. The development of smart contracts involves defining the rules and logic that govern these processes and testing them to ensure they function correctly.

Configuring the blockchain layer involves setting up the Hyperledger Fabric network, defining the network's architecture, and configuring consensus protocols. Hyperledger Fabric's modular architecture allows for customization to meet specific needs, such as defining endorsement policies, configuring channels, and establishing access controls. The network's architecture is designed to include multiple peers, orderers, and certificate authorities, ensuring a secure and scalable environment for transaction processing. The configuration also includes setting up the ledger and chaincode, as well as integrating the blockchain with the backend systems and applications. Consensus protocols are configured to ensure that transactions are validated and recorded accurately. Hyperledger Fabric supports various consensus mechanisms, and the choice of protocol is based on factors such as transaction volume, network size, and performance requirements.

Developing the user interfaces is a crucial part of system implementation. The mobile and web applications are designed to provide an intuitive and seamless user experience. The mobile application allows users to interact with RFID sensors and NFC tags, input data, and access information about sandalwood products. Features such as barcode scanning, real-time notifications, and data validation are incorporated to enhance usability and efficiency. The web application provides a comprehensive dashboard that displays real-time data and analytics. It includes features for monitoring the supply chain, generating reports, and analyzing trends. The dashboard is designed to be visually appealing and easy to navigate, with customizable views and data visualization tools. Training and support materials are developed to assist users in understanding and utilizing the applications. This includes user manuals, video tutorials, and helpdesk support to address any issues or questions that may arise.

Thorough testing and validation are essential to ensure that the system operates correctly and meets performance standards. This phase involves several types of testing, including unit testing, integration testing, and system testing. Each component of the system, such as RFID sensors, NFC tags, and smart contracts, is tested individually to ensure it functions as expected. This includes verifying that the sensors accurately capture and transmit data and that the smart contracts execute the correct logic. The integration of hardware and software components is also tested to ensure that they work together seamlessly. This includes verifying that data collected by RFID sensors and NFC tags is accurately recorded in the blockchain and accessible through the applications. The entire system is finally tested as a whole to ensure that all components work together effectively. This includes testing the system's performance under various conditions, such as high transaction volumes and network failures, to ensure reliability and scalability. User acceptance testing (UAT) is conducted to ensure that the system meets the needs and expectations of stakeholders. Feedback from users is collected and analyzed to make any necessary adjustments or improvements.

Once testing is complete, the system is deployed in a production environment. This involves installing the hardware components, deploying the software applications, and configuring the blockchain network. A phased rollout approach may be used to ensure a smooth transition and minimize disruption to existing operations. Ongoing maintenance and support are provided to ensure the system remains operational and up-to-date. This includes monitoring system performance, addressing any issues or bugs, and implementing updates or enhancements as needed. Regular audits and reviews are conducted to ensure the system continues to meet its objectives and comply with regulatory requirements.

10.3.3 Participants

The implementation of the proposed sandalwood supply chain tracking system is a comprehensive process that involves hardware integration, software development, blockchain configuration, user interface design, and thorough testing. By following a structured approach and focusing on key aspects such as security, usability, and performance, the system is designed to enhance traceability, transparency, and efficiency throughout the sandalwood supply chain. The successful implementation and operation of the proposed sandalwood supply chain tracking system hinge on the active participation and collaboration of various stakeholders. Each participant plays a crucial role in ensuring the system's effectiveness, from initial deployment to ongoing maintenance. This section outlines the key participants involved in the system and their respective responsibilities.

The Forest Department stands as a pivotal entity in the management of sandalwood cultivation and tracking. This department oversees the registration process for sandalwood trees, assigning unique identifiers to each tree, whether situated on private or government land. This registration process is crucial, as it forms the foundation upon which the tracking system is built. The department is also responsible for authorizing the cutting of sandalwood trees, a task that is strictly regulated. Only designated forest officers are permitted to oversee the chopping process, ensuring that it is carried out according to legal and environmental standards. The Forest Department also plays a significant role in monitoring and ensuring compliance with the tracking system, providing oversight to ensure that all procedures align with regulatory requirements.

Private landowners, who manage their own sandalwood plantations, are integral to the tracking system's operation. These landowners are required to register their sandalwood trees with the Forest Department, ensuring that each tree is tagged with an RFID sensor or NFC tag for tracking purposes. Throughout the various stages of the supply chain, landowners are responsible for accurately recording and reporting data related to the volume and location of the sandalwood wood. Compliance with regulations and the proper use of the tracking system are essential responsibilities for private landowners, as they contribute to the overall transparency and traceability of the sandalwood supply chain.

Transporters are key players in the movement of sandalwood from one stage of the supply chain to the next. Their role encompasses the secure and accurate transportation of sandalwood, with a strong emphasis on maintaining data integrity. Transporters are tasked with recording detailed information regarding the movement of sandalwood, including its weight or volume and the start and end locations of each transit phase. The use of NFC-enabled devices allows transporters to update the status of the sandalwood in real time, ensuring that the blockchain ledger reflects the most current and accurate information. In addition to data recording, transporters must ensure the security of the sandalwood during transit, preventing tampering or loss.

Processors and millers are involved in the transformation of raw sandalwood into finished products. At this stage, detailed records are maintained regarding the processing activities, including the identification of the parent tree for each sub-part, the weight of each sub-part, and any specific processing activities performed. This information is crucial for maintaining the integrity of the tracking system, as it ensures that the processed wood can be traced back to its origin. Processors and millers must also adhere to quality assurance protocols, ensuring that the sandalwood meets the required standards. By updating the tracking system with processing details, they help maintain an accurate and comprehensive record of the sandalwood's journey through the supply chain.

Retailers are the final link in the sandalwood supply chain, interacting directly with consumers. They are responsible for providing transparent and accurate information about the origin and quality of the sandalwood products they sell. Retailers use the tracking system to verify the authenticity of the products, ensuring that customers have access to reliable information regarding the provenance of their purchases. Additionally, retailers maintain records of sales and inventory, ensuring that these records are synchronized with the blockchain ledger to reflect accurate stock levels and transaction details.

Technology providers play a crucial role in the development and maintenance of the tracking system. They are responsible for creating and implementing the software applications, blockchain protocols, and user interfaces necessary for the system's operation. Technology providers also supply and maintain the hardware components, such as RFID sensors and NFC tags, ensuring their functionality and performance. Their support extends to providing technical assistance and training for users, addressing any issues that arise, and ensuring that all stakeholders are proficient in utilizing the system.

Regulatory authorities oversee the legal and compliance aspects of the sandalwood supply chain. Their role involves ensuring that all participants adhere to relevant regulations and standards. Regulatory authorities conduct audits to verify the accuracy of the data recorded in the tracking system and review reports to ensure that the system meets legal requirements. They are also involved in developing and updating policies related to the sandalwood industry, aligning them with technological advancements and industry needs.

Consumers, as the end-users of sandalwood products, benefit from the transparency provided by the tracking system. They are empowered to make informed purchasing decisions based on detailed information about the product's origin and quality. Consumers can also provide feedback on the products and report any discrepancies or concerns regarding the tracking information, contributing to the overall integrity and effectiveness of the supply chain. Therefore, the participants in the sandalwood supply chain tracking system each play a vital role in ensuring its success. Every participant contributes to the system's integrity, transparency, and efficiency.

10.3.4 Operations

The operations of the proposed sandalwood supply chain tracking system hinge on the effective implementation and management of smart contracts, which are pivotal for automating processes and ensuring data integrity throughout the supply chain. These smart contracts are designed to facilitate, verify, and enforce the terms of transactions and activities associated with the cultivation, processing, and sale of sandalwood. The following outlines the key smart contracts involved in the system and their functions.

The **Tree Registration and Identification Contract** is fundamental to the system, establishing the initial registry of sandalwood trees. Upon the planting of a sandalwood tree, this contract records essential details, including the tree's unique identifier (such as an RFID tag or NFC chip), location, ownership status, and the date of registration. This contract ensures that each tree is uniquely tracked from its inception, providing a comprehensive record that facilitates subsequent tracking and verification processes. The contract automates the assignment of identifiers and updates the registry with real-time information, ensuring that any changes in tree status or ownership are accurately reflected.

The **Chopping Authorization Contract** governs the authorization process for the cutting of sandalwood trees. It specifies the requirements for obtaining permission to chop a tree, including the need for an application from the owner, approval by a designated forest officer, and adherence to legal and environmental standards. This contract automates the approval process, ensuring that only authorized personnel can approve and record the cutting of trees. By integrating with the Tree Registration and Identification Contract, it updates the tree's status and logs details such as the volume of wood cut, the location of cutting, and the date, ensuring accurate and tamper-proof records.

The **Transportation and Transfer Contract** manages the logistics of moving sandalwood from one stage to another within the supply chain. This contract records critical details such as the start and end locations, the volume or weight of the sandalwood being transported, and the identification of the transporter. It also ensures that any changes in the status of the sandalwood during transit are recorded in real time. By using NFC-enabled devices and blockchain integration, the contract facilitates seamless and accurate updates to the ledger, reducing the risk of data tampering and ensuring transparency throughout the transportation phase.

The **Auction Contract** oversees the auction process for sandalwood, managing bids, sales, and price records. It automates the auction process, ensuring that bids are placed, recorded, and updated in a transparent and fair manner. The contract verifies the identity of participants, records the winning bid, and updates the transaction details to reflect the final sale price and the identity of the buyer. By integrating with other contracts, it ensures that all auction-related data is accurately recorded and accessible, providing a clear audit trail for all transactions.

The **Processing and Milling Contract** manages the conversion of raw sandalwood into processed products. This contract tracks the transformation of the wood, recording details such as the identification of the parent tree for each sub-part, the weight of the processed sub-parts, and the specific processing activities performed. It ensures that all processing activities are logged accurately, maintaining a clear link between the original tree and the final products. By automating the recording of processing details, the contract helps to maintain the integrity of the tracking system and ensures that all processed products can be traced back to their origins.

The **Retail Sales Contract** governs the sale of sandalwood products to consumers. It records details such as the identification of the product, its weight, and the sale price. This contract ensures that all retail transactions are accurately recorded and that consumers have access to reliable information about the provenance and quality of their purchases. By integrating with the Processing and Milling Contract, it verifies the authenticity of the products and provides a transparent record of sales, enhancing consumer trust and confidence in the tracking system.

The **Compliance and Audit Contract** ensures that all participants in the supply chain adhere to regulatory requirements and system protocols. It automates the auditing process, verifying that all data recorded by other contracts is accurate and compliant with legal standards. The contract generates audit reports, flags discrepancies, and facilitates corrective actions if needed. It plays a crucial role in maintaining the overall integrity of the tracking system, providing oversight and ensuring that all activities are conducted in accordance with established regulations.

The **Dispute Resolution Contract** addresses any conflicts or disputes that may arise between participants in the supply chain. It provides a framework for resolving issues related to transactions, data discrepancies, or contractual obligations. The contract outlines the procedures for submitting and adjudicating disputes, ensuring that conflicts are resolved fairly and efficiently. By incorporating a structured dispute resolution mechanism, it helps to maintain the smooth operation of the supply chain and ensures that any issues are addressed promptly.

10.3.5 Advantages and Benefits

The proposed sandalwood supply chain tracking system offers several significant advantages, driven by its integration of blockchain technology and IoT devices. The primary benefit of the system is its enhanced traceability. By utilizing existing identifiers such as RFID sensors and NFC tags, the system provides comprehensive tracking of sandalwood from plantation through to the finished product. This thorough documentation ensures that every stage of the supply chain is recorded, allowing stakeholders to verify the origin and authenticity of the sandalwood. Real-time data collection further supports traceability by capturing information at various stages and updating the blockchain ledger instantaneously. This ensures that all participants have access to the most current data, maintaining the integrity of the supply chain.

In addition to traceability, the system enhances transparency. The use of blockchain technology provides an immutable ledger where all transactions and data entries are securely recorded. This means that once information is entered into the blockchain, it cannot be altered or tampered with, promoting a high level of transparency across the supply chain. The permissioned blockchain model ensures that only authorized stakeholders can access and contribute to the ledger, safeguarding sensitive information while maintaining openness for legitimate participants. Detailed record-keeping at each supply chain stage, from chopping to retailing, offers a transparent view of all activities, further supporting the system's transparency.

The system also significantly improves security. The blockchain's tamper-proof nature ensures that data recorded in the ledger remains intact and secure from manipulation. Smart contracts, which automate and enforce compliance with regulations, add another layer of security by verifying the legitimacy of activities such as tree chopping and transportation. Additionally, data encryption and access controls protect sensitive information from unauthorized access, ensuring that only designated participants can view or modify data.

Efficiency is another key advantage of the proposed system. The integration of RFID sensors and NFC tags with blockchain technology streamlines supply chain processes by automating data collection and entry. This reduces the need for manual record-keeping and minimizes errors, thereby enhancing overall operational efficiency. Real-time updates facilitated by the system allow for immediate information dissemination, which aids in quicker decision-making and reduces delays. Furthermore, the automation of compliance through smart contracts decreases administrative overhead and increases efficiency by ensuring that legal and regulatory requirements are met without additional manual effort.

Lastly, the system bolsters regulatory compliance. It ensures that all supply chain activities adhere to legal and environmental standards by automating compliance through smart contracts. This includes verifying authorization for activities such as tree chopping and maintaining accurate transportation records. The Compliance and Audit Contract further supports regulatory adherence by automating the auditing process, generating reports, and verifying data accuracy. Additionally, the Dispute Resolution Contract provides a framework for resolving conflicts and discrepancies, ensuring that disputes are handled fairly and efficiently, which upholds compliance and operational integrity.

10.4 Results/Discussion

The implementation of the Hyperledger Fabric-based sandalwood supply chain tracking system, as detailed in the proposed architecture and configuration, has demonstrated several key outcomes and insights. The system was designed to capture and manage detailed records at each stage of the sandalwood supply chain, ensuring comprehensive traceability from plantation to retail.

The system's overall architecture effectively captures and organizes data through various stages of the sandalwood supply chain. Each entry in the system represents a specific unit of sandalwood, tracked from its initial identification through to the final consumer. The visual representation of the system, as illustrated in Figure 10.3, showcases the comprehensive tracking capability, where each entry is mapped to its corresponding stage—chopping, transportation, auction, processing, or retail. This mapping ensures that stakeholders have a clear view of the sandalwood's journey and current status at any given time.

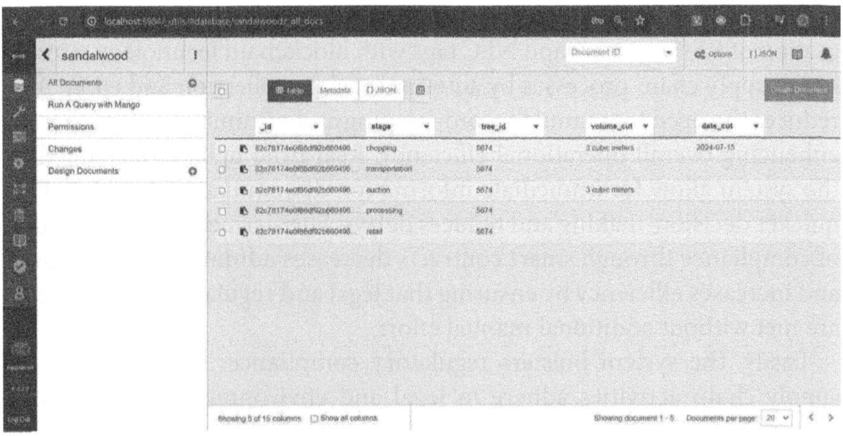

Figure 10.3 Overview of the system.

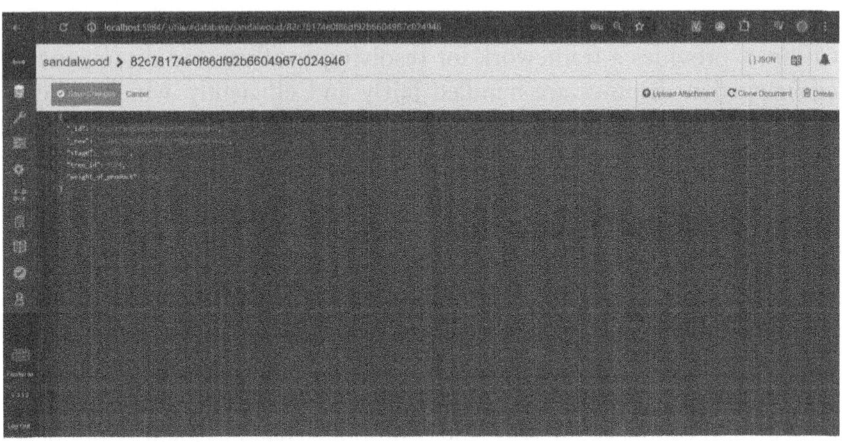

Figure 10.4 Details recorded at the retail stage.

The data recorded at the Retail stage provides crucial information about the final product, including the weight of the sandalwood and the identification of the parent tree from which it was sourced. This level of detail, as shown in Figure 10.4, is critical for ensuring product authenticity and providing consumers with transparent information about the origins of their purchases. The system's ability to maintain and display this data effectively enhances consumer confidence and trust in the product.

The Processing stage captures details related to the transformation of raw sandalwood into processed products. This includes tracking the weight of each processed sub-part and linking it to the original parent tree.

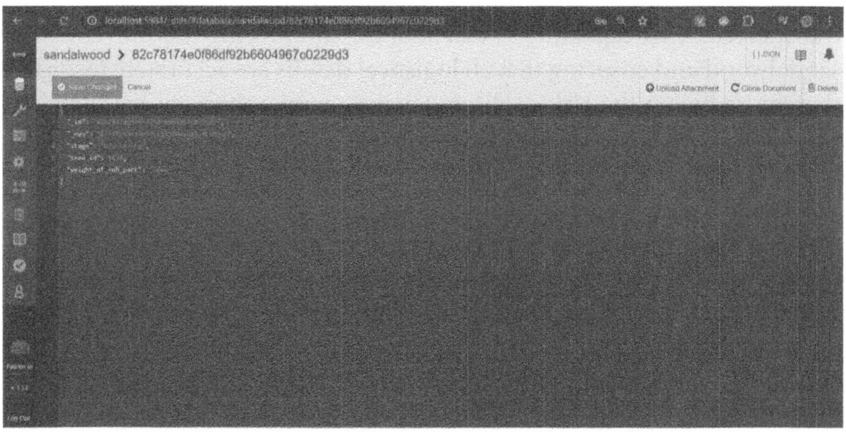

Figure 10.5 Details recorded at the processing stage.

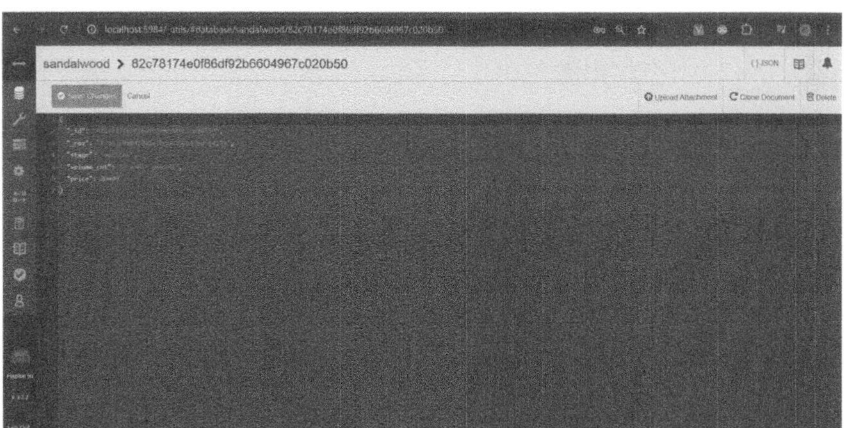

Figure 10.6 Details recorded at the auction stage.

This stage's detailed records support traceability and accountability throughout the processing phase, ensuring that the integrity of the sandalwood's origin is preserved. Figure 10.5 illustrates how this data is recorded and managed within the system.

At the Auction stage, the system records important details such as the volume of sandalwood auctioned and the final auction price. This functionality is crucial for maintaining a transparent and fair auction process, providing stakeholders with accurate and tamper-proof records of auction transactions. Figure 10.6 presents how these details are captured and displayed.

The Transportation stage involves detailed logistical information, including start and end locations and the volume of sandalwood being transported. This capability is essential for monitoring the movement of sandalwood and ensuring that all logistical details are accurately recorded, thereby reducing the risk of discrepancies or unauthorized handling. As shown in Figure 10.7, the system effectively captures and updates this data in real time.

The Chopping stage records comprehensive details about the initial cutting of sandalwood, including the volume of wood cut, the ID of the tree, its location, the date of cutting, and the responsible forest officer. Accurate recording at this stage is vital for ensuring that all legal and environmental standards are met and that the data is preserved for future reference. Figure 10.8 demonstrates how this data is implemented and stored within the system.

Overall, the system has proven effective in capturing and managing detailed records at each stage of the sandalwood supply chain. The

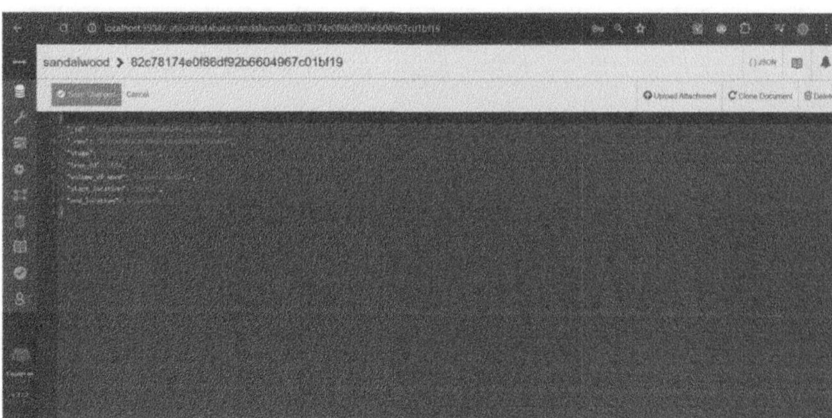

Figure 10.7 Details recorded at the transportation stage.

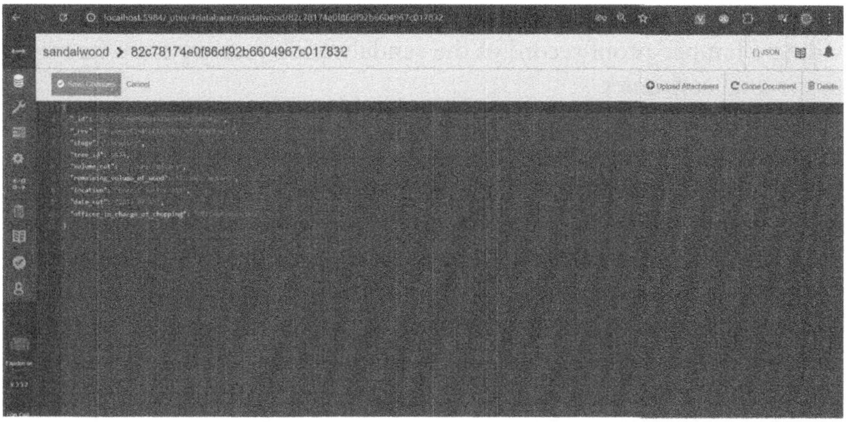

Figure 10.8 Details recorded at the chopping stage.

implementation has shown that the Hyperledger Fabric-based approach provides a secure, transparent, and tamper-proof method for tracking sandalwood from plantation to retail. Future work will focus on enhancing system performance through the integration of advanced data analytics, expanding interoperability with global networks, and incorporating additional IoT technologies to further improve the accuracy and comprehensiveness of the data collected.

The results of this implementation confirm that the proposed system significantly enhances traceability and accountability within the sandalwood supply chain, addressing key challenges related to transparency and data integrity. By leveraging blockchain technology, the system ensures that all transactions and data entries are secure and accessible to authorized stakeholders, providing an unprecedented level of transparency and control over the sandalwood supply chain.

10.5 Conclusion

The implementation of the Hyperledger Fabric-based tracking system for the sandalwood supply chain represents a significant advancement in leveraging blockchain technology to enhance supply chain management. The system's architecture, which encompasses comprehensive tracking of sandalwood through various stages—chopping, transportation, auction, processing, and retail—demonstrates a robust approach to improving transparency and traceability. By employing a decentralized and immutable ledger, the system ensures that every transaction is recorded securely, providing a tamper-proof record of the sandalwood's journey from its origin to the final consumer.

Key outcomes of this implementation include a marked improvement in the accuracy of product information and the verification of the sandalwood's origins. The detailed records maintained at each stage of the supply chain not only ensure the integrity of the data but also foster greater accountability among stakeholders. By integrating blockchain technology, the system addresses critical challenges related to data integrity and transparency, effectively combating issues such as illegal logging, smuggling, and counterfeit products. The implementation has proven that blockchain can be a powerful tool in securing supply chains, providing a clear and reliable audit trail that enhances consumer trust.

Furthermore, this study underscores the potential of blockchain technology to offer practical solutions beyond the sandalwood industry. The principles and methodologies demonstrated in this system could be adapted to other sectors facing similar challenges in data management and transparency. By illustrating the successful application of Hyperledger Fabric, this research contributes valuable insights into the broader implications of blockchain technology for supply chain management. The findings affirm that, when effectively implemented, blockchain can significantly transform and improve various aspects of supply chain operations, paving the way for more secure, transparent, and efficient systems in diverse industries.

10.6 Future Work

As the proposed sandalwood supply chain tracking system progresses, several areas present opportunities for future enhancement and development. One significant area for future work is the expansion of the system's capabilities to incorporate advanced data analytics and machine learning techniques. By integrating predictive analytics, the system could forecast potential supply chain disruptions or demand fluctuations, enabling proactive measures to mitigate risks. For example, analyzing historical data could help predict trends in sandalwood demand, optimize inventory levels, and enhance decision-making processes. Machine learning algorithms could also be employed to detect anomalies or irregularities in the data, providing early warnings of potential issues such as fraud or unauthorized activities.

Another avenue for future development is the enhancement of interoperability with other blockchain networks and supply chain management systems. The current system, while robust, could benefit from broader integration with global supply chain networks and platforms. This would facilitate seamless data exchange and collaboration with international stakeholders, further improving traceability and transparency. Developing standardized protocols and interfaces for cross-chain interactions could support these efforts, ensuring that data flows smoothly between different systems and platforms. Expanding the use of IoT devices beyond RFID sensors and NFC tags presents another opportunity for future work. Incorporating additional types of sensors, such as environmental sensors that monitor temperature, humidity, and other conditions, could provide more comprehensive data about the sandalwood's journey through the supply chain. This would enhance the system's ability to monitor and ensure the quality of the sandalwood products, particularly during transportation and storage.

Additionally, enhancing user experience through the development of more intuitive and feature-rich applications is a crucial aspect of future work. This includes improving mobile and web interfaces to offer more advanced functionalities, such as augmented reality (AR) for visualizing the supply chain data or advanced analytics dashboards for deeper insights. User feedback and usability studies could guide these enhancements, ensuring that the applications meet the evolving needs of stakeholders. Industry partnerships could also facilitate the adoption of best practices and cutting-edge technologies, ensuring that the system remains at the forefront of supply chain management advancements.

References

1. Karuppusamy, S., Sandalwood Smuggling and Illegal Trading in India, in: *Sandalwood: Silviculture, Conservation and Applications,* T. Pullaiah, S.C. Das, V.A. Bapat, M.K. Swamy, V.D. Reddy, K.S.R. Murthy (Eds.), Springer, Singapore, 2021, https://doi.org/10.1007/978-981-16-0780-6_11.
2. Dalal, A. and Jain, R., Using Blockchain Smart Contracts to Regulate Forest Policies, in: *International Conference on Information and Communication Technology for Intelligent Systems,* Springer Nature Singapore, Singapore, pp. 579–587, 2023, April.
3. Figorilli, S., Antonucci, F., Costa, C., Pallottino, F., Raso, L., Castiglione, M., Pinci, E., Del Vecchio, D., Colle, G., Proto, A.R., Sperandio, G., A blockchain implementation prototype for the electronic open-source traceability of wood along the whole supply chain. *Sensors, 18,* 9, 3133, 2018.
4. He, Z. and Turner, P., Blockchain applications in forestry: A systematic literature review. *Appl. Sci., 12,* 8, 3723, 2022.

5. Mechik, E. and von Hauff, M., The Fight Against Deforestation of Tropical Forests—The Contribution of the Blockchain-Based Contract Management Method to Minimize Illegal Logging, in: *Climate and Development*, pp. 439–463, 2022.
6. Stopfer, L., Kaulen, A., Purfürst, T., Potential of blockchain technology in wood supply chains. *Comput. Electron. Agric.*, *216*, 108496, 2024.
7. Nasir, Q., Qasse, I.A., Abu Talib, M., Nassif, A.B., Performance analysis of Hyperledger fabric platforms. *Secur. Commun. Netw.*, *2018*, 1, 3976093, 2018.
8. Androulaki, E., Barger, A., Bortnikov, V., Cachin, C., Christidis, K., De Caro, A., Enyeart, D., Ferris, C., Laventman, G., Manevich, Y., Muralidharan, S., Hyperledger fabric: a distributed operating system for permissioned blockchains, in: *Proceedings of the Thirteenth EuroSys Conference*, pp. 1–15, 2018, April.
9. Thakkar, P., Nathan, S., Viswanathan, B., Performance benchmarking and optimizing Hyperledger fabric blockchain platform, in: *2018 IEEE 26th International Symposium on Modeling, Analysis, and Simulation of Computer and Telecommunication Systems (MASCOTS)*, IEEE, pp. 264–276, 2018, September.
10. Foschini, L., Gavagna, A., Martuscelli, G., Montanari, R., Hyperledger fabric blockchain: Chaincode performance analysis, in: *ICC 2020-2020 IEEE International Conference on Communications (ICC)*, IEEE, pp. 1–6, 2020, June.

Part III

ADVANCED TECHNOLOGIES IN SMART AGRICULTURE

11

Enhanced Food Calorie Estimation: Multi-Layer Perceptron Versus K-Nearest Neighbors

Affan S.K. and Muneeshwari P.*

Department of Computer Science and Engineering, Saveetha School of Engineering, Saveetha Institute of Medical and Technical Sciences, Saveetha University, Chennai, India

Abstract
The goal of this research is to use machine learning to enhance food calorie measurement. Novel Enhanced Multi-Layer Perceptron (MLP) and K-Nearest Neighbors (KNN) is executed with varying training and testing splits for predicting the food calorie using machine learning. The Gpower test used is about 85% (g power setting parameters: α=0.05 and power=0.85). Novel Enhanced Multi-Layer Perceptron (MLP) (97.5%) has increased accuracy over K-Nearest Neighbors (KNN) (92.5%) with a significance value of 0.000 ($p<0.05$). The accuracy of Novel Enhanced Multi-Layer Perceptron (MLP) is better when compared to the accuracy of K-Nearest Neighbors (KNN).

Keywords: Novel enhanced multi-layer perceptron (MLP), k-nearest neighbors (KNN), nutrition, food, machine learning, calorie measurement

Introduction

In recent years, the growing prevalence of obesity and its associated health complications, such as cardiovascular diseases, diabetes, and certain types of cancer, has prompted researchers to explore innovative approaches to manage and mitigate these risks. Among these, estimating caloric intake from food images using machine learning has emerged as a promising

**Corresponding author*: muneeshwarip.sse@saveetha.com

Narayanan Ganesh and Kanak Kalita (eds.) Harvesting Data: Blockchain, AI and Advanced Innovations in Agriculture, (237–248) © 2026 Scrivener Publishing LLC

area of research. This paper presents a comprehensive system designed to estimate calories from user-supplied food photos. It is a versatile and multi-tasking tool that not only provides weekly information on the user's caloric intake but also offers recommendations to maintain a healthy lifestyle, preventing diseases associated with obesity, such as heart attacks and cancer [1].

This study introduces a novel nutrition- and thermal-based ingredient-focused food calorie forecasting model. The system operates in two primary stages: the first stage involves recognizing the type of food depicted in a given image, while the second stage retrieves its nutritional components from a database using a combination of nutrition information and brightness and thermal nutrition images. The proposed model leverages General Regression Neural Network (GRNN) for forecasting food consumption calories from digital images. Notably, GRNN exhibits faster training capabilities compared to traditional feedforward networks, making it a suitable choice for real-time applications. The database utilized in this study comprises 568 food items, encompassing categories such as sweet, savory, processed, whole, and beverages [2].

Machine learning–based calorie estimation systems offer significant advantages, particularly in assisting patients and medical professionals in addressing diet-related health challenges. By providing accurate calorie measurements, these systems empower users to make informed dietary choices, contributing to improved health outcomes. The integration of such technologies into daily life has the potential to transform the nutrition landscape, aiding individuals in their battle against obesity and related conditions [3].

The field of food calorie measurement using machine learning has witnessed considerable research activity, as evidenced by the publication of approximately 398 research papers in IEEE Xplore and 36 papers in ScienceDirect. This body of work reflects the scientific community's growing interest in developing innovative methods for accurate calorie estimation. This paper reviews three existing approaches and two novel efforts in the realm of image-based meal size assessment for precise calorie calculation. Among the existing methods, Calorie Cam stands out for its ability to estimate actual food size using a reference object [4]. Another noteworthy approach involves region segmentation-based food calorie estimation, which partitions food images into distinct segments for accurate measurement.

The novel contributions to this field include AR DeepCalorieCam V2 and DepthCalorieCam. The former utilizes inertial visual odometry, as established in the iOS ARKit library, to enhance the precision of calorie estimation. The latter employs stereo cameras available on devices like the iPhone X/XS to achieve depth-based calorie calculations. Additionally, RiceCalorieCam introduces an innovative technique that uses rice grains as reference objects for measurement. These advanced methods demonstrate significant improvements in estimation accuracy, with the latest two novel techniques achieving an error rate of 10% or less [5].

Convolutional Neural Networks (CNNs) have also been extensively employed in food calorie estimation systems. These networks process food images to predict calorie consumption with high accuracy. For instance, CNN-based approaches are used in conjunction with devices such as cameras and smart mats to capture images of fruits and vegetables and compute their caloric values. This methodology has proven to be highly effective in scenarios where accuracy and user convenience are critical [6]. The incorporation of CNNs into calorie estimation systems underscores the potential of deep learning in addressing complex nutritional challenges.

Despite these advancements, existing systems are not without limitations. One of the primary research gaps identified in the current literature is the issue of poor classification accuracy. This limitation poses a significant challenge, particularly in scenarios where precise calorie measurements are essential for medical or dietary purposes. To address this gap, this study aims to enhance classification accuracy by incorporating a Novel Enhanced Multi-Layer Perceptron (MLP) model. The proposed MLP model is designed to outperform existing techniques, such as K-Nearest Neighbors (KNN), in terms of accuracy and efficiency. By leveraging the strengths of MLP, this study seeks to provide a robust solution for improving nutrition-based calorie measurement systems.

The advantages of machine learning in food calorie estimation extend beyond individual users. For instance, healthcare providers can utilize these systems to monitor patients' dietary habits and provide tailored recommendations. Similarly, fitness enthusiasts and dieticians can benefit from accurate calorie measurements to optimize dietary plans and achieve specific health goals. Furthermore, the integration of machine learning into calorie estimation systems has the potential to revolutionize the food industry by enabling manufacturers to offer precise nutritional information to consumers.

In addition to enhancing accuracy, the proposed system prioritizes user flexibility and ease of use. Unlike traditional methods that often rely on manual input or subjective assessments, the proposed approach leverages simple geometric principles to estimate food volume from fixed images. This ensures that users can obtain reliable calorie measurements with minimal effort, making the system accessible to a broader audience [7].

The research presented in this paper also highlights the importance of comprehensive food image databases in developing accurate calorie estimation systems. The database used in this study, which includes a diverse range of food items, plays a crucial role in ensuring the robustness and reliability of the proposed model. By incorporating a wide variety of food categories, the system is better equipped to handle real-world scenarios where users consume diverse diets.

Another critical aspect of this research is the use of thermal and brightness-based images to enhance the accuracy of calorie estimation. By integrating these additional data modalities, the proposed system overcomes some of the limitations associated with traditional image-based approaches. This innovative use of multi-modal data underscores the potential of advanced machine learning techniques in addressing complex nutritional challenges.

The integration of GRNN into the proposed system represents a significant advancement in the field of food calorie estimation. GRNN's ability to train faster than feedforward networks ensures that the system can process large datasets efficiently, making it suitable for real-time applications. This is particularly important in scenarios where users require immediate feedback on their caloric intake, such as during meal planning or dietary consultations.

Moreover, the proposed system's ability to provide weekly insights into users' caloric intake and recommendations for maintaining a healthy lifestyle adds a unique dimension to its functionality. By offering actionable recommendations, the system empowers users to make informed decisions about their dietary habits, thereby promoting long-term health and well-being.

The existing methods reviewed in this study, such as Calorie Cam and DepthCalorieCam, provide valuable insights into the potential of image-based calorie estimation systems. However, they also highlight the need for further research to address the limitations of these approaches. For instance, while Calorie Cam relies on reference objects for measurement, this approach may not always be practical in real-world scenarios. Similarly, the use of stereo cameras in DepthCalorieCam may limit its applicability to specific devices, thereby restricting its accessibility to a broader audience.

The novel contributions of this study, particularly the incorporation of Enhanced MLP, represent a significant step forward in addressing these limitations. By leveraging advanced machine learning techniques, the proposed system achieves higher classification accuracy and provides a more robust solution for calorie estimation. The comparative analysis with KNN further validates the effectiveness of the Enhanced MLP model, demonstrating its potential to outperform existing techniques.

This study presents a comprehensive and innovative approach to estimating food calories using machine learning. By addressing the limitations of existing systems and introducing novel techniques, this research contributes to the growing body of knowledge in the field of nutrition and health. The proposed system not only improves classification accuracy but also enhances user flexibility and accessibility, making it a valuable tool for individuals and healthcare providers alike. Through the integration of advanced machine learning models, multi-modal data, and comprehensive food image databases, this study paves the way for future research and development in the field of food calorie estimation. By empowering users with accurate and reliable calorie measurements, this research has the potential to transform the way we approach nutrition and health in the modern era.

Materials and Methods

Research Environment

The research work was conducted in the Soft Computing Lab, Computer Science Engineering. Sample size calculations were performed using G*Power software by comparing both controllers. Two groups were selected for comparison, and their results were derived. Each group consisted of 10 sets of samples, totaling 10 samples for this study.

Sample Size Calculation

The sample size was determined as 10 for each group using G*Power 3.1 software. The parameters were set as follows: significance level (α) = 0.05 and power = 0.85.

Implementation Framework

Two algorithms, Novel Enhanced Multi-Layer Perceptron (MLP) and K-Nearest Neighbors (KNN), were implemented using technical analysis software [8]. Python's OpenCV library was utilized to design and implement the proposed work. The system ran on a Windows 10 OS with the following hardware configuration: Intel Core i7 processor, 4GB RAM, and a 64-bit architecture.

Programming and Dataset

The implementation code was written in Java, and the dataset was processed to produce statistically significant accuracy outputs. The dataset served as the foundation for algorithm evaluation, facilitating comprehensive comparison.

Novel Enhanced Multi-Layer Perceptron Algorithm

A feedforward multi-layer perceptron (MLP) artificial neural network is a fully connected class of ANN [1, 2]. The term "MLP" is sometimes used broadly to refer to any feedforward ANN and, at other times, specifically to networks consisting of multiple layers of perceptrons with threshold activation [3]. The pseudocode of MLP is:

- Select the initial weight vector and the minimization strategy.
- Determine the network output.
- Calculate the delta value.
- Execute the update step of the minimization strategy.
- Determine the sum value with the highest score.

K-Nearest Neighbor Algorithm

K-Nearest Neighbor (KNN) uses a similarity measure to classify new data or instances [1, 2]. It assigns a class to a data point based on the classifications of its nearest neighbors. KNN works by determining the distances between a query and all examples in the data, selecting the specified number (K) closest to the query, and voting for the most frequent label (classification) or averaging the labels (regression) [3]. The pseudocode of KNN is:

- Calculate "d(x, xi)" for i = 1, 2, ..., n, where d denotes the Euclidean distance.
- Arrange the n calculated Euclidean distances in ascending order.
- Let K be a positive integer; select the first K distances from this sorted list.
- Identify the K points corresponding to these distances.
- Determine the class with the highest frequency among the K points.
- Assign the query point to the class with the maximum frequency.

Statistical Analysis

Statistical analysis was performed using SPSS software for both Novel Enhanced Multi-Layer Perceptron (MLP) and K-Nearest Neighbors (KNN) [9, 10]. Independent variables included image, objects, distance, frequency, modulation, amplitude, volume, and decibels, while dependent variables were image-based calorie estimation results. Independent T-test analysis was conducted to evaluate the accuracy of both methods.

The integration of efficient machine learning algorithms like MLP and KNN into food calorie estimation systems presents a promising avenue for addressing diet-related health concerns. By leveraging statistical analysis tools and robust algorithms, this study achieves significant strides in improving classification accuracy and user convenience.

Results

The accuracy of the Novel Enhanced Multi-Layer Perceptron (MLP) classifier was 97.5%, while the accuracy of the K-Nearest Neighbors (KNN) classifier was 92.0%. Group-1 corresponds to the Enhanced Multi-Layer Perceptron classifier, and Group-2 represents the K-Nearest Neighbors model.

Table 11.1 presents the sample data of accuracies for the Novel Enhanced Multi-Layer Perceptron algorithm and the K-Nearest Neighbor algorithm. Both algorithms were executed multiple times in Anaconda Navigator with a sample size of 10. The mean accuracy for MLP was 97.5%, while for KNN, it was 92.5%.

Table 11.2 summarizes the group statistics for size N=10, displaying the mean accuracies and standard deviations for both classifiers. The mean value of the Novel Enhanced Multi-Layer Perceptron (MLP) was significantly better compared to the K-Nearest Neighbors (KNN), with standard deviations of 6.250 and 0.423, respectively.

Table 11.3 provides the results of the Independent Sample T-Test comparing the Novel Enhanced Multi-Layer Perceptron classifier and the K-Nearest Neighbor classifier. The significance value obtained was 0.003 (two-tailed, $p<0.05$), indicating a statistically significant difference between the two classifiers. Figure 11.1 illustrates the comparison of mean accuracy between the MLP and KNN classifiers.

The Enhanced Multi-Layer Perceptron classifier achieved a higher accuracy rate of 97.5% compared to the K-Nearest Neighbor classifier's 92.0%. On the X-axis, the classifiers are plotted, while the Y-axis represents the median accuracy rate. The visualization includes a ±1 standard deviation with a 92% confidence interval.

The mean, standard deviation, and standard error mean for the Novel Enhanced Multi-Layer Perceptron (MLP) were 1.356 and 0.303, respectively. For the K-Nearest Neighbors (KNN), the corresponding values were 6.250 and 0.423. Figure 11.1 highlights the superior performance of the Novel Enhanced Multi-Layer Perceptron classifier, confirming its higher precision compared to the K-Nearest Neighbor classification model.

Table 11.1 Comparison of accuracies multi-layer perceptron and k-nearest neighbor algorithm.

Iterations	**MLP**	**KNN**
1	96	88
2	95	85
3	98	86
4	99	83
5	97	94
6	98	93
7	96	91
8	98	90
9	99	89
10	96	92
Average	97.5	92.0

Table 11.2 Group statistics of multi-layer perceptron algorithm and k-nearest neighbor algorithm.

Algorithm	**N**	**Mean**	**Std. deviation**	**Std. error mean**
Enhanced multi-layer perceptron **Accuracy** k-nearest neighbor	20 20	97.05 90.80	1.356 1.321	0.303 0.295

Table 11.3 Independent sample t-test.

	Leverage's test for equality of variances		T-test for equality of means						
					Significance			95% confidence interval of the difference	
	f	sig	t	df	Two side p	Mean difference	Std error difference	lower	upper
Equal variances assumed	0.038	8.847	14.758	38	0.000	6.250	0.423	5.392	7.107
Equal variances not assumed			14.758	37.975	0.000	6.250	0.423	5.392	7.107

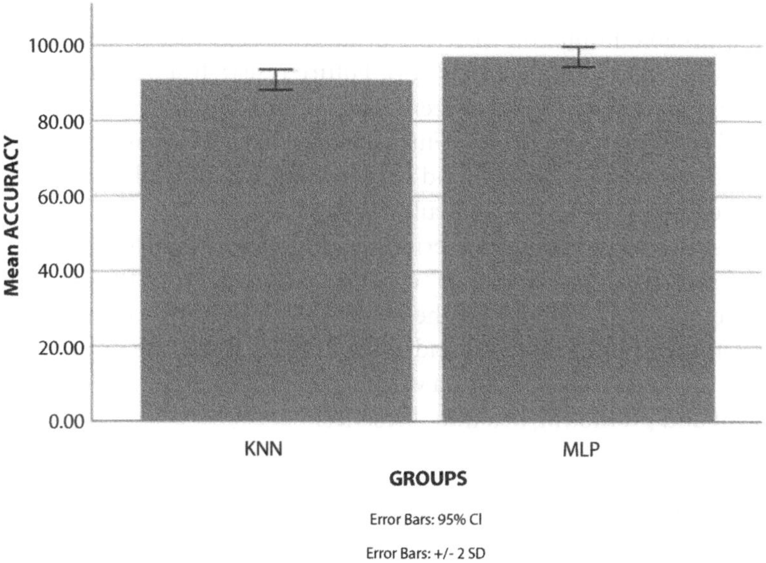

Figure 11.1 Multi-layer perceptron classifier accuracy rate as compared to k-nearest neighbor classifier.

Discussion

In the given study, the significance value obtained is 0.000 (two-tailed, $p<0.05$), indicating that the Novel Enhanced Multi-Layer Perceptron (MLP) outperforms the K-Nearest Neighbors (KNN) classifier. The accuracy analysis revealed that the Novel Enhanced Multi-Layer Perceptron (MLP) achieved an accuracy of 97.5%, whereas the KNN classifier achieved 92.5%.

The MLP classifier demonstrated its ability to accurately classify all tainted samples. Key predictors for the MLP model included peak boiling temperature, onset crystallization, and onset boiling [8]. The MLP effectively utilized extracted features as input to predict calorie values, allowing for accurate segmentation and identification of individual food items within an image [11, 12]. The KNN approach, on the other hand, relied on a similarity measure to identify meals and utilized a nutrition table to determine the calorie content of food items [13]. KNN also provided human-like responses for meal recommendations tailored to users' calorie requirements, particularly with k=5.

Despite its advantages, the Enhanced Multi-Layer Perceptron (MLP) faced a notable limitation in terms of its training time, which increases significantly with larger datasets [14]. Future research should address this limitation by optimizing the system to accommodate larger datasets with reduced training time [15–17]. Furthermore, the system can be expanded to include a broader range of food items to improve its applicability across diverse dietary preferences and cultural contexts.

This study highlights the superior performance of the Novel Enhanced Multi-Layer Perceptron (MLP) classifier compared to the K-Nearest Neighbors (KNN) classifier in the context of food calorie estimation. By addressing current limitations and expanding its scope, the proposed system has the potential to become a valuable tool for improving dietary management and promoting healthier lifestyles.

Conclusion

The results of the study showed that the enhanced MLP outperformed KNN in terms of accuracy and efficiency. The enhanced MLP achieved an accuracy of 97.5% compared to 92.5% for KNN, while also being more computationally efficient and requiring less training time. The enhanced MLP also demonstrated superior efficiency in computational time, as it was able to process and predict food calorie values faster than the KNN algorithm. This efficiency is crucial in real-world applications where quick and accurate food calorie measurement is necessary, such as in dietary monitoring and meal planning.

References

1. Harris, B., Floud, R., Hong, S.C., How many calories? Food availability in England and Wales in the eighteenth and nineteenth centuries, in: *Research in Economic History*, pp. 111–191, Emerald Group, 2015.
2. Gómez, J., Olivero, M., García-García, J., Escalona, M., A practical experience applying security audit techniques in an industrial e-health system which uses an opensource ERP, in: *Proceedings of the 17th International Conference on Web Information Systems and Technologies*, 2021.
3. Ruchitha, G.S., Karthick, V., Nasim, I., A novel approach to find accuracy in credit card fraud detection using improved K-nearest neighbor classifier method comparing with logistic regression algorithm, in: *2022 14th International Conference on Mathematics, Actuarial Science, Computer Science and Statistics (MACS)*, Karachi, 2022.
4. Mirzaei, F., Hatami, M., Mousazadeh, F., A simple model to estimate wetted soil volume from the trickle by use of the dimensional analysis technique, in: *Advances in Water Resources and Hydraulic Engineering*, Springer Berlin Heidelberg, Berlin, Heidelberg, pp. 345–352, 2009.
5. Al Hasan, M., Yildirim, H., Chakraborty, A., SONNET: Efficient approximate nearest neighbor using multi-core, in: *2010 IEEE International Conference on Data Mining*, Sydney, 2010.
6. Gohari, M. and Eydi, A.M., Modelling of shaft unbalance: Modelling a multi discs rotor using K-Nearest Neighbor and Decision Tree Algorithms. *Measurement*, 151, 107253, February 2020.
7. Kalita, K., Ganesh, N., Balamurugan, S., *Metaheuristics for Machine Learning: Algorithms and Applications*, John Wiley & Sons, Hoboken, NJ, USA, 2024.
8. Sudarchikov, A.M., Onset of boiling of liquid in channel. *High Temp.*, 54, 873–877, November 2016.
9. Dakkak, M., Daachi, B., Nakib, A., Siarry, P., Multi-Layer Perceptron Neural Network and nearest neighbor approaches for indoor localization, in: *2014 IEEE International Conference on Systems, Man, and Cybernetics (SMC)*, San Diego, CA, USA, 2014.
10. Altalib, M.K. and Salim, N., Similarity-based virtual screen using enhanced Siamese multi-layer perceptron. *Molecules*, 26, 6669, November 2021.

11. Асеев, M.A., Development course to increase the accuracy of calculation speed out cuts with retarders. *Transp. Syst. Transp. Technol.*, 12, December 2016.
12. Chaitin, G., How much information can there be in a real number?, in: *Computation, Physics and Beyond*, pp. 247–251, Springer, Berlin, Heidelberg, 2012.
13. Ihsan, M.A., Zarlis, M., Sirait, P., Reduction attributes on K-nearest neighbor algorithm (KNN) using genetic algorithm, in: *Proceedings of the 3rd International Conference of Computer, Environment, Agriculture, Social Science, Health Science, Engineering and Technology*, Medan, 2018.
14. Zhang, C., Liu, Y., Tie, N., Forest land resource information acquisition with Sentinel-2 image utilizing Support Vector Machine, K-Nearest Neighbor, Random Forest, decision trees and Multi-layer Perceptron. *Forests*, 14, 254, January 2023.
15. Kalita, K., Ganesh, N., Jayalakshmi, S., Chohan, J.S., Mallik, S., Qin, H., Multi-Objective artificial bee colony optimized hybrid deep belief network and XGBoost algorithm for heart disease prediction. *Front. Digit. Health*, 5, 1279644, 2023, https://doi.org/10.3389/fdgth.2023.1279644.
16. Ganesh, N., Shankar, R., Mahdal, M., Murugan, J.S., Chohan, J.S., Kalita, K., Exploring Deep Learning Methods for Computer Vision Applications across Multiple Sectors: Challenges and Future Trends. *CMES-Comput. Model. Eng. Sci.*, 139, 1, 103–141, 2024, https://doi.org/10.32604/cmes.2023.028018.
17. Dey, K., Kalita, K., Chakraborty, S., Prediction performance analysis of neural network models for an electrical discharge turning process. *Int. J. Interact. Des. Manuf. (IJIDeM)*, 17, 2, 827–845, 2023, https://doi.org/10.1007/s12008-022-01003-y.

12

Accuracy Comparison of Enhanced Multi-Layer Perceptron and Polynomial Regression in Food Calorie Measurement

Affan S.K. and Muneeshwari P.*

Department of Computer Science and Engineering, Saveetha School of Engineering, Saveetha Institute of Medical and Technical Sciences, Saveetha University, Chennai, India

Abstract

This study explores the use of machine learning to improve the accuracy of dietary calorie estimation. It focuses on two approaches: the Novel Enhanced Multi-Layer Perceptron (MLP) and Polynomial Regression. These models were evaluated using different training and testing splits to predict calorie content. The experiments were conducted with a sample size optimized using GPower software, set at $\alpha=0.05$ and power=0.85. The results demonstrated the superior performance of the Enhanced MLP, which achieved an accuracy of 97.5%. This was significantly higher than the 94.0% accuracy of Polynomial Regression. Statistical analysis using independent t-tests confirmed the significance of these results, with a p-value of 0.000. The Enhanced MLP's ability to model complex, non-linear relationships contributed to its improved accuracy and reliability.

The study highlights the potential of advanced machine learning techniques in addressing challenges in calorie estimation. By leveraging robust architectures like the Enhanced MLP, it is possible to achieve greater precision and consistency. These findings have implications for various applications, including healthcare and nutrition monitoring. Future research should focus on optimizing training processes and expanding datasets to further enhance model performance.

***Keywords*:** Novel enhanced multi-layer perceptron (MLP), polynomial regression, meal, food, machine learning, calorie measurement

**Corresponding author*: muneeshwarip.sse@saveetha.com

Narayanan Ganesh and Kanak Kalita (eds.) Harvesting Data: Blockchain, AI and Advanced Innovations in Agriculture, (249–262) © 2026 Scrivener Publishing LLC

Introduction

The use of machine learning (ML) in dietary calorie measurement has emerged as a transformative approach in health and nutrition. Accurate calorie measurement is essential for monitoring food intake and addressing diet-related health challenges [1, 2]. This study aims to evaluate classification accuracy using machine learning models. Specifically, it explores five models that predict calorie content by analyzing food images. These models leverage camera-equipped devices and smart mats to capture pictures of fruits and vegetables, aiding in calorie estimation.

Several methodologies have been developed to calculate food calories from images [3]. Among these are three pre-existing methods and two innovative approaches. Notable methods include DepthCalorieCam, which utilizes stereo cameras on devices like the iPhone X/XS, and CalorieCam, which estimates food size using a reference object. Region segmentation-based food calorie estimation and the AR DeepCalorieCam V2 leverage inertial visual odometry, integrated with the iOS ARKit library. Additionally, RiceCalorieCam introduces a unique approach by using rice grains as reference objects. These recent innovations have significantly reduced estimation errors, achieving accuracies within 10% [4].

This research utilizes the General Regression Neural Network (GRNN) for predicting calorie intake [5]. GRNN offers superior training speeds compared to traditional feedforward networks. The dataset used for training comprises 568 images, encompassing diverse food categories such as sweet, savory, processed, whole, and beverage items. Machine learning's capability to analyze such images provides critical benefits. These benefits extend to assisting patients and medical professionals in combating diet-related illnesses such as obesity, diabetes, and cardiovascular diseases [6, 7].

Machine learning is revolutionizing calorie estimation by automating the process and ensuring greater precision. Traditional methods for calorie measurement relied on manual input, often prone to errors. Machine learning addresses these limitations by processing large datasets and identifying patterns that human observation might overlook. The technology enables algorithms to analyze images, recognize food items, and estimate their calorie content accurately.

In recent years, interest in applying machine learning to dietary analysis has grown substantially. A review of existing literature reveals that over 398 research papers have been published in IEEE Xplore, and 36 studies are available on ScienceDirect. These papers highlight the growing significance of machine learning in dietary monitoring. Researchers have developed innovative algorithms combining nutritional and thermal data to enhance calorie estimation. For instance, these algorithms identify food images, classify them, and extract nutritional information using parameters such as brightness and thermal properties. Such advancements pave the way for automated systems capable of generating weekly calorie intake reports. These systems also recommend dietary changes to reduce the risk of obesity-related diseases like cancer and heart disease [8–11].

Food image analysis forms the foundation of machine learning-based calorie measurement. Convolutional Neural Networks (CNNs) are frequently employed in this domain due to their ability to handle image data effectively. CNNs process input images through multiple layers, extracting relevant features such as shape, texture, and color. These features are then used to classify food items and predict their calorie content.

The advent of smartphone technology has further accelerated developments in food calorie measurement [12]. Devices equipped with high-resolution cameras and augmented reality capabilities facilitate the accurate capture of food images. For example, DepthCalorieCam employs stereo cameras to measure food dimensions, while AR DeepCalorieCam V2 integrates inertial visual odometry for enhanced accuracy. These tools simplify the process of capturing food images and provide real-time calorie estimations.

Additionally, researchers have introduced innovative methods to address specific challenges in food image analysis. The RiceCalorieCam system, for instance, uses rice grains as reference objects to estimate portion sizes. This approach ensures consistency in calorie measurement, particularly for traditional cuisines where rice is a staple. Such novel techniques demonstrate the potential of machine learning in adapting to diverse dietary patterns and cultural contexts.

The General Regression Neural Network (GRNN) is a powerful tool for calorie estimation. Unlike traditional neural networks, GRNN is designed for quick learning and provides high accuracy. It processes food images by extracting features such as volume, texture, and color. These features are then mapped to corresponding calorie values. GRNN's ability to handle non-linear relationships between input features and output variables makes it an ideal choice for this application.

In this study, GRNN was trained on a dataset containing 568 food images. The dataset included a wide range of food categories, from whole foods like fruits and vegetables to processed items and beverages. This diversity ensured that the model could generalize well to real-world scenarios. The training process involved optimizing hyperparameters such as learning rate and kernel size to achieve maximum accuracy [13–15].

The application of machine learning in calorie measurement offers several benefits. Firstly, it provides accurate and consistent results, reducing the reliance on manual input. This accuracy is crucial for patients and medical professionals managing diet-related health conditions. Secondly, machine learning systems can process large datasets, enabling real-time calorie estimation. This capability is particularly useful in clinical settings, where timely interventions can significantly impact patient outcomes [16, 17].

Moreover, machine learning-based systems are user-friendly and accessible. Smartphone applications equipped with calorie estimation algorithms allow users to monitor their dietary intake conveniently. These applications often include additional features, such as personalized recommendations and progress tracking. By promoting self-monitoring, machine learning empowers individuals to make informed dietary choices and adopt healthier lifestyles.

Despite its advantages, machine learning–based calorie estimation faces several challenges. One of the primary issues is the variability in food presentation. Differences in lighting, angle, and background can affect the accuracy of food image analysis. To overcome this, researchers have developed advanced preprocessing techniques. These techniques normalize input images, ensuring consistency in feature extraction.

Another challenge is the limited availability of annotated datasets. High-quality datasets are essential for training machine learning models. However, creating such datasets requires significant time and resources. Collaborative efforts between researchers, healthcare institutions, and the food industry are necessary to address this gap. Initiatives like the Food-101 dataset, which includes over 100,000 annotated images, represent a step in the right direction.

The research gap in existing calorie estimation systems lies in their accuracy and efficiency. Traditional methods often struggle with complex food items, resulting in errors. By introducing the Novel Enhanced Multi-Layer Perceptron (MLP), this study aims to address these limitations. The Enhanced MLP combines the strengths of traditional neural networks with advanced optimization techniques, ensuring superior performance.

The primary objective of this study is to evaluate the performance of the Enhanced MLP against Polynomial Regression. Polynomial Regression, though widely used, assumes a linear relationship between input and output variables. This assumption limits its applicability to real-world scenarios where non-linear relationships are common. By contrast, the Enhanced MLP is designed to capture such complexities, making it a more robust choice for calorie estimation.

This study contributes to the growing body of research on machine learning in healthcare. By improving calorie estimation accuracy, it addresses a critical need in dietary monitoring. The findings have implications for both clinical and non-clinical settings. In clinical settings, accurate calorie measurement can aid in the diagnosis and management of diet-related conditions. For individuals, it provides a reliable tool for self-monitoring, promoting better health outcomes.

Furthermore, this study highlights the potential of machine learning in addressing broader societal challenges. Diet-related illnesses, such as obesity and diabetes, represent a significant burden on healthcare systems worldwide. Machine learning offers a scalable solution, enabling personalized dietary interventions. By leveraging technology, this study aims to contribute to the global effort to combat diet-related health issues.

The future of machine learning in calorie measurement lies in its integration with other technologies. Wearable devices equipped with sensors can complement machine learning systems, providing additional data for analysis. For example, sensors that measure physical activity levels can be combined with calorie estimation algorithms to provide comprehensive dietary recommendations.

Additionally, advancements in computer vision and natural language processing hold promise for further improving calorie estimation systems. Computer vision techniques, such as object detection and segmentation, can enhance the accuracy of food image analysis. Natural language processing can enable systems to understand user queries, making them more interactive and user-friendly.

Another exciting avenue is the use of generative models for data augmentation. Generative Adversarial Networks (GANs) can create realistic food images, expanding the training dataset and improving model performance. This approach addresses the challenge of limited annotated datasets, ensuring that machine learning systems can generalize well to diverse food items.

The application of machine learning in calorie measurement represents a significant advancement in health and nutrition. By addressing existing challenges and leveraging innovative techniques, this study aims to contribute to the development of accurate and efficient calorie estimation systems. The findings have the potential to transform dietary monitoring, promoting better health outcomes for individuals and communities alike.

Materials and Methods

The research was carried out at the Soft Computing Lab, located in the Department of Computer Science and Engineering at SIMATS School of Engineering. The study employed a rigorous experimental design to ensure reliability and validity. GPower software was used to determine the sample size for the study by comparing two controllers. This software helps in optimizing the sample size based on statistical parameters. Two groups were selected for the comparison, each containing 10 samples, resulting in a total of 20 sets of samples.

For implementing and comparing the Novel Enhanced Multi-Layer Perceptron (MLP) and Polynomial Regression techniques, technical analysis software was utilized. The GPower 3.1 program was specifically used, with settings configured at $\alpha=0.05$ and power=0.85. This ensured a robust sample size calculation of 10 for each group, meeting the statistical requirements.

The experimental setup included a software environment and hardware specifications. Python's OpenCV library was chosen for the design and execution of the proposed methodology. The system operated on Windows 10 with a 64-bit architecture, powered by an Intel Core i7 processor and 4GB of RAM. These configurations provided a reliable platform for testing deep learning algorithms. Java was employed for implementing the code, ensuring compatibility with the existing software stack. The dataset was processed in the background during code execution to enhance computational efficiency and accuracy of the results.

Novel Enhanced Multi-Layer Perceptron

The Multi-Layer Perceptron (MLP) is a fully connected type of feedforward artificial neural network (ANN). It consists of multiple layers of perceptrons, each utilizing a threshold activation function. Although the term MLP is often used to describe any feedforward ANN, it is specifically designed for networks with multiple hidden layers. The pseudocode of MLP is:

- Select an initial weight vector and a suitable minimization strategy.
- Compute the network's output based on the input features.
- Calculate the delta value to adjust errors.
- Update weights using the selected minimization algorithm.
- Identify the highest similarity value score.

Polynomial Regression

Polynomial regression is an extension of linear regression, where the relationship between the independent variable ("x") and the dependent variable ("y") is modeled as a polynomial of degree "n". This method is particularly effective in capturing non-linear relationships. Polynomial regression predicts the conditional mean of "y" given "x", denoted as E(y|x). It is widely applied in scenarios involving non-linear phenomena, such as tissue growth rates, epidemic spread, and isotope dispersion in lake sediments. Regression analysis enables the prediction of "y" values based on known "x" values. The pseudocode of polynomial regression is:

- Import the polynomial features module.
- Import the linear regression module.
- Generate polynomial features from the input data.
- Fit the linear regression model using these features.
- Identify the best-fit polynomial equation.

Statistical Analysis

Statistical evaluation of the Novel Enhanced MLP and Polynomial Regression techniques was performed using SPSS software. Several independent variables were analyzed, including images, objects, distance, frequency, modulation, amplitude, volume, and decibels. The dependent variables were primarily related to images and objects.

An independent t-test was conducted to compare the accuracy of the two models. This analysis demonstrated that the Novel Enhanced MLP outperformed Polynomial Regression in food calorie measurement tasks. The MLP's ability to learn complex non-linear relationships between food features and caloric content makes it a more precise and reliable choice.

The materials and methods outlined above establish a robust framework for evaluating machine learning techniques in calorie estimation. The use of advanced statistical tools and well-defined experimental setups ensures the reliability and reproducibility of the findings.

Results

The results of the experiment highlight the superior performance of the Novel Enhanced Multi-Layer Perceptron (MLP) classifier. It achieved an accuracy of 97.5%, compared to the 94.0% accuracy of the Polynomial

Regression classifier. For clarity, Group-1 represents the Novel Enhanced MLP classifier, while Group-2 refers to the Polynomial Regression classifier. The accuracy values for both methods were recorded over ten iterations. Table 12.1 summarizes these results. These results were obtained using Anaconda Navigator for implementing and running the algorithms. The mean accuracy of the Novel Enhanced MLP was consistently higher than Polynomial Regression. Table 12.2 provides group statistics for both models. The Enhanced MLP exhibited a smaller standard deviation, indicating greater consistency in its accuracy measurements.

Figure 12.1 presents a simple bar graph comparing the accuracy rates of the two classifiers. The Enhanced Multi-Layer Perceptron consistently outperformed Polynomial Regression in terms of accuracy.

Table 12.3 provides the results of the independent t-test, comparing the accuracy rates of the two models. The analysis revealed a significant difference between the two classifiers, with a p-value of 0.000 (two-tailed, $p < 0.05$). This confirms that the Enhanced MLP is statistically superior to Polynomial Regression.

The findings of this study emphasize the advantages of the Novel Enhanced Multi-Layer Perceptron (MLP) over Polynomial Regression.

Table 12.1 Accuracy comparison of MLP and PR.

Iterations	MLP	PR
1	96	92
2	95	94
3	98	96
4	99	93
5	97	95
6	98	92
7	96	94
8	98	96
9	99	93
10	96	95
Average	97.5	94.0

Table 12.2 Group statistics.

Algorithm	N	Mean	Std. deviation	Std. error mean
MLP	20	97.15	1.039	0.232
PR	20	94.40	1.313	0.293

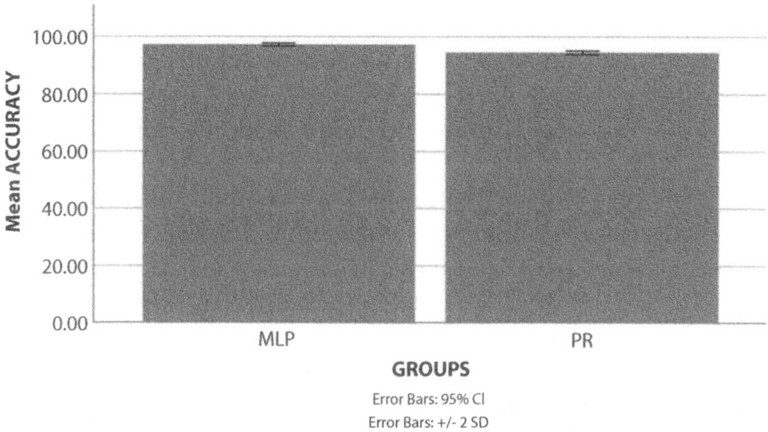

Figure 12.1 Accuracy rate of MLP and PR.

Table 12.3 Independent sample t-test.

	Leverage's test for equality of variances		T-test for equality of means						
					Significance			95% confidence interval of the difference	
	f	sig	t	df	Two side p	Mean difference	Std error difference	lower	upper
Equal variances assumed	1.346	0.25314	7.339	38	0.000	2.750	0.374	1.991	3.508
Equal variances not assumed			7.339	36.097	0.000	2.750	0.374	1.990	3.509

The MLP achieved an accuracy rate of 97.5%, significantly higher than the 94.0% accuracy of Polynomial Regression. This performance gap highlights the MLP's ability to model complex, non-linear relationships between features and outcomes.

The enhanced MLP demonstrated robustness across all iterations, as evidenced by its low standard deviation. This consistency is critical for applications where reliability is paramount. In contrast, Polynomial Regression exhibited greater variability, underscoring its limitations in handling non-linear data.

The t-test analysis further validated these observations. The significant p-value indicates that the difference in performance between the two models is not due to chance. Instead, it reflects the inherent strengths of the Enhanced MLP.

One of the key predictors for the MLP was its ability to adapt to diverse data inputs, such as peak boiling temperature and onset crystallization. These predictors played a crucial role in accurately estimating caloric content. Additionally, the MLP's architecture allowed it to classify tainted samples effectively, ensuring robust performance across varied datasets.

Despite its superior performance, the Enhanced MLP has limitations. Training the model with large datasets requires significant computational resources and time. Future research should focus on optimizing the training process to reduce time consumption. Expanding the dataset to include a wider variety of food items could further enhance the model's applicability.

Future studies should also explore the integration of the Enhanced MLP with other advanced techniques, such as transfer learning and ensemble methods. These approaches could improve accuracy and efficiency, making the model suitable for real-time applications in healthcare and nutrition monitoring.

This study demonstrates the potential of the Novel Enhanced Multi-Layer Perceptron in outperforming traditional methods like Polynomial Regression. Its ability to deliver high accuracy and consistency makes it a valuable tool for food calorie estimation and other machine learning applications.

Conclusion

This study demonstrates the superior performance of the Novel Enhanced Multi-Layer Perceptron (MLP) over Polynomial Regression in food calorie estimation. The accuracy achieved by the Enhanced MLP was 97.5%, significantly higher than the 94.0% accuracy of Polynomial Regression.

These results emphasize the importance of using advanced machine learning techniques to tackle complex, non-linear problems in real-world applications.

The Enhanced MLP's architecture, consisting of multiple interconnected layers of neurons, enables it to model intricate relationships between input features and output variables. This ability to capture non-linear dependencies is a key factor behind its improved performance. In contrast, Polynomial Regression relies on linear approximations, which can lead to inaccuracies when the underlying relationships are more complex.

Another significant advantage of the Enhanced MLP is its robustness and consistency, as evidenced by its lower standard deviation across multiple iterations. This reliability is critical for applications where precision is essential. Polynomial Regression, on the other hand, exhibited greater variability, highlighting its limitations in handling diverse datasets.

Despite its strengths, the Enhanced MLP is not without challenges. Training the model with large datasets requires substantial computational resources and time. Future research should focus on addressing these limitations by optimizing training algorithms and exploring parallel processing techniques. Expanding the dataset to include a wider range of food items could also improve the model's generalizability. The findings of this study highlight the potential of the Novel Enhanced Multi-Layer Perceptron as a powerful tool for calorie estimation and other machine learning applications. Its superior accuracy and consistency make it a promising solution for addressing complex problems in healthcare, nutrition, and beyond.

References

1. Yulita, I.N., Abdullah, A.S., Helen, A., Hadi, S., Sholahuddin, A., Rejito, J., Comparison Multi-Layer Perceptron and Linear Regression for Time Series Prediction of Novel Coronavirus Covid-19 Data in West Java. *J. Phys. Conf. Ser.*, 2021, https://doi.org/10.1088/1742-6596/1722/1/012021.
2. Horne, D., Palermo, R., Neumann, M.F., Housley, R., Bell, J., Can People Accurately Estimate the Calories in Food Images? An Optimised Set of Low- and High-Calorie Images from the Food-Pics Database. *Appetite*, 2019, https://doi.org/10.1016/j.appet.2019.04.017.
3. Taber, J.M. and Aspinwall, L.G., Tasty vs. Healthy: Evaluative Conditioning of Healthy Food with Good Taste Improves Perceived Taste of, Attitudes Toward, and Intentions to Eat Healthy Food. PsycEXTRA Dataset, 2014, https://doi.org/10.1037/e514472015-487.
4. Pradana, M.G., Palilingan, K., Akay, Y.V., Wijaya, D.P., Saputro, P.H., Comparison of Multi-Layer Perceptron, Random Forest & Logistic

Regression on Students Performance Test. *2022 International Conference on Informatics, Multimedia, Cyber and Information System (ICIMCIS)*, 2022, https://doi.org/10.1109/icimcis56303.2022.10017501.

5. Musliha, Bustamam, A., Yanuar, A., Mangunwardoyo, W., Anki, P., Amalia, R., Comparison Accuracy of Multi-Layer Perceptron and DNN in QSAR Classification for Acetylcholinesterase Inhibitors. *2021 International Conference on Artificial Intelligence and Mechatronics Systems (AIMS)*, 2021, https://doi.org/10.1109/aims52415.2021.9466040.
6. Aceeb, M.A., Development course to increase the accuracy of calculation speed cuts with readers. *Transp. Syst. Transp. Technol.*, 2016, https://doi.org/10.15802/tstt2016/85878.
7. Patil, P.C. and Burugapalli, V.C., Food Cuisine Classification by Convolutional Neural Network Based Transfer Learning Approach. *2021 IEEE International Conference on Mobile Networks and Wireless Communications (ICMNWC)*, 2021, https://doi.org/10.1109/icmnwc52512.2021.9688333.
8. Bayman, B.F. and Broadhurst, J.H., Simple Solution to a Problem Arising from the Processing of Finite Accuracy Digital Data Using Integer Arithmetic. https://doi.org/10.2172/5681407, 1980.
9. Tao, Z., Zenghui, W., Ruichang, Y., Study on Model of Onset of Nucleate Boiling in Natural Circulation with Subcooled Boiling Using Unascertained Mathematics. *Nucl. Eng. Des.*, 2005, https://doi.org/10.1016/j.nucengdes.2005.04.003.
10. Badescu, V., How Much Work Can Be Extracted from a Radiation Reservoir? *Phys. A Stat. Mech. Appl.*, 2014, https://doi.org/10.1016/j.physa.2014.05.024.
11. Dey, K., Kalita, K., Chakraborty, S., Prediction Performance Analysis of Neural Network Models for an Electrical Discharge Turning Process. *Int. J. Interact. Des. Manuf.*, 17, 2, 827–845, 2022. Springer. DOI: 10.1007/s12008-022-01003-y.
12. Naftali, T., Dor, A.E., Ruhimovitch, N., Shitrit, A.B., Benjaminov, F.S., Matalon, S., Shirin, H., Konikoff, F.M., Broide, E., Inconsistency Between Electronic Data of Patient's Adherence and Self-Reported Adherence Score. *Gastroenterology*, 2017, https://doi.org/10.1016/s0016-5085(17)32932-3.
13. Heiler, S., Nonparametric Time Series Analysis: Nonparametric Regression, Locally Weighted Regression, Autoregression, and Quantile Regression, in: *Wiley Series in Probability and Statistics*, 2011, https://doi.org/10.1002/9781118032978.ch12.
14. Sudarchikov, A.M., Onset of Boiling of Liquid in Channel. *High Temp.*, 2016, https://doi.org/10.1134/s0018151x16060213.
15. Venkatesh, A. and Saravanan, M.S., Prediction of Crop Yield Production with Novel Lasso Regression against Polynomial Regression Algorithm

to Achieve Higher Accuracy. *2022 International Conference on Edge Computing and Applications (ICECAA)*, 2022, https://doi.org/10.1109/icecaa55415.2022.9936193.

16. Vickram, A.S., Kamini, A.R., Das, R., Pathy, M.R., Parameswari, R., Archana, K., Sridharan, T.B., Validation of artificial neural network models for predicting biochemical markers associated with male infertility. *Syst. Biol. Reprod. Med.*, 62, 4, 258–265, 2016.
17. AS, V., Das, R., MS, S., Rao, K.A., TB, S., Prediction of Zn concentration in human seminal plasma of Normospermia samples by Artificial Neural Networks (ANN). *J. Assist. Reprod. Genet.*, 30, 453–459, 2013.

13

Effective Recommendation of Nutritious Food Using Random Forest Classifier in Comparison with Multi-Layer Perceptron Classifier Algorithm

J. Rishi Kannan and N. Bharatha Devi*

Department of Computer Science and Engineering, Saveetha School of Engineering, Saveetha Institute of Medical and Technical Sciences, Saveetha University, Chennai, India

Abstract

The aim of the study is to predict the nutrient-dense food categories using the Novel Random Forest Classifier in comparison with Multi-Layer Perceptron Classifier. Novel Random Forest Classifier and Multi-Layer Perceptron Classifier are the two algorithms considered for the current research, each with a number of iterations. Twenty are calculated using clincalc software with a G-power value of 80% and 95% confidence level. The dataset for the present work includes 5,250 values linked to the foods, ingredients, and cuisines; the factors considered are reviews, healthy food, snacks, and fast food. The accuracy of Novel Random Forest Classifier is 79.70% over Multi-Layer Perceptron Classifier with accuracy of 72.27% with a significance value of 0.01 (Independent Sample T-test $p<0.05$) and hence there is a statistically significant difference between the two groups. Compared to the accuracy of the Multi-Layer Perceptron Classifier of 72.27%, the Novel Random Forest Classifier's accuracy of 79.70% performs better in the recommendation of nutritious food.

***Keywords*:** Diet, food, food cluster, multi-layer perceptron classifier, machine learning, training, novel random forest

**Corresponding author*: bharathadevin.sse@saveetha.com

Narayanan Ganesh and Kanak Kalita (eds.) Harvesting Data: Blockchain, AI and Advanced Innovations in Agriculture, (263–274) © 2026 Scrivener Publishing LLC

Introduction

The inception of food recommender systems marks a significant advancement in the integration of technology into dietary management. These systems have emerged as pivotal tools in improving dietary choices among various populations, utilizing sophisticated algorithms to minimize errors and enhance precision, even when limited datasets are available. The utilization of the Weighted Slope One predictor in food clustering exemplifies this approach, improving system accuracy and reducing the common errors associated with less sophisticated satisfaction-rating systems [1].

The essence of these recommender systems lies in their ability to process user inputs, which include crucial medical data and dietary preferences, such as the choice between vegetarian and non-vegetarian meals. By analyzing this information, the systems are capable of predicting the most suitable food items for the user, thereby personalizing dietary recommendations to align with individual health needs and preferences [2]. This adaptation not only enhances user experience but also bolsters dietary adherence, which is crucial for managing various health conditions.

One of the noteworthy applications of these systems is the Diet Recommendation System designed specifically for individuals with diabetes. This system leverages food clustering analysis to suggest appropriate replacement foods that meet the nutritional needs of diabetic patients. By utilizing techniques such as K-mean clustering and Self-Organizing Maps, the system assesses the nutritional content of foods, focusing on eight key nutrients that are particularly important for this demographic. The efficacy of this system was validated by nutritionists who praised its utility in providing practical dietary solutions that contribute significantly to the field of nutrition management [3].

The broader aim of employing such dietary advice through technology is to foster a healthier society, free from non-communicable diseases and disorders. By integrating machine learning techniques into dietary recommendations, these systems not only cater to individual dietary needs but also contribute to public health on a larger scale [4].

Recent research underscores the growing interest in the development and refinement of food recommender systems. A survey of literature reveals a wealth of studies, including over 300 articles indexed in IEEE Xplore, that explore various facets of this technology. Notable among these is the DIETOS (Diet Organizer System), which offers adaptive nutritional content management within meal clusters. This system is distinguished by its dynamic profiling capabilities, which utilize real-time questionnaires developed by healthcare professionals to continuously update and refine user health profiles. Such profiles include detailed health and dietary histories, enabling the system to deliver highly personalized dietary advice [5].

Furthermore, the architecture of food recommender systems often incorporates sophisticated data management strategies to optimize daily meal plans. This includes the pre-filtering of inappropriate meals using multi-criteria decision analysis tools like AHPSort, which considers a user's dietary restrictions, preferences, and recent eating history to make nutritional recommendations more precise and tailored [6].

The potential of food recommender systems extends beyond typical dietary management; they are also being explored in therapeutic contexts, such as dietary interventions for children with autism. Studies suggest that dietary modifications can play a crucial role in managing symptoms related to autism, such as speech and sensory processing challenges. By employing machine learning techniques like K-means clustering and association rule mining, researchers are able to propose specific dietary clusters and therapies tailored to the symptomatic needs of autistic children, thereby supporting parents and caregivers in navigating the complexities of dietary management in autism [7, 8].

Moreover, some studies have focused on the direct analysis of grocery purchases to assess nutrient intake, proposing recommendations that enhance nutritional balance without necessitating extensive user input. This approach not only simplifies the user's involvement but also reduces computational costs, making nutritious choices more accessible and feasible for a wider audience [9, 10].

Despite these advancements, the existing systems are not without limitations. The accuracy of food recommendations has been identified as a significant gap in current systems. This chapter delves into the comparative analysis of two machine learning classifiers—the Novel Random Forest Classifier and the Multi-Layer Perceptron Classifier—to address these accuracy concerns. By comparing these methods, the study aims to refine the recommendation processes further, ensuring that the suggestions for healthy food groupings are both accurate and beneficial for users.

Materials and Methods

The exploration and development of advanced food recommender systems necessitate meticulous planning and execution of research methodologies. This research was conducted at the well-equipped Image Processing Lab of the Computer Centre at Saveetha School of Engineering, Saveetha Institute of Medical and Technical Sciences, Chennai, an institution renowned for its rigorous academic environment and state-of-the-art technological facilities. This setting provided the necessary infrastructure to carry out sophisticated image processing and machine learning tasks critical to our study [11].

Study Design and Sample Selection

The foundational step in our research involved a comparative study between two distinct groups, each carefully selected to represent different aspects of food recommendation algorithms. A total of 40 samples, with 20 from each group, were meticulously chosen to ensure a balanced representation of the data. This sample size was determined using a power analysis, where a G power value of 80% was targeted, with an alpha value of 0.05 and a beta value of 0.2, ensuring a 95% confidence interval in the findings. The adequacy of this sample size was confirmed using statistical tools available at ClinCalc, which helped validate the statistical significance of the comparative analysis [11].

Tools and Technologies

The technological backbone of our research comprised the use of the Jupyter notebook, a tool favored for its flexibility in coding and data analysis. The OpenCV software suite, a robust tool for image processing, was employed to handle the vast datasets obtained from the Kaggle platform. These datasets were pivotal as they included 5,250 unique entries spanning various categories such as foods, ingredients, cuisines, and dietary factors like reviews, healthy food labels, snack options, and fast food choices [1].

The experiments were run on a machine equipped with a 4GB RAM and an Intel Core i5 processor, operating on a Windows 10 OS. This hardware setup ensured efficient handling of the large data volumes, utilizing 64-bit system architecture for optimal data processing. Python was the programming language of choice, selected for its wide array of libraries and ease of handling large datasets [11].

Implementation of Novel Random Forest and MLP Classifiers

The core of our methodological framework involved the implementation of two sophisticated algorithms: the Novel Random Forest Classifier and the Multi-Layer Perceptron (MLP) Classifier.

Novel Random Forest Classifier

This algorithm is an advanced version of the conventional random forest method. It involves creating a forest with numerous decision trees to predict the output based on a majority voting system from various subsets of the dataset. This ensemble technique enhances predictive accuracy and robustness, reducing the likelihood of overfitting that is typical of single decision tree models. The Novel Random Forest algorithm incorporates a stacking ensemble method, which combines multiple different models to produce a more accurate and stable prediction [12–14]. The procedure for implementing the Novel Random Forest Classifier is as follows:

- Input: Training Set
- Steps:
  - Randomly select "k" features from a total of "m" features, where k << m.
  - Calculate the best split point to determine the node "d".
  - Split the node into daughter nodes using the best split.
  - Repeat steps 1 to 3 until "l" number of nodes has been reached.
  - Construct the forest by repeating the above steps "n" times to create "n" number of trees [11].

Multi-Layer Perceptron Classifier

The MLP Classifier is designed for complex classification challenges. It uses a feedforward neural network structure with multiple layers, where each layer consists of nodes that are interconnected and carry weighted information. This setup is particularly effective for both classification and regression problems, where it can map inputs to outputs through a series of computational steps involving forward and backward propagation [8, 10, 15, 16]. The procedure for the MLP Classifier is detailed as follows:

- Input: Training Set
- Steps:
  - Define input variables X (Input features) and Y (Target labels).
  - Randomly initialize weights for each layer.
  - Begin iteration count at zero.

- Perform the following until the iteration count reaches max_iter: a. Forward Propagation. b. Back Propagation. c. Increment the iteration count.
- Return the trained MLP Classifier [11].

Statistical Analysis

To quantify the effectiveness and accuracy of these classifiers, we employed SPSS software for statistical analysis. Our study measured various independent variables, including image quality, object recognition, and environmental factors such as distance, frequency, modulation, amplitude, volume, and decibels. The dependent variables were primarily the images and objects recognized and classified by the algorithms. We utilized a separate T-test analysis to statistically evaluate and compare the performance of the Novel Random Forest and MLP classifiers [17–19].

Results and Discussion

The core objective of this study was to evaluate and compare the performance of two machine learning classifiers, the Novel Random Forest Classifier and the Multi-Layer Perceptron Classifier, in their capacity to accurately recommend nutritious foods. This section details the results obtained from the empirical tests and discusses the implications of these findings in the broader context of food recommender systems.

The results of the study revealed that the Novel Random Forest Classifier achieved an accuracy of 79.70%, while the Multi-Layer Perceptron Classifier recorded a slightly lower accuracy of 72.27%. These results are significant as they demonstrate the effectiveness of the Novel Random Forest approach in handling complex datasets and providing reliable food recommendations based on nutritional content.

Detailed statistical analysis was conducted to assess the robustness of the classifiers. Group statistical analysis revealed that the Novel Random Forest Classifier not only outperformed the Multi-Layer Perceptron in terms of accuracy but also showed more consistency in its predictions, as indicated by a standard deviation of 2.46678 compared to 2.03628 for the MLP Classifier (Table 13.1).

An independent sample T-test was performed to determine the statistical significance of the differences observed between the two classifiers (Table 13.2). The results indicated a p-value of 0.01 ($p<0.05$), confirming

Table 13.1 Group statistical analysis of novel random forest classifier and multi-layer perceptron classifier.

	Group	N	Mean	Std. deviation	Std. error mean
Accuracy	Novel Random Forest Classifier	20	79.70	2.46678	.78007
	Multi-Layer Perceptron Classifier	20	72.27	2.03628	.64393
Loss	Novel Random Forest Classifier	20	20.73	2.46678	.78007
	Multi-Layer Perceptron Classifier	20	28.05	2.03628	.64393

that the differences in performance were statistically significant. This analysis substantiates the superior performance of the Novel Random Forest Classifier over the Multi-Layer Perceptron Classifier.

In terms of loss metrics, the Novel Random Forest Classifier recorded a lower loss value of 20.73 compared to 28.05 for the Multi-Layer Perceptron, further affirming its efficiency in predictive accuracy and model stability.

Figure 13.1 visually represents these findings, illustrating the comparative performance of the two classifiers both in terms of mean accuracy and loss, reinforcing the numerical data presented in the tables.

The findings from this study provide compelling evidence of the superiority of the Novel Random Forest Classifier in the context of food recommendation systems. This classifier not only shows higher accuracy but also demonstrates greater reliability in its predictions, which is crucial for applications in dietary recommendations where precision is paramount.

The significance of these findings extends into the realm of curative food recommendations, where accuracy in predicting nutritious food can directly impact individual health outcomes. As the demand for personalized diet plans increases, especially among populations with specific dietary needs such as diabetic patients, the ability of systems like the Novel Random Forest to provide precise recommendations becomes increasingly important.

This research contributes both theoretically and practically to the field of dietary management and machine learning applications in health.

Table 13.2 Independent sample t-test is performed. The significant value obtained is 0.01 (independent sample t-test $p<0.05$), which shows that there is a statistically significant difference between the two groups.

		Levene's test for equality of variances		T-test for equality means with 95% confidence interval						
		f	Sig.	t	df	Sig. (2-tailed)	Mean difference	Std. error difference	Lower	Upper
Accuracy	Equal variances assumed	.398	.536	7.236	18	0.01	7.31900	1.01151	5.1939	9.44409
	Equal Variances not assumed			7.236	17.376	0.01	7.31900	1.01151	5.1884	9.44958
Loss	Equal variances assumed	.398	.536	-7.236	18	0.00	-7.31900	1.01151	- 9.44409	-5.1939
	Equal Variances not assumed			-7.236	17.376	0.00	-7.31900	1.01151	-9.44958	-5.1884

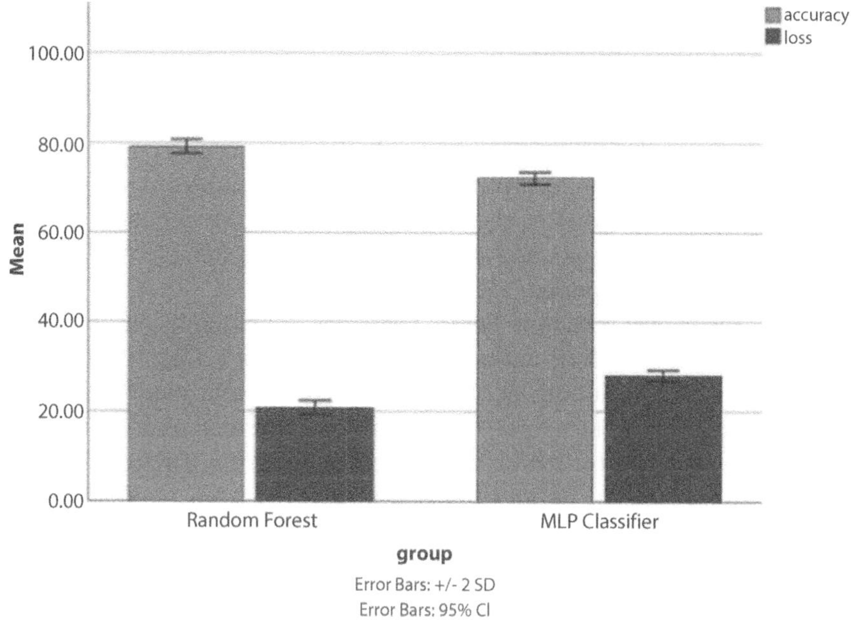

Figure 13.1 Comparison of novel random forest classifier and multi-layer perceptron.

Theoretically, it provides insights into the comparative efficacy of different machine learning algorithms in food recommendation, adding to the existing body of knowledge in the field. Practically, it offers a robust method that can be employed by healthcare providers and dieticians to enhance the nutritional advice given to patients, potentially leading to better health management and disease prevention.

Despite the successes, this study acknowledges certain limitations. The training time for the Novel Random Forest, particularly with large datasets, was noted as a significant challenge. Future research will focus on optimizing the training process to accommodate larger datasets without compromising on speed or accuracy. Additionally, there is potential to expand the system to include a more diverse array of food items and nutritional parameters, thereby broadening the scope and applicability of the food recommendation system.

Conclusion

The comparative analysis between the Novel Random Forest Classifier and the Multi-Layer Perceptron Classifier yielded insightful results, demonstrating clear distinctions in performance. Here are the key conclusions drawn from this study:

- The Novel Random Forest Classifier achieved a higher accuracy of 79.70%, compared to the 72.27% accuracy of the Multi-Layer Perceptron Classifier. This indicates a more robust capability of the Novel Random Forest in handling complex datasets and effectively predicting suitable nutritional food options.
- The Novel Random Forest Classifier consistently outperformed the Multi-Layer Perceptron Classifier across various metrics, including accuracy and loss minimization. This superior performance underscores its potential as a more reliable tool for food recommendation systems, particularly those focusing on nutritional accuracy.
- The study confirms that the Novel Random Forest Classifier not only provides higher accuracy but also enhances the effectiveness of nutritional food recommendations. This makes it a valuable tool for dietary management applications, where precise nutrient-based recommendations are crucial.
- The findings suggest significant implications for the development and optimization of dietary management systems. By integrating the Novel Random Forest Classifier, these systems can offer more accurate and personally tailored food recommendations, thereby supporting better health outcomes for users.
- While the current results are promising, further research is recommended to explore the scalability of the Novel Random Forest Classifier in larger datasets and its integration into real-world dietary management and recommendation platforms.

References

1. Agapito, G., *et al.*, DIETOS: A recommender system for adaptive diet monitoring and personalized food suggestion, in: *12th International Conference on Wireless and Mobile Computing, Networking and Communications (WiMob)*, IEEE, 2016, doi: 10.1109/WiMOB.2016.7763190.

2. Bundasak, S., A healthy food recommendation system by combining clustering technology with the Weighted slope one Predictor, in: *International Electrical Engineering Congress (iEECON)*, Pattaya, pp. 1–5, 2017, doi: 10.1109/IEECON.2017.8075820.
3. Crawford, J., Keynote speech 6, Big data, IoT and the 2nd sustainable development goal, in: *International Workshop on Electromagnetics: Applications and Student Innovation Competition*, London, 2017.
4. Ganesh, P., *et al.*, Random forest regression-based machine learning model for accurate estimation of fluid flow in curved pipes. *Processes*, 9, 11, 2095, Nov. 2021, doi: 10.3390/pr9112095.
5. Gayathri, R., *et al.*, A comparative analysis of machine learning models in prediction of mortar compressive strength. *Processes*, 10, 7, 1387, Jul. 2022, doi: 10.3390/pr10071387.
6. Honda, M. and Nishi, H., Household nutrition analysis and food recommendation Using purchase history, in: *IEEE 30th International Symposium on Industrial Electronics (ISIE)*, Kyoto, 2021, doi: 10.1109/ISIE45552.2021.9576410.
7. Kalita, K., *et al.*, Multi-Objective artificial bee colony optimized hybrid deep belief network and XGBoost algorithm for heart disease prediction. *Front. Digit. Health*, 5, 1279644, Nov. 2023, doi: 10.3389/fdgth.2023.1279644.
8. Lo, C.-C., *et al.*, A semantic web methodology for situation-aware curative food service recommendation system, in: *International Conference on Computer Science and Software Engineering*, Wuhan, 2008, doi: 10.1109/CSSE.2008.519.
9. Luo, J., Analyzing spatial accessibility to foods in GIS: A case of Springfield, MO, in: *25th International Conference on Geoinformatics*, Buffalo, 2017, doi: 10.1109/GEOINFORMATICS.2017.8090923.
10. Nanmaran, R., *et al.*, Investigating the role of image fusion in brain tumor classification models based on machine learning algorithm for personalized medicine. *Comput. Math. Methods Med.*, 2022, 7137524, Feb. 2022, doi: 10.1155/2022/7137524.
11. Phanich, M., *et al.*, Food recommendation system using clustering analysis for diabetic patients, in: *International Conference on Information Science and Applications*, Seoul, South Korea, 2010, doi: 10.1109/ICISA.2010.5480416.
12. Premasundari, M. and Yamini, C., Food and therapy recommendation system for autistic syndrome using machine learning techniques, in: *IEEE International Conference on Electrical, Computer and Communication Technologies (ICECCT)*, Coimbatore, 2019.
13. Ratisoontorn, N., Recipe recommendations for toddlers using integrated nutritional and ingredient similarity measures, in: *19th International Joint Conference on Computer Science and Software Engineering (JCSSE)*, Bangkok, 2022, doi: 10.1109/JCSSE54890.2022.9836248.

14. Shah, M., *et al.*, Diet recommendation system based on different machine learners: A review, in: *Second International Conference on Artificial Intelligence and Smart Energy (ICAIS)*, Coimbatore, 2022, doi: 10.1109/ICAIS53314.2022.9742919.
15. Shaik, K., *et al.*, Big data analytics framework using squirrel search optimized Gradient Boosted Decision Tree for heart disease diagnosis. *Appl. Sci. (Basel)*, 13, 9, 5236, Apr. 2023, doi: 10.3390/app13095236.
16. Shanmugasundar, G., *et al.*, A comparative study of linear, random forest and AdaBoost regressions for modeling non-traditional machining. *Processes*, 9, 11, 2015, Nov. 2021, doi: 10.3390/pr9112015.
17. Vickram, S., *et al.*, Prediction of Zn concentration in human seminal plasma of Normospermia samples by Artificial Neural Networks (ANN). *J. Assist. Reprod. Genet.*, 30, 4, 453–459, Apr. 2013, doi: 10.1007/s10815-012-9926-4.
18. Vickram, S., *et al.*, Validation of artificial neural network models for predicting biochemical markers associated with male infertility. *Syst. Biol. Reprod. Med.*, 62, 4, 258–265, Aug. 2016, doi: 10.1080/19396368.2016.1185654.
19. Wang, C.-L., *et al.*, Survival of Lactobacillus acidophilus encapsulated as freeze-dried culture under extreme conditions, in: *4th International Conference on Bioinformatics and Biomedical Engineering*, Chengdu, 2010, doi: 10.1109/ICBBE.2010.5515772.

14

Smart Pest Identification in Agriculture: Leveraging CNN Classifier Over SVM for Leaf Health Analysis

Bobbilla Ramya Sri and V. Karthick*

Department of Computer Science and Engineering, Saveetha School of Engineering, Saveetha Institute of Medical and Technical Sciences, Saveetha University, Chennai, India

Abstract

The aim of the research is to use CNN Classifier to identify pests impacting leaf health in agricultural crops with more accuracy. Twenty samples were used as the sample size. Both Groups 1 and 2 include 10 samples each, with Group 1 using the Conventional Neural Network (CNN) classifier and Group 2 using the Support Vector Machine (SVM) classifier. The sample size is determined using a G-power pre-test score of 80%, a threshold of 0.05, and a confidence interval of 95%. While doing the study, the alpha and beta were both set to 0.05 and 0.2, respectively. The CNN classifier has an accuracy of 88.93%, which is higher than the SVM classifier's accuracy of 82.81%. The average accuracy detection is two standard deviations above the mean, indicating a significant difference between the two groups based on an independent sample t-test $p=0.000$ ($p<0.05$), which shows that there is a significance between the two groups. The CNN classifier algorithm has an accuracy rate of 88.93%, which is higher than the accuracy rate of the SVM classifier algorithm, which is 82.81%.

Keywords: Pest, leaf, health, agricultural, classification, support vector machine, agriculture, convolutional neural network

**Corresponding author*: karthickv.sse@saveetha.com

Narayanan Ganesh and Kanak Kalita (eds.) Harvesting Data: Blockchain, AI and Advanced Innovations in Agriculture, (275–284) © 2026 Scrivener Publishing LLC

Introduction

Agriculture plays a crucial role in feeding the world's population and providing essential materials for various industries, such as textiles, paper, furniture, and construction. It is also involved in the production of beverages, medicine, and natural rubber [1]. Numerous processes worldwide rely on agricultural products [2]. The productivity of agriculture is reliant on the soil's fertility and the health of plants [3]. Pests can have a detrimental effect on agricultural production by damaging the health of plants, which can be observed in their leaves. These pests can affect various crops, fruits, tree trunks, tea leaves, and herbal plants. To classify pests, object classification techniques are used [4].

More than 900 articles were published from various sources like IEEE Xplore, Google Scholar, Springer and many others in the past five years. The articles published have a unique approach to recognize the objects from the images. Classification can be achieved by using the Object Classification Technique [5]. More than 50,000 pest species and diseases affect agricultural plants [6]. Insects, weeds, birds, rats, fungi, mites, and nematodes are a few kinds of pests creating harm to agricultural plants [7]. Pests like hornworms, aphids, cabbage looper, caterpillars, thrips, cutworms, beetles, and mites may destroy leaves and affect plant growth [8]. Controlling measures are carried out based on the type of pests affecting Leaf Health [9].

To identify and classify pests that affect leaf health in agricultural farms, a database of images of various pests was collected. Object detection techniques were applied to the database, using both CNN and SVM classifiers. The aim was to determine which classifier was more effective in accurately identifying and classifying pests based on their types. The results showed that CNN outperformed SVM in terms of accuracy, as it had better feature extraction capabilities. Overall, the study demonstrated the potential of using image processing techniques to improve pest detection and management in agriculture.

Materials and Methods

This research article was carried out in the Department of Artificial Intelligence Laboratory belonging to Saveetha School of Engineering, Saveetha Institute of Medical and Technical Sciences. This research article has two groups. The two groups are CNN classifier and SVM classifier, which are compared based upon their accuracy of classifying pests from the sample datasets. There are 20 samples in total for the two groups which are divided equally, which is 10 samples per group. The CNN classifier has the first 10 samples of accuracies and the remaining 10 samples of accuracies are for the SVM classifier. The number of samples are taken according to the previous study with confidence interval 95% and enrolment ratio defined as 1 and g power 80% and along with a threshold as 0.05G.

The requirements for this research are a dataset which consists of numerous pest images which are necessary for training the Pest Identification framework. The framework requires a minimum of 8GB of RAM for easy access to the processor. Coming to the processor Intel i5 5th gen or Ryzen 3 are recommended. Hard disk space of at least 500GB is required to store the necessary images of the dataset which is downloaded from kaggle.com and to store the code and to install the plug-in or any software. Graphics card of minimum 4GB is recommended to reduce the load on the CPU which helps in faster processing of the images. The online development environment Kaggle is used to develop the framework for Pest Identification [10].

Support Vector Machine (SVM) Classifier Algorithm

SVM is a supervised machine learning algorithm used for classification and regression analysis. It finds the best hyperplane that maximizes the margin between two classes in a dataset [1, 2]. SVM transforms the input data into a higher-dimensional space using a kernel function to achieve a linear separation between classes [3]. It can handle complex datasets with high accuracy and is used in various fields such as image classification, natural language processing, and bioinformatics. SVM can also be used for multi-class classification by combining binary SVM classifiers.

Support Vector Machine (SVM) Classifier Algorithm Steps

Step 1: Frame the SVM classifier model with libraries necessary for identifying pests.
Step 2: Read Data set of containing images of pests and train the SVM model.
Step 3: Initialize the dimension parameters for image mapping with Train data set.
Step 4: Extract Features from Data points in the Hyperplane.
Step 5: Determine the values filtered for test data set and Store the Feature values.
Step 6: Compile the model till all the images are identified.
Step 7: Write the results of the SVM model of Identifying pests.

Convolutional Neural Network (CNN) Classifier Algorithm

Convolutional Neural Networks (CNN) is a type of deep learning algorithm used for image and video classification, object detection, and image recognition [3]. It works by passing input images through multiple convolutional and pooling layers to extract relevant features. These features are then used to classify the input image. The use of convolutional layers helps in preserving the spatial relationships between the features of the image, leading to higher accuracy in image classification tasks. CNNs have shown impressive performance in various computer vision tasks, including face recognition, object detection, and autonomous driving [5, 6].

Convolutional Neural Network (CNN) Classifier Algorithm Steps

Step 1: Construct CNN model with Image Detection and Feature extraction Libraries.
Step 2: Get data set for training the CNN Model for Classifying and identifying pests.
Step 3: Obtain the Image filter values from Convolutional layer and Feature map coefficients from Pooling Layers for train data set.
Step 4: Compare the similarities of the Test image set with Logistic functional Module of CNN classifier.
Step 5: Record the similarity values of Features collected.
Step 6: Iterate the layers of CNN model for complete analysis of pest identification.
Step 7: Write the results executed from CNN Model.

Statistical Analysis

IBM SPSS Version 26 is used to implement the Statistical Analysis. The Independent Sample T-test is performed with the help of comparison made between mean accuracies. The Independent variables are accuracy and number of images in [11] whereas the dependent variable is image size.

Results

The accuracy of the CNN classifier is 88.93% and the accuracy of the SVM classifier is 82.81%. The Group-1 is referred to as the CNN classifier and Group-2 is referred to as the SVM Classifier. Here both the groups are compared in the terms of accuracy. So, the CNN classifier model performed better than the SVM classifier model.

Table 14.1 shows the sample data of the accuracies of CNN algorithm and SVM algorithm. Table 14.2 shows the group statistics for size N=20, which contains mean accuracies and standard deviations for CNN and SVM classifier methods. Table 14.3 Shows the Independent sample T-test that compares CNN classifier as well as SVM algorithm with confidence interval 95%. These results showed that there was a statistically significant

Table 14.1 Comparison of accuracies of sample size 10 for convolutional neural network algorithm and support vector machine algorithm.

S. no.	CNN classifier	SVM classifier
1	90.36	84.24
2	89.27	83.12
3	88.30	82.26
4	87.60	81.35
5	88.20	82.14
6	86.21	80.70
7	90.29	84.19
8	88.90	82.39
9	90.57	84.24
10	89.63	83.50

Table 14.2 The following table gives group statistics which shows a sample size of n=10 for each group. The mean percentage of the convolutional neural network algorithm is 88.93% whereas the accuracy percentage of the support vector machine algorithm is 82.81%. Standard deviation 1.38 and 1.25 as well as standard error rate is also shown.

	Groups	N	Mean	Std. deviation	Std. error mean
	CNN	10	88.9330	1.38595	.43827
ACCURACY	SVM	10	82.8130	1.25068	.39550

Table 14.3 The following table shows the analysis of the independent sample t-test and the equal variance assumed is compared with equal variances in the accuracy with 95% confidence interval of the difference and the significant value as 0.000 ($p<0.05$).

		Levene's test for equality of variances		T-test for equality of means					95% confidence interval of the difference	
		F	Sig.	t	df	Sig. (2-tailed)	Mean difference	Std. error difference	Lower	Upper
ACCURACY	Equal variances assumed	.022	.003	10.367	18	.000	6.12000	.59034	4.87974	7.36026
	Equal variances not assumed			10.367	17.813	.000	6.12000	.59034	4.87880	7.36120

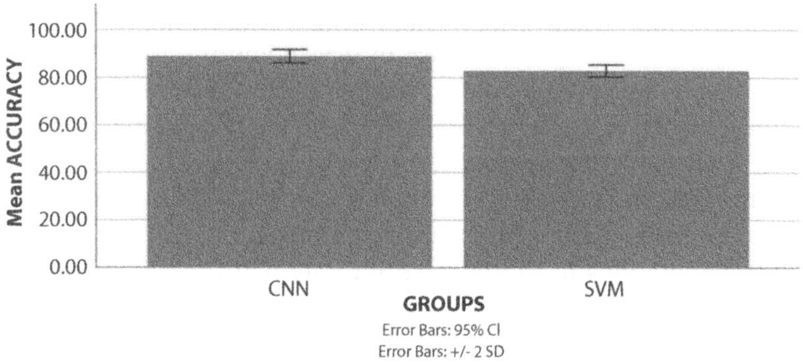

Figure 14.1 The above bar chart compares the mean accuracies of both the existing and proposed algorithms. The accuracy is taken on the y-axis while the proposed and existing algorithms are taken on x-axis. The accuracy of the convolutional neural network algorithm is 88.93% and support vector machine algorithm is 82.81%. The mean accuracy detection is ± 2SD.

difference between the two groups with the $p=0.000$ ($p<0.05$). Figure 14.1 is a graph that shows the comparison between the mean accuracy of the CNN and mean accuracy of the SVM algorithm along with the error bars.

Discussion

As mentioned in the results it is evident that the Convolutional Neural Network (CNN) algorithm has performed significantly better than that of SVM algorithm [12]. The accuracy percentage of CNN model is found to be 88.93% while that of the SVM model is 82.81%.

Similar research work shows that SVM works with better precision accuracy for reduced input size and CNN sometimes requires more computational time for filtering images [4]. The CNN model lacks retaining the defined position and the orientation of the objects present in image and requires numerous trainings for better classification of the objects. Three similar research papers use a dataset consisting of images of crops affected by different types of pests [13] and demonstrate that the CNN classifier outperforms the SVM classifier in terms of accuracy and robustness [1]. The opposite finding could be that using machine learning algorithms such as CNN and SVM for pest identification in agricultural farms is less accurate and efficient than traditional manual methods [14]. The study could conclude that manual identification methods are more effective and reliable in identifying pests and protecting plant health in agricultural farms [15]. CNN model has its use in developing the Face Recognition frameworks, Fingerprint analysis, Weather forecasts networks. To detect pest images when they are not totally visible to the system, the system must manage occlusion scenarios and consistently recognize the object. Because the model lacks correct object location and orientation in pictures, effective item categorization needs extensive training.

All the limitations in the research indicate that the system could face confusion due to varied perspectives on objects. Future research can focus on improving the CNN and SVM classifiers by refining algorithms and increasing training data to overcome these challenges. The scope of the study can be expanded by integrating these classifiers with other technologies like drones, sensors, and automation to create an intelligent pest identification and management system for farms. This system can enable farmers to take proactive measures to prevent crop damage by providing real-time monitoring and alerts for pest outbreaks. The research can also extend to identifying and managing plant diseases and environmental stress factors affecting crop yields, with potential use in other industries such as forestry, horticulture, and landscaping.

Conclusion

The Convolutional Neural Network (CNN) classifier algorithm, which has an accuracy of 88.93%, performed better than Support Vector Machine (SVM) algorithm with an accuracy of 82.81%. So, using CNN algorithm in Identifying Pests affecting Leaf Health gives better accuracy compared to SVM algorithm.

References

1. Zhang, Z., Liu, S., Liu, M., A multi-task fully deep convolutional neural network for contactless fingerprint minutiae extraction. *Pattern Recognit.*, 120, 108189, December 2021.
2. Agulhon, R., Prediction of risk, control methods and application of integrated pest control, in: *Integrated Pest Control in Viticulture*, pp. 337–342, CRC Press, 2021.
3. Munson, R.D., Soil fertility, fertilizers, and plant nutrition, in: *Handbook of Soils and Climate in Agriculture*, pp. 269–294, CRC Press, 2018.

4. Wagle, S.A., Harikrishnan, R., Ali, S.H.M., Faseehuddin, M., Classification of plant leaves using new compact convolutional neural network models. *Plants*, 11, 24, December 2021.
5. Sahoo, S.K., Saidulu, B., Shyam Prasad, D., Defective object classification using advanced optimization technique. *Mater. Today*, 38, 2695–2699, 2021.
6. World Health Organization, and Food and Agriculture Organization of the United Nations, *Guidance on pesticide licensing schemes: International code of conduct on pesticide management*, 2021.
7. Harris, P., Weeds (insects and mites): Biological control, in: *Managing Biological and Ecological Systems*, pp. 277–280, CRC Press, 2020.
8. Gupta, G. and Kumar, N.R., Efficacy of pomegranate peel against aphids, Thrips and spider mites in Rose. *Indian J. Entomol.*, 83, 332–338, 2021.
9. Mills, N.J., Plant health management: Biological control of insect pests, in: *Reference Module in Food Science*, Elsevier, 2018.
10. Kaggle, Paddy Image Classification, 2022.
11. George, D. and Mallery, P., *IBM SPSS statistics 26 step by step*, Routledge, 2019.
12. Michelucci, U., *Advanced applied deep learning*, 1st ed., APress, Berlin, Germany, 2019.
13. Tungo, A.K., Padhan, R., Pradhan, T.P., Dehury, M., Jena, R.K., Fuzzy C-means clustering and Pseudo-coloring-based pest detection of ripe-fruit health monitoring system using 2-D aggrotech images. *Grad. Res. Eng. Technol.*, 40–44, May 2022.
14. Shetty, B., Fernandes, R., Rodrigues, A.P., Chengoden, R., Bhattacharya, S., Lakshmanna, K., Author Correction: Skin lesion classification of dermoscopic images using machine learning and convolutional neural network. *Sci. Rep.*, 12, 21919, December 2022.
15. Vaishali, and Thangaraj, D.S.J.J., Innovative facial expression identification for criminal identification using unsupervised machine learning and compare the accuracy with CNN classifiers, in: *2022 International Conference on Business Analytics for Technology and Security (ICBATS)*, Dubai, United Arab Emirates, 2022.

15

Role of Artificial Intelligence in Weed Detection and Prevention

K. Arunkumar, S. Leninisha* and M. Sandhya

School of Computer Science and Engineering, Vellore Institute of Technology, Chennai, India

Abstract

Survival of any form of life needs energy for existence. The energy can come in many forms, including oxygen, water, proteins, vitamins, starch, and fat. However, consumption of these energies has paved the way for hunting, fishing and agriculture. Today agriculture plays a major role in addressing the food demand of human lives and others. Due to factors like disease, storage, and transportation, most of the crops are useless. Plant disease is the major factor, because of which 15% of cultivation is wasted. However, development of technology has paveda way to overcome the disease issue. Another important problem in farming is weed. Farmers have followed the conventional method of identifying the weeds with the naked eye,but it not possible for all the farmers to identify these weeds if the size of the farming land is large. Computer vision facilities need to be incorporated into agriculture with the advancementof artificial intelligence in order to identify weeds earlier. This work presents a review of weedidentification and removal from the classic method to recent methods. The effort will allow researchers, especially those who are new to this field, to get a quick introduction to weeddetection and identification.

***Keywords*:** Weed, machine learning, deep learning, precision agriculture, smart farming, blockchain

**Corresponding author*: leninisha.shanmugam@vit.ac.in; ORCID: 0000-0002-8205-1447
K. Arunkumar: ORCID: 0000-0002-7300-2168
M. Sandhya: ORCID: 0000-0003-1208-2990

Narayanan Ganesh and Kanak Kalita (eds.) Harvesting Data: Blockchain, AI and Advanced Innovations in Agriculture, (285–324) © 2026 Scrivener Publishing LLC

Introduction

Agricultural yield has a great effect on weed, a word that's short and sweet. Overall, weed produced the highest potential loss of around 34% in the total yield. Weed mapping is much more needed from day one of the agricultures. Manual weed identification is a classic technique used by farmers, which is time consuming, requiring more manpower. It remains a challenge to detect a weed within the row, despite the many techniquesused. Weeds are plants that negatively impact the economy, the environment, human health, or amenity. Weeds are a major danger to the natural environment and main production businesses. It's important to note that there are many different weed species [126]. As well as outgrowing crops, weeds consume quite a bit of water and nutrients, resulting in a decrease in crop production. There is a threat to native species and displacing them, causing significant deforestation and land degradation, increasing the cost of cultivation and reducing the quality of the product, harboring insects and pathogens and emitting toxic secretions [79]. Preventing weeds, detecting them early, and identifying them are essential. The manual weeding method iscumbersome, inefficient, and costly, making it impractical for modern weeding [7]. Mostly, the weedsare controlled or removed by mechanical method (hand pulling, hand weeding, tillage, hoeing, flooding, smothering), cropping or cultural method (crop rotation), chemical method and biological method. An herbicide application is less expensive and more efficient than mechanical weeding for controlling weeds on a field, so it is chosen as the method of choice [76]. Moreover, hand hoeing weeds is widely used, but most of the time plants are mistaken as weeds or weeds are missed, which results in only 65% to 85% of weeds being eradicated. Hand weeding also has the disadvantage of being labor-intensive and expensive. Due to the weed's high resemblance to plants, extracting and discriminating features is difficult [12]. Farm products are reduced in quality, irrigation water is lost, and cultivated crops lose their commercial value as a result of weeds [99, 137]. The development of AI has led to the need for incorporating computer vision into agriculture to identify weeds earlier. An important and recurring issue is the automatic identification of weeds [129]. Numerous advancements in crop growth monitoring, soil status monitoring, and crop/weed discrimination, at rates appropriate to site-specific field operations, are now based on close-range sensing of the morphologies.

Various Methods of Weed Control

The primary factor causing crops to be ruined in any field, which lowers crop productivity, are weed plants [102]. There are several methods of weeding, including manual weeding by hand or using simple hand tools, which has been used for centuries and continues to be used in small fields today [100]. Classification is based on characterization of pixels as crop, soil, and weed [30]. Controlling established weeds is possible, but preventing them from becoming established can prevent weed infestations. Various methods of weed control are depicted in Figure 15.1.

1. Biological Method

The goal of this method is to control non-native species by releasing natural enemies. Bio-agents like pathogen, insects, and other animals are used to control weeds. Insects and illnesses that infest weeds may stunt their growth or cause them to die. Biological control techniques can diminish weeds, but they cannot completely remove them. Also, this process is slow. The biological agents take a great deal of time and patience to work.

2. Chemical Method

Chemicals which are used to kill plants or weeds are called herbicides. An option in integrated weed management is chemical weed control, which consists of a combination of cultural, mechanical, and chemical methods. Chemicals are generally used to control weeds in combination with tillage operations and hand weeding. Commercial operations need to control weeds chemically and apply herbicides both at planting and after harvest.

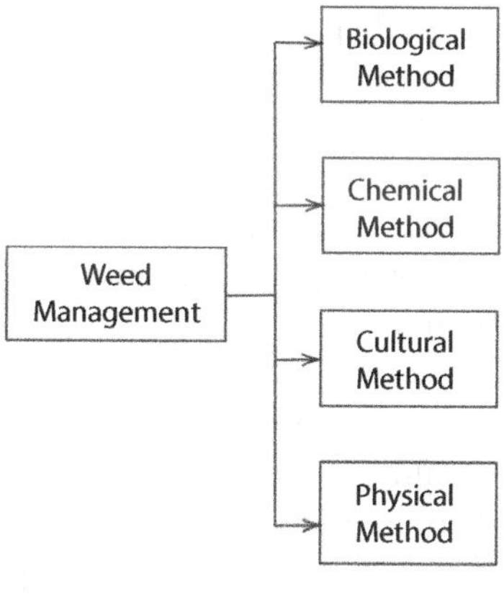

Figure 15.1 Weed management.

Table 15.1 Different chemical methods.

Chemical method	
Soil application	**Foliar application**
Soil surface application: Herbicides sprayed on the soil's top to create a consistent herbicide layer. **Sub-surface application:** Herbicides are injected into the soil's deeper layers. **Band application:** Over or along the crop row, herbicides are administered.	**Blanket application:** Applying herbicide to all of the leaf's surface. **Directed Application:** Weeds between crop rows are treated with herbicide immediately. **Spot application:** Small weed areas receive an application or pouring of herbicides.

Unwise use of herbicides can reduce yield, pollute the environment, and adversely affect the biotic and abiotic environments, posing a threat to human health and well-being. There is no one herbicide that can be used for all soil types and weed populations due to the fact that most herbicides are specific for certain soil types and weed populations. Also, chemicals cannot be used in organic farming. Soil and Foliar application chemical methods are illustrated in Table 15.1.

Use of Herbicides

Although the use of agrochemicals can significantly improve agricultural yield and quality, recent years have seen an increase in environmental concerns. With regard to production increase, cost effectiveness, and environmental protection, conventional agricultural pesticide application methods have created a conflict. In order to prevent negative impacts on the environment and human health, pesticides must be administered using the proper spraying systems. Environmental damage and a rise in weed control costs are caused by the usage of large doses of herbicide [71]. As a result, spraying techniques and technology have been continuously evolving in recent years. Traditional sprayers required a lot of work and heavy equipment to operate them in the field.

Use of Sprayers

As a result of the lack of path planning and field GPS survey, the maximum volume of spray could not be achieved at the target, and spray drift and field turn resulted in spray loss. The lack of accuracy in broadcast sprayers is the cause of this inefficiency. Farmers faced difficulties in the past because weeds, a nuisance, were causing agricultural yield to suffer.

A smart spraying technique that makes use of sensors and artificial intelligence has recently been introduced (variable sprayer, drone sprayers). When this technology recognizes plants, weeds, and pests, it can then apply chemicals selectively where they are needed. First, a picture is captured using a camera or a sensor to recognize a plant; next, deep learning algorithms are employed to identify various plants, weeds, and illnesses, which aids the decision support system in determining the target. The algorithms automatically choose the plant/herbicide to spray. Different conventional sprayers are

1. Hand-operated sprayer
2. Backpack sprayers
3. PTO driven boom sprayers
4. Knapsack sprayer
5. Boom sprayer
6. Smart sprayer
7. Orchard sprayer
8. Steam power sprayer
9. Pressure regulator engine sprayer
10. Conventional VRT sprayer
11. Tunnel sprayer
12. Tower sprayer
13. Multi-channel air blast sprayer
14. Vehicle mounted ultra-low volume sprayer

3. Cultural Method

Ploughing

Soil is turned and loosened before seeds are sown. After plowing, the soil is evened out and leveled with a processcalled leveling. By ploughing, manure is integrated, weeds are uprooted, infectious pathogens and insects are removed.Tractors or bullocks are used to pull this plough.

Crop Rotation

Planning crop rotations on agricultural lands is a method of increasing soil productivity, crop yield, and weed/pest resistance through the selection and succession of crops. By considering agronomic, environmental, ecological and economic factors, choosing successor crops for various years is done [1]. By inhibiting the growth of weeds, crop rotation reduces the use of pesticides and herbicides, which means less harmful ingredients are released into the environment [33]. In addition to affecting soil microbial diversity and activity, crop rotation may also affect soil enzyme activity by releasing enzymes from living and dead cells, thus altering soil microbial composition and activity. The soil bacterial community composition, abundance, and diversity in rotation systems were significantly different from those in monocrops [49].

4. Physical Method

Hand-Weeding and Hand Hoeing

By using a small hand tool (sickle, shovel, etc.), the weeds are pulled out by hand or uprooted. Some vegetable plantations are being done using hand weeding as a means of weed control [112].

Two aspects are important in hand weeding:

- How many hand weedings must be performed and how long must pass between each hand weeding.
- Crop growth, weed growth, and the key period of crop-weed competition all affect how many hand weedings need to be done, for example: finger millet, pearl millet, onion, etc.

Nevertheless, manual weeding is time-consuming, inefficient, and labor-intensive, making it unsuitable for modern weeding.

Digging

To remove underground storage organs, weeds must be dug up to deeper layers. This is done by using a simple toollike shovel or spade. If the ratio of weeds in the field is high, then digging process becomes tedious as it will affect adjacent crops too.

Apart from these techniques, Mowing, Cutting, Dredging and Chaining, Burning and Flaming, and Mulchesare some of the other physical weed removal methodologies which are involved in non-cropped areas, roadsides, lawns and gardens.

Tillage

Soil structure and soil fertility are maintained or improved through primary tillage. Furthermore, weeds are stronglyaffected by the tillage strategy and operation. Weed control strategies in conjunction with tillage systems are an integrated approach to weed management [2]. Tillage controls weed in four phases: stubble cultivation occurs in the first and second phases. In this step, weed seeds, and crop residue are buried inside the ground with a mouldboard plough. Tillage is used to prepare seedbeds, and inter-row weed control is used to finalize weed control on seed beds. First and second phase operations can be categorized as preventive, while third and fourth phase operations can be categorized as repressive.

Introduction to UAV

Weed mapping by UAV was introduced by Maria *et al.* [78]. The effects of backpack weedicide spraying on human health are felt. Tractor spraying creates pollution and is impossible when there is no access for the tractors. Crop health can sometimes be negatively impacted by equal spraying of weeds and crops, and crops may sometimes absorb dangerous chemicals [48]. This new technology can help farmers work more efficiently and in less time. For farmers and agricultural production organizations, spraying crops is typically a difficult and taxing task. Agricultural UAVs have made crop spraying easier for farmers because they can quickly cover vast expanses of territory. UAVs may automatically change their height when spraying across uneven areas. This improves spraying accuracy while conserving resources. Since they can reach both the plants and the soil below, UAVs are an effective way to spray crops. They also protect farmers from prolonged contact to potentially hazardous chemicals that have traditionally been linked to manual spraying. Vegetation patterns in images are identified by rows, after which optimum chemical distribution may be made possible [94]. Small-scale unmanned aerial vehicle (UAV) crop protection operations, in contrast, offer the benefits of a low flight height, flight velocity control, and good field adaptability, primarily for small fields and diversified crop planting zones. Precision agriculture can utilize aerial images in a widerange of fields. For the purpose of obtaining the photographs in some UAVs, the free software program Pix4D Capture was utilized. Planning the AOF in advance is made possible through this application, which gives an estimate of how long the flight will take [101].

Due to its high resolution, light weight, and low cost, the Unmanned Aerial Vehicle (UAV) method has shown potential for more fine-grained recognition and analysis in recent years. UAV images have been widely applied to many domains [25, 51, 124], including environment analysis [16, 117, 121, 136], precise agriculture [14, 26, 77, 135], forest monitoring [47, 68], wildlife protection [55, 56, 98], etc. Unmanned aerial vehicle (UAV), sometimes known as a drone, is an airborne system or an aircraft that may be flown remotely by a human operator or automatically by an onboard computer. Aerial robots that fly themselves are available from identified technologies. You can choose the region you want to map or survey, and the robot will take off, collect your data, land, upload it to the cloud, and change out and recharge its own batteries for you. The ability to record cropped photos and transmit them to an information centre has been made possible by

Table 15.2 List of various sensors used in weed detection.

Sensor	Usage	Author
Electronic	sensor proved effective spraying over weed patches	Hagger *et al.*, 1983 [37]
Ultrasonic	marketed with a claimed accuracy of 25mm	McRae *et al.*, 1985 [81]
Infrared	to measure the row at three different heights	Bontsema *et al.*, 1991 [18]
Magnetic	to measure mechanical quantities	Zwiggelaar, 1996 [138]
Electronic gas	to measure humidity in agricultural environment	Zwiggelaar, 1996 [138]
Hoe	distinguish beet plants from weeds by counting synchronous contacts	Kouwenhoven, 1997 [59]
Light	summation of the 3 signals to a single signal where FFT is performed	Bontsema *et al.*, 1998 [19]
Optoelectronic	detection of weeds against a soil or plant residue background	Rainer, 1998 [97]
Optical	detection of diseases and weeds	Josse, 2000 [54]
Inertia	used as alternative to odometers for dead reckoning	Hague *et al.*, 2000 [38]
Hyperspectral	soil-crop segmentation	Victor *et al.*, 2005 [122]
Displacement	for determining sprayer location	Loghavi *et al.*, 2008 [69]
Tactile	indicate the relative position and orientation of the crop rows	Tijmen *et al.*, 2010 [119]
Spectrometric	discrimination between crops and weeds	Lopez-Granados, 2011 [70]
Wireless	to obtain weed leaf image	Zhang *et al.*, 2012 [132]
Temperature	detection of temperature of soil	Shivam *et al.*, 2020 [108]

recent developments in image acquisition equipment like UAV and data transmission technology [66]. The combination of UAV-based imagery and DL techniques in recent scientific studies has substantially benefitted precision agriculture applications [72].

Different UAVs are

1) Single rotor UAV
2) Four rotor UAV (Quadcopter, [9])
3) Six rotor UAV
4) Eight rotor UAV (Oktokopter, [42])

Sensors and Their Usage

Sensors play a very important role in IoT-based systems. A sensor is used to measure temperature, humidity, plant health, pH level, wind flow, moisture, etc. Additionally, the sensor monitors, controls, secures, warns, and analyzes realistic and non-realistic data. Agricultural operations are simpler, smarter, and more efficient with sensors because they require less human intervention [75]. Apart from sensors given in Table 15.2, we have dielectric soil moisture sensor, agricultural weather sensor, airflow sensor, fire sensor and smoke sensors which are widely used in precision agriculture.

Dataset

Dataset is an important aspect while examining the crop field. Many datasets are publicly available while some datasets charge a fee. Previously, the plants and weeds were examined physically for classification and study, whereas with the improvement of image processing technology, picture annotations are enough to analysis and retrievevarious information. Plant leaves preserve much information about plant species recognition [23]. For instance, while the majority of plants' leaves are green or brown, their forms are typically different and can be used toidentify them [53]. The crop field image was taken using a digital camera, UAV, Satellites, etc. Table 15.3 enumerates the list of various data sets used in weed identification.

Table 15.3 Dataset table. *Values may change because of prolonged updating.

Dataset	Agency	Species	Samples	Images	URL
Flavia	SourceForge	32	-	1970	http://flavia.sourceforge.net/
ICL	Computing academy, China	-	220	16,848	http://intelengine.cn/English/dataset/
Swedish leaf	Linköping University	15	75	1125	https://www.cvl.isy.liu.se/
MEW	Central European woody plants	153	-	9745	http://zoi.utia.cas.cz/download
GitHub	GitHub	-	200M	200M+	https://github.com/collections
PlantVillage	TensorFlow	55	24	82,161	https://www.tensorflow.org/datasets/
Digipathos	Embrapa	-	-	3000	https://www.digipathos-rep.cnptia.embrapa.br/
figshare	figshare	-	-	-	https://figshare.com/articles/dataset/
Pl@ntLeaves	Chorus	126	88	5340	http://www.ifs.tuwien.ac.at/Pl@ntLeaves.html
MalayaKew	Royal Botanic Gardens	44	-	36,960	https://web.fsktm.um.edu.my/
Apple leaf dataset	Quantitative-Plant		-	9000	https://www.quantitative-plant.org/dataset/
Smithsonian	Smithsonian Libraries	-	-	-	https://library.si.edu/data

(*Continued*)

Table 15.3 Dataset table. *Values may change because of prolonged updating. (*Continued*)

Dataset	Agency	Species	Samples	Images	URL
Plumbers island	data.world	249	-	7313	https://data.world/datasets/environment
Gross-Broadleaf	Mendeley data	-	-	-	https://data.mendeley.com/research-data/?
kaggle	Kaggle	-	13	10000+	https://www.kaggle.com/datasets

Data Augmentation

Many authors utilized artificially extending the dataset using augmentation techniques to increase its performance. There are a number of fundamental enhancement techniques including rotation, cropping, noise addition, and grayscale conversion. By feeding the model with different data, this improves the learning process and performance, as well asgeneralization. For papers training DL models with only small datasets, this augmentation process is crucial. Various image augmentation techniques are represented in the 3D pie chart in Figure 15.2.

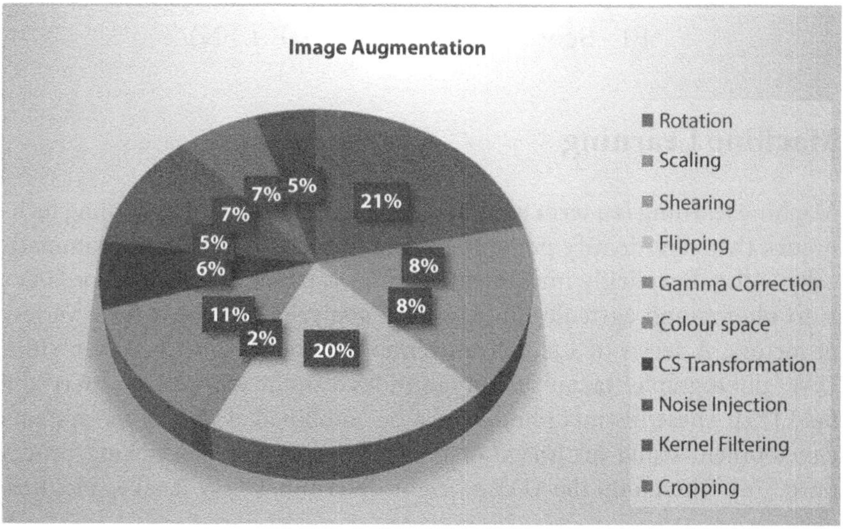

Figure 15.2 Various image augmentation techniques.

Evaluation Parameters

On desktop computers, weed recognition algorithms have been evaluated using a variety of metrics. In terms of different types of recognition approaches, these metrics may be defined differently. Binary image classification, where positive (P) or negative (N) classification results are represented for an input sample, four possible outcomes can be derived: (1) An accurate prediction is defined as true positive (TP) when a positive sample is classified as positive; (2) a false positive (FP) is a prediction made based on a negative sample being classified as positive; (3) the prediction is true negative (TN) when a negative sample is classified as negative; and (4) false negatives (FNs) are predictions basedon positive samples that are classified as negatives. The accuracy of a prediction is determined by the percentage of correct predictions (TP + TN) over all the predictions (P + N). A sensitivity test is used to determine how many caseswere correctly predicted as positive, also known as recall (TP) over all the positive cases (TP + FN). The specificity ofa prediction is the percentage of negative cases predicted correctly (TN) over all predicted negative cases (TN + FP).Taking precision and recall into account equally, the F-score (also known as F1 score) combines their values.

$$\text{Accuracy} = (\text{TP})/(\text{Total number of classifications})$$

$$\text{Sensitivity (SN)} = \text{TP}/(\text{TP} + \text{FN})\ \text{Specificity (SP)} = \text{TN}/(\text{TN} + \text{FP})$$

$$\text{F1 - Score} = (2\text{TP})/(2\text{TP} + \text{FP} + \text{FN})$$

Machine Learning

Machine learning is a term used to describe computerized modelling techniques that can identify patterns in data and make judgments automatically without explicitly implementing rules [7]. One application for UAVs is to photograph agricultural fields and analyze the images for a variety of factors. A series of successive overlapped photos must be taken since UAV photographs taken at low altitudes cannot completely cover the field [27]. These distinct photos must be combined as part of the system's development using an image orthorectification and mosaicking procedure [78]. Therefore, the UAV's height determines how it takes pictures.

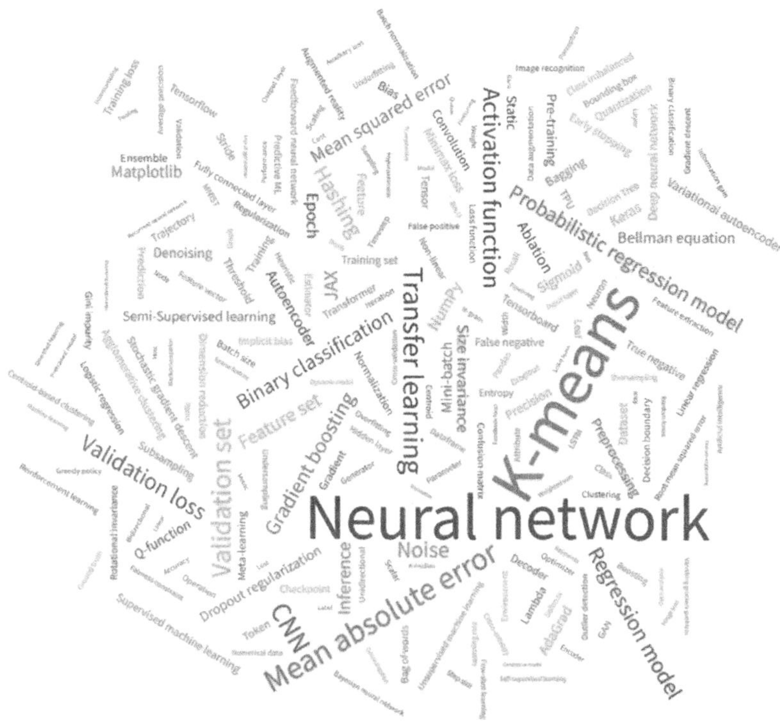

Figure 15.3 Word-cloud of different literature-revision papers relation to the "Machine learning".

Unsupervised and supervised learning are two categories for traditional machine learning. Word-cloud of different literature-revision papers relation to the "Machine learning" depicted in Figure 15.3.

1. Supervised Learning

Using samples that have already been labelled, supervised learning is concerned with the idea of creating a prediction model [78]. A tagged set of data is necessary for supervised classification algorithms to train their learning models [80]. As a result, the classification model performs effectively for images that share attributes with the training samples, and its effectiveness is strongly influenced by the chosen examples [7]. The creation of a prediction model using tagged samples is the focus of supervised learning. Labeled data are used for the training phase of supervised classification, and the remaining information (i.e., the sub-image) is only taken into account for prediction [80]. In other words, using the labelled dataset, the model learns how to map a given input to a specific output during supervised training [12, 110].

Regression

In order to handle classification and regression issues, supervised learning is frequently used [22]. Regression is a technique for determining the relationships among various metrics, datasets, or fields. The technique also involves examining data items and predicting the value of the data using a real-valued prediction figure. There are two approaches to regression or prediction. Both the Linear Regression (LR) and NonlinearRegression (NLR) methods [89].

Linear Regression

A linear method for simulating the relationship between the input and the result is linear regression, an integratedweed management approach using tillage systems and weed control strategies. Despite the fact that linear regression, which was developed by statisticians as a way to understand the relationship between input and output numerical variables, has been replaced by machine learning methods, multiple linear regression is a useful method for modellingthe relationship between two or more explanatory variables and a response variable that entails fitting a linear equationto the observed data [74]. In addition to being a statistical algorithm, it is also a machine learning algorithm.

Decision Tree

The most widely used algorithms in research and particular operations of data analysis are decision trees [92]. Using a decision tree, one can break up a vast amount of data into more manageable chains of data. It iscarried out in accordance with a set ofbasic decision rules. The individuals in the resulting sets are more or less similarto one another in each subsequent division. This cluster is constructed to partition a large and heterogeneous population into smaller, more homogeneous groups with regard to a certain aim variable [28]. Overlapping nodesand data overfitting are two more significant drawbacks of decision trees [32].

Random Forest

A large number of decision trees are used to generate the random forest method, which then uses the findings to anticipate how each tree will be classified *via* regression [21]. A modern ensemble approach called random forests (RF) uses a collection of de-correlated trees as each classifier [76]. In addition to being extremely quick, they perform on par with other cutting-edge classifiers. Estimating the significance of input variables is also possible with random forests [83]. Multiple separate regression trees make up the predictor known as the random forest algorithm [43].

Neural Network

Neural networks are a subset of machine learning that are used in deep learning techniques. In a neural network, its incoming edges provide numerical inputs and its outgoing edges provide numerical outputs [106]. Each node has a threshold and weight that are linked to one another. A node is activated and starts sending data to the network's top tiers when its output surpasses a certain threshold value. Otherwise, no data is transferred to the network's next tier.

Classification

On the basis of training data, a supervised learning method called the classification algorithm is used to classify fresh observations. Classification is the process of classifying fresh observations into various classes or groups usingdata or observations that have already been provided by the program.

Logistic Regression

Logistic regression performs better for smaller data sets [24]. For many classification issues, logistic regression is a useful place to start [31, 57]. A classification between weed/crop can be done using LR.

K-Nearest Neighbor

By taking into account how much space there is between the input data for each class, K-nearest neighbor classification may be used on the dataset of choice. Consequently, it is necessary to carry out a more functional and error-free classification technique [107]. With these methods, it is possible to create a ranking of species based on the matches' order. This is a simple yet effective solution, but it involves a lot of calculation that gets more difficult as the database gets bigger, especially considering the quadratic complexity of the edit distance [36]. The Nearest Neighbor approach was used to analyze each unique leaf feature also [133].

Support Vector Machine

The support vector machine (SVM) was invented by Vladimir Vapnik in 1998, and it uses the principles of modern statistical le rning theory to generate input-output mapping functions from labeled training data [3]. The theory of statistical learning was the basis for the development of SVM. By maximizing the margin between two (or more) classes and minimizing generalization errors, it finds the optimal separating hyperplane [67]. There are many data points in two training sets, but support vectors are the shortest distance between points from each set [133]. SVM has been used for crop/weeds identification in maize fields [8, 35, 67], weed/corn seedling recognition [125], weeds detection from a chilli field [5] and distinguishing broad and narrow leafed weeds [109]. Even SVM performed well in classification of aquatic weeds [95]. In summary, the SVM is a powerful classification algorithm that is capable of solving a wide range of complex classification problems [93].

Naive Bayes

The term naive refers to immature. A straightforward technique based on probability is the naive bayes classifier. It uses Bayes theorem. It assumes that instances are independent of each other. They work very well in complex real-world scenarios also. A classifier that measures morphological, color, and textural characteristics of an image is used to classify it [88]. An extremely scalable classifier is the Naive Bayes classifier, which requires uniform parameters depending on the number of variables involved. Naive Bayes along with adaboost classified monocot and dicot weeds at an accuracy of 98.4% with the help of edge and shape orientation, it is possible to evaluate a closed-form expression to perform maximum likelihood training, which requires linear processing time [6].

2. Unsupervised learning

Unsupervised learning begins with unlabeled data and searches for unidentified patterns that allow for a fresh, more thorough representation of the information present. Clustering is by far the most important unsupervised learning [10, 15]. Figure 15.4 depicts implementation of various techniques in machine learning.

Clustering

The inherent groupings in the data are discovered. The unlabeled data is organized into similar groups known as clusters. And the process of partitioning of a set of observations into subsets (or clusters) so that observation in the same cluster is similar is called as clustering. One of the most fundamental unsupervised machine learning problems is clustering data into clusters of similar data points [10]. So, a cluster consists of data items which are similar in comparison to other clusters which contain dissimilar items.

K-means Clustering

K-means in machine learning or data science, clustering is an unsupervised learning process that is used to address clustering problems by categorizing the unlabeled data into clusters. Due to its simplicity and speed,

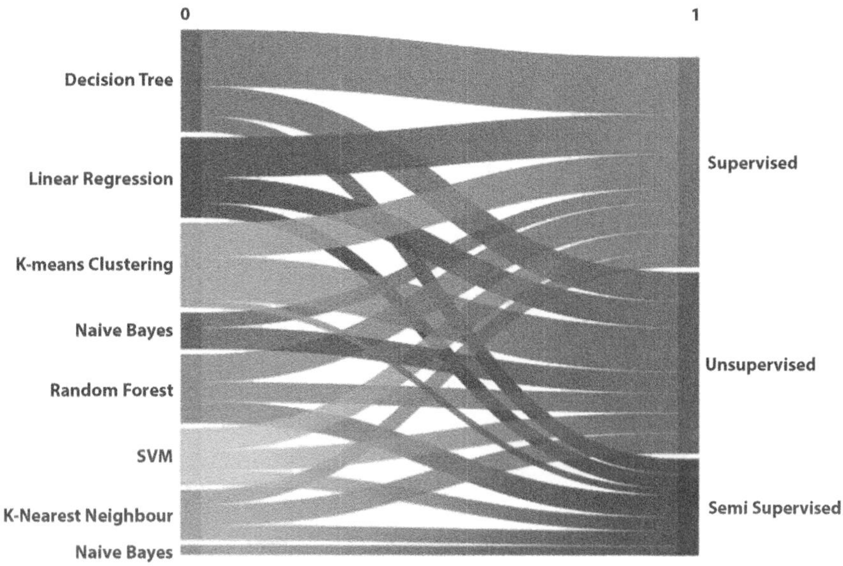

Figure 15.4 Representation of implementation between various techniques in machine learning.

K-means clustering is frequently employed in picture segmentation [114]. Using K as a parameter, we can define how many predefined clusters need to be created in the process, so if K=2, we'd need to create two clusters, and so on. Kumar and Prema [61] used K-means algorithm for filtering images and separating soil from plants. In the K-means clustering technique, three key aspects need to be taken into consideration: the choice of k, the initialization of the clustering centre, and the creation of the feature dictionary [52]. The centroid-based technique connects each cluster to a centroid. An algorithm such as this minimizes the total distance between data points and their clusters by minimizing the sum of the squares of the distance between the item and the cluster it is related to [105]. Before CNN is optimized, weights of the network are learned using K-means clustering algorithm. Convolutional neural networks and K-means feature learning classify data objects as members of the nearest category. The error of network weights will be reduced after further parameter fine-tuning [52]. Using a data set without labels as input, the algorithm divides it into k clusters and repeats the process until it runs out of clusters. Figure 15.5 elaborates various techniques in weed taxonomy and some of its abbreviations are given in Table 15.4.

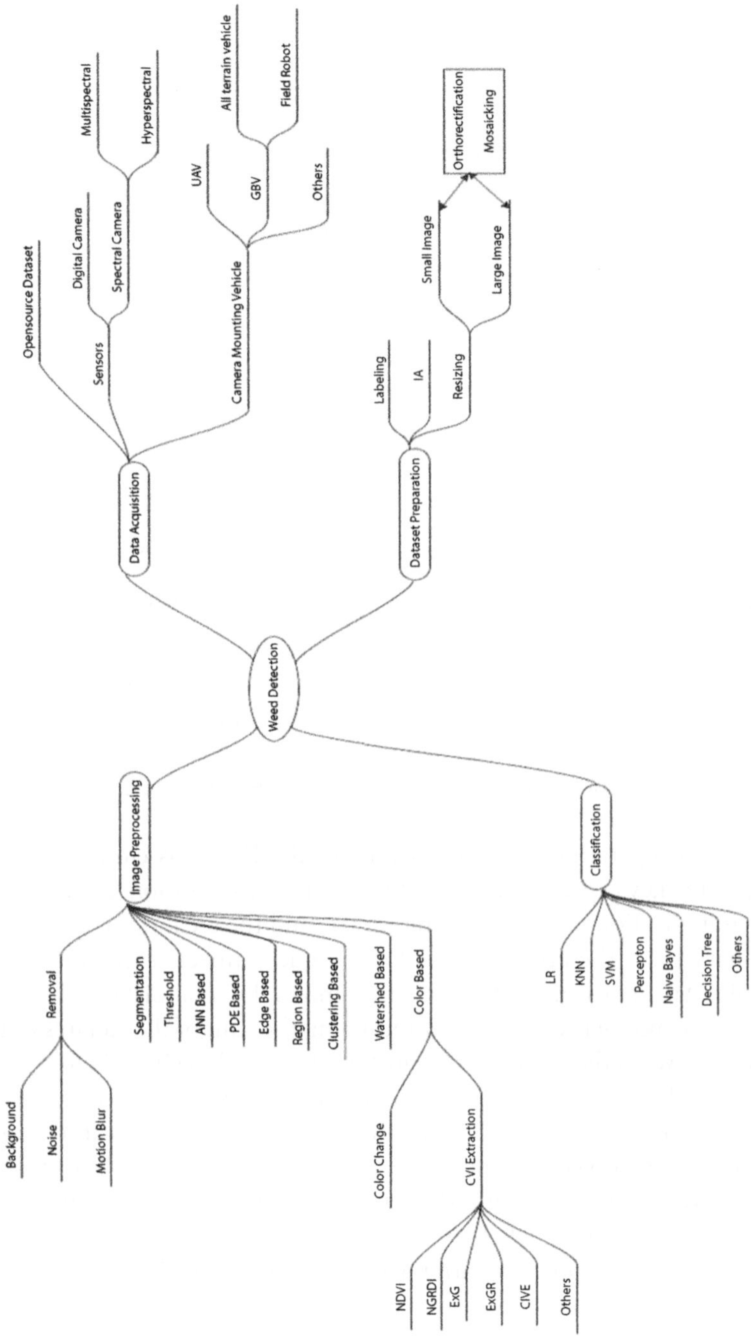

Figure 15.5 Taxonomy of weed detection.

Table 15.4 Abbreviation table for Figure 15.5.

Abbr	Description
NDVI	Normalized Difference Vegetation Index
ExG	Excess Green Index
ExGR	Excess Green minus Excess Red Index
CIVE	Color Index of Vegetation Extraction
NGRDI	Normalized Green-Red Difference Index
CVI	Color Vegetation Index
NIR	Near Infra-Red
UAV	Unmanned Aerial Vehicle
GBV	Ground-Based Vehicle
IA	Image Augmentation
PDE	Partial Differential Equation
ANN	Artificial Neural Network
LR	Logistic Regression
KNN	K-Nearest Neighbor
SVM	Support Vector Machine
RGB	Red, Green and Blue
HSI	Hue, Saturation and Intensity
HSV	Hue, Saturation and Value
HT	Hough Transform
GCN	Graph Convolutional Network

Deep Learning

When deep learning is used as a learning module, it creates a network with many layers; it is generally believed that deep learning works best when learning modules are applied recursively, finding more complex patterns each time [86]. By expanding the range and volume of the data utilized for training deep learning models,augmentation techniques are used [62]. Lawrence *et al.* [64] also proposed a new approach to identifyleaf diseases from individual lesions using deep learning.

Convolutional Neural Network

For classifying plants, deep learning methods were examined, and CNN in particular has garnered a lot of interest. Caffe, a CCC-based framework for deep learning and CNN-related algorithms has various benefits, including quick updates and adaptable scalability. It offers a full toolkit for instruction, testing, and fine-tuning [127]. Convolution layers are the foundation of convolution neural networks, pooling layers are the next layers, and fully linking layers are the final layers, as in the example shown in Figure 15.6. By disentangling high-level representations across several processing layers, convolutional neural networks (CNN) excel above DL approaches. CNN identified weeds in soybean crop photos and separated them into grass and broadleaf weeds [4, 11]. Convolutional, ReLU, and max-pooling layers make up the convolutional block. Through the use of a number of parallel filters that process small portions of the input space, each set of convolutional layers diversifies the features. Low-level local characteristics from the earliest layers are combined with higher-level representations from the most recent levels in the feature vector [34]. Each layer of the CNN's multilayer structure network generates a response. The layers separate the fundamental visual feature and move on to the following layer [96]. Increasing the size and variety of training samples could generally improve the ability of the recognition systems to represent the images [128]. Convolutional neural networks have improved dramatically in the past several years in terms of their ability to recognize objects [60, 131] and classify images [40]. However, convolutional neural networks now offer a more scalable method

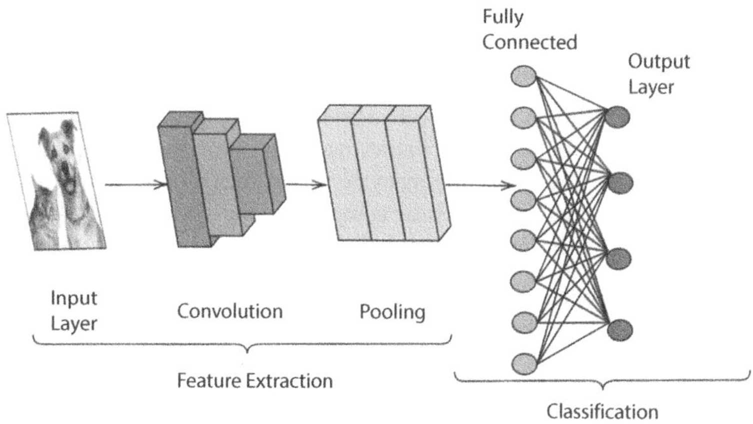

Figure 15.6 Diagrammatic representation of CNN.

for classifying images and identifying objects by utilizing the ideas of linear algebra, particularly matrix multiplication, to find patterns in images. CNN identified weeds in soybean crop photos and separated them into grass and broadleaf weeds [4]. Dian Bah *et al.* [13] examined how well a CNN-based approach performed at predicting weeds in various crops' plantation lines. That said, they can be computationally demanding, requiring graphical processing units (GPUs) to train models. Using RGB vision obtained with a UAV-based remote system, a CNN method was developed to simultaneously recognize plants and plantation-rows in various datasets [73]. Deep learning methods typically require more data to train them, as is widely acknowledged [23, 50, 104]. Apart from this, graph convolutional network (GCN) was also used to improve crop and weed recognition [44]. A four-layer CNN was constructed specifically for weed dataset [84]. Semantic segmentation-based CNN was used to detect weeds in sugar beet crop [82]. A fully connected Neural network is used to identify weed among sugar beet and Oilseed [123]. FCN was used by Huang *et al.* [46] to identify various weed varieties in rice field. Sarvini *et al.* [103] implemented SVM, ANN and CNN for distinguishing chrysanthemum and paragrass. Mads *et al.* [76] used CNN to distinguish between Knotweed family, chickweed, etc., among wheat, maize, sugar beet, cabbage, etc.

Table 15.5 Terminologies used in CNN.

<table>
<tr><th>Terms</th><th>Explanation</th></tr>
<tr><td>Filter/Kernel</td><td>Moves across respective fields in the image and checks for the feature present in the image. An entire image is swept over by the kernel over many iterations. Each time the filter is applied, the input pixels are compared to the result of the dot product. The final output is called feature map/convolved feature.</td></tr>
<tr><td>Depth</td><td>A neural network's depth is determined by its amount of layers/ number of filters applied during convolution.</td></tr>
<tr><td>Stride</td><td>Number of pixel jump.</td></tr>
<tr><td>Padding</td><td>Adding corresponding number of rows and column on each side of the input pixels.
Two types of padding are:
<table>
<tr><th>Valid Padding</th><th>Same Padding</th></tr>
<tr><td>Don't add any extra rows or columns</td><td>Extra zeros to the edges of the input matrix</td></tr>
</table></td></tr>
<tr><td>Pooling</td><td>In addition to reducing the size of feature maps, pooling also reduces the number of training parameters, which would otherwise slow down computation.
<table>
<tr><th>Max Pooling</th><th>Min Pooling</th><th>Average Pooling</th></tr>
<tr><td>The maximum value in a region summarizes thefeatures in that region, i.e., brighter pixel.</td><td>The minimum value in a region summarizes thefeatures in that region, i.e., lighter pixel.</td><td>The average value in a region summarizes thefeatures in that region, i.e., smooths the harsh edges of a picture</td></tr>
</table></td></tr>
<tr><td>Fully Connected layer</td><td>Fully connected layers are fed by the outputs from the last pooling or convolutional layer, which are flattened.</td></tr>
</table>

(*Continued*)

Table 15.5 Terminologies used in CNN. (*Continued*)

Terms	Explanation			
Activation Function	Applied to each neuron in the neuron. By summing all the inputs, it creates an output that is passed On to the next layer.			
	ReLU	Sigmoid	Tanh	Softmax
	It allows non-linearity, pixels with negative values are replaced with zero.	0 to 1 is the output value of the function which takes any real value as input.	-1 to 1 is the output value of the function which takes any real value as input.	Analyzes neural network outputs and transforms them into probabilities.
Cost function	Essentially, a cost function is a measure of how close your model is to the actual value.			
Backpropagation	To determine how much the output contributes to the overall loss, reverse the forward pass and find the gradient of each neuron with respect to the loss function.			

Apart from terminologies represented in Table 15.5, a crossword comprising various terms in deep learning is built as shown in Figure 15.7. This gives a short introduction to various terms involved in convolutional neural network. The definition of the various terms in the crossword is given under Across and Down topics.

Across

1 Convolutional neural network that is 19 layers deep (5)11 The number of pixels shifts over the input matrix (7)
27 Model which utilized swish activation function and depth wise separable convolutions (11)48 Deep convolutional neural networks with 22-layer (9)
102 Configurable hyperparameter used in the training of neural networks (12)172 Feed forward neural networks, to put it simply (19)
319 Network architecture for deep learning (3)
338 Convolutional neural network that is 16 layers deep (5)345 Matching the output with input (15)

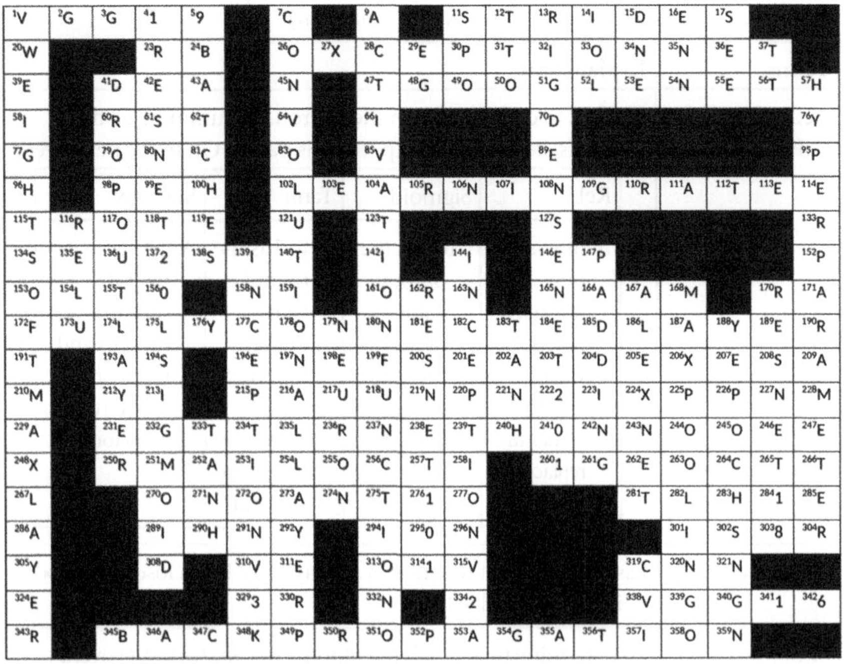

Figure 15.7 CNN crossword.

Down

7 Building blocks used in convolutional neural networks (18)
9 A node that is put at the end of or in between Neural Networks (18)
20 Parameter that transforms input data within the network's hidden layers (7)23 Deep learning model with 20 parameter layers (8)
24 Number of samples that will be propagated through the network (7)
41 A mask that nullifies the contribution of some neurons towards the next layer and leaves others (12) 57 Number of neurons, activation function, optimizer, learning rate, batch size, and epochs is called (14)70 CNN that is 201 layers deep (11)
116 Prevent the emergence of the so-called "vanishing gradient" problem (4) 134 Layer just before the output layer whose probabilities added up to 1.0 (12)139 Model that has been shown greater accuracy on the ImageNet dataset (11)144 Second generation of Inception CNN architectures (11)
147 The number of pixels added to an image (7)162 CNN that is 101 layers deep (9)
167 It has eight layers with learnable parameters (7)
168 Operation that selects the maximum element from the feature map covered by the filter (10)170 CNN that is 18 layers deep (8)

179 That have learnable weights and biases (6)
183 It is superior to the logistic sigmoid in every way (4)194 Function good for representing a probability (7)
207 Using all of the training data to train the neural network for one cycle (6)233 logistic sigmoid with range from -1 to 1 (4)

VGG Net Model

Simonyan and Zisserman [111] designed a CNN model called VGG net for the ILSVRC-2014 challenge. Their work shows the inclusion of a softmax classifier, two completely connected layers with a total of 4,096 nodes each, and twofully connected layers. By deleting the original softmax layer and adding ours in its place, the VGG 16 was made better. Also used was a pre-trained model with weights from ImageNet. Finally, the model's accuracy on the test set and cross-entropy loss was used to evaluate it. The model's performance on the validation set resulted in a top-5 error rate of 7.5%, which earned them second place in the competition. The CNN model with just three three-layer convolutionspiled on top of one another in increasing depth. The capacity is reduced by max pooling handles (down sampling). Hang *et al.* [39] proposed an updated VGG16 which addressed 10 different stresses from apple, cherry, and corn. VGG19focuses on shape and venation; also it has produced remarkable results in different leaf image processing. Fawakherji *et al.* [29] used semantic segmentation for weed detection in sunflower crop. They separated vegetation and backgroundusing UNet with VGG-16, the extracted vegetation blobs, finally reapplied DL using VGG-16 neural networkto classifycrop and weed blobs. VGGNet, Inception-ResNet architectures was applied to distinguish weed species like black nightshade, velvetleaf among tomato and cotton [20]. VGG16, VGG19 models were usedto distinguish weeds among canola, corn, and radish [65]. VGG16 was used to distinguish grasslands and weeds [63]. ResNet-50, ResNet-101 and other architectures have been applied by Partel *et al.* [90] to distinguish blueberry and weeds. Yu *et al.* [130] applied a VGG model to distinguish between Bermuda grass and weeds, also perennial ryegrass, and dandelion.

Inception and ResNet Module

Szegedy *et al.* [116] first incorporated the "Inception" concept into the Google LeNet design. Inception vN isthe name given to the subsequent iterations of the Google Net architecture, where N stands for the version number. In order to improve the accuracy of ImageNet categorization,

Szegedy *et al.* [116] suggested the Inception V3 architecture,which encourages altering the Inception module. Szegedy *et al.* [115] improved the architecture even more, resultingin Inception V4. Remaining connections are added to the Inception architecture in this design. They want to hasten the Inception networks' training. The Inception module is made up of convolution layers and a pooling layer put together. 1×1, 3×3, and 5×5 are the various sizes of convolutions.1×1 convolution bottleneck layer is another salient featureof the Inception module. The bottleneck layer assists in lowering the amount of computing needed. Additionally, themodule's pooling layer is utilized for dimension reduction. Szegedy *et al.* [116] used concatenation filter to combinelayers. Inception v4 substitutes residual connections for the Inception architecture's filter concatenation stage [115]. Use of pre-trained weights from ImageNet was used to fine-tune Google Net Inception V4. Teimouri *et al.* [118] distinguished various weeds using Inception v3 architecture, meanwhile, Suh *et al.* [113] distinguished sugar beetand volunteer potato; also Kounalakis *et al.* [58] used inception v1 to distinguish Cloves and weed. Xijian *et al.* [128] used inception v3 as the backbone for transfer learning, also it achieves high accuracy in plant disease detection [34]. The ResNet model, which served as the basis for the 2015 ILSVRC and COCO classification challenges, was introduced by He *et al.* [40]. Their model placed first in the ImageNet classification with an error rate of 3.57%. The deep residual learning approach was driven by the numerous non-linear layers' failure to learn identity mappingsand the degradation problem. A ResNet is constructed by stacking basic building blocks on top of each other. In some blocks, there is no connection or a loose connection between the convolution layers of these building blocks. Aremaining mapping is set in all piled layers, whereas identity mapping is set in skip connections [91]. The residual units consist of the convolution, pooling, and layer components. Although ResNet is made up of 33 filtersand has a similar design to the VGG net, it is around 8 times deeper [111]. This is thoughtto be caused by employing fully connected layers instead of global average pooling. In order to obtain more accuracyfurther update of ResNet was done by updating the residual module to use identity mappings [41]. A ResNet model with 50,101 and 152 layers as in [41] and it was made to have pre-trained weights fromImageNet loaded into it. Trong *et al.* [120] applied Inception-Resnet architecture for 21 species ofCNN weeds dataset. Binguitcha-Fare *et al.* [17] distinguished maize, common wheat, sugar beet and other weed species using ResNet-101architecture which was previously classified by Nkemelu *et al.* [85] using KNN, SVM and CNN. ResNet-18 was usedby Bah *et al.* [13] to distinguish between spinach, bean, and weeds.

DenseNet

A convolutional network design with dense connections was introduced by Huang *et al.* [45]. All layers of the network are directly connected to one another in a feed-forward fashion to enable maximum information flow between them. Layers before and after it use the feature-maps of all layers preceding them, and their own feature-maps are used for all layers following them. With a significantly smaller number of parameters, Huang *et al.* [45] described DenseNets model with 121 layers for the task of plant disease identification was created. Additionally, the model had ImageNet pre-trained weights added to it. Finally, a new fully connected model was developed, featuring a top-layer softmax. Also, DenseNets reduces the vanishing-gradient problem's difficulty.

YOLO

With YOLO, fast object detection is achieved with convolutional neural networks, which makes the algorithm useful in real time [87]. Detection and recognition of weeds can be performed with deep learning models based on YOLO. A weed detection model based on YOLO v3-tiny was developed by Zhang R in wheat field. YOLO v3-tiny was used by Sharpe to detect goosegrass in strawberry and tomato. An improved the YOLO v3-tiny model was applied in sugar beet fields for weed detection by Gao. The smart system developed by Jabir and Falih uses YOLO v5 to detect weeds in wheat fields using a Raspberry Pi. Research cases like these demonstrate the YOLO model's potential. Figure 15.8 illustrates the number of articles published in reputed journals between 2020 and 2024.

Blockchain

An agricultural product's journey from farm to table can be tracked using blockchain technology. A range of challenges can be addressed with blockchain technology, providing farmers, supply chains, and consumers with new opportunities. Agricultural data can be stored securely using blockchain, enabling farmers to make informed decisions based on reliable data. As a result, farmers, researchers, and agribusinesses are able to share data more easily, allowing collaboration and innovation to take place. A blockchain can facilitate collaboration between farmers and aid the pooling of

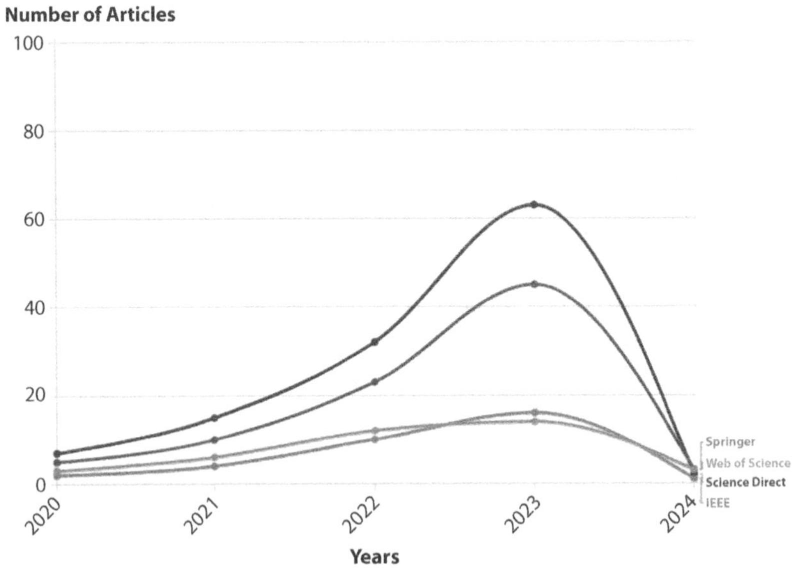

Figure 15.8 Articles published using YOLO in respective years.

resources, sharing of knowledge, or collective marketing of products. In addition to improving supply chain management, it is also likely to improve practices around financial inclusion and sustainability. While blockchain adoption in agriculture is still in its early stages, it could transform the agricultural system in the long run to create one that is more efficient, resilient, and equitable.

Discussions and Conclusion

Despite numerous recent deep learning-based attempts to identify weed and crop, some unresolved issues remain, such as the use of real-world data, background removal that is automatic, and the use of portable devices to train and test complex convolutional neural networks with millions of parameters. After combining the information on differences in position, texture, size, shape and color or spectrum of weeds and crops, weed detection by computer vision method is performed. This survey elaborates various methods of weed detection and identification from scratch. The majority of the research has been based on publicly accessible datasets, such as Flavia, PlantVillage, Kaggle, etc. Most of the dataset contains more than 50,000 images sufficient to train any convolutional neural network. Some authors employed fewer than 1,000 original photos, but data augmentation was their go-to strategy to achieve an adequate number of images needed to train a deep model.

Almost all types of plants and weeds are accurately recognized using deep networks proposed recently. All of the deep networks analyzed for this work have outperformed conventional machine learning-based feature extraction and classification techniques, which make up a significant class of techniques. This survey has examined various machine and deep learning concepts which have been widely used in weed detection and identification.

Bibliography

1. Ahmad, A., Saraswat, D., Aggarwal, V., Aaron Etienne, Benjamin Hancock, Performance of deep learning models for classifying and detecting common weeds in corn and soybean production systems. *Comput. Electron. Agric.*, 184, 106081, 2021, DOI: https://doi.org/10.1016/j.compag.2021.106081.
2. Khaliq, A., Shakeel, M., Matloob, A., Hussain, S., Tanveer, A., Murtaza, G., Influence of Tillage and Weed Control Practices on Growth and Yield of Wheat. *Philipp. J. Crop Sci. (PJCS)*, 38, 3, December 2013, Copyright 2013, Crop Science Society of the Philippines.
3. Bakhshipoura, A. and Jafari, A., Evaluation of support vector machine and artificial neural networks in weed detection using shape features. *Comput. Electron. Agric.*, 145, 153–160, 2018, DOI: https://doi.org/10.1016/j.compag.2017.12.032.
4. dos Santos Ferreira, A., Freitas, D.M., Silva, G.G.D., Pistori, H., Folhes, M.T., Weed detection in soybean crops using ConvNets. *Comput. Electron. Agric.*, 143, 314–324, Dec 2017, DOI: https://doi.org/10.1016/j.compag.2017.10.027.
5. Ahmed, F., Al-Mamun, H.A., Bari, A.S.M.H., Hossain, E., Kwan, P., Classification of crops and weeds from digital images: A support vector machine approach. *Crop Prot.*, 40, 98–104, Oct. 2012, DOI: https://doi.org/10.1016/j.cropro.2012.04.024.
6. Ahmad, J., Muhammad, K., Ahmad, I., Ahmad, W., Smith, M.L., Smith, L.N., Jain, D.K., Wang, H., Mehmood, I., Visual features based boosted classification of weeds for real-time selective herbicide sprayer systems. *Comput. Ind.*, 98, 23–33, 2018, DOI: https:// doi.org/10.1016/j.compind.2018.02.005.
7. Wang, A., Zhang, W., Wei, X., A review on weed detection using ground-based machine vision and image processing techniques. *Comput. Electron. Agric.*, 158, 226–240, 2019, DOI: https://doi.org/10.1016/j.compag.2019.02.005.
8. Akbarzadeh, S., Paap, A., Ahderom, S., Apopei, B., Alameh, K., Plant discrimination by Support Vector Machine classifier based on spectral reflectance.

Comput. Electron. Agric., 148, 250–258, 2018, DOI: https://doi.org/10.1016/J.COMPAG.2018.03.026.

9. Pandey, A. and Jain, K., An intelligent system for crop identification and classification from UAV images using conjugated dense convolutional neural network. *Comput. Electron. Agric.*, 192, 106543, 2022, DOI: https://doi.org/10.1016/j.compag.2021.106543.
10. dos Santos Ferreira, A., Freitas, D.M., da Silva, G.G., Pistori, H., Folhes, M.T., Unsupervised deep learning and semi-automatic data labeling in weed discrimination. *Comput. Electron. Agric.*, 165, 104963, 2019, DOI: https://doi.org/10.1016/j.compag.2019.104963.
11. Beikmohammadi, A., Faez, K., Motallebi, A., SWP-LeafNET: A novel multistage approach for plant leaf identification based on deep CNN. *Expert Syst. Appl.*, 202, 117470, 2022, DOI: https://doi.org/10.1016/j.eswa.2022.117470.
12. Mahmudul Hasan, A.S.M., Sohel, F., Diepeveen, D., Laga, H., Jones, M.GK., A survey of deep learning techniques for weed detection from images. *Comput. Electron. Agric.*, 184, 106067, 2021, DOI: https://doi.org/10.1016/j.compag.2021.106067.
13. Bah, M.D., Hafiane, A., Canals, R., Deep learning with unsupervised data labeling for weed detection in line crops in UAV images. *Remote Sens.*, 10, 11, 1690, 2018.
14. Bayraktar, E., Basarkan, M.E., Celebi, N., A low-cost UAV framework towards ornamental plant detection and counting in the wild. *ISPRS J. Photogramm. Remote Sens.*, 167, 1–11, 2020, DOI: https://doi.org/10.1016/j.isprsjprs.2020.06.012.
15. Behmann, J., Mahlein, A.K., Rumpf, T., Römer, C., Plümer, L., A review of advanced machine learning methods for the detection of biotic stress in precision crop protection. *Precis. Agric.*, 2015, DOI: https://doi.org/10.1007/s11119-014-9372-7.
16. Bhardwaj, A., Sam, L., Martín-Torres, F.J., Kumar, R., UAVs as remote sensing platform in glaciology: Present applications and future prospects. *Remote Sens. Environ.*, 175, 196–204, 2016, DOI: https://doi.org/10.1016/j.rse.2015.12.029.
17. Binguitcha-Fare, A.-A. and Sharma, P., Crops and weeds classification using convolutional neural networks *via* optimization of transfer learning parameters. *Int. J. Eng. Adv. Technol. (IJEAT)*, 8, 5, 2284–2294, 2019.
18. Bontsema, J., Grift, T., Pleijsier, K., Mechanical weed control in sugar beet growing: the detection of a plant in a row. *IFAC Mathematical and Control Applications in Agriculture and Horticulture*, Matsuyama, Japan, 1991.
19. Bontsema, J., van Asselt, C.J., Lempens, P.W.J., van Straten, G., Intra-row weed control: a mechatronics approach. *IFAC Control Applications and Ergonomics in Agriculture*, Athens, Greece, 1998.
20. Espejo-Garcia, B., Mylonas, N., Athanasakos, L., Fountas, S., Vasilakoglou, I., Towards weeds identification assistance through transfer learning. *Comput.*

Electron. Agric., 171, 105306, April 2020, DOI: https://doi.org/10.1016/j.compag.2020.105306.

21. Bosch, A., Zisserman, A., Munoz, X., Image classification using random forests and ferns, in: *2007 IEEE 11th International Conference on Computer Vision*, 2007, October, IEEE, pp. 1–8.
22. Caruana, R. and Niculescu-Mizil, A., An empirical comparison of supervised learning algorithms, in: *Proceedings of the 23rd International Conference on Machine Learning*, pp. 161–168, 2006.
23. Yang, C., Plant leaf recognition by integrating shape and texture features. *Pattern Recognit.*, 112, 107809, https://doi.org/10.1016/j.patcog.2020.107809.
24. Perlich, C., Provost, F., Simonoff, J.S., Tree Induction vs. Logistic Regression: A Learning-Curve Analysis. *J. Mach. Learn. Res.*, 4, 211–255, 2003.
25. Colomina, I. and Molina, P., Unmanned aerial systems for photogrammetry and remote sensing: a review. *ISPRS J. Photogramm. Remote Sens.*, 92, 79–97, 2014, DOI: https://doi.org/10.1016/j.isprsjprs.2014.02.013.
26. Deng, L., Mao, Z., Li, X., Hu, Z., Duan, F., Yan, Y., UAV-based multispectral remote sensing for precision agriculture: a comparison between different cameras. *ISPRS J. Photogramm. Remote Sens.*, 146, 124–136, 2018, DOI: https://doi.org/10.1016/j.isprsjprs.2018.09.008.
27. Shanmugam, L., Adline, AL Agasta, Aishwarya, N., Krithika, G., Disease detection in crops using remote sensing images. *IEEE Technological Innovations in ICT for Agriculture and Rural Development (TIAR)*, 2017. 10.1109/TIAR.2017.8273696
28. Fayyad, U.M. and Irani, K.B., On the handling of continuous-valued attributes in decision tree generation. *Mach. Learn.*, 8, 1, 87–102, 1992, DOI: https://doi.org/10.1007/BF00994007.
29. Fawakherji, M., Youssef, A., Bloisi, D., Pretto, A., Nardi, D., Crop and weeds classification for precision agriculture using context-independent pixel-wise segmentation, in: *Proc. 3rd IEEE Int. Conf. Robotic Comput. (IRC)*, Feb. 2019, pp. 146–152, DOI: 10.1109/IRC.2019.00029.
30. Knoll, F.J., Czymmek, V., Harders, L.O., Hussmann, S., Real-time classification of weeds in organic carrot production using deep learning algorithms. *Comput. Electron. Agric.*, 167, 105097, 2019, DOI: https://doi.org/10.1016/j.compag.2019.105097.
31. Friedman, J., Hastie, T., Tibshirani, R., *The Elements of Statistical Learning*, 2008.
32. Geetharamani, G. and Arun Pandian, J., Identification of plant leaf diseases using a nine-layer deep convolutional neural network. *Comput. Electr. Eng.*, 76, 323–338, June 2019, DOI: https://doi.org/10.1016/j.compeleceng.2019.04.011.
33. Hu, G., Xiaowei, Y., Mingzhu, Z.Y.W., Identification of tea leaf diseases by using an improved deep convolutional neural network. *Sustain. Comput.*

Inform. Syst., 24, 100353, December 2019, DOI: https://doi.org/10.1016/j.suscom.2019.100353.

34. Vizcarra, G., Bermejo, D., Mauricio, A., Gomez, R.Z., The Peruvian Amazon forestry dataset: A leaf image classification corpus. *Ecol. Inform.*, 62, 101268, DOI: https://doi.org/10.1016/j.ecoinf.2021.101268.
35. Guerrero, J.M., Pajares, G., Montalvo, M., Romeo, J., Guijarro, M., Support Vector Machines for crop/weeds identification in maize fields. *Expert Syst. Appl.*, 39, 11149–11155, 2012, DOI: https://doi.org/10.1016/j.eswa.2012.03.040.
36. Cerutti, G., Tougne, L., Coquin, D., Vacavant, A., Leaf margins as sequences: A structural approach to leaf identification. *Pattern Recognit. Lett.*, 49, 177–184, 2014, DOI: http://dx.doi.org/10.1016/j.patrec.2014.07.016.
37. Hagger, R.J., Stent, C.J., Isaac, S., A prototype hand-held patch sprayer for killing weeds, activated by spectral differences in crop/weed canopies. *J. Agric. Eng. Res.*, 28, 4, 349–358, July 1983, DOI: https://doi.org/10.1016/0021-8634(83)90066-5.
38. Hague, T., Marchant, J.A., Tillett, N.D., Ground based sensing systems for autonomous agricultural vehicles. *Comput. Electron. Agric.*, 25, 1–2, 11–28, January 2000, DOI: https://doi.org/10.1016/S0168-1699(99)00053-8.
39. Hang, J., Zhang, D., Chen, P., Zhang, J., Wang, B., Classification of plant leaf diseases based on improved convolutional neural network. *Sensors*, 19, 19, 4161, 2019, DOI: https://doi.org/10.3390/s19194161.
40. He, K., Zhang, X., Ren, S., Sun, J., Deep residual learning for image recognition. arXiv:1512.03385, 2015.
41. He, K., Zhang, X., Ren, S., Sun, J., Deep residual learning for image recognition, in: *Proceedings of the IEEE Conference on Computer Vision and Pattern Recognition (CVPR '16)*, Las Vegas, Nev, USA, June 2016, pp. 770–778.
42. Zheng, H., Zhou, X., He, J., Yao, X., Cheng, T., Zhu, Y., Cao, W., Tian, Y., Early season detection of rice plants using RGB, NIR-G-B and multispectral images from unmanned aerial vehicle (UAV). *Comput. Electron. Agric.*, 169, 105223, February 2020, DOI: https://doi.org/10.1016/j.compag.2020.105223.
43. Hethcoat, M.G., Edwards, D.P., Carreiras, J.M.B., Bryant, R.G., França, F.M., Quegan, S., A machine learning approach to map tropical selective logging. *Remote Sens. Environ.*, 221, 569–582, 2019, DOI: https://doi.org/10.1016/j.rse.2018.11.044.
44. Jiang, H., Zhang, C., Qiao, Y., Zhang, Z., Zhang, W., Song, C., CNN feature based graph convolutional network for weed and crop recognition in smart farming. *Comput. Electron. Agric.*, 174, 105450, 2020, DOI: https://doi.org/10.1016/j.compag.2020.105450.
45. Huang, G., Weinberger, K.Q., Van Der Maaten, L., Densely connected convolutional networks, 2016.
46. Huang, H., Lan, Y., Yang, A., Zhang, Y., Wen, S., Deng, J., Deep learning versus object-based image analysis (obia) in weed mapping of UAV imagery. *Int. J. Remote Sens.*, 41, 9, 3446–3479, 2020.

47. Hyyppa, E., Hyyppa, J., Hakala, T., Kukko, A., Wulder, M.A., White, J.C., *et al.*, Under-canopy UAV laser scanning for accurate forest field measurements. *ISPRS J. Photogramm. Remote Sens.*, 164, 41–60, 2020, DOI: https://doi.org/10.1016/j.isprsjprs.2020.03.021.
48. Imran Moazzam, S., Khan, U.S., Qureshi, W.S., Tiwana, M., Rashid, N., Alasmary, W.S., Iqbal, J., Hamza, A., A Patch-Image Based Classification Approach for Detection of Weeds in Sugar Beet Crop. *IEEE Access*, August 30, 2021.
49. Ioffe, S. and Szegedy, C., Batch normalization: Accelerating deep network training by reducing internal covariate shift. Arxiv. DOI: http://arxiv.org/abs/1502.03167, 2015.
50. Barbedo, J.GA., Factors influencing the use of deep learning for plant disease recognition. *Biosyst. Eng.*, 172, 84–91, August 2018, DOI: https://doi.org/10.1016/j.biosystemseng.2018.05.013.
51. Jiang, S., Jiang, C., Jiang, W., Efficient structure from motion for large-scale UAV images: a review and a comparison of SfM tools. *ISPRS J. Photogramm. Remote Sens.*, 167, 230–251, 2020, DOI: https://doi.org/10.1016/j.isprsjprs.2020.04.016.
52. Tang, J., Wang, D., Zhang, Z., He, L., Xin, J., Xu, Y., Weed identification based on K-means feature learning combined with convolutional neural network. *Comput. Electron. Agric.*, 135, 63–70, 1 April 2017, DOI: https://doi.org/10.1016/j.compag.2017.01.001.
53. Park, J.K., Hwang, E.J., Nam, Y.Y., Utilizing venation features for efficient leaf image retrieval. *J. Syst. Software*, 81, 71–82, 2008. DOI: 10.1016/j.jss.2007.05.001.
54. De Baerdemaeker, J., Process monitoring and control for precision agriculture. *IFAC Bio-Robotics, Information Technology and Intelligent Control for Bio-Production Systems*, Sakai, Osaka, Japan, 2000.
55. Kellenberger, B., Marcos, D., Tuia, D., Detecting mammals in UAV images: Best practices to address a substantially imbalanced dataset with deep learning. *Remote Sens. Environ.*, 216, 139–153, 2018, DOI: https://doi.org/10.1016/j.rse.2018.06.028.
56. Kellenberger, B., Marcos, D., Lobry, S., Tuia, D., Half a percent of labels is enough: Efficient animal detection in UAV imagery using deep CNNs and active learning. *IEEE Trans. Geosci. Remote Sens.*, 57, 12, 9524–9533, 2019, DOI: https://doi.org/10.1109/TGRS.2019.2927393.
57. Kleinbaum, D.G. and Klein, M., *Logistic Regression: A self-learning text*, Springer-Verlag, NY, 1994.
58. Kounalakis, T., Triantafyllidis, G.A., Nalpantidis, L., Deep learning-based visual recognition of rumex for robotic precision farming. *Comput. Electron. Agric.*, 165, 104973, 2019.
59. Kouwenhoven, J.K., Intra-row mechanical weed control-possibilities and problems. *Soil Tillage Res.*, 41, 1–2, 87–104, March 1997, DOI: https://doi.org/10.1016/S0167-1987(96)01076-8.

60. Krizhevsky, A., Sutskever, I., Hinton, G.E., Imagenet classification with deep convolutional neural networks, in: *Advances in Neural Information Processing Systems*, F. Pereira, C.J.C. Burges, L. Bottou, K.Q. Weinberger (Eds.), pp. 1097–1105, Curran Associates, Inc., 2012.
61. Kumar, D.A. and Prema, P., A novel wrapping curvelet transformation based angular texture pattern (WCTATP) extraction method for weed identification. *ICTACT J. Image Video Process.*, 6, 2016.
62. Lalitha, V. and Latha, B., A review on remote sensing imagery augmentation using deep learning. *Mater. Today Proc.*, 62, Part 7, 4772–4778, 2022, DOI: https://doi.org/10.1016/j.matpr.2022.03.341.
63. Lam, O.H.Y., Dogotari, M., Priim, M., Vithlani, H.N., Roers, C., Melville, B., Zimmer, F., Becker, R., An open source workflow for weed mapping in native grassland using unmanned aerial vehicle: Using rumex obtusifolius as a case study. *Eur. J. Remote Sens.*, 1–18, 2020.
64. Ngugi, L.C., Abdelwahab, M., Abo-Zahhad, M., A new approach to learning and recognizing leaf diseases from individual lesions using convolutional neural networks. *Inf. Process. Agric.*, Available online 26 October 2021. In press, DOI: https://doi.org/10.1016/j.inpa.2021.10.004.
65. Le, V.N.T., Ahderom, S., Alameh, K., Performances of the LBP based algorithm over CNN models for detecting crops and weeds with similar morphologies. *Sensors*, 20, 8, 2193, 2020.
66. Liankuan, Z., Weckler, P., Wang, N., Xiao, D., Chai, X., Individual leaf identification from horticultural crop images based on the leaf skeleton. *Comput. Electron. Agric.*, 127, 184–196, 2016, DOI: https://doi.org/10.1016/j.compag.2016.06.017.
67. Lin, C., A support vector machine embedded weed identification system, University of Illinois at Urbana-Champaign, 2009.
68. Liu, K., Shen, X., Cao, L., Wang, G., Cao, F., Estimating forest structural attributes using UAV-LiDAR data in Ginkgo plantations. *ISPRS J. Photogramm. Remote Sens.*, 146, 465–482, 2018, DOI: https://doi.org/10.1016/j.isprsjprs.2018.11.001.
69. Loghavi, M. and Behzadi Mackvandi, B., Development of a target oriented weed control system. *Comput. Electron. Agric.*, 63, 112–118, 2008, DOI: 10.1016/j.compag.2008.01.020.
70. Lopez-Granados, F., Weed detection for site-specific weed management: mapping and real-time approaches. *Weed Res.*, 51, 1–11, 2011, DOI: https://doi.org/10.1111/j.1365-3180.2010.00829.x.
71. Parra, L., Marin, J., Yousfi, S., Rincón, G., Mauri, P.V., Lloret, J., Edge detection for weed recognition in lawns. *Comput. Electron. Agric.*, 176, 105684, September 2020, DOI: https://doi.org/10.1016/j.compag.2020.105684.
72. Osco, L.P., Junior, J.M., Ramos, A.P.M., Jorge, L.A.C., Fatholahi, S.N., de Andrade Silva, J., Matsubara, E.T., Pistori, H., Gonçalves, W.N., Li, J., A review on deep learning in UAV remote sensing. *Int. J. Appl. Earth Obs. Geoinf.*, 102, 102456, October 2021a, DOI: https://doi.org/10.1016/j.jag.2021.102456.

73. Osco, L.P., de Arruda, M.S., Gonçalves, D.N., Alexandre, D., Batistoti, J., de Souza, M., Gomes, F.D.G., Ramos, A.P.M., de Castro Jorge, L.A., Liesenberg, V., Li, J., Ma, L., Munior, J., Gonçalves, W.N., A CNN approach to simultaneously count plants and detect plantation-rows from UAV imagery. *ISPRS J. Photogramm. Remote Sens.*, 174, 1–17, April 2021b, DOI: https://doi.org/10.1016/j.isprsjprs.2021.01.024.
74. Luminto, H., Weather analysis to predict rice cultivation time using multiple linear regression to escalate farmer's exchange rate. *2017 International Conference on Advanced Informatics, Concepts, Theory, and Applications (ICAICTA)*, IEEE, DOI: 10.1109/ICAICTA.2017.8090974.
75. Wang, L., Shen, Y., Liu, H., Guo, Z., An accurate and efficient multi-category edge detection method. *Cognit. Syst. Res.*, 58, 160–172, December 2019, DOI: https://doi.org/10.1016/j.cogsys.2019.06.002.
76. Dyrmann, M., Karstoft, H., Midtiby, H.S., Plant species classification using deep convolutional neural network. *Biosyst. Eng.*, 151, 72–80, November 2016, DOI: https://doi.org/10.1016/j.biosystemseng.2016.08.024.
77. Maimaitijiang, M., Sagan, V., Sidike, P., Hartling, S., Esposito, F., Fritschi, F.B., Soybean yield prediction from UAV using multimodal data fusion and deep learning. *Remote Sens. Environ.*, 237, 111599, 2020, DOI: https://doi.org/10.1016/j.rse.2019.111599.
78. Pérez-Ortiz, M., Peña, J.M., Gutiérrez, P.A., Torres-Sánchez, J., Hervás-Martínez, C., López-Granados, F., A semi-supervised system for weed mapping in sunflower crops using unmanned aerial vehicles and a crop row detection method. *Appl. Soft Comput.*, 37, 533–544, December 2015, DOI: https://doi.org/10.1016/j.asoc.2015.08.027.
79. Pérez-Ortiz, M., Peña, J.M., Gutiérrez, P., Torres-Sánchez, J., Hervás-Martíne, C., López-Granados, F., Machine learning paradigms for weed mapping *via* unmanned aerial vehicles. *2016a IEEE Symposium Series on Computational Intelligence (SSCI)*, 13 February 2017, DOI: https://DOI: 10.1109/SSCI.2016.7849987.
80. Pérez-Ortiz, M., Peña, J.M., Torres-Sánchez, J., Hervás-Martínez, C., López-Granados, F., Selecting patterns and features for between- and within- crop-row weed mapping using UAV-imagery. *Expert Syst. Appl.*, 47, 85–94, 2016b, DOI: https://doi.org/10.1016/j.eswa.2015.10.043.
81. McRae, D.C., A review of developments in potato handling and grading. *J. Agric. Eng. Res.*, 31, 2, 115–138, February 1985, DOI: https://doi.org/10.1016/0021-8634(85)90065-4.
82. Milioto, A., Lottes, P., Stachniss, C., Real-time semantic segmentation of crop and weed for precision agriculture robots leveraging background knowledge in CNNs, in: *Proc. IEEE Int. Conf. Robot. Automat. (ICRA)*, May 2018, pp. 2229–2235, DOI: 10.1109/ICRA.2018.8460962.
83. Larese, M.G., Namías, R., Craviotto, R.M., Arango, M.R., Gallo, C., Granitto, P.M., Automatic classification of legumes using leaf vein image features.

Pattern Recognit., 47, 158–168, 2014, DOI: https://doi.org/10.1016/j.patcog.2013.06.012.

84. Razfar, N., True, J., Bassiouny, R., Venkatesh, V., Kashef, R., Weed detection in soybean crops using custom lightweight deep learning models. *J. Agric. Food Res.*, 8, 100308, June 2022, DOI: https://doi.org/10.1016/j.jafr.2022.100308.
85. Nkemelu, D.K., Omeiza, D., Lubalo, N., Deep convolutional neural network for plant seedlings classification. *arXiv preprint arXiv:1811.08404*, 2018.
86. Liu, N. and Kan, J.-M., Improved deep belief networks and multi-feature fusion for leaf identification. *Neurocomputing*, 16, 30823–2, DOI: http://dx.doi.org/10.1016/j.neucom.2016.08.005.
87. Nwankpa, C., Ijomah, W., Gachagan, A., Marshall, S., Activation functions:-Comparison of trends in practice and research for deep learning. arXiv preprint arXiv:1811.03378, 2018.
88. Granitto, P.M., Navone, H.D., Verdes, P.F., Ceccatto, H.A., de Física Rosario, I., Weed Seeds Identification by Machine Vision. CONICET and Universidad Nacional de Rosario, Boulevard 27 de Febrero 210 Bis, 2002 Rosario, Argentina.
89. Jirapure, P.V. and Deshkar, P.A., Qualitative data analysis using regression method for agricultural data. *IEEE Sponsored World Conference on Futuristic Trends in Research and Innovation for Social Welfare (WCFTR'16)*, IEEE, 2016, 978-1-4673-9214-3/16/©.
90. Partel, V., Kakarla, S.C., Ampatzidis, Y., Development and evaluation of a low-cost and smart technology for precision weed management utilizing artificial intelligence. *Comput. Electron. Agric.*, 157, 339–350, 2019.
91. Panchal, A.V., Patel, S.C., Bagyalakshmi, K., *et al.*, Image-based Plant Diseases Detection using Deep Learning. *Mater. Today Proc.*, DOI: https://doi.org/10.1016/j.matpr.2021.07.281.
92. Mekha, P. and Teeyasuksaet, N., Image Classification of Rice Leaf Diseases Using Random Forest Algorithm, in: *The 6th International Conference on (DAMT) and 4th ECTI Northern Section Conference on(NCON)*, IEEE, 2021, 978-1-6654-1569-9/21/.
93. Patil, V., Suryawanshi, S., Saner, M., Patil, V., Student performance prediction using classification data mining techniques. *Int. J. Res. Emerg. Sci. Technol.*, 4, 15–18, 2017.
94. Júnior, P.C.P., Monteiro, A., Da Luz Ribeiro, R., Sobieranski, A.C., Von Wangenheim, A., Comparison of Supervised Classifiers and Image Features for Crop Rows Segmentation on Aerial Images. *Appl. Artif. Intell.*, 34, 4, 271–291, 2020, DOI: https://doi.org/10.1080/08839514.2020.1720131.
95. Pereira, L.A.M., Nakamura, R.Y.M., de Souza, G.F.S., Martins, D., Papa, J.P., Aquatic weed automatic classification using machine learning techniques. *Comput. Electron. Agric.*, 87, 56–63, 2012.
96. Sethy, P.K., Barpanda, N.K., Rath, A.K., Behera, S.K., Deep feature based rice leaf disease identification using support vector machine. *Comput. Electron. Agric.*, 175, 105527, DOI: https://doi.org/10.1016/j.compag.2020.105527.

97. Biller, R.H., Reduced Input of Herbicides by Use of Optoelectronic Sensors. *J. Agric. Eng. Res.*, 71, 4, 357–362, December 1998, DOI: https://doi.org/10.1006/jaer.1998.0334.
98. Rey, N., Volpi, M., Joost, S., Tuia, D., Detecting animals in African Savanna with UAVs and the crowds. *Remote Sens. Environ.*, 200, 341–351, 2017, DOI: https://doi.org/ 10.1016/j.rse.2017.08.026.
99. Rizzardi, M. and Fleck, N., Methods of quantification of weeds and soybean leaf covers. *Cienc. Rural*, 34, 1, 13–18, 2004.
100. Saber, M., Lee, W.S., Burks, T.F., Schueller, J.K., Chase, C.A., MacDonald, G.E., Salvador, G.A., Performance and Evaluation of Intra-Row Weeder Ultrasonic Plant Detection System and Pinch-Roller Weeding Mechanism for Vegetable Crops, in: *2015 ASABE International Meeting. American Society of Agricultural and Biological Engineers*, p. 1, 2015, DOI: https://doi.org/10.13031/aim.20152188868.
101. Bhatnagar, S., Gill, L., Regan, S., Waldren, S., Ghosh, B., A nested drone-satellite approach to monitoring the ecological conditions of wetlands. *ISPRS J. Photogramm. Remote Sens.*, 174, 151–165, April 2021, DOI: https://doi.org/10.1016/j.isprsjprs.2021.01.012.
102. Hameed, S. and Amin, I., Detection of Weed and Wheat Using Image Processing. *2018 IEEE 5th International Conference on Engineering Technologies & Applied Sciences*, Bangkok, Thailand, 22–23 Nov. 2018.
103. Sarvini, T., Sneha, T., GS, S.G., Sushmitha, S., Kumaraswamy, R., Performance comparison of weed detection algorithms, in: *2019 International Conference on Communication and Signal Processing (ICCSP)*, pp. 843–847, 2019.
104. Noon, S.K., Amjad, M., Qureshi, M.A., Mannan, A., Use of deep learning techniques for identification of plant leaf stresses: A review. *Sustain. Comput. Inform. Syst.*, 28, 100443, 2020, DOI: https://doi.org/10.1016/j.suscom.2020.100443.
105. Javidan, S.M., Banakar, A., Vakilian, K.A., Ampatzidis, Y., Diagnosis of grape leaf diseases using automatic K-means clustering and machine learning. *Smart Agric. Technol.*, 3, 100081, 2023, DOI: https://doi.org/10.1016/j.atech.2022.100081.
106. Mohanty, S.P., Hughes, D.P., Salathé, M., Using Deep Learning for Image-Based Plant Disease Detection. *Front. Plant Sci.*, 7, Article 1419, September 2016, DOI: 10.3389/fpls.2016.01419.
107. Aggarwal, S. and Bhatia, M., Anatomy of Leaf Classification Techniques. *2019 International Conference on Machine Learning, Big Data, Cloud and Parallel Computing (Com-IT-Con)*, 978-1-7281-0211-5/19/IEEE.
108. Pareek, S., Shrivastava, S., Jhala, S., Siddiqui, J.A., Patidar, S., IoT and Image Processing based Forest Monitoring and Counteracting System. *Proceedings of the Fourth International Conference on Trends in Electronics and Informatics (ICOEI 2020)*, IEEE Xplore Part Number: CFP20J32-ART; ISBN: 978-1-7281-5518-0.

109. Siddiqi, M.H. and Seok-Won Lee, A.M.K., Weed image classification using wavelet transform, stepwise linear discriminant analysis and support vector machines for an automatic spray control system. *J. Inf. Sci. Eng.*, 30, 1253–1270, 2014.
110. Cox, S., Information technology: the global key to precision agriculture and sustainability. *Comput. Electron. Agric.*, 36, 93–111, 2002, DOI: https://doi.org/10.1016/S0168-1699(02)00095-9.
111. Simonyan, K. and Zisserman, A very deep convolutional networks for large-scale image recognition. *ICLR*, pp. 1–14, 2015, arXiv:1409.1556.
112. Slaughter, D.C., Giles, D.K., Downey, D., Autonomous robotic weed control systems: A review. *Comput. Electron. Agric.*, 61, 1, 63–78, Apr. 2008, DOI: https://doi.org/10.1016/j.compag.2007.05.008.
113. Suh, H.K., Ijsselmuiden, J., Hofstee, J.W., van Henten, E.J., Transfer learning for the classification of sugar beet and volunteer potato under field conditions. *Biosyst. Eng.*, 174, 50–65, 2018.
114. Sulaiman, S.N. and Mat Isa, N.A., Adaptive fuzzy-K-means clustering algorithm for image segmentation. *IEEE Trans. Consum. Electron.*, 56, 4, 2661–2668, 2010.
115. Szegedy, C., Vanhoucke, V., Ioffe, S., Shlens, J., Wojna, Z., Rethinking the inception architecture for computer vision, in: *Proceedings of the 2016 IEEE Conference on Computer Vision and Pattern Recognition, CVPR*, pp. 2818–2826, 2016July 2016.
116. Szegedy, C., Liu, W., Jia, Y., Sermanet, P., Reed, S., Anguelov, D., *et al.*, Going deeper with convolutions, in: *Proceedings of the IEEE Conference on Computer Vision and Pattern Recognition*, 2015.
117. Tan, Y., Wang, S., Xu, B., Zhang, J., An improved progressive morphological filter for UAV-based photogrammetric point clouds in river bank monitoring. *ISPRS J. Photogramm. Remote Sens.*, 146, 421–429, 2018, DOI: https://doi.org/10.1016/j.isprsjprs.2018.10.013.
118. Teimouri, N., Dyrmann, M., Nielsen, P.R., Mathiassen, S.K., Somerville, G.J., Jørgensen, R.N., Weed growth stage estimator using deep convolutional neural networks. *Sensors*, 18, 5, 1580, 2018.
119. Bakker, T., van Asselt, K., Bontsema, J., Muller, J., van Straten, G., Systematic design of an autonomous platform for robotic weeding. *J. Terramech.*, 47, 63–73, 2010, DOI: 10.1016/j.jterra.2009.06.002.
120. Trong, V.H., Gwang-hyun, Y., Vu, D.T., Jin-young, K., Late fusion of multimodal deep neural networks for weeds classification. *Comput. Electron. Agric.*, 175, 105506, 2020.
121. Tu, Y., Zhou, H., Lang, W., Chen, T., Li, X., Xu, B., A novel cross-sensor calibration method to generate a consistent night-time lights time series dataset. *Int. J. Remote Sens.*, 41, 14, 5482–5502, 2020, DOI: https://doi.org/10.1080/01431161.2020.1731935.

122. Alchanatis, V., Ridel, L., Hetzroni, A., Yaroslavsky, L., Weed detection in multi-spectral images of cotton fields. *Comput. Electron. Agric.*, 47, 3, 243–260, June 2005, DOI: https://doi.org/10.1016/j.compag.2004.11.019.
123. Wang, A., Xu, Y., Wei, X., Cui, B., Semantic segmentation of crop and weed using an encoder-decoder network and image enhancement method under uncontrolled outdoor illumination. *IEEE Access*, 8, 81724–81734, 2020.
124. Wu, H., Xu, Z., Wu, G., A novel method of missing road generation in city blocks based on big mobile navigation trajectory data. *ISPRS Int. J. Geo-Inf.*, 8, 3, 142, 2019, DOI: https://doi.org/10.3390/ijgi8030142.
125. Wu, L. and Wen, Y., Weed/corn seedling recognition by support vector machine using texture features. *Afr. J. Agric. Res.*, 4, 840–846, 2009, DOI: https://doi.org/10.5897/AJAR.
126. Jin, X., Che, J., Chen, Y., Weed Identification Using Deep Learning and Image Processing in Vegetable Plantation. *IEEE Access*, January 8, 2021.
127. Zhang, X., Qiao, Y., Meng, F., Fan, C., Zhang, M., Identification of Maize Leaf Diseases Using Improved Deep Convolutional Neural Networks. 2169-3536. 2018 IEEE, DOI: 10.1109/ACCESS.2018.2844405.
128. Fan, X., Luo, P., Mu, Y., Zhou, R., Tjahjadi, T., Ren, Y., Leaf image based plant disease identification using transfer learning and feature fusion Author links open overlay panel. *Comput. Electron. Agric.*, 196, 106892, May 2022, DOI: https://doi.org/10.1016/j.compag.2022.106892.
129. Xinshao, W. and Cheng, C., Weed seeds classification based on pcanet deep learning baseline, in: *2015 Asia-Pacific Signal and Information Processing Association Annual Summit and Conference (APSIPA)*, IEEE, pp. 408–415, 2015.
130. Yu, J., Sharpe, S.M., Schumann, A.W., Boyd, N.S., Deep learning for image-based weed detection in turfgrass. *Eur. J. Agron.*, 104, 78–84, 2019.
131. Zeiler, M.D. and Fergus, R., Visualizing and understanding convolutional networks, in: *Computer Vision–ECCV*, D. Fleet, T. Pajdla, B. Schiele, T. Tuytelaars (Eds.), pp. 818–833, Springer, 2014.
132. Zhang, L. and Xiao, D., Collaborative image compression with error bounds in wireless sensor networks for crop monitoring. *Comput. Electron. Agric.*, 89, 1–9, 2012.
133. Zhong, D., Novais, J., Grift, T.E., Bohn, M., Han, J., Maize root complexity analysis using a Support Vector Machine method. *Comput. Electron. Agric.*, 69, 46–50, 2009, DOI: 10.1016/j.compag.2009.06.013.
134. Zhao, Z.-Q., Ma, L.-H., Cheung, Y.-M., Wu, X., Tang, Y., Chen, C.L.P., ApLeaf: An Efficient Android-based Plant Leaf Identification System. *Neurocomputing*, 151, 1, 1112–1119, 2015.
135. Zhou, X., Zheng, H.B., Xu, X.Q., He, J.Y., Ge, X.K., Yao, X., *et al.*, Predicting grain yield in rice using multi-temporal vegetation indices from UAV-based multispectral and digital imagery. *ISPRS J. Photogramm. Remote Sens.*, 130, 246–255, 2017, DOI: https://doi.org/10.1016/j.isprsjprs.2017.05.003.

136. Zhu, X., Hou, Y., Weng, Q., Chen, L., Integrating UAV optical imagery and LiDAR data for assessing the spatial relationship between mangrove and inundation across a subtropical estuarine wetland. *ISPRS J. Photogramm. Remote Sens.*, 149, 146–156, 2019, DOI: https://doi.org/10.1016/j.isprsjprs.2019.01.021.
137. Zimdahl, R.L., *Fundamentals of Weed Science*, 5th ed., Academic Press Elsevier Inc., 2018.
138. Zwiggelaar, R. and Bull, C.R., The VIIth International Conference on Sensors and their Applications: Relevance to the Agricultural Community. *Comput. Electron. Agric.*, 1996.

About the Editors

Narayanan Ganesh, PhD is a Senior Associate Professor at the Vellore Institute of Technology's Chennai Campus with nearly two decades of experience in teaching, training, and research. He has published more than 30 articles, written eight textbooks, and filed two Australian patents. His research encompasses a range areas, including software engineering, agile software development, prediction and optimization techniques, deep learning, image processing, and data analytics.

Kanak Kalita, PhD is an Associate Professor in the Department of Mechanical Engineering at Vel Tech University with more than ten years of experience. He has authored more than 200 articles and edited more than eight book volumes. His research interests encompass machine learning, fuzzy decision making, metamodeling, process optimization, and composites.

Index

Also of Interest

Check out these other related titles from Scrivener Publishing

Sustainable Agriculture Production Using Blockchain Technology, Edited by Rekh Ram Janghel, Rajesh Doriya, Jaykumar Lachure, and Yogesh Kumar Rathore, ISBN: 9781394248674. Revolutionize the agricultural supply chain with this essential guide, which provides the practical knowledge to leverage blockchain technology for transparency, traceability, and trust, alongside AI for overcoming modern farming challenges.

Mathematical Modeling in Agriculture, Edited by Sabyasachi Pramanik, Niranjanamurthy M., Ankur Gupta, and Ahmed J. Obaid, ISBN: 9781394233717. The main goal of the book is to explore the idea behind data modeling in smart agriculture using information and communication technologies and tools to make agricultural practices more functional, fruitful and profitable.

Agroforestry, Edited by Abhishek Raj, Manoj Kumar Jhariya, Arnab Banerjee, Ramesh Kumar Jha, and Krishan Pal Singh, ISBN: 9781394231133. This book offers comprehensive insights into the management of agroforestry for livelihood security and sustainable development in the tropics, addressing ecological interactions, productivity, and the monetization of carbon credits, while also outlining a future roadmap and policy challenges.

Smart Agritech: Robotics, AI, and Internet of Things (IoT) in Agriculture, Edited by Santosh Kumar Srivastava, Durgesh Srivastava, Korhan Cengiz, and Pramod Gaur, ISBN: 9781394302959. The main goal of *Smart Agritech: Robotics, AI, and the Internet of Things (IoT) in Agriculture* is to explore how emerging technologies such as robotics, artificial intelligence (AI), and IoT can be leveraged to improve efficiency, sustainability, and productivity in agriculture.

DIGITAL AGRICULTURAL ECOSYSTEM: Revolutionary Advancements in Agriculture, Edited by Kuldeep Singh and Prasanna Kolar, ISBN: 9781394242931. The book comprehensively explores the dynamic synergy between modern technology and agriculture, showcasing how advancements such as artificial intelligence, data analytics, and smart farming practices are reshaping the landscape to ensure food security in the era of climate change, as well as bridging the gap between cutting-edge research and practical implementation.

THE DIGITAL AGRICULTURAL REVOLUTION: Innovations and Challenges in Agriculture through Technology Disruptions, Edited by Roheet Bhatnagar, Nitin Kumar Tripathi, Nitu Bhatnagar and Chandan Kumar Panda, ISBN: 9781119823339. The book integrates computational intelligence, applied artificial intelligence, and modern agricultural practices and will appeal to scientists, agriculturists, and those in plant and crop science and management.

HANDBOOK OF AGRICULTURAL BIOTECHNOLOGY: Volume I Nanopesticides, Edited by Charles Oluwaseun Adetunji and Julius Kola Oloke, ISBN: 9781119836148. The book provides detailed information on the application of nanopesticides for the management of numerous agricultural pests and pathogens, as well as to foster an innovative pathway toward future sustainable agriculture and food systems.

HANDBOOK OF AGRICULTURAL BIOTECHNOLOGY: Volume II Nanobioherbicides, Edited by Charles Oluwaseun Adetunji, Julius Kola Oloke, ISBN: 9781119836155. The book provides a detailed examination of the application of nanobioherbicides that come from plants including information on the different metabolites derived from numerous plants that could become bioherbicides.

HANDBOOK OF AGRICULTURAL BIOTECHNOLOGY: Volume III Nanofungicides, Edited by Charles Oluwaseun Adetunji and Julius Kola Oloke, ISBN: 9781119836162. This book provides state-of-the-art information about recent advancements in the application of nanobiofungicides for effective management of post-harvest diseases and agricultural fungal diseases, including blights, mildews, molds, and rusts.

HANDBOOK OF AGRICULTURAL BIOTECHNOLOGY: Volume IV Nanoinsecticides, Edited by Charles Oluwaseun Adetunji and Julius Kola Oloke, ISBN: 9781119836179. The book provides detailed information about the application of repellent products that contain plant-based ingredients known as nanobioinsecticides, including the pesticide evaluation scheme guidelines for repellent testing, relevant information about the procedures to evaluate several repellent compounds, the development of new products that offer high repellency, and guidelines for consumer safety.

ECORESTORATION FOR SUSTAINABILITY, Edited by Arnab Banerjee, Manoj Kumar Jhariya, Surendra Singh Bargali, and Debnath Palit, ISBN: 9781119879718. With climate change and land degradation advancing at an alarming rate, the state of the global ecosystem and how it can be restored in our march toward sustainability is incredibly important, and this new, groundbreaking volume tackles these important issues head on.

FUNCTIONAL POLYMERS IN FOOD SCIENCE, Part 1: Food Packaging, Edited by Giuseppe Cirillo, Umile Gianfranco Spizzirri, and Francesca Iemma, ISBN: 9781118594896. Provides an extensive overview of the link between polymer properties and food quality. *NOW AVAILABLE!*

FUNCTIONAL POLYMERS IN FOOD SCIENCE, Part 2: Food Processing, Edited by Giuseppe Cirillo, Umile Gianfranco Spizzirri, and Francesca Iemma, ISBN: 9781118595183. Provides an extensive overview of the link between polymer properties and food quality. *NOW AVAILABLE!*

ADVANCES IN FOOD SCIENCE AND TECHNOLOGY Volume 1, Edited by Visakh, P.M., Sabu Thomas, Laura B. Iturriaga, and Pablo Daniel Ribotta, ISBN: 9781118121023. Written in a systematic and comprehensive manner the book reports recent advances in the development of food science and food technology areas. *NOW AVAILABLE!*

ADVANCES IN FOOD SCIENCE AND NUTRITION Volume 2, Edited by Visakh P.M., Laura B. Iturriaga, and Pablo Daniel Ribotta, ISBN: 9781118137093. This important book comprehensively reviews research on new developments in all areas of food chemistry/science and nutrition. *NOW AVAILABLE!*

Applied Water Science Volume 1: Fundamentals and Applications, Edited by Inamuddin, Mohd Imran Ahamed, Rajender Boddula and Tauseef Ahmad Rangreez, ISBN: 9781119724766. Edited by one of the most well-respected and prolific engineers in the world and his team, this is the first volume in a two-volume set that is the most thorough, up-to-date, and comprehensive volume on applied water science available today. *COMING IN SUMMER 2021*

Sustainable Water Purification, by Safiur Rahman and M. R. Islam, ISBN: 9781119650997. This is the only book that takes a zero-waste approach to propose 100% sustainable water purification techniques. *NOW AVAILABLE!*

Books in the series, "Bioprocessing in Food Science"

NUTRACEUTICALS FROM FRUIT AND VEGETABLE WASTE, Edited by Vidisha Tomer, Navnidhi Chhikara, Ashwani Kumar, and Anil Panghal, ISBN: 9781119803508. Nutraceuticals from Fruit and Vegetable Waste, the latest volume in the series, "Bioprocessing in Food Science," is an essential reference on the valorization of fruit and vegetable waste and the state of the art for fruit and vegetable processing.

NUTRITIONAL SCIENCE AND TECHNOLOGY: Concept to Application, Edited by Tejpal Dhewa, Anil Kumar Puniya, and Anil Panghal, ISBN: 97811198089. This new volume in the groundbreaking series, "Bioprocessing in Food Science," Nutritional Science and Technology, is a comprehensive resource covering topics such as human nutrition, food safety concerns, and emerging technologies like nanotechnology, and it also addresses the need for innovative food products, contamination, and regulatory challenges in the global food market.

HARVESTING FOOD FROM WEEDS, Edited by Prerna Gupta, Navnidhi Chhikara, and Anil Panghal, ISBN: 9781119791973. An exciting new volume in the groundbreaking new series, "Bioprocessing in Food Science," Harvesting Food from Weeds focuses on the latest processes, industrial applications, and leading research on this important, evolving new area, for engineers, scientists, students, and other industry professionals.

MICROBES IN THE FOOD INDUSTRY, Edited by Navnidhi Chhikara, Anil Panghal, and Gaurav Chaudhary, ISBN: 9781119775584. This newest volume in the groundbreaking new series, "Bioprocessing in Food Science," focuses on the latest processes, industrial applications, and leading research on microbes in the food industry, for engineers, scientists, students, and other industry professionals.

NOVEL TECHNOLOGIES IN FOOD SCIENCE, Edited by Navnidhi Chhikara, Anil Panghal, and Gaurav Chaudhary, ISBN: 9781119775584. The third book in the series, "Bioprocessing in Food Science," covers the latest and greatest new technologies in food science.

FUNCTIONAL FOODS, Edited by Navnidhi Chhikara, Anil Panghal, and Gaurav Chaudhary, ISBN: 9781119775560. Presenting cutting-edge information on new and emerging food engineering processes, *Functional Foods*, the second volume in the groundbreaking new series, "Bioprocessing in Food Science," is an essential reference on the modeling, quality, safety, and technologies associated with food processing operations today.

THERMAL FOOD ENGINEERING OPERATIONS, Edited by Nitin Kumar, Anil Panghal, and M. K. Garg, ISBN: 9781119775591. Presenting cutting-edge information on new and emerging food engineering processes, Thermal Food Engineering Operations, the first volume in the new series, "Bioprocessing in Food Science," is an essential reference on the modeling, quality, safety, and technologies associated with food processing operations today.

Printed and bound by CPI Group (UK) Ltd, Croydon, CR0 4YY

24/08/2026

14947831-0003